Effective Panda

Patterns for Data Manip

Effective Pandas

Patterns for Data Manipulation

Matt Harrison

Technical Editors: Lawrence Gray, Alexandre Batisse, Edward Krueger,

hairysun.com

Contents

Contents

Contents

Contents

Contents

Forward

Python is easy to learn. You can learn the basics in a day and be productive. With only an understanding of Python, moving to pandas can be difficult or confusing. It borrows some ideas from NumPy that are not common in the wider Python ecosystem. This book is meant to aid you in mastering pandas.

I have taught Python and pandas to many people over the years, in large corporate environments, small startups, and in Python and Data Science conferences. I have seen what trips people up, and confuses them. With the correct background, an attitude of acceptance, and a deep breath, much of this confusion evaporates.

Having said this, pandas is an excellent tool. Many use it around the world to great success. I hope to empower you to do this as well.

Cheers!

Matt

Chapter 1

Introduction

I have been using Python in some professional capacity or another since the turn of the century. One of the trends that I have seen in that time is the uptake of Python for various aspects of data science—gathering data, cleaning data, analysis, machine learning, and visualization. The pandas library has seen much uptake in this area.

pandas[1] is a data analysis library for Python that has exploded in popularity over the past years. The website describes it like this:

> "pandas is an open-source, BSD-licensed library providing high-performance, easy-to-use data structures and data analysis tools for the Python programming language."
>
> -pandas.pydata.org

My description of pandas is: pandas is an in-memory analysis tool, which has SQL-like constructs, essential statistical and analytic support, as well as graphing capability. Because pandas is built on top of Cython and NumPy, it has less memory overhead and runs quicker than pure Python code. Many people use pandas to replace Excel, perform ETL (extract transform load processing to move data from one place to another), process tabular data, load CSV or JSON files, prep for machine learning, and more. Though it grew out of the financial sector (for time series analysis), it is now a general-purpose data manipulation library.

---

[1]pandas (http://pandas.pydata.org) refers to itself in lowercase, so this book will follow suit. When I'm referring to specific code, I will set it in a monospace font.

With its NumPy lineage, pandas adopts some NumPy'isms that regular Python programmers may not be aware of or familiar with. Yes, one could go out and use Cython to perform fast typed data analysis with a Python-like dialect, but with pandas, you don't need to. This work is done for you. If you use pandas and the vectorized operations, you are getting close to C-level speeds for numeric work but writing Python.

1.1   Who this book is for

This guide is intended to introduce pandas and patterns for best practices. If you work with tabular data and need capabilities beyond Excel, this is for you. This book covers many (but not all) aspects of the library, as well as some gotchas or details that may be counter-intuitive or even non-pythonic to longtime users of Python.

This book assumes a basic knowledge of Python. The author has written *Illustrated Guide to Python 3* that provides all the background necessary.

1.2   Data in this Book

Every attempt has been made to use data that illustrates real-world pandas usage. As a visual learner, I appreciate seeing where data is coming and going. As such, I try to shy away from just showing tables of random numbers that have no meaning. I will show best practices gleaned from years of using pandas.

I have selected a variety of datasets to show that the advice given in this book is applicable in most situations you may encounter.

1.3   Hints, Tables, and Images

The hints, tables, and graphics found in this book have been collected over my years of using pandas. They come from hang-ups, notes, and cheat sheets that I have developed after using pandas and teaching others how to use the library.

In the physical version of this book, there is an index that has also been battle-tested during development. Inevitably, when I was doing analysis for consulting or clients, I would check that the index had the information I needed. If it didn't, I added it.

If you enjoy this book, please consider writing a review on Amazon. That is one of the best ways to thank an author.

Chapter 2

Installation

This book will use Python 3 throughout! Please do not use Python 2 unless you have a compelling reason to. Python 3 is the future of the language, and the current pandas releases do not support Python 2.

2.1 Anaconda

With that out of the way, let's address the installation of pandas. The easiest and least painful way to install pandas on most platforms is to use the Anaconda distribution[2]. Anaconda is a meta-distribution of Python, which contains many additional packages that have traditionally been annoying to install unless you have the necessary toolchains to compile Fortran and C code. Anaconda allows you to skip the compile step because it provides binaries for most platforms. The Anaconda distribution itself is freely available, though commercial support is available as well.

After installing the Anaconda package, you should have a conda executable. Running the following command will install pandas:

```
$ conda install pandas
```

> **Note**
>
> This book shows commands run from the UNIX command prompt. They are prefixed by the prompt $. Unless otherwise noted, these commands will run on the Windows command prompt as well. Do not type the

prompt. It is included to distinguish commands run via a terminal or command prompt from Python code.

We can verify that this works by trying to import the pandas package:

```
$ python
>>> import pandas
>>> pandas.__version__
'1.3.2'
```

> **Note**
>
> The command above shows a Python prompt, >>>. Do not type the Python prompt. It is included to make it easy to distinguish Python code from the output of Python code. For example, the output of the above, '1.3.2' does not have the prompt in front of it. The book also includes the secondary Python prompt, ... for code that is longer than a single line.
> Note that Jupyter does not use the Python prompt in its cells.

If the library successfully imports, you should be good to go.

2.2 Pip

If you aren't using Anaconda, I recommend you use pip[3] to install pandas. The pandas library will install on Windows, Mac, and Linux via pip.

It may be necessary to prepare the operating system for building pandas from source by installing dependencies and the proper header files for Python. On Ubuntu, this is straightforward, other environments may be different:

```
$ sudo apt-get install build-essential python-all-dev
```

Using *virtualenv*[4] will alleviate the need for superuser access during installation. Because virtualenv uses pip, it can download and install newer releases of pandas if the version found on the distribution is lagging.

---

[2]https://anaconda.com/downloads

[3]http://pip-installer.org/

[4]http://www.virtualenv.org

On Mac and Linux platforms, the following commands create a virtualenv sandbox and install the latest pandas in it (assuming that the prerequisite files are also installed):

```
$ python3 -m venv pandas-env
$ source pandas-env/bin/activate
(pandas-env)$ pip install pandas
```

Once you have pandas installed, confirm that you can import the library and check the version:

```
$ source pandas-env/bin/activate
(pandas-env)$ python
>>> import pandas
>>> pandas.__version__
'1.3.2'
```

On Windows, you will open a Command Prompt and run the following to create a virtual environment:

```
> python -m venv pandas-env
> pandas-env/Scripts/activate
(pandas-env)> pip install pandas
```

Note

The Windows command prompt, >, is shown in the previous command. Do not type it. Only type the commands following the prompt.

Try to import the library and check the version:

```
(pandas-env)> python
>>> import pandas
>>> pandas.__version__
'1.3.2'
```

2.3 Jupyter Overview

I recommend you use Jupyter (or a program that connects to it) as a data exploration tool. I use Jupyter classic, though there are other options: JupyterLab, connecting to Jupyter via PyCharm, VSCode, Emacs, as well as Google Colab. Jupyter classic will give you basic functionality and is included in many cloud environments.

Figure 2.1: Jupyter home page.

Jupyter notebook is an environment for combining interactive coding and text in a web browser. This allows us to easily share code and narrative around that code. An example that was popular in the scientific community was the discovery of gravitational waves.[5]

The name Jupyter is a rebranding of an open-source project previously known as iPython Notebook. The rebranding was to emphasize that although the backend is written in Python, Jupyter supports various *kernels* to run other languages, including Julia (the "Ju" portion), Python ("pyt"), and R ("er"). All popular data science programming languages.

The architecture of Jupyter includes a server running various kernels. Using a *notebook* we can interact with a kernel. Typically we use a web browser to do this, but other interfaces exist, such as an emacs mode (ein), PyCharm, or VSCode.

To install Jupyter, type:

```
$ pip install notebook
```

Once Jupyter is installed, launch it with this command:

```
$ jupyter-notebook
```

Then navigate to https://localhost:8888 and you should be presented with the Jupyter home page.

---

[5]https://losc.ligo.org/s/events/GW150914/GW150914_tutorial.html

Figure 2.2: Creating a Python 3 Jupyter notebook.

Click on the dropdown button on the right that says "New" and select Python 3.

At this point, you are presented with a notebook with an empty cell. Jupyter is a *modal* environment. There are two modes, command mode and edit mode. Command mode is for creating and manipulating cells. Edit mode is for changing what is inside of a single cell.

There are many commands for both modes. If you are in command mode (and you will know that because the box around the cell is blue), you can type "h", and it will bring up a pop-up with the keyboard shortcuts for both command and edit mode. Don't worry about memorizing all of them. Here are the commands you will be using most of the time in command mode:

- h - Bring up help (ESC to dismiss)

- a - Create cell above

- b - Create cell below

- x - Cut cell

- c - Copy cell

- v - Paste cell below

- Enter - Go into Edit Mode

- m - Change cell type to Markdown

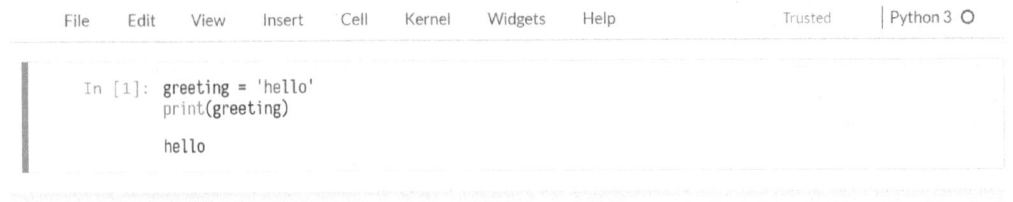

Figure 2.3: Running a cell in Jupyter with basic Python commands.

- y - Change cell type to code

- ii - Interrupt kernel

- 00 - Restart kernel

- Ctr-Enter - Execute cell

When you click on a cell or type Enter, you go into *edit mode*. You will see that the outline turns green if you are in edit mode. In edit mode, you have basic editing functionality. A few keys to know:

- Ctr-Enter - Run cell (execute Python code, render Markdown)

- ESC - Go back to command mode

- TAB - Tab completion

- Shift-TAB - Bring up tooltip (ESC to dismiss)

2.4 Summary

In this chapter, we saw how to set up a Python environment using Anaconda or Pip. We also introduced the Jupyter notebook. I recommend that you get comfortable with Jupyter. Not only is it free and open-source, but many large cloud providers also offer Jupyter in their environments.

2.5 Exercises

1. Install pandas on your machine (using Anaconda or pip).

2. Install Jupyter on your machine.

3. Launch Jupyter and run the following in a cell:
   ```
   import pandas
   pandas.show_versions()
   ```

Chapter 3

Data Structures

One of the keys to understanding pandas is to understand the data model. At the core of pandas are two data structures. The most widely used data structures are the `Series` and the `DataFrame` for dealing with array data and tabular data. This table shows their analogs in the spreadsheet and database world.

Data Structure	Dimensionality	Spreadsheet Analog	Database Analog	Linear Algebra
Series	1D	Column	Column	Column Vector
DataFrame	2D	Single Sheet	Table	Matrix

Figure 3.1: Different dimensions of pandas data structures

An analogy with the spreadsheet world illustrates the basic differences between these types. A `DataFrame` is similar to a sheet with rows and columns, while a `Series` is similar to a single column of data (when we refer to a column of data in this text, we are referring to a `Series`).

Diving into these core data structures a little more is helpful because a bit of understanding goes a long way towards better use of the library. We will spend a good portion of time discussing the `Series` and `DataFrame`. Both the `Series` and `DataFrame` share features. For example, they both have an index, which we will need to examine to understand how pandas works.

Also, because the `DataFrame` can be thought of as a collection of columns that are really `Series` objects, it is imperative that we have a comprehensive study of the `Series` first. Additionally (and perhaps odd to some), we will see this

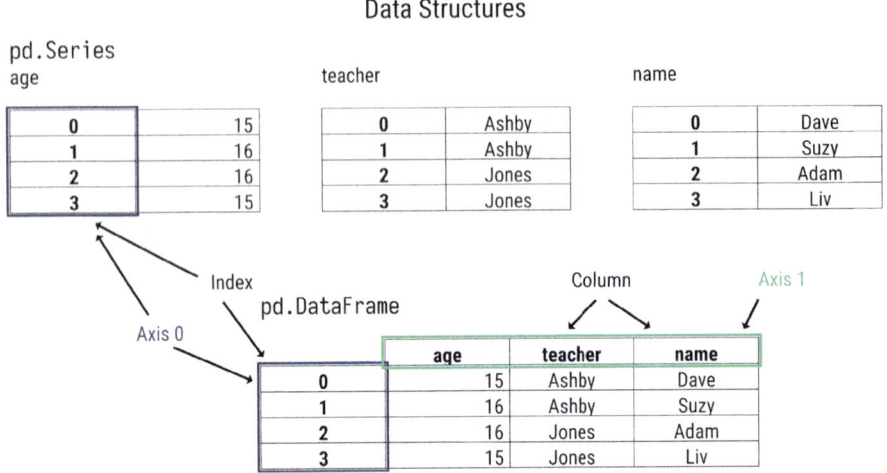

Figure 3.2: Figure showing the relation between the main data structures in pandas. Namely, that a dataframe can have one or many series.

when we iterate over rows, and the rows are represented as Series (however, if you find yourself consistently dealing with rows instead of columns, you are probably not using pandas in an optimal way).

Some have compared the data structures to Python lists or dictionaries, and I think this is a stretch that doesn't provide much benefit. Mapping the list and dictionary methods on top of pandas' data structures just leads to confusion.

3.1 Summary

The pandas library includes two main data structures and associated functions for manipulating them. This book will focus on the Series and DataFrame. First, we will look at the Series as the DataFrame can be considered a collection of columns represented as Series objects.

3.2 Exercises

1. If you had a spreadsheet with data, which pandas data structure would you use to hold the data? Why?

2. If you had a database with data, which pandas data structure would you use to hold the data? Why?

Chapter 4

Series Introduction

A Series is used to model one-dimensional data. The Series object also has a few more bits of data, including an index and a name. A common idea through pandas is the notion of an axis. Because a series is one-dimensional, it has a single *axis*—the index.

Below is a table of counts of songs artists composed. We will use this to explore the series:

Artist	Data
0	145
1	142
2	38
3	13

If you wanted to represent this data in pure Python, you could use a data structure similar to the one that follows. The dictionary, series, has a list of the data points stored under the 'data' key. In addition to an entry in the dictionary for the actual data, there is an explicit entry for the corresponding index values for the data (in the 'index' key), as well as an entry for the name of the data (in the 'name' key):

```
>>> series = {
...     'index':[0, 1, 2, 3],
...     'data':[145, 142, 38, 13],
...     'name':'songs'
...     }
```

The get function defined below can pull items out of this data structure based on the index:

```
>>> def get(series, idx):
...     value_idx = series['index'].index(idx)
...     return series['data'][value_idx]

>>> get(series, 1)
142
```

> **Note**
>
> The code samples in this book are shown as if they were typed directly into an interpreter. Lines starting with >>> and ... are interpreter markers for the *input prompt* and *continuation prompt* respectively. Lines that are not prefixed by one of those sequences are the output from the interpreter after running the code.
>
> In Jupyter (and IPython) you do not see the prompts. I include them to help distinguish between code and output.
>
> The Python interpreter will print the return value of the last invocation (even if the print statement is missing) automatically. If you desire to use the code samples found in this book, leave the interpreter prompts out.

4.1   The index abstraction

This double abstraction of the index seems unnecessary at first glance—a list already has integer indexes. But there is a trick up pandas' sleeves. By allowing non-integer values, the data structure supports other index types such as strings, dates, as well as arbitrarily ordered indices, or even duplicate index values.

Below is an example that has string values for the index:

```
>>> songs = {
...     'index':['Paul', 'John', 'George', 'Ringo'],
...     'data':[145, 142, 38, 13],
...     'name':'counts'
...     }

>>> get(songs, 'John')
142
```

The index is a core feature of pandas'data structures given the library's past in analysis of financial data or *time-series data*. Many of the operations performed on a Series operate directly on the index or by index lookup.

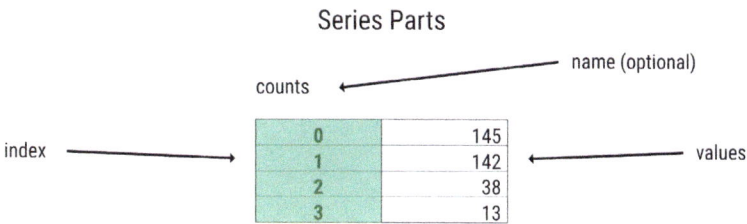

Figure 4.1: The parts of a Series.

4.2 The pandas Series

With that background in mind, let's look at how to create a Series in pandas. It is easy to create a Series object from a list:

```
>>> import pandas as pd
>>> songs2 = pd.Series([145, 142, 38, 13],
...         name='counts')

>>> songs2
0    145
1    142
2     38
3     13
Name: counts, dtype: int64
```

When the interpreter prints our series, pandas makes a best effort to format it for the current terminal size. The series is one-dimensional. However, this looks like it is two-dimensional. The leftmost column is the *index*, which contains entries for the index. The index is not part of the values. The generic name for an index is an *axis*, and the values of the index—0, 1, 2, 3—are called *axis labels*. The data—145, 142, 38, and 13—is also called the *values* of the series. The two-dimensional structure in pandas—a DataFrame—has two axes, one for the rows and another for the columns.

The rightmost column in the output contains the *values* of the series—145, 142, 38, and 13. In this case, they are integers (the console representation says dtype: int64, dtype meaning data type, and int64 meaning 64-bit integer), but in general, the values of a Series can hold strings, floats, booleans, or arbitrary

Python objects. To get the best speed (and to leverage vectorized operations), the values should be of the same type, though this is not required.

It is easy to inspect the index of a series (or data frame), as it is an attribute of the object:

```
>>> songs2.index
RangeIndex(start=0, stop=4, step=1)
```

The default values for an index are monotonically increasing integers. songs2 has an integer-based index.

> **Note**
>
> The index can be string-based as well, in which case pandas indicates that the datatype for the index is object (not string):
>
> ```
> >>> songs3 = pd.Series([145, 142, 38, 13],
> ...       name='counts',
> ...       index=['Paul', 'John', 'George', 'Ringo'])
> ```
>
> Note that the dtype that we see when we print a Series is the type of the values, not the index. Even though this looks two-dimensional, remember that the index is not part of the values:
>
> ```
> >>> songs3
> Paul       145
> John       142
> George      38
> Ringo       13
> Name: counts, dtype: int64
> ```
>
> When we inspect the index attribute, we see that the dtype is object:
>
> ```
> >>> songs3.index
> Index(['Paul', 'John', 'George', 'Ringo'],
> dtype='object')
> ```

The actual data (or values) for a series does not have to be numeric or homogeneous. We can insert Python objects into a series:

```
>>> class Foo:
...       pass

>>> ringo = pd.Series(
...       ['Richard', 'Starkey', 13, Foo()],
...       name='ringo')
```

```
>>> ringo
0                          Richard
1                          Starkey
2                               13
3    <__main__.Foo instance at 0x...>
Name: ringo, dtype: object
```

In the above case, the dtype-*datatype*-of the Series is object (meaning a Python object). This can be good or bad.

The object data type is also used for a series with string values. In addition, it is also used for values that have heterogeneous or mixed types. If you have just numeric data in a series, you wouldn't want it stored as a Python object, but rather as an int64 or float64, which allow you to do vectorized numeric operations.

If you have time data and it says it has the object type, you probably have strings for the dates. Using strings instead of date types is bad as you don't get the date operations that you would get if the type were datetime64[ns]. A series with string data, on the other hand, has the type of object. Don't worry; we will see how to convert types later in the book.

4.3 The NaN value

A value that may be familiar to NumPy users, but not Python users in general, is NaN. When pandas determines that a series holds numeric values but cannot find a number to represent an entry, it will use NaN. This value stands for *Not A Number* and is usually ignored in arithmetic operations. (Similar to NULL in SQL).

Here is a series that has NaN in it:

```
>>> import numpy as np
>>> nan_series = pd.Series([2, np.nan],
...     index=['Ono', 'Clapton'])
>>> nan_series
Ono        2.0
Clapton    NaN
dtype: float64
```

Note

One thing to note is that the type of this series is float64, not int64! The type is a float because float64 supports NaN, while int64 does not. When pandas sees numeric data (2) as well as the np.nan, it coerced the 2 to a float value.

Below is an example of how pandas ignores NaN. The .count method, which counts the number of values in a series, disregards NaN. In this case, it indicates that the count of items in the series is one, one for the value of 2 at index location Ono, ignoring the NaN value at index location Clapton:

```
>>> nan_series.count()
1
```

You can inspect the number of entries (including missing values) with the .size property:

```
>>> nan_series.size
2
```

Note

If you load data from a CSV file, an empty value for an otherwise numeric column will become NaN. Later, methods such as .fillna and .dropna will explain how to deal with NaN.

None, NaN, nan, <NA>, and null are synonyms in this book when referring to empty or missing data found in a pandas series or dataframe.

4.4 Optional Integer Support for NaN

The int64 type does not support missing data. Many considered that a wart of pandas. As of pandas 0.24, there is optional support for another integer type that can hold missing values denoted as <NA> below. The documentation calls this type the *nullable integer type*. When you create a series, you can pass in dtype='Int64' (note the capitalization):

```
>>> nan_series2 = pd.Series([2, None],
...      index=['Ono', 'Clapton'],
...      dtype='Int64')
>>> nan_series2
Ono          2
```

```
Clapton     <NA>
dtype: Int64
```

Operations on these series still ignore NaN or <NA>:

```
>>> nan_series2.count()
1
```

> **Note**
>
> You can use the `.astype` method to convert columns to the nullable integer type. Just use the string `'Int64'` as the type:
>
> ```
> >>> nan_series.astype('Int64')
> Ono             2
> Clapton      <NA>
> dtype: Int64
> ```

I generally ignore `'Int64'` as I tend to clean up missing data. Also, when you ingest data in pandas, most functions use `'int64'` (in lowercase) by default.

4.5 Similar to NumPy

The `Series` object behaves similarly to a NumPy array. As shown below, both types respond to index operations:

```
>>> import numpy as np
>>> numpy_ser = np.array([145, 142, 38, 13])
>>> songs3[1]
142
>>> numpy_ser[1]
142
```

They both have methods in common:

```
>>> songs3.mean()
84.5
>>> numpy_ser.mean()
84.5
```

They also both have a notion of a *boolean array*. A boolean array is a series with the same index as the series you are working with that has boolean values, and it can be used as a mask to filter out items. Normal Python lists do not support such fancy index operations, like sticking a list into an index operation.

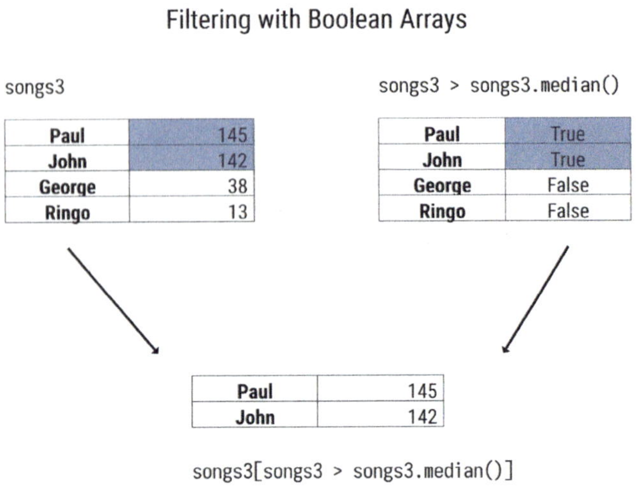

Filtering with Boolean Arrays

Figure 4.2: Filtering a series with a boolean array.

In this example, we will make a mask:

```
>>> mask = songs3 > songs3.median()  # boolean array
```

```
>>> mask
Paul       True
John       True
George     False
Ringo      False
Name: counts, dtype: bool
```

Once we have a mask, we can use that as a filter. We just need to pass the mask into an index operation. If the mask has a True value for a given index, the value is kept. Otherwise, the value is dropped. The mask above represents the locations that have a value higher than the median value of the series.

```
>>> songs3[mask]
Paul     145
John     142
Name: counts, dtype: int64
```

NumPy also has filtering by boolean arrays, but lacks the .median method on an array. Instead, NumPy provides a median function in the NumPy namespace. The equivalent version in NumPy looks like this:

```
>>> numpy_ser[numpy_ser > np.median(numpy_ser)]
array([145, 142])
```

Note

Both NumPy and pandas have adopted the convention of using import statements in combination with an `as` statement to rename their imports to two letter acronyms. This is called *aliasing*:

```
>>> import pandas as pd
>>> import numpy as np
```

Renaming imports provides a slight typing benefit (four fewer characters) while still allowing the user to be explicit with their namespaces.

Be careful, as you may see the following cast about in code samples, blogs, or documentation:

```
>>> from pandas import *
```

Though you see *star imports* frequently used in examples online, I would advise not to use star imports. I never use them in my book examples or code that I write for clients. They have the potential to clobber items in your namespace and make tracing the source of a definition more difficult (especially if you have multiple star imports). As the Zen of Python states, "Explicit is better than implicit"[6].

4.6 Categorical Data

When you load data, you can indicate that the data is categorical. If we know that our data is limited to a few values; we might want to use categorical data. Categorical values have a few benefits:

- Use less memory than strings

- Improve performance

- Can have an ordering

---

[6]Type `import this` into an interpreter to see the Zen of Python. Or search for "PEP 20".

- Can perform operations on categories

- Enforce membership on values

Categories are not limited to strings; we can also convert numbers or datetime values to categorical data.

To create a category, we pass dtype="category" into the Series constructor. Alternatively, we can call the .astype("category") method on a series:

```
>>> s = pd.Series(['m', 'l', 'xs', 's', 'xl'], dtype='category')
>>> s
0     m
1     l
2    xs
3     s
4    xl
dtype: category
Categories (5, object): ['l', 'm', 's', 'xl', 'xs']
```

If this series represents the size, there is a natural ordering as a small is less than a medium. By default, categories don't have an ordering. We can verify this by inspecting the .cat attribute that has various properties:

```
>>> s.cat.ordered
False
```

To convert a non-categorical series to an ordered category, we can create a type with the CategoricalDtype constructor and the appropriate parameters. Then we pass this type into the .astype method:

```
>>> s2 = pd.Series(['m', 'l', 'xs', 's', 'xl'])
>>> size_type = pd.api.types.CategoricalDtype(
...     categories=['s','m','l'], ordered=True)
>>> s3 = s2.astype(size_type)
...
>>> s3
0      m
1      l
2    NaN
3      s
4    NaN
dtype: category
Categories (3, object): ['s' < 'm' < 'l']
```

In this case, we limited the categories to just 's', 'm', and 'l', but the data had values that were not in those categories. Converting the data to a category type replaces those extra values with NaN.

If we have ordered categories, we can do comparisons on them:

```
>>> s3 > 's'
0      True
1      True
2      False
3      False
4      False
dtype: bool
```

The prior example created a new Series from existing data that was not categorical. We can also add ordering information to categorical data. We just need to make sure that we specify all of the members of the category or pandas will throw a ValueError:

```
>>> s.cat.reorder_categories(['xs','s','m','l', 'xl'],
...                          ordered=True)
0      m
1      l
2      xs
3      s
4      xl
dtype: category
Categories (5, object): ['xs' < 's' < 'm' < 'l' < 'xl']
```

Note

String and datetime series have a str and dt attribute that allow us to perform common operations specific to that type. If we convert these types to categorical types, we can still use the str or dt attributes on them:

```
>>> s3.str.upper()
0      M
1      L
2      NaN
3      S
4      NaN
dtype: object
```

29

Method	Description
pd.Series(data=None, index=None, dtype=None, name=None, copy=False)	Create a series from data (sequence, dictionary, or scalar).
s.index	Access index of series.
s.astype(dtype, errors='raise')	Cast a series to dtype. To ignore errors (and return original object) use errors='ignore'.
s[boolean_array]	Return values from s where boolean_array is True.
s.cat.ordered	Determine if a categorical series is ordered.
s.cat.reorder_categories(new_categories, ordered=False)	Add categories (potentially ordered) to the series. new_categories must include all categories.

Table 4.1: Series Overview Attributes and Methods

4.7 Summary

The Series object is a one-dimensional data structure. It can hold numerical data, time data, strings, or arbitrary Python objects. If you are dealing with numeric data, using pandas rather than a Python list will benefit you. Pandas is faster, consumes less memory, and comes with built-in methods that are very useful to manipulate the data. Also, the index abstraction allows for accessing values by position or label. A Series can also have empty values and has some similarities to NumPy arrays. It is the primary workhorse of pandas; mastering it will pay dividends.

4.8 Exercises

1. Using Jupyter, create a series with the temperature values for the last seven days. Filter out the values below the mean.

2. Using Jupyter, create a series with your favorite colors. Use a categorical type.

Chapter 5

Series Deep Dive

There are many operations you can do with a Series. In this chapter, we will introduce many of them.

We will pull data from the US Fuel Economy website[7]. This site has data on the efficiency of makes and models of cars sold in the US since 1984.

5.1 Loading the Data

I have a copy of this data in my GitHub repository. One of the nice features of pandas is that the read_csv function can accept not only URLs but also ZIP files. Because this ZIP file contains only a single file, we can use this function. If it was a ZIP file with multiple files, we would need to decompress the data to pull out the file we were interested in.

The first columns in the dataset we will investigate are *city08* and *highway08*, which provide information on miles per gallon usage while driving around in the city and highway respectively:

```
>>> import pandas as pd
>>> url = 'https://github.com/mattharrison/datasets/raw/master/data/' \
....        'vehicles.csv.zip'
>>> df = pd.read_csv(url)
>>> city_mpg = df.city08
>>> highway_mpg = df.highway08
```

Let's look at the data:

---

[7]https://www.fueleconomy.gov/feg/download.shtml

```
>>> city_mpg
0          19
1           9
2          23
3          10
4          17
           ..
41139      19
41140      20
41141      18
41142      18
41143      16
Name: city08, Length: 41144, dtype: int64

>>> highway_mpg
0          25
1          14
2          33
3          12
4          23
           ..
41139      26
41140      28
41141      24
41142      24
41143      21
Name: highway08, Length: 41144, dtype: int64
```

It looks like each series has around 40,000 integer entries. Because the type of this series is int64, we know that none of the values are missing.

5.2 Series Attributes

The pandas library provides a lot of functionality. The built-in dir function will list the attributes of an object. Let's examine how many attributes there are on a series:

```
>>> len(dir(city_mpg))
457
```

Wow! There are over 400 attributes on a series. In contrast, a Python list or dictionary has around 40 attributes. Do not fret; you will not need to memorize all of these if you get comfortable with a tool like Jupyter. If you have a Series

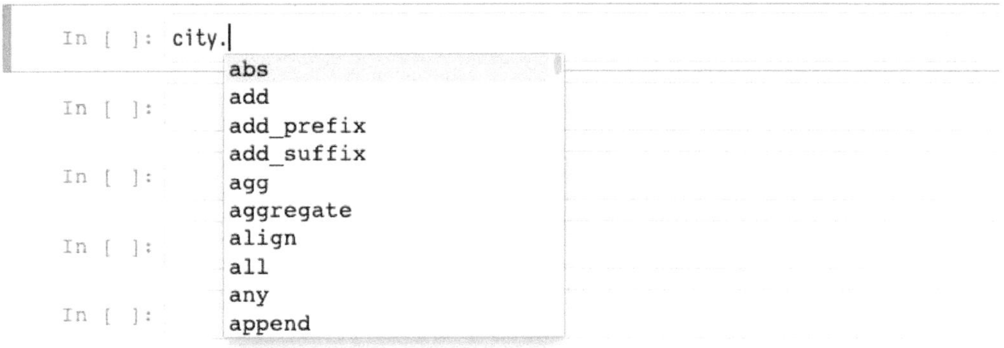

```
In [ ]: city.|
                abs
In [ ]:         add
                add_prefix
                add_suffix
In [ ]:         agg
                aggregate
In [ ]:         align
                all
                any
In [ ]:         append
```

Figure 5.1: Jupyter will pop up a list of options for completions when you hit TAB following a period.

object, you can hit TAB after a period, and it will pop up a list of completions. (Other tools are also able to do this for Python objects).

What functionality do all of these attributes provide? Here is a summary. There are many ways to categorize these, and I'm roughly going to do it by what the result of the method is:

- Dunder methods (.__add__, .__iter__, etc) provide many numeric operations, looping, attribute access, and index access. For the numeric operations, these return Series.

- Corresponding operator methods for many of the numeric operations allow us to tweak the behavior (there is an .add method in addition to .__add__).

- Aggregate methods and properties which reduce or aggregate the values in a series down to a single scalar value. The .mean, .max, and .sum methods and .is_monotonic property are all examples.

- Conversion methods. Some of these start with .to_ and export the data to other formats.

- Manipulation methods such as .sort_values, .drop_duplicates, that return Series objects with the same index.

- Indexing and accessor methods and attributes such as .loc and .iloc. These return Series or scalars.

- String manipulation methods using .str.

- Date manipulation methods using .dt.

- Plotting methods using .plot.

- Categorical manipulation methods using .cat.

- Transformation methods such as .unstack and .reset_index, .agg, .transform.

- Attributes such as .index and .dtype.

- A bunch of *private* attributes that we will ignore (around 130 of them).

We will cover many of these in the following chapters.

5.3 Summary

In this chapter, we introduced the notion that pandas objects have a large number of attributes and methods. Do not let this overwhelm you. You don't need to memorize all of the methods.

5.4 Exercises

1. Explore the documentation for five attributes of a series from Jupyter.

2. How many attributes are found on the .str attribute? Look at the documentation for three of them.

3. How many attributes are found on the .dt attribute? Look at the documentation for three of them.

Chapter 6

Operators (& Dunder Methods)

6.1 Introduction

This chapter, will review some of the operators and magic or *dunder methods* found in series. In short, these are the protocols that determine how the Python language reacts to operations. For example, when you use the + operation, Python is dispatching to the .__add__ method. When you use a loop with a for statement, Python dispatches to the .__iter__ method.

This will not be a deep treatise on the dunder methods (double underscore methods) or magic methods.

Let's look at how this works with a pandas series.

6.2 Dunder Methods

Here is an example in pure Python. When you run this code:

```
>>> 2 + 4
6
```

Under the covers, Python runs this:

```
>>> (2).__add__(4)
6
```

A Python integer object that has a .__add__ method responds to the + operation. Because a Series object has this method, you can call + on it. There is also a .__div__ method that supports division. One way to calculate the average of the two series is the following:

```
>>> (city_mpg + highway_mpg)/2
0           22.0
1           11.5
2           28.0
3           11.0
4           20.0
             ...
41139       22.5
41140       24.0
41141       21.0
41142       21.0
41143       18.5
Length: 41144, dtype: float64
```

Note that the type of the result is float64.

6.3 Index Alignment

Of note, you can apply most math operations on a series with another series, and you can also use a scalar (as we did with the division). When you operate with two series, pandas will *align* the index before performing the operation. Aligning will take each index entry in the left series and match it up with every entry with the same name in the index of the right series. In the above case, values with the same index name are added together and then divided by 2. These operations return a Series object.

Because of index alignment, you will want to make sure that the indexes:

- Are unique (no duplicates)

- Are common to both series

If these situations do not exist you will get missing values or a combinatoric explosion of results. Here is a simple example of two series that have repeated index entries as well as non-common entries:

```
>>> s1 = pd.Series([10, 20, 30], index=[1,2,2])
>>> s2 = pd.Series([35, 44, 53], index=[2,2,4], name='s2')
>>> s1
1    10
2    20
2    30
dtype: int64
```

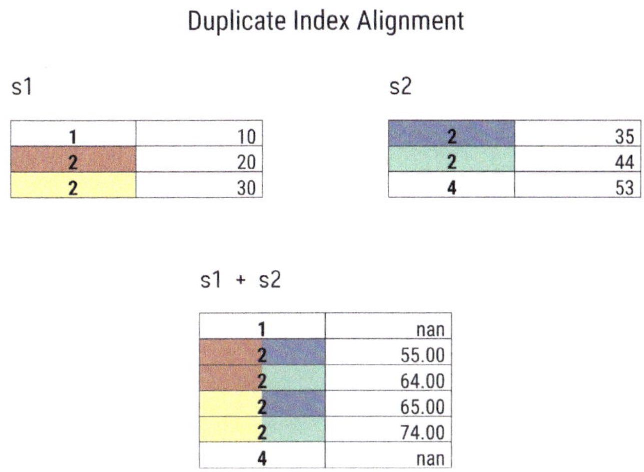

Duplicate Index Alignment

Figure 6.1: The index entries align before operating. If they are not unique, you will get a combinatoric explosion of index entries. Notice that each 2 name from s1 matches each 2 name from the index in s2.

```
>>> s2
2    35
2    44
4    53
Name: s2, dtype: int64

>>> s1 + s2
1     NaN
2    55.0
2    64.0
2    65.0
2    74.0
4     NaN
dtype: float64
```

Note that index names 1 and 4 have NaN while index name 2 has four results —every 2 from s1 is matched up with every 2 from s2.

6.4 Broadcasting

When you perform math operations with a scalar, pandas *broadcasts* the operation to all values. In the above case, the values are added together. This

Duplicate Index Alignment

s1

1	10
2	20
2	30

s2

2	35
2	44
4	53

s1.add(s2, fill_value=0)

1	10.00
2	55.00
2	64.00
2	65.00
2	74.00
4	53.00

Figure 6.2: One upside to the operation methods like .add is that you can specify a fill value. The index entries will still align before performing the operation.

makes it easy to write mathematical operations. It also makes the code easy to read.

There is another advantage to broadcasting. With many math operations, these are optimized and happen very quickly in the CPU. This is called *vectorization*. (A numeric pandas series is a block of memory, and modern CPUs leverage a technology called Single Instruction/Multiple Data (SIMD) to apply a math operation to the block of memory.)

Operations that are available include: +, -, /, // (floor division), % (modulus), @ (matrix multiplication), ** (power), <, <=, ==, !=, >=, >, & (binary and), ^ (binary xor), | (binary or).

6.5 Iteration

Note that there is also a .__iter__ method on a series, and you can loop over the items in a series. However, I recommend avoiding using a for loop with a series. That is a *code smell*, indicating that you are probably doing things the wrong way. You are removing one of the benefits of pandas—vectorization and operating at the C level. If you use a loop to search or filter for values, we will see that there are other ways to do that that are usually faster and they make the code easier to understand.

6.6 Operator Methods

You might wonder why pandas also provides methods for the standard operators. In general, functions and methods have parameters to allow you to *parameterize* or change the behavior based on the parameters. The dunder methods generally fill in NaN (or <NA> for Int64) when one of the operands is missing following index alignment. The operator methods have a fill_value parameter that changes this behavior. If one of the operands is missing, it will use the fill_value instead.

If we call the .add method with the default parameters, we will have the same result as the + operator:

```
>>> s1 + s2
1     NaN
2    55.0
2    64.0
2    65.0
2    74.0
4     NaN
dtype: float64

>>> s1.add(s2)
1     NaN
2    55.0
2    64.0
2    65.0
2    74.0
4     NaN
dtype: float64
```

However, we can use the fill_value parameter to specify that we use zero instead:

```
>>> s1.add(s2, fill_value=0)
1    10.0
2    55.0
2    64.0
2    65.0
2    74.0
4    53.0
dtype: float64
```

6.7 Chaining

Another stylistic reason to prefer the method to the operator is that it makes
chaining manipulations easier. Because most pandas methods do not mutate
data in place but instead return a new object, we can keep tacking on method
calls to the returned object. We will see many examples of this throughout
the book. Chaining makes the code easy to read and understand. We can
chain with operators as well, but it requires that we wrap the operation with
parentheses.

Below, we calculate the average of city and highway mileage using
operators:

```
>>> ((city_mpg +
...     highway_mpg)
...    / 2
... )
0          22.0
1          11.5
2          28.0
3          11.0
4          20.0
          ...
41139      22.5
41140      24.0
41141      21.0
41142      21.0
41143      18.5
Length: 41144, dtype: float64
```

Here is an example of chaining to calculate the average of city and highway
mileage:

```
>>> (city_mpg
...     .add(highway_mpg)
...     .div(2)
... )
0          22.0
1          11.5
2          28.0
3          11.0
4          20.0
          ...
41139      22.5
41140      24.0
41141      21.0
```

```
41142    21.0
41143    18.5
Length: 41144, dtype: float64
```

This is a simple example, but I really like how chaining can lead to understanding your code. I like to put these operations in their own line. I read this as "we are taking the *city_mpg* series, then we are adding the *highway_mpg* series to it. Finally, we are dividing by two."

Method	Operator	Description
s.add(s2)	s + s2	Adds series
s.radd(s2)	s2 + s	Adds series
s.sub(s2)	s - s2	Subtracts series
s.rsub(s2)	s2 - s	Subtracts series
s.mul(s2) s.multiply(s2)	s * s2	Multiplies series
s.rmul(s2)	s2 * s	Multiplies series
s.div(s2) s.truediv(s2)	s / s2	Divides series
s.rdiv(s2) s.rtruediv(s2)	s2 / s	Divides series
s.mod(s2)	s % s2	Modulo of series division
s.rmod(s2)	s2 % s	Modulo of series division
s.floordiv(s2)	s // s2	Floor divides series
s.rfloordiv(s2)	s2 // s	Floor divides series
s.pow(s2)	s ** s2	Exponential power of series
s.rpow(s2)	s2 ** s	Exponential power of series
s.eq(s2)	s2 == s	Elementwise equals of series
s.ne(s2)	s2 != s	Elementwise not equals of series
s.gt(s2)	s > 2	Elementwise greater than of series
s.ge(s2)	s >= 2	Elementwise greater than or equals of series
s.lt(s2)	s < 2	Elementwise less than of series
s.le(s2)	s <= 2	Elementwise less than or equals of series
np.invert(s)	~s	Elementwise inversion of boolean series (no pandas method).

41

np.logical_and(s, s2)	s & s2	Elementwise logical and of boolean series (no pandas method).
np.logical_or(s, s2)	s | s2	Elementwise logical or of boolean series (no pandas method).

Table 6.1: Math Methods and Operators

6.8 Summary

Pandas series respond to most common math operations. You can use the operator directly, and will broadcast the operation to all the values. Alternatively, you can also call the corresponding method for the operator if you want to make chaining easier or parameterize the behavior of the operation.

6.9 Exercises

With a dataset of your choice:

1. Add a numeric series to itself.

2. Add 10 to a numeric series.

3. Add a numeric series to itself using the .add method.

4. Read the documentation for the .add method.

Chapter 7

Aggregate Methods

Aggregate methods collapse the values of a series down to a scalar. Aggregations are the numbers that your boss wants to be reported. If you worked at a burger joint and the boss came in and asked how the restaurant was doing, you wouldn't answer, "Sally ordered a burger and fries. Joe ordered a cheeseburger and shake. Tom ordered ...".

Your boss doesn't care about that level of detail. They care about:

- How many people came in (count)

- How much food was ordered (count)

- What was the total revenue (sum)

- When did people come (skew)

- What was the average purchase amount (mean)

Aggregations allow you to take detailed data and collapse it to a single value. This chapter will explore how to do that on a series.

7.1 Aggregations

If we want to calculate the mean value of a series, we can use an aggregation method, `.mean`:

```
>>> city_mpg.mean()
18.369045304297103
```

There are also a few aggregate properties. These start with .is_. You do not call them; they will evaluate to True or False:

```
>>> city_mpg.is_unique
False
```

```
>>> city_mpg.is_monotonic_increasing
False
```

One method to be aware of is the .quantile method. By default, it returns the 50% quantile. You can specify another level, or you can pass in a list of levels. In the latter case, the result of calling .quantile no longer returns a scalar but a Series object:

```
>>> city_mpg.quantile()
17.0
```

```
>>> city_mpg.quantile(.9)
24.0
```

```
>>> city_mpg.quantile([.1, .5, .9])
0.1     13.0
0.5     17.0
0.9     24.0
Name: city08, dtype: float64
```

7.2 Count and Mean of an Attribute

Here is a neat trick in pandas to calculate aggregates. If you want the count of values that meet some criteria, you can use the .sum method. For example, if we want the count and percent of cars with mileage greater than 20, we can use the following code:

```
>>> (city_mpg
...    .gt(20)
...    .sum()
... )
10272
```

If you want to calculate the percentage of values that meet some criteria, you can apply the .mean method:

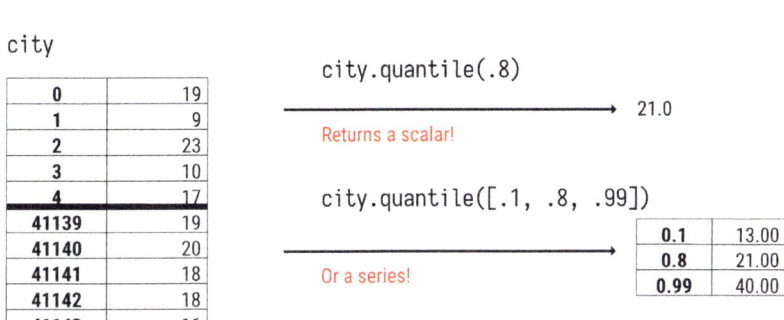

Figure 7.1: Aggregation collapses a series to a scalar value. However, the .quantile method also accepts a list of quantile levels and will return a Series object in that case.

```
>>> (city_mpg
...    .gt(20)
...    .mul(100)
...    .mean()
... )
24.965973167412017
```

This trick comes from the fact that Python treats True as 1 and False as 0. (In earlier versions of the language, True and False did not exist, so programmers used 1 and 0 as stands ins for them). To maintain backward compatibility, the language maintained math operations on booleans. If you sum up a series of boolean values, the result is the count of True values. If you take the mean of a series of boolean values, the result is the fraction of values that are True. You can use this trick with any series of boolean values.

There are a bunch of aggregate methods found on a series, and they are listed later in the chapter.

7.3 .agg and Aggregation Strings

Finally, the .agg method does aggregations (not too much of a surprise given the name). But like .quantile, it also transforms the data in other ways depending on how it is called.

You can use .agg to calculate the mean:

```
>>> city_mpg.agg('mean')
```

However, that is easier with city_mpg.mean(). Where .agg shines is in the ability to perform multiple aggregations. In that case, it returns a series. You can pass in the names of aggregations methods, NumPy reduction functions, Python aggregations, or define your own aggregation function. Here is an example calling all of these types of reductions:

```
>>> import numpy as np
>>> def second_to_last(s):
...     return s.iloc[-2]

>>> city_mpg.agg(['mean', np.var, max, second_to_last])
mean              18.369045
var               62.503036
max              150.000000
second_to_last    18.000000
Name: city08, dtype: float64
```

Below are strings that the .agg method accepts. You can pass in other strings as well, but they will return non-aggregating results. When you pass in a string to .agg pandas will map it to a method found on the Series:

Method	Description
'all'	Returns True if every value is truthy.
'any'	Returns True if any value is truthy.
'autocorr'	Returns Pearson correlation of series with shifted self. Can override lag as keyword argument(default is 1).
'corr'	Returns Pearson correlation of series with other series. Need to specify other.
'count'	Returns count of non-missing values.
'cov'	Return covariance of series with other series. Need to specify other.
'dtype'	Type of the series.
'dtypes'	Type of the series.
'empty'	True if no values in series.

`'hasnans'`	True if missing values in series.
`'idxmax'`	Returns index value of maximum value.
`'idxmin'`	Returns index value of minimum value.
`'is_monotonic'`	True if values always increase.
`'is_monotonic_decreasing'`	True if values always decrease.
`'is_monotonic_increasing'`	True if values always increase.
`'kurt'`	Return "excess" kurtosis (0 is normal distribution). Values greater than 0 have more outliers than normal.
`'mad'`	Return the mean absolute deviation.
`'max'`	Return the maximum value.
`'mean'`	Return the mean value.
`'median'`	Return the median value.
`'min'`	Return the minimum value.
`'nbytes'`	Return the number of bytes of the data.
`'ndim'`	Return the number of dimensions (1) of the data.
`'nunique'`	Return the count of unique values.
`'quantile'`	Return the median value. Can override q to specify other quantile.
`'sem'`	Return the unbiased standard error.
`'size'`	Return the size of the data.
`'skew'`	Return the unbiased skew of the data. Negative indicates tail is on the left side.
`'std'`	Return the standard deviation of the data.
`'sum'`	Return the sum of the series.

Table 7.1: Aggregation strings and descriptions

Below is a table of various aggregation methods and properties.

Method	Description
`s.agg(func=None, axis=0, *args, **kwargs)`	Returns a scalar if func is a single aggregation function. Returns a series if a list of aggregations are passed to func.
`s.all(axis=0, bool_only=None, skipna=True, level=None)`	Returns True if every value is truthy. Otherwise False
`s.any(axis=0, bool_only=None, skipna=True, level=None)`	Returns True if at least one value is truthy. Otherwise False

`s.autocorr(lag=1)`	Returns Pearson correlation between s and shifted s
`s.corr(other, method='pearson')`	Returns correlation coefficient for 'pearson', 'spearman', 'kendall', or a callable.
`s.cov(other, min_periods=None)`	Returns covariance.
`s.max(axis=None, skipna=None, level=None, numeric_only=None`	Returns maximum value.
`s.min(axis=None, skipna=None, level=None, numeric_only=None)`	Returns minimum value.
`s.mean(axis=None, skipna=None, level=None, numeric_only=None)`	Returns mean value.
`s.median(axis=None, skipna=None, level=None, numeric_only=None)`	Returns median value.
`s.prod(axis=None, skipna=None, level=None, numeric_only=None, min_count=0)`	Returns product of s values.
`s.quantile(q=.5, interpolation='linear')`	Returns 50% quantile by default. *Note* returns Series if q is a list.
`s.sem(axis=None, skipna=None, level=None, ddof=1, numeric_only=None)`	Returns unbiased standard error of mean.
`s.std(axis=None, skipna=None, level=None, ddof=1, numeric_only=None)`	Returns sample standard deviation.
`s.var(axis=None, skipna=None, level=None, ddof=1, numeric_only=None)`	Returns unbiased variance.
`s.skew(axis=None, skipna=None, level=None, numeric_only=None)`	Returns unbiased skew.
`s.kurtosis(axis=None, skipna=None, level=None, numeric_only=None)`	Returns unbiased kurtosis.
`s.nunique(dropna=True)`	Returns count of unique items.
`s.count(level=None)`	Returns count of non-missing items.
`s.size`	Number of items in series. (Property)
`s.is_unique`	True if all values are unique
`s.is_monotonic`	True if all values are increasing
`s.is_monotonic_increasing`	True if all values are increasing
`s.is_monotonic_decreasing`	True if all values are decreasing

Table 7.2: Aggregation methods and properties

7.4 Summary

In this chapter, we discussed ways to summarize data in a series. As you begin to analyze data, you will find many of these keep popping up. One thing to keep in mind is that they also apply to a DataFrame.

7.5 Exercises

With a dataset of your choice:

1. Find the count of non-missing values of a series.

2. Find the number of entries of a series.

3. Find the number of unique entries of a series.

4. Find the mean value of a series.

5. Find the maximum value of a series.

6. Use the .agg method to find all of the above.

Chapter 8

Conversion Methods

Sometimes you will need to change the type of the data. This may be due to formats that do not include type information, or it may be that you can have better performance (more manipulation options or use less memory) by changing types.

In this chapter, we will look at various conversions that you might want to do to a Series.

8.1 Automatic Conversion

In pandas 1.0, a new conversion method was introduced, .convert_dtypes. This tries to convert a Series to a type that supports pd.NA. In the case of our city_mpg series, it will change the type from int64 to Int64:

```
>>> city_mpg.convert_dtypes()
0          19
1           9
2          23
3          10
4          17
           ..
41139      19
41140      20
41141      18
41142      18
41143      16
Name: city08, Length: 41144, dtype: Int64
```

I find that .convert_dtypes is a little too magical for me. I prefer more explicit control over what happens to my data.

To specify a type for a series, you can try to use the .astype method. Our city mileage can be held in a 16-bit integer, however an 8-bit integer will not work, as the maximum value for that signed type is 127, and we have some cars with a value of 150:

```
>>> city_mpg.astype('Int16')
0          19
1           9
2          23
3          10
4          17
           ..
41139      19
41140      20
41141      18
41142      18
41143      16
Name: city08, Length: 41144, dtype: Int16
```

```
>>> city_mpg.astype('Int8')
Traceback (most recent call last):
  ...
TypeError: cannot safely cast non-equivalent int64 to int8
```

Using the correct type can save significant amounts of memory. The default numeric type is 8 bytes wide (64 bits, ie int64 or float64). If you can use a narrower type, you can cut back on memory usage, giving you memory to process more data.

You can use NumPy to inspect limits on integer and float types:

```
>>> np.iinfo('int64')
iinfo(min=-9223372036854775808, max=9223372036854775807, dtype=int64)
```

```
>>> np.iinfo('uint8')
iinfo(min=0, max=255, dtype=uint8)
```

```
>>> np.finfo('float16')
finfo(resolution=0.001, min=-6.55040e+04, max=6.55040e+04, dtype=float16)
```

```
>>> np.finfo('float64')
finfo(resolution=1e-15, min=-1.7976931348623157e+308,
      max=1.7976931348623157e+308, dtype=float64)
```

8.2 Memory Usage

To calculate memory usage of the Series, you can use the .nbytes property or the .memory_usage method. The latter is useful when dealing with object types as you can pass deep=True to include the amount of memory used by the Python objects in the Series.

Here we compare memory usage of default numeric integers to Int16:

```
>>> city_mpg.nbytes
329152
```

```
>>> city_mpg.astype('Int16').nbytes
123432
```

Using .nbytes with object types only shows how much memory the Pandas object is taking. The *make* of the autos has strings and is stored as an object. To get the amount of memory that includes the strings, we need to use the .memory_usage method:

```
>>> make = df.make
>>> make.nbytes
329152
```

```
>>> make.memory_usage()
329280
```

```
>>> make.memory_usage(deep=True)
2606395
```

The value of .nbytes is just the memory that the data is using and not the ancillary parts of the Series. The .memory_usage includes the index memory and can include the contribution from object types.

In the next section, we discuss converting to a categorical. We can see that we will save a lot of memory for the make data:

```
>>> (make
...    .astype('category')
...    .memory_usage(deep=True)
... )
95888
```

8.3   String and Category Types

The .astype method can also convert numeric series to strings if you pass str
into it. Note the dtype in the example below:

```
>>> city_mpg.astype(str)
0          19
1           9
2          23
3          10
4          17
           ..
41139      19
41140      20
41141      18
41142      18
41143      16
Name: city08, Length: 41144, dtype: object
```

To convert to a categorical type, you can pass in 'category' as a type:

```
>>> city_mpg.astype('category')
0          19
1           9
2          23
3          10
4          17
           ..
41139      19
41140      20
41141      18
41142      18
41143      16
Name: city08, Length: 41144, dtype: category
Categories (105, int64): [6, 7, 8, 9, ..., 137, 138, 140, 150]
```

A categorical series is useful for string data and can result in large memory
savings. This is because pandas stores Python strings when you have string
data. When you convert it to categorical data, pandas no longer uses Python
strings for each value but optimizes it, so repeating values are not duplicated.
You still have all of the functionality found off of the .str attribute, but it
comes with potentially large memory savings (if you have many duplicate
values) and performance boosts as you do not need to perform as many string
operations.

8.4 Ordered Categories

To create ordered categories, you need to define your own `CategoricalDtype`:

```
>>> values = pd.Series(sorted(set(city_mpg)))
>>> city_type = pd.CategoricalDtype(categories=values,
...        ordered=True)
>>> city_mpg.astype(city_type)
0          19
1           9
2          23
3          10
4          17
           ..
41139      19
41140      20
41141      18
41142      18
41143      16
Name: city08, Length: 41144, dtype: category
Categories (105, int64): [6 < 7 < 8 < 9 ... 137 < 138 < 140 < 150]
```

The section on categories below will discuss more of their features.
The following table lists the types that you can pass into `.astype`.

String or Type	Description
str 'str'	Convert type to Python string
'string'	Convert type to pandas string (supports pd.NA)
int 'int' 'int64'	Convert type to NumPy int64
'int32' 'uint32'	Convert type to 32 signed or unsigned NumPy integer (can also use 16 and 8).
'Int64'	Convert type to pandas Int64 (supports pd.NA). Might complain when you convert floats or strings.
float 'float' 'float64'	Convert type to NumPy float64 (can also support 32 or 16).
'category'	Convert type to categorical (supports pd.NA). Can also use instance of CategoricalDtype.

dates	Don't use this for date conversion, use pd.to_datetime.

Table 8.1: Type and strings for column conversion

8.5 Converting to Other Types

The .to_numpy method (or the .values property) will give us a NumPy array of values, and the .to_list will return a Python list of values. I recommend staying away from these unless necessary. Sometimes there is a speed increase if you use straight NumPy, but there are drawbacks as well. I find pandas objects to be a lot more user-friendly, and the code reads easier. Using Python lists will slow down your code significantly.

As was mentioned before, a Series object is a column from a DataFrame. However, you might need to turn a Series back into a DataFrame. When we discuss dataframes, we will show how to add columns to them, but if you just want a dataframe with a single column, you can use the .to_frame method:

```
>>> city_mpg.to_frame()
       city08
0          19
1           9
2          23
3          10
4          17
...       ...
41139      19
41140      20
41141      18
41142      18
41143      16

[41144 rows x 1 columns]
```

Also, there are many conversion methods to export data into other formats, including CSV, Excel, HDF5, SQL, JSON, and more. These also exist on dataframes, and I find that I use them there and never use them on a Series object. We will talk more about them in the dataframe serialization chapter. Be aware of these methods, and realize that if you understand how they work with dataframes, that knowledge will map back to series.

Finally, to convert to a datetime, use the to_datetime function in pandas. If you want to add timezone information, it is a little more involved. The section on dates will discuss this.

Method	Description
s.convert_dtypes(infer_objects=True, convert_string=True, convert_integer=True, convert_boolean=True, convert_floating=True)	Convert types to appropriate pandas 1 types (that support NA). Doesn't try to reduce size of integer or float types.
s.astype(dtype, copy=True, errors='raise')	Cast series into particular type. If errors='ignore' then return original series on error.
pd.to_datetime(arg, errors='raise', dayfirst=False, yearfirst=False, utc=None, format=None, exact=True, unit=None, infer_datetime_format=False, origin='unix', cache=True)	Convert arg (a series) into datetime. Use format to specify strftime string.
s.to_numpy(dtype=None, copy=False,na_value=object, **kwargs)	Convert the series to a NumPy array.
s.values	Convert the series to a NumPy array.
s.to_frame(name=None)	Return a dataframe representation of the series.
pd.CategoricalDtype(categories=None, ordered=False)	Create a type for categorical data.

Table 8.2: Aggregation methods and properties

8.6 Summary

Having the correct types is very convenient. Not only does it save memory, but it also enables operations that are otherwise tedious. Whenever I teach students the fundamentals of data analysis, I make sure that they go through each column and determine what the correct type for that column is.

8.7 Exercises

With a dataset of your choice:

8. Conversion Methods

1. Convert a numeric column to a smaller type.

2. Calculate the memory savings by converting to smaller numeric types.

3. Convert a string column into a categorical type.

4. Calculate the memory savings by converting to a categorical type.

Chapter 9

Manipulation Methods

I consider manipulation methods to be the workhorses of pandas. When I have a dataset that I am trying to understand, clean up, and model, I use methods that operate on a series and return a new series (usually with the same index) to stick it back in the dataframe I'm working on. Most of the methods we discuss here manipulate the series values but preserve the index. In this chapter, we will explore these methods.

9.1 `.apply` and `.where`

The `.apply` is a curious method, and I often tell my students to avoid it, but sometimes it comes in handy. This method allows you to apply a function element-wise to every value. If you pass in a NumPy function that works on an array, it will broadcast the operation to the series.

However, usually, when I see this method is used, it is a code smell. How so? Because the `.apply` method typically operates on each individual value in the series, the function is called once for every value. If you have one million values in a series, it will be called one million times. It breaks out of the fast vectorized code paths we can leverage in pandas and puts us back to using slow Python code.

For example, we previously checked whether the values in the mileage were greater than 20. We can also do this with the `.apply` method. I'll use the Jupyter `%%timeit` cell magic to microbenchmark this (note this will only work in Jupyter or IPython):

```
>>> def gt20(val):
...     return val > 20
```

```
>>> %%timeit
>>> city_mpg.apply(gt20)
7.32 ms ± 390 µs per loop (mean ± std. dev. of 7 runs, 100 loops each)
```

In contrast if we use the broadcasted .gt method, it runs almost 50 times faster:

```
>>> %%timeit
>>> city_mpg.gt(20)
156 µs ± 30.2 µs per loop (mean ± std. dev. of 7 runs, 10000 loops each)
```

Here's another example. I'm going to look at the *make* column from my dataset. This has the company that made each car. There are quite a few makes in there. I might want to limit my dataset to show the top five makes and label everything else as *Other*. To do that, I would use the .value_counts method to get the frequencies:

```
>>> make = df.make

>>> make
0          Alfa Romeo
1             Ferrari
2               Dodge
3               Dodge
4              Subaru
              ...
41139          Subaru
41140          Subaru
41141          Subaru
41142          Subaru
41143          Subaru
Name: make, Length: 41144, dtype: object

>>> make.value_counts()
Chevrolet                        4003
Ford                             3371
Dodge                            2583
GMC                              2494
Toyota                           2071
                                  ...
Superior Coaches Div E.p. Dutton    1
Vixen Motor Company                 1
London Coach Co Inc                 1
Panoz Auto-Development              1
Qvale                               1
```

```
Name: make, Length: 136, dtype: int64
```

The first five entries in the index are the values I want to keep, everything else I want to replace with *Other*. Here is an example using .apply:

```
>>> top5 = make.value_counts().index[:5]
>>> def generalize_top5(val):
...     if val in top5:
...         return val
...     return 'Other'

>>> make.apply(generalize_top5)
0        Other
1        Other
2        Dodge
3        Dodge
4        Other
         ...
41139    Other
41140    Other
41141    Other
41142    Other
41143    Other
Name: make, Length: 41144, dtype: object
```

Note that when we have already defined a function to pass into .apply that we do not call that function. In the above example, we are not calling generalize_top5, just passing it into .apply. The .apply method will call the function for us.

In the above example, generalize_top5 is called once for every value. A faster, more idiomatic manner of doing this is using the .where method. This method takes a *boolean array* to mark where a condition is true. The .where method keeps values from the series it is called on (make in the example below) where the boolean array is true, if the boolean array is false, it uses the value of the second parameter, other:

```
>>> make.where(make.isin(top5), other='Other')
0        Other
1        Other
2        Dodge
3        Dodge
4        Other
         ...
41139    Other
41140    Other
```

The .where Method

make			make.isin(top5)			make.where(make.isin(top5), other='Other')		
0	Oldsmobile		0	False		0	Other	
1	Chrysler		1	False		1	Other	
2	Ford		2	True		2	Ford	
3	Jeep		3	False		3	Other	
4	BMW		4	False		4	Other	
15	Chevrolet		15	True		15	Chevrolet	
16	Mitsubishi		16	False		16	Other	
17	GMC		17	True		17	GMC	
18	Chevrolet		18	True		18	Chevrolet	
19	Suzuki		19	False		19	Other	

```
top5
['Chevrolet', 'Ford', 'Dodge', 'GMC', 'Toyota']
```

Figure 9.1: The .where method keeps the values where the index is True and uses the other parameter to specify values for False.

```
41141    Other
41142    Other
41143    Other
Name: make, Length: 41144, dtype: object
```

The .where method is optimized and if you look at the timings it is about six times faster:

```
>>> %%timeit
>>> make.apply(generalize_top5)
23.3 ms ± 3.31 ms per loop (mean ± std. dev. of 7 runs, 10 loops each)

>>> %%timeit
>>> make.where(make.isin(top5), 'Other')
4.49 ms ± 1.94 ms per loop (mean ± std. dev. of 7 runs, 100 loops each)
```

The complement of the .where method is the .mask method. Wherever the condition is False it keeps the original values; if it is True it replaces the value with the other parameter. Here is the .mask version of our where statement:

```
>>> make.mask(~make.isin(top5), other='Other')
0        Other
1        Other
2        Dodge
3        Dodge
```

```
4          Other
           ...
41139      Other
41140      Other
41141      Other
41142      Other
41143      Other
Name: make, Length: 41144, dtype: object
```

The tilde, ~, performs an inversion of the boolean array, switching all true values to false and vice versa.

In pandas, there is often more than one way to do something. My take is to prefer using .where and ignore .mask since it is the complement.

9.2 If Else with Pandas

I'm going to show one more piece of code that illustrates what I consider a shortcoming of pandas. If I wanted to keep the top five makes and use *Top10* for the remainder of the top ten makes, with *Other* for the rest, there is no built-in pandas method to do that. I could use the following function in combination with .apply:

```
>>> vc = make.value_counts()
>>> top5 = vc.index[:5]
>>> top10 = vc.index[:10]
>>> def generalize(val):
...      if val in top5:
...           return val
...      elif val in top10:
...           return 'Top10'
...      else:
...           return 'Other'

>>> make.apply(generalize)
0          Other
1          Other
2          Dodge
3          Dodge
4          Other
           ...
41139      Other
41140      Other
41141      Other
41142      Other
```

```
41143    Other
Name: make, Length: 41144, dtype: object
```

To replicate this in pandas, I would need to chain calls to .where:

```
>>> (make
...     .where(make.isin(top5), 'Top10')
...     .where(make.isin(top10), 'Other')
... )
0          Other
1          Other
2          Dodge
3          Dodge
4          Other
          ...
41139      Other
41140      Other
41141      Other
41142      Other
41143      Other
Name: make, Length: 41144, dtype: object
```

Another option is to use the select function found in the NumPy library. This function works with a pandas series. The interface takes a list of boolean arrays and a list with corresponding replacement values. Finally, you can give it a default value:

```
>>> import numpy as np
>>> np.select([make.isin(top5), make.isin(top10)],
...     [make, 'Top10'], 'Other')
array(['Other', 'Other', 'Dodge', ..., 'Other', 'Other', 'Other'],
      dtype=object)
```

Note that this returns a NumPy array. You can wrap it in a Series if you desire. I like this syntax for longer if statements than chaining .where calls because I think it is easier to understand:

```
>>> pd.Series(np.select([make.isin(top5), make.isin(top10)],
...     [make, 'Top10'], 'Other'), index=make.index)
0          Other
1          Other
2          Dodge
3          Dodge
4          Other
          ...
41139      Other
41140      Other
```

```
41141     Other
41142     Other
41143     Other
Length: 41144, dtype: object
```

9.3 Missing Data

Filling in missing data is another common operation, and this is important because many machine learning algorithms do not work if there is missing data. Also, it is prudent to be aware of how much data is missing to make sure you are getting the full story from your data.

The *cylinders* column has missing values. Remember our trick to calculate the count of items that have some property? We can use it here to determine the count of entries that are missing. We convert the property to booleans (using .isna), then call .sum on it:

```
>>> cyl = df.cylinders
>>> (cyl
...    .isna()
...    .sum()
... )
206
```

From the *cylinders* series alone, it is hard to determine why these values are missing. Typically we will have more context, and a dataframe gives that to us. We will use the *make* column which corresponds with the cylinder values to give us some insight. First, let's find the index where the values are missing in the *cylinders* column and then show what those makes are:

```
>>> missing = cyl.isna()
>>> make.loc[missing]
7138     Nissan
7139     Toyota
8143     Toyota
8144       Ford
8146       Ford
          ...
34563     Tesla
34564     Tesla
34565     Tesla
34566     Tesla
34567     Tesla
Name: make, Length: 206, dtype: object
```

Note

We often use the same term to represent different items. In pandas, both a series and a data frame have an *index*, the value that names each row. In addition, we use an *index operation*, performed with square brackets ([and]), to select values from a series or a data frame.

I will try to use the noun "index" to discuss the member of the series or data frame. If I use "index" as a verb, or say "index operation", it is referring to selecting out subsets of data. Below, I am indexing off of the .loc attribute. I could also say that I'm doing an indexing operation:

```
make.loc[missing]
```

We will talk about the .loc attribute when we discuss indexing. For now, realize that if we index .loc with a boolean array, it returns the rows where the boolean array is true.

9.4 Filling In Missing Data

It looks like the cylinder information is missing from cars that are electric. A Tesla car-because it has an electric engine, not a combustion engine-has zero cylinders. The .fillna method allows you to specify a replacement value for any missing data. To fill in the missing values with 0 we can do the following:

```
>>> cyl[cyl.isna()]
7138     NaN
7139     NaN
8143     NaN
8144     NaN
8146     NaN
          ..
34563    NaN
34564    NaN
34565    NaN
34566    NaN
34567    NaN
Name: cylinders, Length: 206, dtype: float64

>>> cyl.fillna(0).loc[7136:7141]
7136     6.0
7137     6.0
7138     0.0
7139     0.0
```

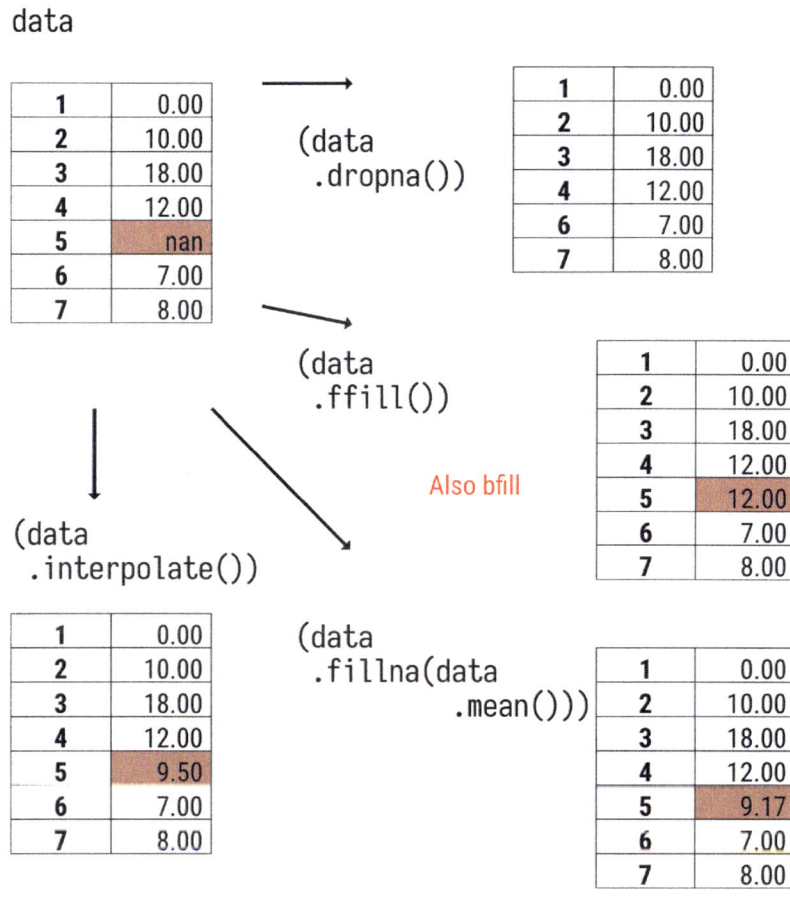

Figure 9.2: We can drop missing data or fill it in with other values.

```
7140    6.0
7141    6.0
Name: cylinders, dtype: float64
```

> **Note**
>
> Almost every operation that I show in this book does not mutate data. In other words, the above operation returns a new series with the missing values replaced by zero. If I want to update my cyl variable, I would need to assign it to this new result. Usually, I end up chaining each command and build up a sequence of operations.

9.5 Interpolating Data

Another option for replacing missing data is the .interpolate method. This comes in handy if the data is ordered (as time series data often is) and there are holes in the data. For example if you had temperature measurements, temp, you could fill in the values using this:

```
>>> temp = pd.Series([32, 40, None, 42, 39, 32])
>>> temp
0    32.0
1    40.0
2     NaN
3    42.0
4    39.0
5    32.0
dtype: float64
```

```
>>> temp.interpolate()
0    32.0
1    40.0
2    41.0
3    42.0
4    39.0
5    32.0
dtype: float64
```

Notice that the value for index label 2 was missing, however, there are values for index labels 1 and 3. After interpolation, the missing value becomes *41.0*, the interpolation of the values around the missing value.

9.6 Clipping Data

If you have outliers in your data, you might want to use the .clip method. In the example below, the first 447 entries in *city* range from 9 to 31:

```
>>> city_mpg.loc[:446]
0        19
1         9
2        23
3        10
4        17
          ..
442      15
443      15
444      15
445      15
446      31
Name: city08, Length: 447, dtype: int64
```

We can trim the values to be between the 5th (11.0) and 95th quantile (27.0) with the following code:

```
>>> (city_mpg
...      .loc[:446]
...      .clip(lower=city_mpg.quantile(.05),
...            upper=city_mpg.quantile(.95))
... )
0        19
1        11
2        23
3        11
4        17
          ..
442      15
443      15
444      15
445      15
446      27
Name: city08, Length: 447, dtype: int64
```

In fact, if you dig into the implementation of .clip, you will see a call to .where. Below is a portion of the ._clip_with_scalar method that .clip calls:

```
if upper is not None:
    subset = self.to_numpy() <= upper
    result = result.where(subset, upper)
if lower is not None:
    subset = self.to_numpy() >= lower
    result = result.where(subset, lower)
```

The .sort_values Method

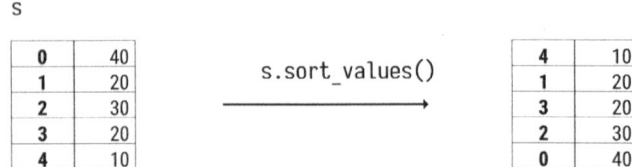

Figure 9.3: The .sort_values method will return a new series with the values sorted (and the original labels in the corresponding order).

9.7   Sorting Values

There are other manipulation methods that might return objects with different index entries. The .sort_values method will sort the values in ascending order and also rearrange the index accordingly:

```
>>> city_mpg.sort_values()
7901         6
34557        6
37161        6
21060        6
35887        6
           ...
34563      138
34564      140
32599      150
31256      150
33423      150
Name: city08, Length: 41144, dtype: int64
```

Note that because of index alignment, you can still do math operations (and many other operations) on a sorted series:

```
>>> (city_mpg.sort_values() + highway_mpg) / 2
0         22.0
1         11.5
2         28.0
3         11.0
4         20.0
          ...
```

```
41139    22.5
41140    24.0
41141    21.0
41142    21.0
41143    18.5
Length: 41144, dtype: float64
```

9.8 Sorting the Index

If you want to sort the index of a series, you can use the `.sort_index` method.
Below we unsort the index by sorting the values, then essentially revert that:

```
>>> city_mpg.sort_values().sort_index()
0           19
1            9
2           23
3           10
4           17
            ..
41139       19
41140       20
41141       18
41142       18
41143       16
Name: city08, Length: 41144, dtype: int64
```

9.9 Dropping Duplicates

Many datasets have duplicate entries. The `.drop_duplicates` method will
remove values that appear more than once. You can determine whether to
keep the first or last duplicate value found using the `keep` parameter. If you
set it to `'last'` it will use the last value. The default value is `'first'`. If you set
it to `False` it will remove any duplicated values (including the initial value).
Notice that this call keeps the original index. However, there are only 105
results (down from 41144) now that duplicates are removed:

```
>>> city_mpg.drop_duplicates()
0           19
1            9
2           23
3           10
4           17
```

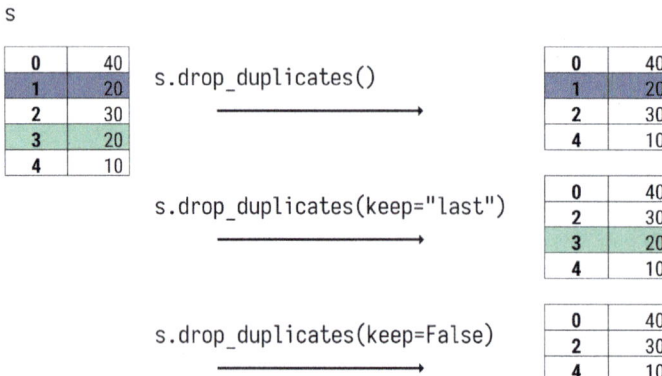

The .drop_duplicates Method

Figure 9.4: The .drop_duplicates method will return a new series that drops the values after they appear more than once by default. The behavior can be changed with the keep parameter.

```
        ...
34364    127
34409    114
34564    140
34565    115
34566    104
Name: city08, Length: 105, dtype: int64
```

9.10 Ranking Data

The .rank method will return a series that keeps the original index but uses the ranks of values from the original series. You can control how ranking occurs with the method parameter. By default, if two values are the same, their rank will be the average of the positions they take. You can specify 'min' to put equal values in the same rank, and 'dense' to not skip any positions:

```
>>> city_mpg.rank()
0          27060.5
1            235.5
```

```
2          35830.0
3            607.5
4          19484.0
              ...
41139      27060.5
41140      29719.5
41141      23528.0
41142      23528.0
41143      15479.0
Name: city08, Length: 41144, dtype: float64

>>> city_mpg.rank(method='min')
0          25555.0
1            136.0
2          35119.0
3            336.0
4          17467.0
              ...
41139      25555.0
41140      28567.0
41141      21502.0
41142      21502.0
41143      13492.0
Name: city08, Length: 41144, dtype: float64

>>> city_mpg.rank(method='dense')
0            14.0
1             4.0
2            18.0
3             5.0
4            12.0
              ...
41139        14.0
41140        15.0
41141        13.0
41142        13.0
41143        11.0
Name: city08, Length: 41144, dtype: float64
```

9.11 Replacing Data

The .replace method allows you to map values to new values. There are many ways to specify how to replace the values. You can specify a whole string to

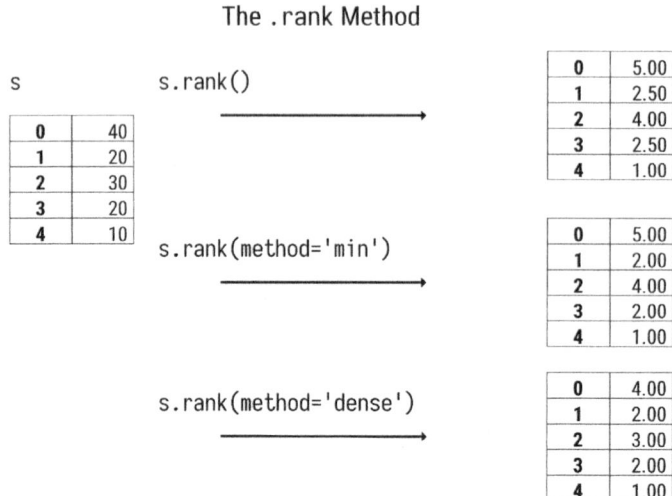

Figure 9.5: The .rank method has various options for dealing with ties.

replace a string or use a dictionary to map old values to new values. This
example uses the former:

```
>>> make.replace('Subaru', 'スバル')
0          Alfa Romeo
1             Ferrari
2               Dodge
3               Dodge
4               スバル
              ...
41139           スバル
41140           スバル
41141           スバル
41142           スバル
41143           スバル
Name: make, Length: 41144, dtype: object
```

The to_replace parameter's value can contain a regular expression if you
provide the regex=True parameter. In this example we use regular expression
capture groups (they are specified in the expression by the parentheses). In
value parameter we refer to these groups (\1 refers to the contents inside the

The .replace Method

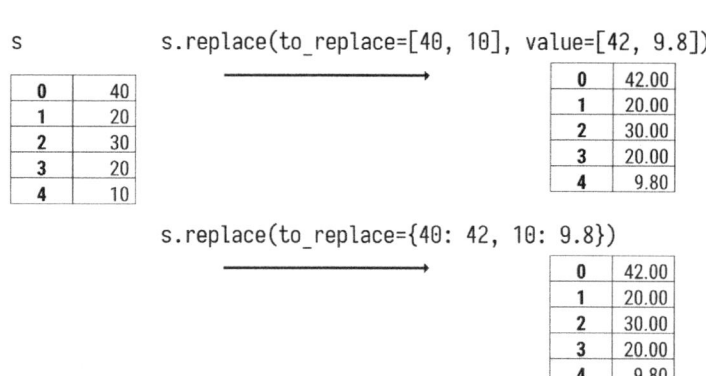

Figure 9.6: The .replace method illustrating lists and dictionaries.

first parentheses and \2 refers to the contents in the second parentheses) when replacing the original value:

```
>>> make.replace(r'(Fer)ra(r.*)',
...     value=r'\2-other-\1', regex=True)
0           Alfa Romeo
1         ri-other-Fer
2                Dodge
3                Dodge
4               Subaru
            ...
41139           Subaru
41140           Subaru
41141           Subaru
41142           Subaru
41143           Subaru
Name: make, Length: 41144, dtype: object
```

9.12 Binning Data

You can bin data as well. Using the cut function, you can create bins of equal width:

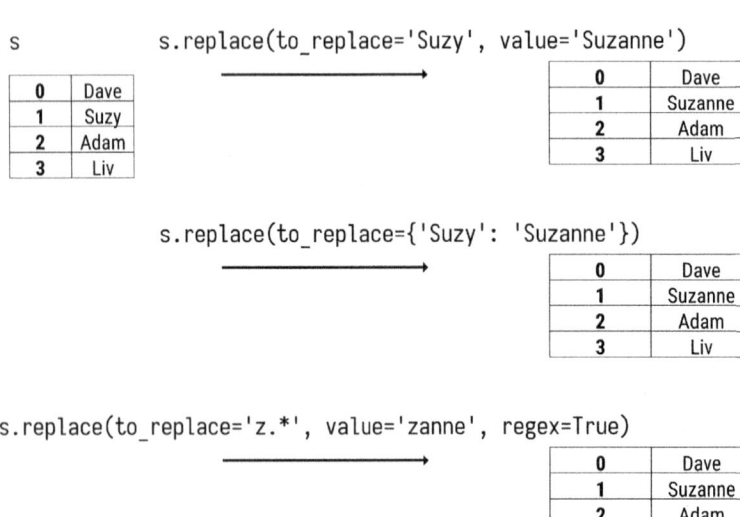

Figure 9.7: The .replace method illustrating different replacement mechanisms.

```
>>> pd.cut(city_mpg, 10)
0         (5.856, 20.4]
1         (5.856, 20.4]
2          (20.4, 34.8]
3         (5.856, 20.4]
4         (5.856, 20.4]
              ...
41139     (5.856, 20.4]
41140     (5.856, 20.4]
41141     (5.856, 20.4]
41142     (5.856, 20.4]
41143     (5.856, 20.4]
Name: city08, Length: 41144, dtype: category
Categories (10, interval[float64]): [(5.856, 20.4] < (20.4, 34.8] < ...
    (121.2, 135.6] < (135.6, 150.0]]
```

Notice that the results of this call is a series with categorical values.

If you have specific sizes for bin edges, you can specify those. In the following example five bins are created (so you need to provide six edges):

```
>>> pd.cut(city_mpg, [0, 10, 20, 40, 70, 150])
0         (10, 20]
1          (0, 10]
2         (20, 40]
3          (0, 10]
4         (10, 20]
            ...
41139     (10, 20]
41140     (10, 20]
41141     (10, 20]
41142     (10, 20]
41143     (10, 20]
Name: city08, Length: 41144, dtype: category
Categories (5, interval[int64]): [(0, 10] < (10, 20] < (20, 40]
    < (40, 70] < (70, 150]]
```

Note the bins have a half-open interval. They do not have the start value but do include the end value. If the city_mpg series had values with 0 or values above 150, they would be missing after binning the series.

You can bin data with quantiles instead. If you wanted 10 bins that had approximately the same number of entries in each bin (rather that each bin width being the same), use the qcut function:

```
>>> pd.qcut(city_mpg, 10)
0         (18.0, 20.0]
1         (5.999, 13.0]
2         (21.0, 24.0]
3         (5.999, 13.0]
4         (16.0, 17.0]
            ...
41139     (18.0, 20.0]
41140     (18.0, 20.0]
41141     (17.0, 18.0]
41142     (17.0, 18.0]
41143     (15.0, 16.0]
Name: city08, Length: 41144, dtype: category
Categories (10, interval[float64]): [(5.999, 13.0] < (13.0, 14.0] < ...
    (18.0, 20.0] < (20.0, 21.0] < (21.0, 24.0] < (24.0, 150.0]]
```

Both of these functions allow you to set the labels to use instead of the categorical intervals they generate:

```
>>> pd.qcut(city_mpg, 10, labels=list(range(1,11)))
0          7
1          1
2          9
3          1
4          5
          ..
41139      7
41140      7
41141      6
41142      6
41143      4
Name: city08, Length: 41144, dtype: category
Categories (10, int64): [1 < 2 < 3 < 4 ... 7 < 8 < 9 < 10]
```

Method	Description
s.apply(func, convert_dtype=True, args=(), **kwds)	Pass in a NumPy function that works on the series, or a Python function that works on a single value. args and kwds are arguments for func. Returns a series, or dataframe if func returns a series.
s.where(cond, other=nan, inplace=False, axis=None, level=None, errors='raise', try_cast=False)	Pass in a boolean series/dataframe, list, or callable as cond. If the value is True, keep it, otherwise use other value. If it is a function, it takes a series and should return a boolean sequence.
np.select(condlist, choicelist, default=0)	Pass in a list of boolean arrays for condlist. If the value is true use the corresponding value from choicelist. If multiple conditions are True, only use the first. Returns a NumPy array.
s.fillna(value=None, method=None, axis=None, inplace=False, limit=None, downcast=None)	Pass in a scalar, dict, series, or dataframe for value. If it is a scalar, use that value, otherwise use the index from the old value to the new value.
s.interpolate(method='linear', axis=0, limit=None, inplace=False, limit_direction=None, limit_area=None, downcast=None, **kwargs)	Perform interpolation with missing values. method may be linear, time among others.

`s.clip(lower=None, upper=None, axis=None, inplace=False, *args, **kwargs)`	Return a new series with values clipped to `lower` and `upper`.
`s.sort_values(axis=0, ascending=True, inplace=False, kind='quicksort', na_position='last', ignore_index=False, key=None)`	Return a series with values sorted. The kind option may be `'quicksort'`, `'mergesort'` (stable), or `'heapsort'`. `na_position` indicates location of NaNs and may be `'first'` or `'last'`.
`s.sort_index(axis=0, level=None, ascending=True, inplace=False, kind='quicksort', na_position='last', sort_remaining=True, ignore_index=False, key=None)`	Return a series with index sorted. The kind option may be `'quicksort'`, `'mergesort'` (stable), or `'heapsort'`. `na_position` indicates location of NaNs and may be `'first'` or `'last'`.
`s.drop_duplicates(keep='first', inplace=False)`	Drop duplicates. `keep` may be `'first'`, `'last'`, or `False`. (If `False`, it removes all values that were duplicated).
`s.rank(axis=0, method='average', numeric_only=None, na_option='keep', ascending=True, pct=False)`	Return a series with numerical ranks. `method` allows you to specify tie handling. `'average'`, `'min'`, `'max'`, `'first'` (uses order they appear in series), `'dense'` (like `'min'`, but rank only increases by one after tie). `na_option` allows you to specify NaN handling. `'keep'` (stay at NaN), `'top'` (move to smallest), `'bottom'` (move to largest).
`s.replace(to_replace-None, value=None, inplace=False, limit=None, regex=False, method='pad')`	Return a series with new values. `to_replace` can be many things. If it is a string, number, or regular expression, you can replace it with a scalar value. It can also be a list of those things which requires values to be a list of the same size. Finally, it can be a dictionary mapping old values to new values.

`pd.cut(x, bins, right=True,`
`  labels=None, retbins=False,`
`  precision=3,`
`  include_lowest=False,`
`  duplicates='raise',`
`  ordered=True)`
	Bin values from x (a series). If bins is an integer, use equal-width bins. If bins is a list of numbers (defining minimum and maximum positions) use those for the edges. right defines whether the right edge is open or closed. labels allows you to specify the bin names. Out of bounds values will be missing.

`pd.qcut(x, q, labels=None,`
`  retbins=False, precision=3,`
`  duplicates='raise')`
	Bin values from x (a series) into q equal sized bins (10 for quantiles, 4). Alternatively, can pass in a list of quantile edges. Out of bounds values will be missing.

Table 9.1: Manipulation methods and properties

9.13 Summary

In this chapter, we explored many methods and functions that are useful for changing the data. We saw how to use function application with the .apply method, but try to avoid that and use np.select instead to get better performance. We discussed various ways to deal with missing data. We saw that we can sort both the values and the index. We can replace data and we can bin data. These operations will come in useful as you begin to analyze data.

9.14 Exercises

With a dataset of your choice:

1. Create a series from a numeric column that has the value of 'high' if it is equal to or above the mean and 'low' if it is below the mean using .apply.

2. Create a series from a numeric column that has the value of 'high' if it is equal to or above the mean and 'low' if it is below the mean using np.select.

3. Time the differences between the previous two solutions to see which is faster.

4. Replace the missing values of a numeric series with the median value.

5. Clip the values of a numeric series to between to 10th and 90th percentiles.

6. Using a categorical column, replace any value that is not in the top 5 most frequent values with 'Other'.

7. Using a categorical column, replace any value that is not in the top 10 most frequent values with 'Other'.

8. Make a function that takes a categorical series and a number (n) and returns a replace series that replaces any value that is not in the top n most frequent values with 'Other'.

9. Using a numeric column, bin it into 10 groups that have the same width.

10. Using a numeric column, bin it into 10 groups that have equal sized bins.

Chapter 10

Indexing Operations

Indexing is an overloaded term in the pandas world. Both a series and a dataframe have an index (the labels down the left side for each row). In addition, both types support the Python indexing operator ([]). But that is not all! They both have attributes (.loc and .iloc) that you can index against (using the Python indexing operator). This section will address both changing the index and accessing parts of a series with the indexing operators.

10.1   Prepping the Data and Renaming the Index

To ease explaining the various operations, I'm going to take the automobile mileage data series with the city miles per gallon values and insert each car's make as the index. This is because many operations work on the index position while others work on the index label. If these are both integer values, it can be a little confusing but becomes more clear if the index has string labels.

   We will use the .rename method to change the index labels. We can pass in a dictionary to map the previous index label to the new label:

```
>>> city2 = city_mpg.rename(make.to_dict())
>>> city2
Alfa Romeo    19
Ferrari        9
Dodge         23
Dodge         10
Subaru        17
              ..
Subaru        19
Subaru        20
```

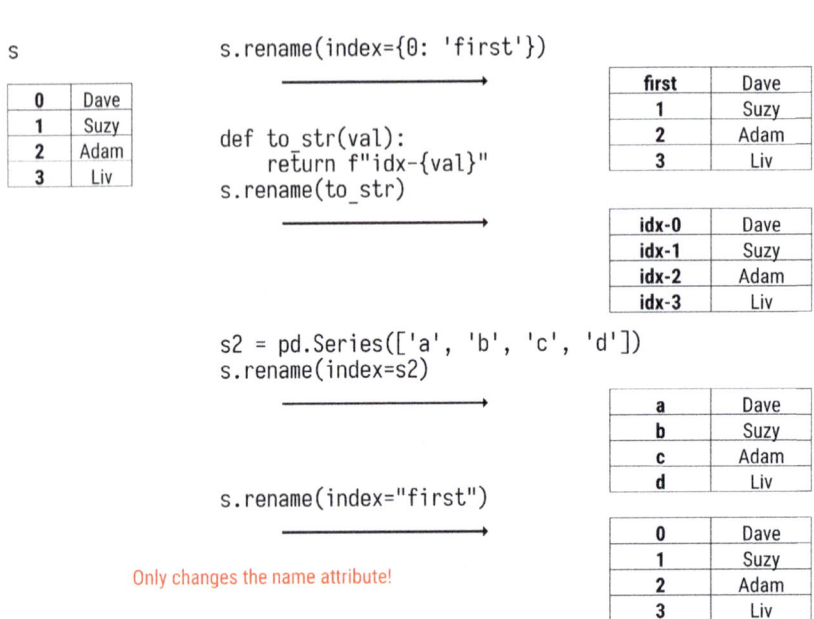

Figure 10.1: The .rename method will return a new series with the original values but new index labels. If you pass in a scalar value it will change the .name attribute of the series on the new series it returns, leaving the index intact.

```
Subaru          18
Subaru          18
Subaru          16
Name: city08, Length: 41144, dtype: int64
```

To view the index you can access the .index attribute:

```
>>> city2.index
Index(['Alfa Romeo', 'Ferrari', 'Dodge', 'Dodge', 'Subaru', 'Subaru',
       'Toyota', 'Toyota', 'Toyota',
       ...
       'Saab', 'Saturn', 'Saturn', 'Saturn', 'Saturn', 'Subaru', 'Subaru',
       'Subaru', 'Subaru', 'Subaru'],
      dtype='object', length=41144)
```

The .rename method also accepts a series, a scalar, a function that takes an old label and returns a new label or a sequence. When we pass in a series and the index values are the same, the values from the series that we passed in are used as the index:

```
>>> city2 = city_mpg.rename(make)
>>> city2
Alfa Romeo    19
Ferrari        9
Dodge         23
Dodge         10
Subaru        17
              ..
Subaru        19
Subaru        20
Subaru        18
Subaru        18
Subaru        16
Name: city08, Length: 41144, dtype: int64
```

Careful though! If you pass a scalar value (a single string) into .rename, the index will stay the same, but the .name attribute of the series will update:

```
>>> city2.rename('citympg')
Alfa Romeo    19
Ferrari        9
Dodge         23
Dodge         10
Subaru        17
              ..
Subaru        19
Subaru        20
Subaru        18
Subaru        18
Subaru        16
Name: citympg, Length: 41144, dtype: int64
```

10.2 Resetting the Index

Sometimes you need a unique index to perform an operation. If you want to set the index to monotonic increasing, and therefore unique integers starting at zero, you can use the .reset_index method. By default, this method will return a dataframe, moving the current index into a new column:

```
>>> city2.reset_index()
          index  city08
0    Alfa Romeo      19
```

```
1           Ferrari      9
2            Dodge      23
3            Dodge      10
4           Subaru      17
...            ...     ...
41139       Subaru      19
41140       Subaru      20
41141       Subaru      18
41142       Subaru      18
41143       Subaru      16

[41144 rows x 2 columns]
```

To drop the current index and return a Series, use the drop=True parameter:

```
>>> city2.reset_index(drop=True)
0           19
1            9
2           23
3           10
4           17
            ..
41139       19
41140       20
41141       18
41142       18
41143       16
Name: city08, Length: 41144, dtype: int64
```

Note that you can sort the values and the index with .sort_values and .sort_index respectively. Because those keep the same index, but just rearrange the order, they do not impact operations that align on the index.

10.3   The .loc Attribute

Let's shift the focus onto pulling data out by using indexing operators. You can index directly on a series object, but I recommend not doing it. I prefer to be a little more explicit. I would index off of the .loc or .iloc attributes.

The .loc attribute deals with index *labels*. It allows you to pull out pieces of the series. You can pass in the following into an index operation on .loc:

- A scalar value of one of the index labels

- A list of index labels.

The .reset_index Method for Series

s

Paul	145
John	142
George	38
Ringo	13

s.reset_index()

Returns a dataframe!

	index	counts
0	Paul	145
1	John	142
2	George	38
3	Ringo	13

```
(s
 .rename_axis("first")
 .reset_index()
)
```

Rename index column

	first	counts
0	Paul	145
1	John	142
2	George	38
3	Ringo	13

s.reset_index(drop=True)

Returns a series!

0	145
1	142
2	38
3	13

Figure 10.2: The .reset_index method will return a dataframe or a series with the index changed to a monotonically increasing index.

- A slice of labels (closed interval so it includes the stop value).

- An index.

- A boolean array (same index labels as the series, but with True or False values.

- A function that accepts a series and returns one of the above.

If you pass in a scalar with the label of an index, you need to be careful. If there are duplicate labels in the index, it will return a series, but if there is only one value for that label, it will return a scalar. In the example below 'Subaru' has multiple index entries, but 'Fisker' only has one. Note the types they return. One returns a series while the other returns a scalar:

```
>>> city2.loc['Subaru']
Subaru     17
Subaru     21
Subaru     22
```

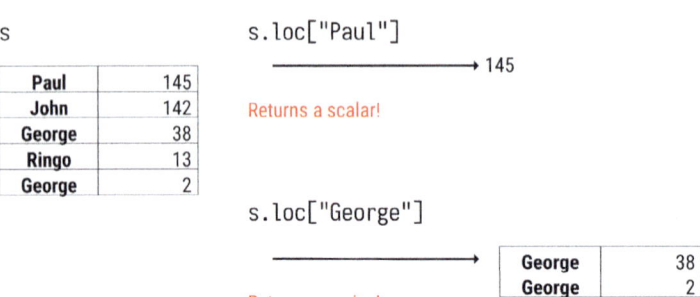

Figure 10.3: Indexing off of the .loc attribute will return a series if the index label is duplicated.

```
Subaru    19
Subaru    20
           ..
Subaru    19
Subaru    20
Subaru    18
Subaru    18
Subaru    16
Name: city08, Length: 885, dtype: int64

>>> city2.loc['Fisker']
20
```

If you want to guarantee that a series is returned, pass in a list rather than passing in a scalar value. It can be a list with a single value or a list with multiple values:

```
>>> city2.loc[['Fisker']]
Fisker    20
Name: city08, dtype: int64

>>> city2.loc[['Ferrari', 'Lamborghini']]
Ferrari        9
Ferrari       12
Ferrari       11
Ferrari       10
```

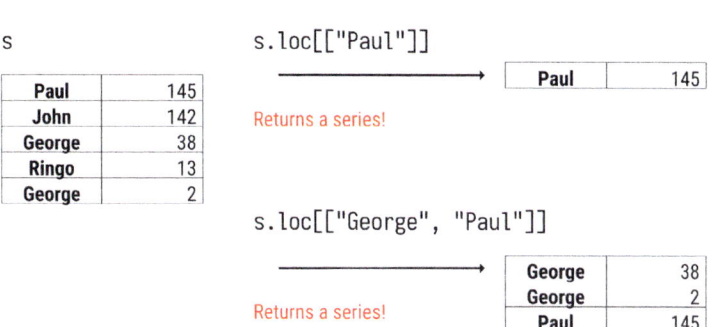

Figure 10.4: Indexing off of the .loc attribute with a list of index names will return a series.

```
Ferrari         11
                ..
Lamborghini      6
Lamborghini      8
Lamborghini      8
Lamborghini      8
Lamborghini      8
Name: city08, Length: 357, dtype: int64
```

This next option might seem a little weird if you are used to normal list slicing with Python. When we slice sequences, we use integer index position, however with .loc we can use a slice with string values. You need to be aware that if join will first need to sort the index if you are slicing with duplicate index labels. Otherwise, you will see a KeyError:

```
>>> city2.loc['Ferrari':'Lamborghini']
Traceback (most recent call last):
  ...
KeyError: "Cannot get left slice bound for non-unique label: 'Ferrari'"

>>> city2.sort_index().loc['Ferrari':'Lamborghini']
Ferrari         10
Ferrari         13
Ferrari         13
Ferrari          9
Ferrari         10
```

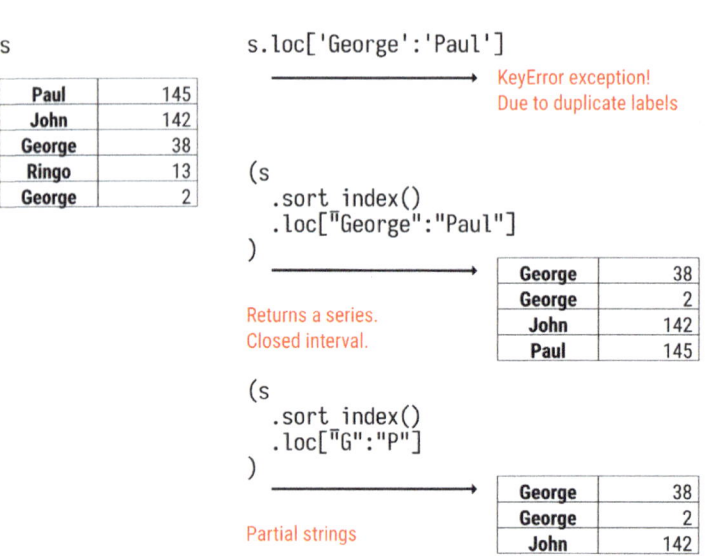

Figure 10.5: Indexing off of the .loc attribute with a slice will return a series. Note that slicing with labels is *closed* and includes the end value.

```
               ..
Lamborghini    12
Lamborghini     9
Lamborghini     8
Lamborghini    13
Lamborghini     8
Name: city08, Length: 11210, dtype: int64
```

Note that when slicing with .loc, it follows the *closed interval*. The closed interval includes both the start index and the final index. This behavior differs from the *half-open interval* found in Python's slicing behavior for strings and lists (which includes the start index, going up to but not including the final index). We will see that the .iloc attribute supports slicing with the half-open interval as well.

There is another trick up the label slicing sleeve. If you have a sorted index, you can slice with strings that are not actual labels. For example, if I wanted all the labels in city2 that start with *F* and go up to those index labels that

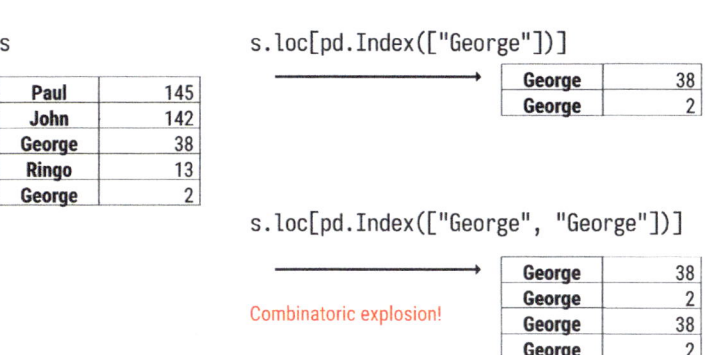

Figure 10.6: The .loc attribute will accept an Index in an indexing operation (no pun intended). Be careful with duplicate index labels, as that may lead to a combinatoric explosion.

also start with *G H I*, and including precisely `'J'`, but not anything else that happens to start with *J*, I could do the following. Note, that no label has the literal value of either the start or stop, so these are not included:

```
>>> city2.sort_index().loc["F":"J"]
Federal Coach    15
Federal Coach    13
Federal Coach    13
Federal Coach    14
Federal Coach    13
                 ..
Isuzu            15
Isuzu            15
Isuzu            15
Isuzu            27
Isuzu            18
Name: city08, Length: 9040, dtype: int64
```

You can also pass in a pandas Index to .loc. This is useful when you have parallel pandas objects with the same index. If you have already filtered one of them, you can get the other to conform by passing its index into .loc. However, you need to be aware of duplicate index labels.

An example will make this more clear. Our `city2` series has many
duplicated index labels. If we index into `.loc` with a simple `Index` with only
`'Dodge'` in it, we get back every value for the label. Using an index is useful if
we want to align a series to a new index:

```
>>> idx = pd.Index(['Dodge'])
>>> city2.loc[idx]
Dodge     23
Dodge     10
Dodge     12
Dodge     11
Dodge     11
          ..
Dodge     18
Dodge     17
Dodge     14
Dodge     14
Dodge     11
Name: city08, Length: 2583, dtype: int64
```

However, if we duplicate `'Dodge'` in the `Index`, the previous operation has
twice as many values, a combinatoric explosion:

```
>>> idx = pd.Index(['Dodge', 'Dodge'])
>>> city2.loc[idx]
Dodge     23
Dodge     10
Dodge     12
Dodge     11
Dodge     11
          ..
Dodge     18
Dodge     17
Dodge     14
Dodge     14
Dodge     11
Name: city08, Length: 5166, dtype: int64
```

You can also pass in a boolean array to `.loc`. Remember that a boolean array
is a series with the same index labels as the series (or dataframe) that you are
manipulating that has boolean values. If you do an indexing operation off
of `.loc` with a boolean array it will return only the values where the boolean
array was true.

In the example below, we will filter out values where the city mileage is above 50. First, I will create a boolean array and store it in a variable called mask:

```
>>> mask = city2 > 50
>>> mask
Alfa Romeo      False
Ferrari         False
Dodge           False
Dodge           False
Subaru          False
                ...
Subaru          False
Subaru          False
Subaru          False
Subaru          False
Subaru          False
Name: city08, Length: 41144, dtype: bool
```

Then I will use that boolean array in an index operation off of .loc:

```
>>> city2.loc[mask]
Nissan      81
Toyota      81
Toyota      81
Ford        74
Nissan      84
            ...
Tesla      140
Tesla      115
Tesla      104
Tesla       98
Toyota      55
Name: city08, Length: 236, dtype: int64
```

You can see that there were only 236 entries with mileage above 50.

Note

The .loc attribute supports pulling out values by specifying index name as well by providing a boolean array. By using a boolean array, you can extract almost any data from a series. This becomes even more powerful when you use it with dataframes and can combine logic based on different columns.

Finally, you can use a function with the .loc attribute. This will come in handy when chaining operations. After multiple operations, the intermediate object you are operating on might have a completely different index than the original object. By using a function, you will have access to the intermediate series and be able to create a row filter based on it. For series objects, this might seem like overkill, but it comes in very handy with dataframes.

Here is an example. I have a series with old pricing information from last year. I know that there was a 10% increase in cost during that time. If I want to find all of the new prices that are above $3 after inflation, we can chain these operations together:

```
>>> cost = pd.Series([1.00, 2.25, 3.99, .99, 2.79],
...       index=['Gum', 'Cookie', 'Melon', 'Roll', 'Carrots'])
>>> inflation = 1.10
>>> (cost
...       .mul(inflation)
...       .loc[lambda s_: s_ > 3]
... )
Melon      4.389
Carrots    3.069
dtype: float64
```

If I calculate the boolean array before taking into account the inflation, (ie using the old series instead of the chained intermediate values) I get the wrong answer:

```
>>> cost = pd.Series([1.00, 2.25, 3.99, .99, 2.79],
...       index=['Gum', 'Cookie', 'Melon', 'Roll', 'Carrots'])
>>> inflation = 1.10
>>> mask = cost > 3
>>> (cost
...       .mul(inflation)
...       .loc[mask]
... )
Melon    4.389
dtype: float64
```

The .loc Attribute for Series

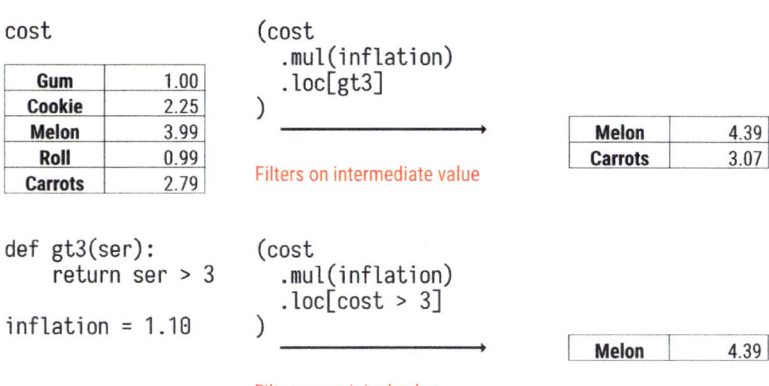

Figure 10.7: The .loc attribute will accept a function. This function accepts the current series it was called on and should return a scalar, list, slice, or index.

Note

The correct example above uses a *lambda function*. This is a syntax that Python provides for making a function in a single line of code. We could have defined a regular Python function instead. The following are equivalent:

```
>>> def gt3(s):
...     return s > 3

>>> gt3 = lambda s: s > 3
```

The basic rule for creating a lambda function is that you use the lambda statement followed by the parameters (s in this case). The parameters are followed by a colon and whatever you want to return. Note that there is an implicit return statement in the lambda function. Also, you can only put an *expression* in it, you can have a *statement*. So it is limited to a single line of code.

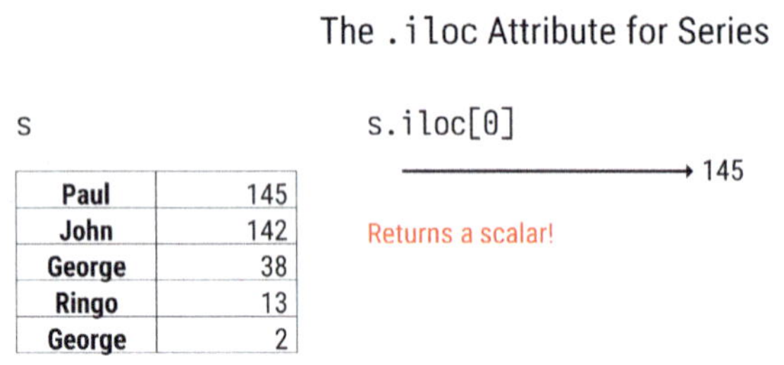

The .iloc Attribute for Series

s   s.iloc[0]

Paul	145
John	142
George	38
Ringo	13
George	2

→ 145

Returns a scalar!

Figure 10.8: Indexing off of the .iloc attribute will return a scalar by location in the series.

10.4   The .iloc Attribute

The series also supports indexing off of the .iloc attribute. This attribute is analogous to .loc but with a few differences. When we slice off of this attribute, we pull out items by index position. The .iloc attribute supports indexing with the following:

- A scalar index position (an integer)

- A list of index positions

- A slice of positions (half-open interval so it does not include stop value).

- A NumPy array (or Python list) of boolean values.

- A function that accepts a series and returns one of the above.

In the examples below we will pull out the first value and last value by slicing off of .iloc with a scalar. Note that because index positions are unique, we will always get the scalar value when indexing with .iloc at a position:

```
>>> city2.iloc[0]
19
```

We can also use negative indexing to pull out the last value:

```
>>> city2.iloc[-1]
16
```

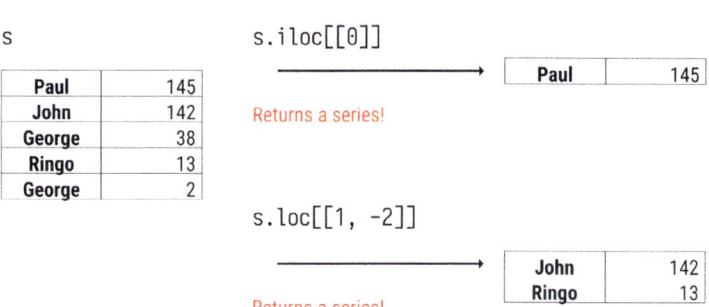

Figure 10.9: Indexing off of the .iloc attribute with a list will return a series of values at the locations in the list.

If we want to return a series object, we can index it with a list of positions. This can be a list with a single index in it or multiple index values. The following code will return a series with the first, second, and last values:

```
>>> city2.iloc[[0,1,-1]]
Alfa Romeo    19
Ferrari        9
Subaru        16
Name: city08, dtype: int64
```

We can also use slices with .iloc. In this case, slices behave as they do in Python lists and follow the half-open interval. That is, they include the first index and go up to but do not include the last index. If we want to return the first five items, we can use the .head method or the following code, which takes index positions starting at 0 and includes 1, 2, 3, and 4, but does not include 5:

```
>>> city2.iloc[0:5]
Alfa Romeo    19
Ferrari        9
Dodge         23
Dodge         10
Subaru        17
Name: city08, dtype: int64
```

To return the last eight values, you could use the following code. In Python, negative index positions start counting from the end. The position -1 is the last

The `.iloc` Attribute for Series

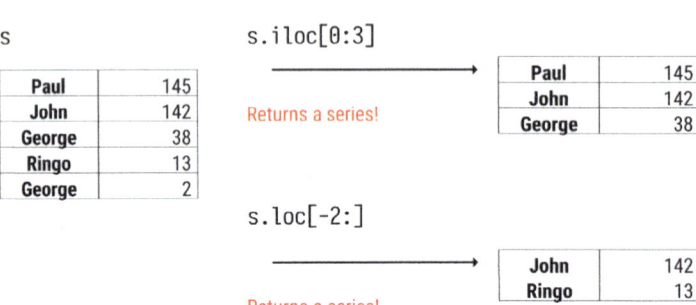

Figure 10.10: Indexing off of the `.iloc` attribute with a slice uses the half-open interval of positions.

index, -2 is the second to last, etc. If we do not include a final index, the slice goes up to the end:

```
>>> city2.iloc[-8:]
Saturn     21
Saturn     24
Saturn     21
Subaru     19
Subaru     20
Subaru     18
Subaru     18
Subaru     16
Name: city08, dtype: int64
```

You can also use a NumPy array of booleans (or a Python list), but if you use what we call a boolean array (a pandas series with booleans), this will fail:

```
>>> mask = city2 > 50
>>> city2.iloc[mask]
Traceback (most recent call last):
  ...
ValueError: iLocation based boolean indexing cannot use an indexable as a mask
```

We can convert the mask to a NumPy array or Python list and the `.iloc` selection will work:

```
>>> city2.iloc[mask.to_numpy()]
Nissan     81
```

```
Toyota       81
Toyota       81
Ford         74
Nissan       84
            ...
Tesla       140
Tesla       115
Tesla       104
Tesla        98
Toyota       55
Name: city08, Length: 236, dtype: int64

>>> city2.iloc[list(mask)]
Nissan       81
Toyota       81
Toyota       81
Ford         74
Nissan       84
            ...
Tesla       140
Tesla       115
Tesla       104
Tesla        98
Toyota       55
Name: city08, Length: 236, dtype: int64
```

Finally, you can pass in a function to .iloc that accepts the series on which it is called. This function can return any of the above options for .iloc. I have not found a real-life use case for passing in a function. Because I would use such functionality to pull out values on the result of a chained method call, using .loc is preferred as it accepts a boolean array.

10.5 Heads and Tails

The .head and .tail methods are useful for pulling out values at the start or end of the series, respectively. These methods are used to quickly inspect a chunk of the data. The following code inspects the three values at the start and end:

```
>>> city2.head(3)
Alfa Romeo     19
Ferrari         9
Dodge          23
Name: city08, dtype: int64
```

```
>>> city2.tail(3)
Subaru     18
Subaru     18
Subaru     16
Name: city08, dtype: int64
```

10.6 Sampling

While the previous two methods allow us to inspect the data, sampling the data can be a better choice. Often the first few entries of the data may be incomplete, test data, or not representative of all of the values. Sampling might be a better option. The code below randomly pulls out six values:

```
>>> city2.sample(6, random_state=42)
Volvo           16
Mitsubishi      19
Buick           27
Jeep            15
Land Rover      13
Saab            17
Name: city08, dtype: int64
```

10.7 Filtering Index Values

The .filter method will filter index labels by exact match, substring, or regular expression. These are controlled with the mutually exclusive items, like, and regex parameters, respectively.

Note that exact match (with items) fails with duplicate index labels:

```
>>> city2.filter(items=['Ford', 'Subaru'])
Traceback (most recent call last):
  ...
ValueError: cannot reindex from a duplicate axis
```

Using like we can do substring matches:

```
>>> city2.filter(like='rd')
Ford     18
Ford     16
Ford     17
Ford     17
Ford     15
  ..
```

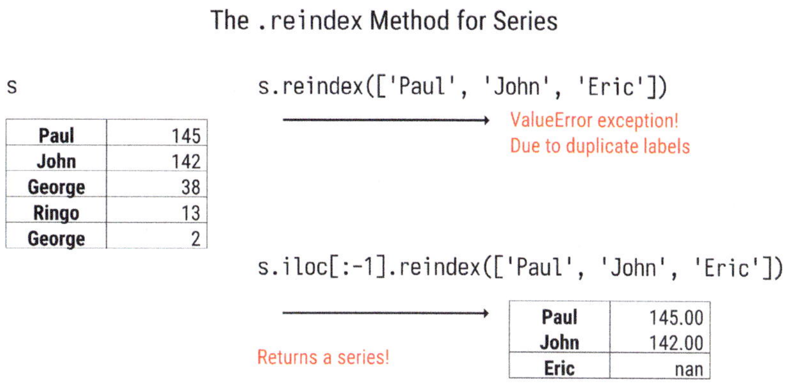

The .reindex Method for Series

Figure 10.11: The .reindex method will *conform* an index to a new index.

```
Ford     26
Ford     19
Ford     21
Ford     18
Ford     19
Name: city08, Length: 3371, dtype: int64
```

We can also specify a regular expression to match against index values:

```
>>> city2.filter(regex='(Ford)|(Subaru)')
Subaru   17
Subaru   21
Subaru   22
Ford     18
Ford     16
         ..
Subaru   19
Subaru   20
Subaru   18
Subaru   18
Subaru   16
Name: city08, Length: 4256, dtype: int64
```

10.8 Reindexing

The .reindex method allows you to pull out values by index label. It will *conform* the series or return a series with the order of the index labels provided. Unlike .loc and .filter, you can pass in labels that are not in the index, and it will not throw an error. Rather it will insert missing values. However, the .reindex method does not like duplicate index labels in the series and will throw an error if you have them:

```
>>> city2.reindex(['Missing', 'Ford'])
Traceback (most recent call last):
  ...
ValueError: cannot reindex from a duplicate axis
```

Note that even though this will not work with duplicate index labels in a series, you can pass in the index label multiple times in the call and it will repeat that index (city has a numeric index that is unique):

```
>>> city_mpg.reindex([0,0, 10, 20, 2_000_000])
0            19.0
0            19.0
10           23.0
20           14.0
2000000      NaN
Name: city08, dtype: float64
```

This method is a lifesaver if you have series that have portions of index labels that are the same and you want one to have the index of the other:

```
>>> s1 = pd.Series([10,20,30], index=['a', 'b', 'c'])
>>> s2 = pd.Series([15,25,35], index=['b', 'c', 'd'])

>>> s2
b    15
c    25
d    35
dtype: int64

>>> s2.reindex(s1.index)
a     NaN
b    15.0
c    25.0
dtype: float64
```

Method	Description
s.rename(index=None, *, level=None, errors='ignore')	Return a series with updated .name attribute if index is a scalar. If index is a function series, or dictionary, return a series with updated index mapped from input (functions work on index name, series and dictionaries map the index name to a new value).
s.index	Returns the index of the series.

s.reset_index(level=None,
    drop=False, name=None,
    inplace=False)
	Return a dataframe (or series when drop=True) with a new integer index.

s.sort_index(axis=0, level=None,
    ascending=True, inplace=False,
    kind='quicksort',
    na_position='last',
    sort_remaining=True,
    ignore_index=False, key=None)
	Return a series with the index sorted. The kind option may be 'quicksort', 'mergesort' (stable), or 'heapsort'. na_position indicates the location of NaNs and may be 'first' or 'last'.

s.loc[idx]	Slice series by names. idx can be a scalar (pull out value at that name), list of names, slice with names (including end position), a boolean array, an index, or a function (that accepts the series and returns one of the previous items).
s.iloc[idx]	Slice series by index position. idx can be a scalar (pull out value at that index), list of indices, slice with index positions (half-open including start but not end index), a list of booleans, or a function (that accepts the series and returns one of the previous items).
s.head(n=5)	Return a series with the first n values.
s.tail(n=5)	Return a series with the last n values.

s.sample(n=None, frac=None,
    replace=False, weights=None,
    random_state=None, axis=None)
	Return a series with n random entries. Can also specify a fraction with frac (if frac > 1 specify replace=True).

s.filter(items=None, like=None, regex=None, axis=None)	Return a series with index values from items list, matching like substring, or when regex (regular expression) search matches.

`s.reindex(index=None,`
`  method=None, copy=True,`
`  level=None, limit=None,`
`  tolerance=None)`
	Return a series with a conformed index.

Table 10.1: Indexing operation, methods, and properties

10.9 Summary

The index is a fundamental structure of pandas. Both a series and dataframe have an index. To get the most out of pandas, it is important that you understand how to manipulate the index. We often have two pandas objects, and if we want to perform operations on them, we might need them to have similar index values. For example, when we add a series to another series, pandas will align the index values and add the corresponding values for each index entry.

We also saw that we could index off of .loc and .iloc to pull out values by name and position, respectively. You will use both of these attributes often when dealing with pandas dataframes and series.

10.10 Exercises

With a dataset of your choice:

1. Inspect the index.

2. Sort the index.

3. Set the index to monotonically increasing integers starting from 0.

4. Set the index to monotonically increasing integers starting from 0, then convert these to the string version. Save this a s2.

5. Using s2, pull out the first 5 entries.

6. Using s2, pull out the last 5 entries.

7. Using s2, pull out one hundred entries starting at index position 10.

8. Using s2, create a series with values with index entries '20', '10', and '2'.

Chapter 11

String Manipulation

In this chapter, we will explore series that have string data. String data is commonly used to hold free-form text, semi-structured text, categorical data, and data that should have another type (typically numeric or datetime). We will look at common operations of textual data.

11.1 Strings and Objects

Before pandas 1.0, if you stored strings in a series the underlying type of the series was object. This is unfortunate as the object type can be used for other series that have Python types in them (such as a list, a dictionary, or a custom class). Also, the object type is used for mixed types. If you have a series that has numbers and strings in it, the type is also object.

Pandas 1.0 introduced the new 'string' type. In addition to being more explicit than object, it supports missing values that are not NaN.

The *make* column has an object type by default:

```
>>> make
0          Alfa Romeo
1             Ferrari
2               Dodge
3               Dodge
4              Subaru
               ...
41139          Subaru
41140          Subaru
41141          Subaru
41142          Subaru
```

```
41143        Subaru
Name: make, Length: 41144, dtype: object
```

You can convert it to a string type by using the .astype method:

```
>>> make.astype('string')
0          Alfa Romeo
1             Ferrari
2               Dodge
3               Dodge
4              Subaru
             ...
41139          Subaru
41140          Subaru
41141          Subaru
41142          Subaru
41143          Subaru
Name: make, Length: 41144, dtype: string
```

The main difference between the 'string' type and strings stored in object (and category) type series is that the string methods return the nullable type when you use a 'string' series. If the result of the string method is missing, pandas will use the newer types that have native pandas nullable types. Otherwise, the behavior is similar.

11.2 Categorical Strings

If you have low cardinality string columns, consider using a categorical type for them. You will have access to many of the same string manipulation methods (though some are not available in this case). The main advantage here is memory savings and performance improvements, as the operations need to be done only on the individual categories and not each value in the series:

```
>>> make.astype('category')
0          Alfa Romeo
1             Ferrari
2               Dodge
3               Dodge
4              Subaru
             ...
41139          Subaru
41140          Subaru
41141          Subaru
```

```
41142        Subaru
41143        Subaru
Name: make, Length: 41144, dtype: category
Categories (136, object): [AM General, ASC Incorporated,
  Acura, Alfa Romeo, ..., Volvo, Wallace Environmental,
  Yugo, smart]
```

We will dive into categories later.

11.3 The .str Accessor

The object, 'string', and 'category' types have a .str accessor that provides
string manipulation methods. Most of these methods are modeled after the
Python string methods. If you are adept at the Python string methods, many
of the pandas variants should be second nature. Here is the Python string
method .lower:

```
>>> 'Ford'.lower()
'ford'
```

And here is the pandas method .lower that works on a series:

```
>>> make.str.lower()
0        alfa romeo
1           ferrari
2             dodge
3             dodge
4            subaru
          ...
41139        subaru
41140        subaru
41141        subaru
41142        subaru
41143        subaru
Name: make, Length: 41144, dtype: object
```

Here is another example of the Python .find method:

```
>>> 'Alfa Romeo'.find('A')
0
```

And here is the pandas version:

```
>>> make.str.find('A')
0          0
1         -1
2         -1
```

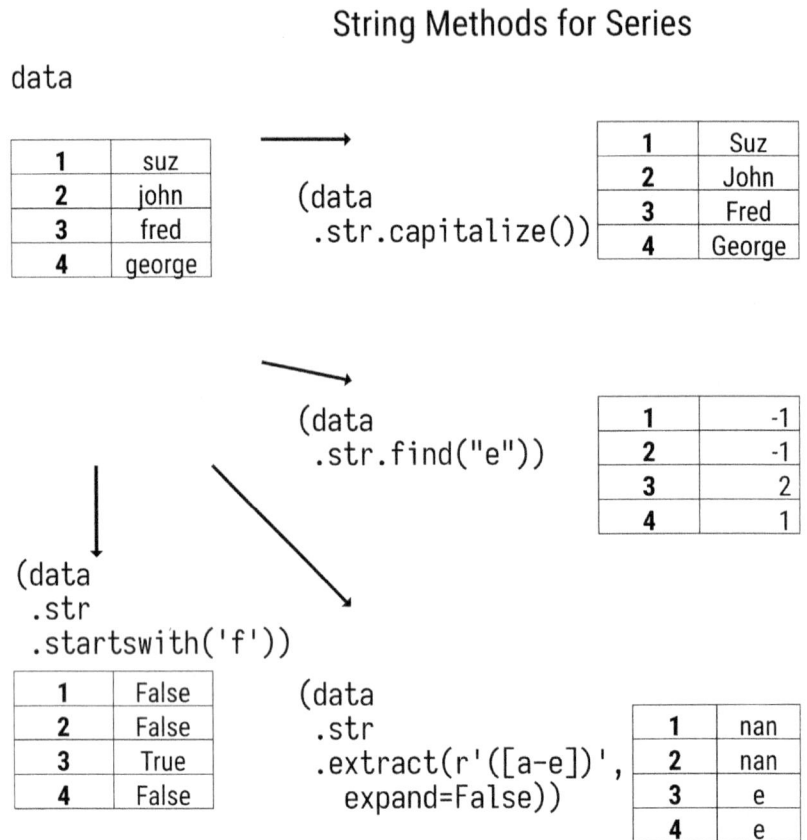

Figure 11.1: The .str accessor will allow you to manipulate strings in a series much like you can manipulate Python strings.

```
3          -1
4          -1
           ..
41139      -1
41140      -1
41141      -1
41142      -1
41143      -1
Name: make, Length: 41144, dtype: int64
```

Many methods are common to both strings and pandas series. They are found in a table later in this chapter.

11.4 Searching

There are a few methods that leverage regular expressions to perform searching, replacing, and splitting. This book will not go deep into regular expressions as there are books solely devoted to that subject.

To find all of the non alphabetic characters (disregarding space), you could use this code:

```
>>> make.str.extract(r'([^a-z A-Z])')
           0
0        NaN
1        NaN
2        NaN
3        NaN
4        NaN
...      ...
41139    NaN
41140    NaN
41141    NaN
41142    NaN
41143    NaN

[41144 rows x 1 columns]
```

This returns a dataframe that has mostly missing values and by inspection is not very useful. If we collapse it into a series (with the parameter expand=False), we can chain the .value_counts method to view the count of non-missing values:

```
>>> (make
...     .str.extract(r'([^a-z A-Z])', expand=False)
...     .value_counts()
```

```
... )
-     1727
.       46
,        9
Name: make, dtype: int64
```

Hint

I like to use a similar technique to the above to search for non-numeric characters that pop up from reading a CSV file. If a column in a CSV file contains non-numeric characters, use the following code to find them:

```
(col
    .str.extract(r'([^0-9.])', expand=False)
    .value_counts()
)
```

After diagnosing the bad actors, you can replace them or drop them and convert the column to the appropriate numeric type.

11.5 Splitting

When dealing with survey data, you may come across binned numeric values. The survey probably had a drop-down of different ranges. It might have said, what is your age? And have options for *20-29, 30-39, 40-49*, etc. Those survey results come in as strings because pandas cannot handle the dash. Hence we cannot perform math operations on the ages, like calculating the minimum or mean values.

Here is an example of pulling out the value before the dash and converting it to a number using the .split method:

```
>>> age = pd.Series(['0-10', '11-15', '11-15', '61-65', '46-50'])
>>> age
0     0-10
1    11-15
2    11-15
3    61-65
4    46-50
dtype: object
```

If we just call .split on the series, we get back a series that has lists in it:

```
>>> age.str.split('-')
0     [0, 10]
```

```
1    [11, 15]
2    [11, 15]
3    [61, 65]
4    [46, 50]
dtype: object
```

Having a series with a Python list makes it hard to manipulate the data. To remedy that, we can provide the expand=True parameter to retrieve a dataframe. If I just wanted to use the first column as an age value, I could chain together an .iloc operation to pull out the first column, and then convert the strings to integers with the .astype method:

```
>>> (age
...     .str.split('-', expand=True)
...     .iloc[:,0]
...     .astype(int)
... )
0     0
1    11
2    11
3    61
4    46
Name: 0, dtype: int64
```

This will bias our ages towards the low side. If you wanted to just use the tail end of the binned value, you can use the .slice method or just do a slice operation off of .str:

```
>>> (age
...     .str.slice(-2)
...     .astype(int)
... )
0    10
1    15
2    15
3    65
4    50
dtype: int64

>>> (age
...     .str[-2:]
...     .astype(int)
... )
0    10
1    15
2    15
```

```
3     65
4     50
dtype: int64
```

We can take the average of the bin ranges using this code:

```
>>> (age
...     .str.split('-', expand=True)
...     .astype(int)
...     .mean(axis='columns')
... )
0     5.0
1     13.0
2     13.0
3     63.0
4     48.0
dtype: float64
```

We have not really dived into dataframes, but in short, the above will convert the columns to numbers, then apply the .mean method across each row (manipulating across the row is accomplished with the axis='columns' parameter). This will make more sense when we discuss the dataframe axis.

Finally, if you wanted to get a random number between the ranges, you could do this:

```
>>> import random
>>> def between(row):
...         return random.randint(*row.values)

>>> (age
...     .str.split('-', expand=True)
...     .astype(int)
...     .apply(between, axis='columns')
... )
0     7
1     15
2     15
3     63
4     49
dtype: int64
```

11.6 Optimizing .apply with Cython

The previous example uses .apply and by now, you should know that I'm generally against that method because it is slow. Let's divert from strings for a minute and look at making the .apply operation quicker using Cython.

Cython is a superset of Python that can compile to native code. To enable it in Jupyter, you will need to run the following cell magic:

```
%load_ext Cython
```

Then you can define functions with Cython. I'm going to "cythonize" the between function as a first step:

```
%%cython
import random
def between_cy(row):
    return random.randint(*row.values)
```

When I benchmark this it is no faster than my current code. If you add types to Cython code, you can get a speed increase. I'll try that here:

```
%%cython
import random
cpdef int between_cy3(int x, int y):
    return random.randint(x, y)
```

Because I'm calling .apply across the columns axis, the between function needs to work on a row (converted into a series) of data. I'm going to use a lambda to pull apart the series and then call between_cy3:

```
(age
  .str.split('-', expand=True)
  .astype(int)
  .apply(lambda row: between_cy3(row[0], row[1]), axis=1)
)
```

I'm still not getting much of a boost. Using prun I see that I'm spending a good deal of time doing index operations (row[0] and row[1]):

```
%prun -l 10 (age.str.split('-', expand=True).astype(int)
    .apply(lambda row: between_cy3(row[0], row[1]), axis=1))

31786620 function calls (31786601 primitive calls) in 12.334 seconds

 Ordered by: internal time
 List reduced from 308 to 10 due to restriction <10>

 ncalls  tottime  percall  cumtime  percall filename:lineno(function)
```

```
1000000    1.533    0.000    5.190    0.000  series.py:928(__getitem__)
1000000    0.708    0.000    2.908    0.000  series.py:1034(_get_value)
1000006    0.674    0.000    2.075    0.000  generic.py:5489(__setattr__)
 500001    0.607    0.000    3.311    0.000  apply.py:937(series_generator)
1000000    0.591    0.000    1.390    0.000  base.py:5175(_get_values_for_loc)
1000000    0.534    0.000    0.809    0.000  range.py:379(get_loc)
 500006    0.501    0.000    0.501    0.000  {method 'split' of 'str' objects}
 500000    0.494    0.000    0.557    0.000  managers.py:1712(set_values)
 500003    0.461    0.000    1.327    0.000  series.py:627(name)
 500000    0.439    0.000    6.832    0.000  <string>:1(<lambda>)
```

I'm going to change the plan of attack and just send in two NumPy arrays and return a NumPy array:

```
%%cython
cimport numpy as np
import numpy as np
import random
cpdef np.ndarray[int] apply_between_cy4(np.ndarray[int] x, np.ndarray[int] y):
    cdef np.ndarray[int] res = np.empty(len(x), dtype='int32')
    for i in range(len(x)):
        res[i] = random.randint(x[i], y[i])
    return res
```

I can run this with the following code and it runs 8x faster on a dataset with 500,000 values:

```
(age
  .str.split('-', expand=True)
  .astype(int)
 .pipe(lambda df_: apply_between_cy4(df_.iloc[:, 0].to_numpy(dtype='int32'),
                                     df_.iloc[:, 1].to_numpy(dtype='int32')))
)
```

11.7   Replacing Text

Both the series and the .str attribute have a .replace method, and these methods have overlapping functionality. If I want to replace single characters, I typically use .str.replace, but if I have complete replacements for many of the values I use .replace.

If I wanted to replace a capital "A" with the Unicode letter a with a ring above it, I could use this code:

```
>>> make.str.replace('A', 'Å')
0          Ålfa Romeo
```

```
1              Ferrari
2               Dodge
3               Dodge
4              Subaru
               ...
41139          Subaru
41140          Subaru
41141          Subaru
41142          Subaru
41143          Subaru
Name: make, Length: 41144, dtype: object
```

This would replace all the "A"s in Audi, Acura, Ashton Martin, Alfa Romeo etc.

However, the version below, calling .replace directly on the series, does not replace anything because it tries to replace the whole string 'A', and there are no makes with that name:

```
>>> make.replace('A', 'Å')
0          Alfa Romeo
1             Ferrari
2               Dodge
3               Dodge
4              Subaru
               ...
41139          Subaru
41140          Subaru
41141          Subaru
41142          Subaru
41143          Subaru
Name: make, Length: 41144, dtype: object
```

You can use a dictionary to specify complete replacements. (This is very explicit, but it might be problematic if you had 20,000 numeric values that had dashes in them, and you wanted to strip out the dashes for all 20,000 numbers. You would have to create a dictionary with all the entries, tedious work.):

```
>>> make.replace({'Audi': 'Åudi', 'Acura': 'Åcura',
...     'Ashton Martin': 'Åshton Martin',
...     'Alfa Romeo': 'Ålfa Romeo'})
0          Ålfa Romeo
1             Ferrari
2               Dodge
3               Dodge
4              Subaru
```

```
          ...
41139          Subaru
41140          Subaru
41141          Subaru
41142          Subaru
41143          Subaru
Name: make, Length: 41144, dtype: object
```

Alternatively, you can specify that you mean to use a regular expression to replace just a portion of the strings with the regex=True parameter:

```
>>> make.replace('A', 'Å', regex=True)
0          Ålfa Romeo
1             Ferrari
2               Dodge
3               Dodge
4              Subaru
          ...
41139          Subaru
41140          Subaru
41141          Subaru
41142          Subaru
41143          Subaru
Name: make, Length: 41144, dtype: object
```

I use .str.replace to replace substrings, and .replace to replace mappings of complete strings.

Note

In pandas, we often refer to vectorized operations. It turns out that pandas is not very optimized for dealing with strings. The string operations are not vectorized. I'm generally against using the .apply method because unless you use NumPy functions, you lose vectorization, and operations take a slow path through Python rather than SIMD instructions on the CPU. Because strings are already slow, this is one place where I'm ok with .apply.

There are a bunch of other string operations. Below is a table with the string methods.

Method	Description
.str.capitalize()	Capitalize strings
.str.casefold()	Lowercase Unicode / caseless strings.

`.str.cat(others=None, sep='',` `  na_rep=None, join='inner')`	If others is None, return a string with values separated by sep. Otherwise, align the index (if others series) and concatenate values.
`.str.center(width, fillchar=' ')`	Center align strings

`.str.contains(pat, case=True,`
`  flags=0, na=np.nan,`
`  regex=True)`
	Return a boolean array if pat matches values.

`.str.count(pat, flags=0)`	Return series with the count of how many times pat occurs in each value.
`.str.decode(encoding)`	Works with bytestrings to decode them to Unicode strings.
`.str.encode(encoding)`	Encode Unicode string to bytestring.
`.str.endswith(pat, na=np.nan)`	Return boolean array if value ends with pat.
`.str.extract(pat, flags=0,` `  expand=True)`	Return a dataframe with the first match from each regular expression capture group in its own column (use named groups for column names). Returns a series if expand=False.
`.str.extractall(pat, flags=0)`	Return a dataframe with all matches from each regular expression capture group in its own column (use named groups for column names). The dataframe has a multiindex, where the inner index is named *match* and has match number.
`.str.find(sub, start=None,` `  end=None)`	Return the lowest index of sub. -1 if not found.
`.str.findall(pat, flags=0)`	Return a series with a list of matches for each value.
`.str.get(i)`	Return a series with the result of val[i] for each value (val) in the series.
`.str.get_dummies(sep='|')`	Return a dataframe with each value in its own column and a 0/1 indicating if the value is absent/appeared for that index label. If a string has multiple values they can be separated with sep.
`.str.index(sub, start=None,` `  end=None)`	Return the lowest index of sub. ValueError if not found.

`.str.isalnum()`	Return boolean array if characters are alphanumeric.
`.str.isalpha()`	Return boolean array if characters are alphabetic.
`.str.isdecimal()`	Return boolean array if characters are decimal.
`.str.isdigit()`	Return boolean array if characters are digits.
`.str.islower()`	Return boolean array if characters are lowercase.
`.str.isnumeric()`	Return boolean array if characters are numeric.
`.str.isspace()`	Return boolean array if characters are whitespace.
`.str.istitle()`	Return boolean array if characters are titlecase.
`.str.isupper()`	Return boolean array if characters are uppercase.
`.str.join(sep)`	Given a series with a list of strings in it, join each element with sep.
`.str.len()`	Return a series with length of each value (works with lists or collections).
`.str.ljust(width, fill=' ')`	Return a left justified series.
`.str.lower()`	Return a lowercase series.
`.str.lstrip(to_strip=None)`	Return a series with left stripped to_strip (whitespace default).
`.str.match(pat, case=True, flags=0, na=np.nan)`	Return a boolean array if pat matches values (anchored at the beginning). Use `.str.contains` to match anywhere in the string. (Use `.str.extract` to pull out the string.)
`.str.normalize(form)`	Return Unicode normal form for series. form can be `'NFC'`, `'NFKC'`, `'NFD'`, or `'NFKD'`.
`.str.pad(width, side='left', fill=' ')`	Return a padded series of length width. side can be `'left'`, `'right'`, or `'both'`.
`.str.partition(sep, expand=True)`	Return a dataframe with three columns: element before first sep, the sep, and the part after.

`.str.repeat(repeats)`	Return a series with values repeated repeats times. repeats can be a scalar or list.
`.str.replace(pat, repl, n=-1, case=True, flags=0, regex=True)`	Return a series where pat is replaced by repl. n is the number of times to replace a value. repl can be a string or a callable that takes a match object and returns a string.
`.str.rfind(sub, start=None, end=None)`	Return highest index of sub. -1 if not found.
`.str.rindex(sub, start=None, end=None)`	Return highest index of sub. ValueError if not found.
`.str.rjust(width, fill=' ')`	Return a right justified series.
`.str.rpartition(sep, expand=True)`	Return a dataframe with three columns: element before last sep, the sep, and the part after.
`.str.rsplit(pat, n=-1, expand=False)`	Return a Series (if expand=False) with a list of values split from the right side limited to n splits.
`.str.rstrip(to_strip=None)`	Return a series with rightstripped to_strip (whitespace default).
`.str.slice(start=None, stop=None, step=None)`	Return a series. Equivalent to s[start:stop:step].
`.str.slice_replace(start=None, stop=None, repl=None)`	Return a series with slice replaced by the value of repl.
`.str.split(pat, n=-1, expand=False)`	Return a Series (if expand=False) with a list of values split by sep limited to n splits.
`.str.startswith(pat, na=np.nan)`	Return boolean array if value starts with pat.
`.str.strip(to_strip=None)`	Return a series with left and right stripped to_strip (whitespace default).
`.str.swapcase()`	Return swapcase series.
`.str.title()`	Return titlecase series.
`.str.translate(table)`	Return series using a dictionary table to replace characters. table maps code points to new code points (numbers not strings). Keys mapped to None are deleted.
`.str.upper()`	Return uppercase series.

.str.wrap(width)	Return a line wrapped series limited to width.
.str.zfill(width)	Return a series limited to width left padded with '0'.

Table 11.1: String methods

11.8 Summary

The object, 'string', and 'category' type series all can be used to store string data. They all have the .str accessor. If you are familiar with Python strings, you get much of the same functionality. In addition, there is the ability to manipulate with regular expressions.

11.9 Exercises

With a dataset of your choice:

1. Using a string column, lowercase the values.

2. Using a string column, slice out the first character.

3. Using a string column, slice out the last three characters.

4. Using a string column, create a series extracting the numeric values.

5. Using a string column, create a series extracting the non-ASCII values.

6. Using a string column, create a dataframe with the dummy columns for every character in the column.

Chapter 12

Date and Time Manipulation

Pandas allows you to create series with date and time information in them. In this chapter, we will explore common operations that you will need to perform with date data.

12.1 Date Theory

Let's talk about dates in brief. Coordinated Universal Time (UTC) is the time standard at 0 degrees longitude. It has an excellent property, that it is monotonically increasing. I live in Salt Lake City, Utah, the *America/Denver* timezone, which is 6 or 7 hours offset of UTC depending on the time of year.

In short, a timezone may contain one or more offsets (depending on if they observe daylight savings time or political whimsy). There is a standardized format, ISO 8601, for representing dates. It does not include the timezone but optionally an offset.

A note on timezone names. The public domain timezone database (also known as the Olsen database) from iana.org provides code and data regarding timezones and their history. From their documentation:

> Timezones are typically identified by continent or ocean and then by the name of the largest city within the region containing the clocks. For example, America/New_York represents most of the US eastern time zone; America/Phoenix represents most of Arizona, which uses mountain time without daylight saving time (DST); America/Detroit represents most of Michigan, which uses eastern time but with different DST rules in 1975; and other

entries represent smaller regions like Starke County, Indiana, which switched from central to eastern time in 1991 and switched back in 2006.

https://data.iana.org/time-zones/tz-link.html

Getting the correct timezone name is important and might be confusing or difficult. As I said, I live in Salt Lake City. If I search for "Timezone for Salt Lake City", I get "Mountain Daylight Time" or "GMT-6". Neither of which is a timezone. You might also see "US/Mountain", "MST", or "MDT". These are not timezones either. These are deprecated names or offsets. The correct timezone name is "America/Denver". However, many applications support erroneous names.

I recommend prefacing your search with "IANA" (ie. "IANA Timezone for Salt Lake City") and then double checking your result in this Wikipedia article (which shows deprecated names)[8].

It is important to have the offset information as well. Timezones that have daylight savings time can have "ambiguous time" in the fall when the time goes back. For example, in Salt Lake on Nov 1, 2015 after 1:59 AM (MDT), the clock goes to 1:00 AM (MST). On that date there are two 1:30 AMs. One at MDT and another an hour later at MST.

For this reason, if you are dealing with local times, you will want three things: the time, the timezone, and an offset. If you are only concerned with duration, you can just use UTC time or seconds since UNIX epoch.

Let's introduce a few more terms before jumping to an example. A time without a timezone or offset is called "naive" time. A time specified in local time is also called "civil time" or "wall time".

UTC time is unambiguous. It does not repeat.

Naive time is ambiguous. 2:37 PM happens multiple times per day for each timezone.

1:29 AM US/Mountain might seem specific enough, but it is context-dependent. On the first Sunday in November, you also need offset information because it is ambiguous. There is 1:29 AM MDT, then after 1:59 AM MDT comes 1:00 AM MST, and there is another 1:29 AM for MST!

A general recommendation for programmers is to store dates in UTC times and then convert them to local time as needed. The ISO 8601 format is not

---

[8]https://en.wikipedia.org/wiki/List_of_tz_database_time_zones

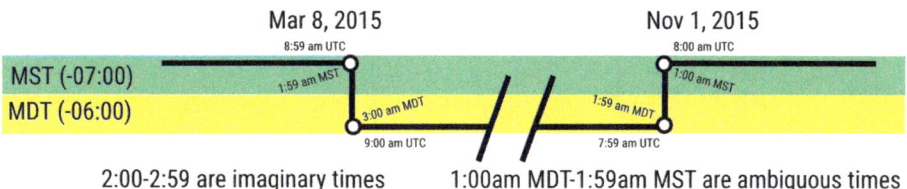

Figure 12.1: When daylight savings begins in the spring, it creates imaginary times. When daylight savings ends in the fall, there are ambiguous times (unless you include the offset).

sufficient to store precise local dates as it supports offset but not timezone. If you need local times I suggest you store one of these two options:

- UTC date and timezone

- Local date, offset, and timezone

Note

The pandas library can support dates stored in UTC values using the datetime64[ns] type. It also supports local times from a single timezone. It appears to (and by appear, I mean the operation goes without failure) support multiple timezones in a single series. However, the underlying datatype will be a pd.Timestamp object that does not support the .dt accessor.

If you have time data and you need to deal with multiple timezones, I would probably break up the data by timezone, put each timezone in its own dataframe or series.

12.2 Loading UTC Time Data

Here is a series of strings with UTC dates. Let's convert it to a date series. You need to remember to pass the utc=True parameter to pd.to_datetime:

123

```
>>> col = pd.Series(['2015-03-08 08:00:00+00:00',
...        '2015-03-08 08:30:00+00:00',
...        '2015-03-08 09:00:00+00:00',
...        '2015-03-08 09:30:00+00:00',
...        '2015-11-01 06:30:00+00:00',
...        '2015-11-01 07:00:00+00:00',
...        '2015-11-01 07:30:00+00:00',
...        '2015-11-01 08:00:00+00:00',
...        '2015-11-01 08:30:00+00:00',
...        '2015-11-01 08:00:00+00:00',
...        '2015-11-01 08:30:00+00:00',
...        '2015-11-01 09:00:00+00:00',
...        '2015-11-01 09:30:00+00:00',
...        '2015-11-01 10:00:00+00:00'])

>>> utc_s = pd.to_datetime(col, utc=True)
>>> utc_s
0     2015-03-08 08:00:00+00:00
1     2015-03-08 08:30:00+00:00
2     2015-03-08 09:00:00+00:00
3     2015-03-08 09:30:00+00:00
4     2015-11-01 06:30:00+00:00
                ...
9     2015-11-01 08:00:00+00:00
10    2015-11-01 08:30:00+00:00
11    2015-11-01 09:00:00+00:00
12    2015-11-01 09:30:00+00:00
13    2015-11-01 10:00:00+00:00
Length: 14, dtype: datetime64[ns, UTC]
```

Notice the type of the result. It indicates that the dates are stored as UTC. Once you have converted a series into a datetime64[ns] object, you have the ability to leverage the .dt attribute.

Let's convert this series to the *America/Denver* timezone:

```
>>> utc_s.dt.tz_convert('America/Denver')
0     2015-03-08 01:00:00-07:00
1     2015-03-08 01:30:00-07:00
2     2015-03-08 03:00:00-06:00
3     2015-03-08 03:30:00-06:00
4     2015-11-01 00:30:00-06:00
                ...
9     2015-11-01 01:00:00-07:00
10    2015-11-01 01:30:00-07:00
11    2015-11-01 02:00:00-07:00
12    2015-11-01 02:30:00-07:00
```

```
13   2015-11-01 03:00:00-07:00
Length: 14, dtype: datetime64[ns, America/Denver]
```

Note that if you have data with offsets that are not 00:00, you can still use the same code to load the data:

```
>>> s = pd.Series(['2015-03-08 01:00:00-07:00',
...   '2015-03-08 01:30:00-07:00',
...   '2015-03-08 03:00:00-06:00',
...   '2015-03-08 03:30:00-06:00',
...   '2015-11-01 00:30:00-06:00',
...   '2015-11-01 01:00:00-06:00',
...   '2015-11-01 01:30:00-06:00',
...   '2015-11-01 01:00:00-07:00',
...   '2015-11-01 01:30:00-07:00',
...   '2015-11-01 01:00:00-07:00',
...   '2015-11-01 01:30:00-07:00',
...   '2015-11-01 02:00:00-07:00',
...   '2015-11-01 02:30:00-07:00',
...   '2015-11-01 03:00:00-07:00'])

>>> pd.to_datetime(s, utc=True).dt.tz_convert('America/Denver')
0    2015-03-08 01:00:00-07:00
1    2015-03-08 01:30:00-07:00
2    2015-03-08 03:00:00-06:00
3    2015-03-08 03:30:00-06:00
4    2015-11-01 00:30:00-06:00
            ...
9    2015-11-01 01:00:00-07:00
10   2015-11-01 01:30:00-07:00
11   2015-11-01 02:00:00-07:00
12   2015-11-01 02:30:00-07:00
13   2015-11-01 03:00:00-07:00
Length: 14, dtype: datetime64[ns, America/Denver]
```

12.3 Loading Local Time Data

If we want to load local date information, we need to have the date, the offset, and the timezone. Let's assume that we have localtime information in one series, and offset in another:

```
>>> time = pd.Series(['2015-03-08 01:00:00',
...   '2015-03-08 01:30:00',
...   '2015-03-08 02:00:00',
...   '2015-03-08 02:30:00',
```

```
...    '2015-03-08 03:00:00',
...    '2015-03-08 02:00:00',
...    '2015-03-08 02:30:00',
...    '2015-03-08 03:00:00',
...    '2015-03-08 03:30:00',
...    '2015-11-01 00:30:00',
...    '2015-11-01 01:00:00',
...    '2015-11-01 01:30:00',
...    '2015-11-01 02:00:00',
...    '2015-11-01 02:30:00',
...    '2015-11-01 01:00:00',
...    '2015-11-01 01:30:00',
...    '2015-11-01 02:00:00',
...    '2015-11-01 02:30:00',
...    '2015-11-01 03:00:00'])

>>> offset = pd.Series([-7, -7, -7, -7, -7, -6, -6,
...    -6, -6, -6, -6, -6, -6, -6, -7, -7, -7, -7, -7])
```

We want to apply the offset to the corresponding time. The mechanism in pandas is to use .groupby with .transform to do this. (We will explain these in detail later in the grouping chapter.) The basic idea is that we group all dates from one offset together and call .dt.tz_localize on them. We repeat this for each offset. Calling the .transform method allows us to work on a group and then return a result in the original length of the grouped object (that has not been aggregated):

```
>>> (pd.to_datetime(time)
...      .groupby(offset)
...      .transform(lambda s: s.dt.tz_localize(s.name)
...                          .dt.tz_convert('America/Denver'))
... )
0     2015-03-07 18:00:07-07:00
1     2015-03-07 18:30:07-07:00
2     2015-03-07 19:00:07-07:00
3     2015-03-07 19:30:07-07:00
4     2015-03-07 20:00:07-07:00
                ...
14    2015-10-31 19:00:07-06:00
15    2015-10-31 19:30:07-06:00
16    2015-10-31 20:00:07-06:00
17    2015-10-31 20:30:07-06:00
18    2015-10-31 21:00:07-06:00
Length: 19, dtype: datetime64[ns, America/Denver]
```

Note that this operation did not error out and appeared to run successfully. However, it you look closely, the offsets were incorrect and moved the minute by 7 or 6 minutes instead of the hours. We need to use different offsets, we want them to be '-07:00' and '-06:00' respectively:

```
>>> offset = offset.replace({-7:'-07:00', -6:'-06:00'})
>>> local = (pd.to_datetime(time)
...          .groupby(offset)
...          .transform(lambda s: s.dt.tz_localize(s.name)
...                     .dt.tz_convert('America/Denver'))
... )

>>> local
0     2015-03-08 01:00:00-07:00
1     2015-03-08 01:30:00-07:00
2     2015-03-08 03:00:00-06:00
3     2015-03-08 03:30:00-06:00
4     2015-03-08 04:00:00-06:00
                 ...
14    2015-11-01 01:00:00-07:00
15    2015-11-01 01:30:00-07:00
16    2015-11-01 02:00:00-07:00
17    2015-11-01 02:30:00-07:00
18    2015-11-01 03:00:00-07:00
Length: 19, dtype: datetime64[ns, America/Denver]
```

12.4 Converting Local time to UTC

If you have a series with local time information (stored as datetime64[ns] and not a string), you can use the .dt.tz_convert method to change it to UTC time:

```
>>> local.dt.tz_convert('UTC')
0     2015-03-08 08:00:00+00:00
1     2015-03-08 08:30:00+00:00
2     2015-03-08 09:00:00+00:00
3     2015-03-08 09:30:00+00:00
4     2015-03-08 10:00:00+00:00
                 ...
14    2015-11-01 08:00:00+00:00
15    2015-11-01 08:30:00+00:00
16    2015-11-01 09:00:00+00:00
17    2015-11-01 09:30:00+00:00
18    2015-11-01 10:00:00+00:00
Length: 19, dtype: datetime64[ns, UTC]
```

12.5 Converting to Epochs

If you have a series with UTC or local time information, you can get the seconds past the UNIX epoch using this code:

```
>>> secs = local.view(int).floordiv(1e9).astype(int)
>>> secs
0     1425801600
1     1425803400
2     1425805200
3     1425807000
4     1425808800
         ...
14    1446364800
15    1446366600
16    1446368400
17    1446370200
18    1446372000
Length: 19, dtype: int64
```

To load epoch information into UTC use the following:

```
>>> (pd.to_datetime(secs, unit='s')
...     .dt.tz_localize('UTC'))
0     2015-03-08 08:00:00+00:00
1     2015-03-08 08:30:00+00:00
2     2015-03-08 09:00:00+00:00
3     2015-03-08 09:30:00+00:00
4     2015-03-08 10:00:00+00:00
         ...
14    2015-11-01 08:00:00+00:00
15    2015-11-01 08:30:00+00:00
16    2015-11-01 09:00:00+00:00
17    2015-11-01 09:30:00+00:00
18    2015-11-01 10:00:00+00:00
Length: 19, dtype: datetime64[ns, UTC]
```

12.6 Manipulating Dates

To further demo date manipulation, I am going to read in a dataset with snowfall levels from a local ski resort.

```
>>> url = 'https://github.com/mattharrison/datasets '+\
...      '/raw/master/data/alta-noaa-1980-2019.csv'
>>> alta_df = pd.read_csv(url)
```

I'm going to show working with a series with date information in them. Then we will look at a series that has dates in the index. The date series will be pulled from the *DATE* column. Remember that when you read a CSV, it does not convert columns to dates by default. You can use the parse_dates parameter to try and convert to dates when reading a CSV, but the to_datetime function is more powerful. I generally recommend messing around with dates outside of the read_csv function:

```
>>> dates = pd.to_datetime(alta_df.DATE)
>>> dates
0        1980-01-01
1        1980-01-02
2        1980-01-03
3        1980-01-04
4        1980-01-05
            ...
14155    2019-09-03
14156    2019-09-04
14157    2019-09-05
14158    2019-09-06
14159    2019-09-07
Name: DATE, Length: 14160, dtype: datetime64[ns]
```

A series with a date in it is a little boring. However, you will see dataframes with date columns in them. Remember that a column is just a series and being able to manipulate that column as part of a dataframe will be useful.

Note that the type of date is datetime64[ns]. This gives us some super powers. It adds a .dt attribute to the series that allows us to perform various date manipulations.

To get the weekdays in Spanish, I can specify the appropriate locale:

```
>>> dates.dt.day_name('es_ES')
0          Martes
1        Miércoles
2          Jueves
3          Viernes
4          Sábado
            ...
14155      Martes
14156    Miércoles
14157      Jueves
14158      Viernes
14159      Sábado
Name: DATE, Length: 14160, dtype: object
```

Note

To get a list of locales on Linux, run the `locale` command from the terminal. My output looks like this:

```
$ locale -a
C
C.UTF-8
POSIX
en_US.utf8
es_ES
es_ES.iso88591
spanish
```

Many of the attributes of the `.dt` attribute are properties and are not methods. Many ask me why are they properties and not methods? A property is not parameterizable. You just get back the results. Also note, that you do not put parentheses at the end of a property (ie, you do not *call* it). If you do, you will get an error stating that it is not callable.

The creators of the properties felt that there were no options to them. For example, `.is_month_end` just tells you whether a day is the last of the month so it is a property. However, `.strftime` requires that we parameterize it with a formatting string, so it is a method:

```
>>> dates.dt.is_month_end
0         False
1         False
2         False
3         False
4         False
          ...
14155     False
14156     False
14157     False
14158     False
14159     False
Name: DATE, Length: 14160, dtype: bool
```

Here we format the date as a string:

```
>>> dates.dt.strftime('%d/%m/%y')
0         01/01/80
1         02/01/80
2         03/01/80
3         04/01/80
```

```
4           05/01/80
              ...
14155       03/09/19
14156       04/09/19
14157       05/09/19
14158       06/09/19
14159       07/09/19
Name: DATE, Length: 14160, dtype: object
```

Code	Meaning	Sample
%y	Year (decimal)	14
%Y	Year (century)	2014
%m	Month (padded)	08
%b	Month (Abbrev locale)	Aug
%B	Month	August
%d	Day (padded)	04
%a	Weekday (Abbrev locale)	Mon
%A	Weekday (locale)	Monday
%H	Hour (24 padded)	22
%I	Hour (12 padded)	10
%M	Minutes (padded)	25
%S	Seconds (padded)	24
%p	AM/PM	PM
%-d	Day (unpadded unix*)	4
%e	Day (unpadded unix*)	4
%c	Locale representation	Mon Aug 4 22:25:24 2014
%x	Locale date	08/04/14
%X	Locale time	22:25:24
%W	Week num (Mon 1st)	31
%U	Week num (Sun 1st)	31
%j	Day of year (padded)	216
%z	UTC offset	+0000
%Z	Time Zone	MDT
%%	Percent sign	%

Figure 12.2: Table of strftime codes

Below is a table of .dt methods and properties.

Method	Description

`.ceil(freq=None,`
`  ambiguous=None,`
`  nonexistent=None)`
	Return ceiling according to offset alias in `freq`. The `nonexistent` parameter controls DST time issues.

`.date`	Property with a series of Python `datetime.date` objects.
`.day`	Property with a series of day of month.
`.day_name(locale='en_us')`	Return the string day of week.
`.dayofweek`	Property with a series of date of week as number (0 is Monday).
`.dayofyear`	Property with a series of day of the year.
`.days_in_month`	Property with a series of number of days in month.
`.daysinmonth`	Property with a series of number of days in month.

`.floor(freq=None,`
`  ambiguous=None,`
`  nonexistent=None)`
	Return floor according to offset alias in `freq`. The `nonexistent` parameter controls DST time issues.

`.hour`	Property with a series of hour of date.
`.is_leap_year`	Property with a series of booleans if date is leap year.
`.is_month_end`	Property with a series of booleans if date is end of month.
`.is_month_start`	Property with a series of booleans if date is start of month.
`.is_quarter_end`	Property with a series of booleans if date is end of quarter.
`.is_quarter_start()`	Property with a series of booleans if date is start of quarter.
`.is_year_end`	Property with a series of booleans if date is end of year.
`.is_year_start`	Property with a series of booleans if date is start of year.
`.microsecond`	Property with a series of microseconds of date.
`.minute`	Property with a series of minutes of date.
`.month`	Property with a series of month of date (numeric).
`.month_name(locale='en_us')`	Return a series of month of date (string).
`.nanosecond`	Property with a series of nanoseconds of date.
`.normalize()`	Return a series of dates converted to midnight.
`.quarter`	Property with series of quarter of date (numeric 1-4).

`.round(freq=None,`
`  ambiguous=None,`
`  nonexistent=None)`
	Return round according to fixed frequency (cannot be end like `'ME'`) in `freq`. The `nonexistent` parameter controls DST time issues.

`.second`	Property with a series of seconds of date (numeric).
`.strftime(date_format)`	Return a series with string dates. Formatted using strftime format codes.
`.time`	Property with a series of Python `datetime.time` objects.
`.timetz`	Property with a series of Python `datetime.time` objects with timezone information.
`.to_period(freq)`	Return a series with pandas `Period` objects.
`.to_pydatetime()`	Return a numpy array with `datetime.datetime` objects.
`.tz`	Property with timezone.
`.tz_convert(tz)`	Convert from one timezone aware series to another.

`.tz_localize(tz,`
`  ambiguous=None,`
`  nonexistent=None)`
	Convert from naive to timezone aware.

`.week`	Property with a series of week of date (numeric 1-53).
`.weekday`	Property with a series of date of week as number 0 is Monday.
`.weekofyear`	Property with a series of week of date (numeric 1-53).
`.year`	Property with a series of year of date.

Table 12.1: .dt methods and Properties

12.7 Summary

In the chapter, we explored converting series into date series. We discussed timezones, offsets, local time, and UTC time. If you have UTC time, you can convert it into a timezone. If you have local time, you will need an offset information to convert it into a timezone (as many local times have ambiguous times). If you have a series with multiple timezone dates in it, I recommend leaving it as UTC because pandas will not allow you to work on the dates unless you split them out into one timezone.

12.8 Exercises

With a dataset of your choice:

1. Convert a column with date information to a date.

2. Convert a date column into UTC dates.

3. Convert a date column into local dates with a timezone.

4. Convert a date column into epoch values.

5. Convert an epoch number into UTC.

Chapter 13

Dates in the Index

If you have dates in the index, you can do some powerful manipulation and aggregation of your data.

We are going to shift gears and look at data that has a date as an index. We will look at the amount of snow that fell each day at the ski resort:

```
>>> url = 'https://github.com/mattharrison/datasets '+\
...      '/raw/master/data/alta-noaa-1980-2019.csv'
>>> alta_df = pd.read_csv(url)
>>> dates = pd.to_datetime(alta_df.DATE)

>>> snow = (alta_df
...      .SNOW
...      .rename(dates)
... )

>>> snow
1980-01-01    2.0
1980-01-02    3.0
1980-01-03    1.0
1980-01-04    0.0
1980-01-05    0.0
              ...
2019-09-03    0.0
2019-09-04    0.0
2019-09-05    0.0
2019-09-06    0.0
2019-09-07    0.0
Name: SNOW, Length: 14160, dtype: float64
```

13. Dates in the Index

13.1 Finding Missing Data

Let's look for missing data. There are a few methods that help with dealing with missing data in time data. We can check is any values are missing using .any:

```
>>> snow.isna().any()
True
```

There is missing data. Let's look where it is:

```
>>> snow[snow.isna()]
1985-07-30    NaN
1985-09-12    NaN
1985-09-19    NaN
1986-02-07    NaN
1986-06-26    NaN
               ..
2017-04-26    NaN
2017-09-20    NaN
2017-10-02    NaN
2017-12-23    NaN
2018-12-03    NaN
Name: SNOW, Length: 365, dtype: float64
```

With a date index, we can provide partial date strings to the .loc indexing attribute. This will let us inspect around the missing data and see if that gives us any insight into why it is missing:

```
>>> snow.loc['1985-09':'1985-09-20']
1985-09-01    0.0
1985-09-02    0.0
1985-09-03    0.0
1985-09-04    0.0
1985-09-05    0.0
               ...
1985-09-16    0.0
1985-09-17    0.0
1985-09-18    0.0
1985-09-19    NaN
1985-09-20    0.0
Name: SNOW, Length: 20, dtype: float64
```

13.2 Filling In Missing Data

Often we have time series data with missing values. For example, in the snow data, the value for the date 1985-09-19 is missing. (See previous code.)

This value looks like it could be filled in with zero (as this is the end of summer):

```
>>> (snow
...     .loc['1985-09':'1985-09-20']
...     .fillna(0)
... )
1985-09-01    0.0
1985-09-02    0.0
1985-09-03    0.0
1985-09-04    0.0
1985-09-05    0.0
              ...
1985-09-16    0.0
1985-09-17    0.0
1985-09-18    0.0
1985-09-19    0.0
1985-09-20    0.0
Name: SNOW, Length: 20, dtype: float64
```

However, these values in January, the middle of the winter, might not be zero. (It is not clear to me why these values are missing. Did a sensor fail? Did someone forget to write down the amount? Was it really zero?) The best way to do with missing data is the talk to a subject matter expert and determine why it is missing:

```
>>> snow.loc['1987-12-30':'1988-01-10']
1987-12-30    6.0
1987-12-31    5.0
1988-01-01    NaN
1988-01-02    0.0
1988-01-03    0.0
              ...
1988-01-06    6.0
1988-01-07    4.0
1988-01-08    9.0
1988-01-09    5.0
1988-01-10    2.0
Name: SNOW, Length: 12, dtype: float64
```

Pandas has various tricks for dealing with missing data. Let's demonstrate them with the missing data from the end of December through January. Notice what happens to the January 1 value as we demo these.

We can do a forward fill or back fill using `.ffill` and `.bfill` respectively:

```
>>> (snow
...     .loc['1987-12-30':'1988-01-10']
...     .ffill()
... )
1987-12-30    6.0
1987-12-31    5.0
1988-01-01    5.0
1988-01-02    0.0
1988-01-03    0.0
                ...
1988-01-06    6.0
1988-01-07    4.0
1988-01-08    9.0
1988-01-09    5.0
1988-01-10    2.0
Name: SNOW, Length: 12, dtype: float64

>>> (snow
...     .loc['1987-12-30':'1988-01-10']
...     .bfill()
... )
1987-12-30    6.0
1987-12-31    5.0
1988-01-01    0.0
1988-01-02    0.0
1988-01-03    0.0
                ...
1988-01-06    6.0
1988-01-07    4.0
1988-01-08    9.0
1988-01-09    5.0
1988-01-10    2.0
Name: SNOW, Length: 12, dtype: float64
```

13.3 Interpolation

We can also interpolate using `.interpolate`. By default this does a linear interpolation for the missing values:

Snow/Winter Truth Table

	Snow Missing	Snow Not Missing
Winter	I	II
Not Winter	III	IV

Figure 13.1: Truth table for snow and winter options.

```
>>> (snow
...      .loc['1987-12-30':'1988-01-10']
...      .interpolate()
... )
1987-12-30    6.0
1987-12-31    5.0
1988-01-01    2.5
1988-01-02    0.0
1988-01-03    0.0
              ...
1988-01-06    6.0
1988-01-07    4.0
1988-01-08    9.0
1988-01-09    5.0
1988 01-10    ?.0
Name: SNOW, Length: 12, dtype: float64
```

We can use the code below to fill in the missing winter values (if the quarter is 1 or 4) with interpolated values and the other values with zero. (Because the index is a datetime, we can access .dt attributes directly on it.)

This is a good example of the .where method. In the figure is a truth table for *winter* and *snow* values.

When it is winter and we are missing snow values, we will interpolate. This corresponds to sections I. When it is not winter and snow values are missing we will fill in 0 (section III). Recall that the .where method keeps values where the first parameter is True, so we invert the conditions with ~:

```
>>> winter = (snow.index.quarter == 1) | (snow.index.quarter== 4)
>>> (snow
...      .where(~(winter & snow.isna()), snow.interpolate())
...      .where(~(~winter & snow.isna()), 0)
... )
```

```
1980-01-01    2.0
1980-01-02    2.5
1980-01-03    1.0
1980-01-04    0.0
1980-01-05    0.0
               ...
2019-09-03    0.0
2019-09-04    0.0
2019-09-05    0.0
2019-09-06    0.0
2019-09-07    0.0
Name: SNOW, Length: 14160, dtype: float64
```

And we can validate the values to make sure that it worked:

```
>>> (snow
...      .where(~(winter & snow.isna()), snow.interpolate())
...      .where(~(~winter & snow.isna()), 0)
...      .loc[['1985-09-19','1988-01-01']]
... )
1985-09-19    0.0
1988-01-01    2.5
Name: SNOW, dtype: float64
```

Note

These .where statements can get confusing with double negatives. I like to work in Jupyter, where I can quickly try code and validate the results. Please do likewise!

13.4 Dropping Missing Values

We can also just drop the missing data using the .dropna method:

```
>>> (snow
...      .loc['1987-12-30':'1988-01-10']
...      .dropna()
... )
1987-12-30    6.0
1987-12-31    5.0
1988-01-02    0.0
1988-01-03    0.0
1988-01-05    2.0
1988-01-06    6.0
1988-01-07    4.0
```

```
1988-01-08    9.0
1988-01-09    5.0
1988-01-10    2.0
Name: SNOW, dtype: float64
```

Be careful with the method and only use it after talking to a subject matter expert who confirms that it is ok to drop the data. It can be hard to tell later if the data is missing. For example, if you plotted this data, you might not see that data was dropped unless you pay close attention.

13.5 Shifting Data

We can shift data up or down, which is useful for sequence data like time series. This method works on any pandas series but comes in really useful with time series when we want to compare to the previous or subsequent entry. Here is a forward and backward shift:

```
>>> snow.shift(1)
1980-01-01    NaN
1980-01-02    2.0
1980-01-03    3.0
1980-01-04    1.0
1980-01-05    0.0
               ...
2019-09-03    0.0
2019-09-04    0.0
2019-09-05    0.0
2019-09-06    0.0
2019-09-07    0.0
Name: SNOW, Length: 14160, dtype: float64

>>> snow.shift(-1)
1980-01-01    3.0
1980-01-02    1.0
1980-01-03    0.0
1980-01-04    0.0
1980-01-05    1.0
               ...
2019-09-03    0.0
2019-09-04    0.0
2019-09-05    0.0
2019-09-06    0.0
2019-09-07    NaN
Name: SNOW, Length: 14160, dtype: float64
```

13.6 Rolling Average

To calculate the five day moving average, we can leverage `.shift` and do the following:

```
>>> (snow
...     .add(snow.shift(1))
...     .add(snow.shift(2))
...     .add(snow.shift(3))
...     .add(snow.shift(4))
...     .div(5)
... )
1980-01-01    NaN
1980-01-02    NaN
1980-01-03    NaN
1980-01-04    NaN
1980-01-05    1.2
             ...
2019-09-03    0.0
2019-09-04    0.0
2019-09-05    0.0
2019-09-06    0.0
2019-09-07    0.0
Name: SNOW, Length: 14160, dtype: float64
```

That was a little tedious to write. Thankfully, pandas has a trick up its sleeve. There is a `.rolling` method that allows us to specify a window size. This method returns a `Rolling` object that we can apply various aggregate methods to. If we apply `.mean` to it, we get a very similar result to above:

```
>>> (snow
...     .rolling(5)
...     .mean()
... )
1980-01-01    NaN
1980-01-02    NaN
1980-01-03    NaN
1980-01-04    NaN
1980-01-05    1.2
             ...
2019-09-03    0.0
2019-09-04    0.0
2019-09-05    0.0
2019-09-06    0.0
2019-09-07    0.0
Name: SNOW, Length: 14160, dtype: float64
```

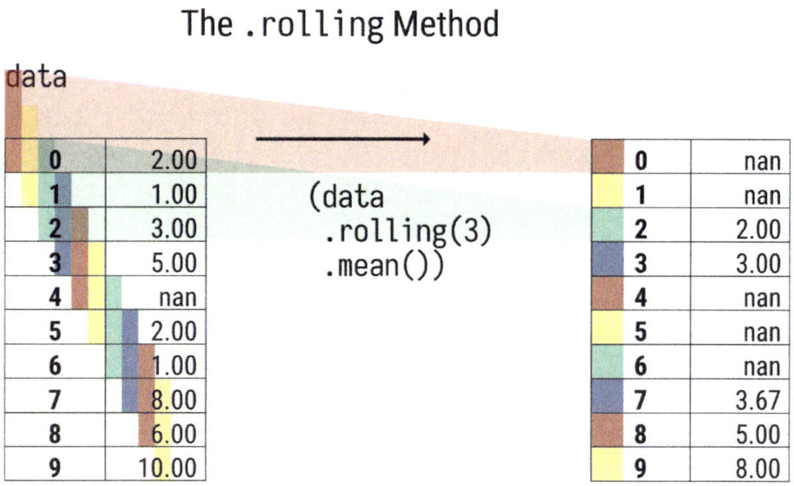

The .rolling Method

Figure 13.2: The .rolling method slides a window along the data, allowing you to call an aggregate function.

Below are methods that work on a Rolling object:

Method	Description
r.agg(func=None, axis=0, *args, **kwargs)	Returns a scalar if func is a single aggregation function. Returns a series if a list of aggregations are passed to func. (aggregate is a synonym.)
r.apply(func, args=None, kwargs=None)	Apply custom aggregation function to rolling group.
r.corr(other, method='pearson')	Returns correlation coefficient for 'pearson', 'spearman', 'kendall', or a callable.
r.count(other, method='pearson')	Returns count of non NaN values.
r.cov(other, min_periods=None)	Returns covariance.
r.max(axis=None, skipna=None, level=None, numeric_only=None	Returns maximum value.
r.min(axis=None, skipna=None, level=None, numeric_only=None)	Returns minimum value.

`r.mean(axis=None, skipna=None, level=None, numeric_only=None)`	Returns mean value.
`r.median(axis=None, skipna=None, level=None, numeric_only=None)`	Returns median value.
`r.quantile(q=.5, interpolation='linear')`	Returns 50% quantile by default. *Note* returns Series if q is a list.
`r.sem(axis=None, skipna=None, level=None, ddof=1, numeric_only=None)`	Returns unbiased standard error of mean.
`r.std(axis=None, skipna=None, level=None, ddof=1, numeric_only=None)`	Returns sample standard deviation.
`r.var(axis=None, skipna=None, level=None, ddof=1, numeric_only=None)`	Returns unbiased variance.
`r.skew(axis=None, skipna=None, level=None, numeric_only=None)`	Returns unbiased skew.

Table 13.1: Rolling methods and properties

13.7 Resampling

Because this series has dates as the index, it has more super powers. We can use the `.resample` method to aggregate values at different levels. At a high level, we group date entries by some interval (yearly, monthly, weekly) and then aggregate the values at that interval.

For example, to find the maximum snowfall by month, we can use this code:

```
>>> (snow
...     .resample('M')
...     .max()
... )
1980-01-31    20.0
1980-02-29    25.0
1980-03-31    16.0
1980-04-30    10.0
1980-05-31     9.0
               ...
2019-05-31     5.1
2019-06-30     0.0
2019-07-31     0.0
```

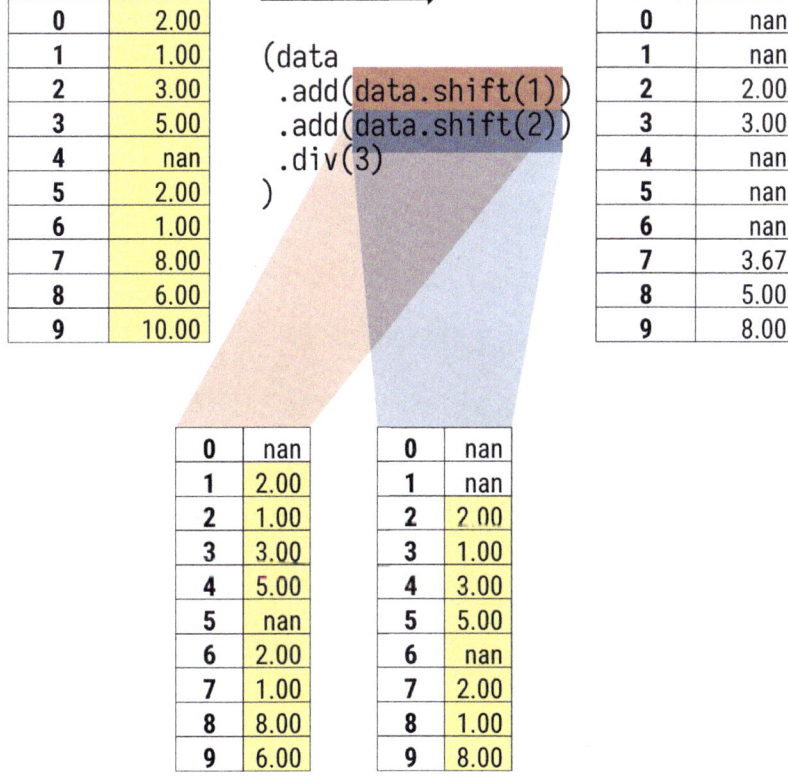

Figure 13.3: The .rolling method slide is similar to shifting the data for N-1 window size and then applying an aggregation.

```
2019-08-31    0.0
2019-09-30    0.0
Freq: M, Name: SNOW, Length: 477, dtype: float64
```

The 'M' string in the .resample call is what pandas calls an *offset alias*. This is a string that specifies a grouping frequency. Using *M* means group all values by the end of the month. If you look at the index for the result, you will see that each date is the end of the month. If we want to aggregate at the end of every two months, we can use '2M' as the offset alias:

```
>>> (snow
...      .resample('2M')
...      .max()
... )
1980-01-31    20.0
1980-03-31    25.0
1980-05-31    10.0
1980-07-31     1.0
1980-09-30     0.0
                ...
2019-01-31    19.0
2019-03-31    20.7
2019-05-31    18.0
2019-07-31     0.0
2019-09-30     0.0
Freq: 2M, Name: SNOW, Length: 239, dtype: float64
```

If we want to aggregate the maximum value for each ski season, which normally ends in May, we could use the following code. This offset alias, 'A-MAY', indicates that we want an annual grouping ('A'), but ending in May of each year:

```
>>> (snow
...      .resample('A-MAY')
...      .max()
... )
1980-05-31    25.0
1981-05-31    26.0
1982-05-31    34.0
1983-05-31    38.0
1984-05-31    25.0
                ...
2016-05-31    15.0
2017-05-31    26.0
2018-05-31    21.8
2019-05-31    20.7
```

```
2020-05-31    0.0
Freq: A-MAY, Name: SNOW, Length: 41, dtype: float64
```

Below is a table of the offset aliases.

Offset Alias	Date Offset	Description
None	DateOffset	Default 1 day
'B'	BDay	Business day (weekday)
'C'	CDay	Custom business day
'W'	Week	Week (Can add -MON to end on Monday)
'WOM'	WeekOfMonth	Nth day of Mth week of month
'LWOM'	LastWeekOfMonth	Nth day of last week of month
'M'	MonthEnd	Month end
'MS'	MonthBegin	Month start
'BM'	BMonthEnd	Business month end
'BMS'	BMonthBegin	Business month start
'CBM'	CBMonthEnd	Custom business month end
'CBMS'	CBMonthBegin	Custom business month start
'SM'	SemiMonthEnd	Semi-month end (15th and month end)
'SMS'	SemiMonthBegin	Semi-month start (15th and month start)
'Q'	QuarterEnd	Quarter end (Can specify -JAN to end quarter in January)
'QS'	QuarterBegin	Quarter start
'BQ'	BQuarterEnd	Business quarter end
'BQS'	BQuarterBegin	Business quarter start
'REQ'	FY5253Quarter	Retail quarter end (52-53 week)
'A'	YearEnd	Calendar year end (Can specify -MAY to end year in May)
'AS' / 'BYS'	YearBegin	Calendar year start
'BA'	BYearEnd	Business year end
'BAS'	BYearBegin	Business year start
'RE'	FY5253	Retail year end (52-53 week)
'BH'	BusinessHour	Business hour
'CBH'	CustomBusinessHour	Custom business hour
'D'	Day	Day
'H'	Hour	Hour
'T' / 'min'	Minute	Minute
'S'	Second	Second

`'L' /` `'ms'`	`Milli`	Millisecond
`'U' /` `'us'`	`Micro`	Microsecond
`'N'`	`Nano`	Nanosecond

Table 13.2: Offset aliases and date offset classes for `Grouper` and `.resample`

The result of calling `.resample` is a `DateTimeIndexResampler` object. It can perform many operations in addition to taking the maximum value (as shown in the examples). See the table in the next section.

13.8 Gathering Aggregate Values (But Keeping Index)

Below, instead of performing an aggregation with `.resample`, we leverage the `.transform` method, which works on aggregation groups but returns a series with the original index. This makes it easy to do things like calculate the percentage of quarterly snowfall that fell in a day:

```
>>> (snow
...     .div(snow
...             .resample('Q')
...             .transform('sum'))
...     .mul(100)
...     .fillna(0)
... )
1980-01-01    0.527009
1980-01-02    0.790514
1980-01-03    0.263505
1980-01-04    0.000000
1980-01-05    0.000000
                ...
2019-09-03    0.000000
2019-09-04    0.000000
2019-09-05    0.000000
2019-09-06    0.000000
2019-09-07    0.000000
Name: SNOW, Length: 14160, dtype: float64
```

To compute the percentage of a season's snowfall that fell during each month, we could do the following:

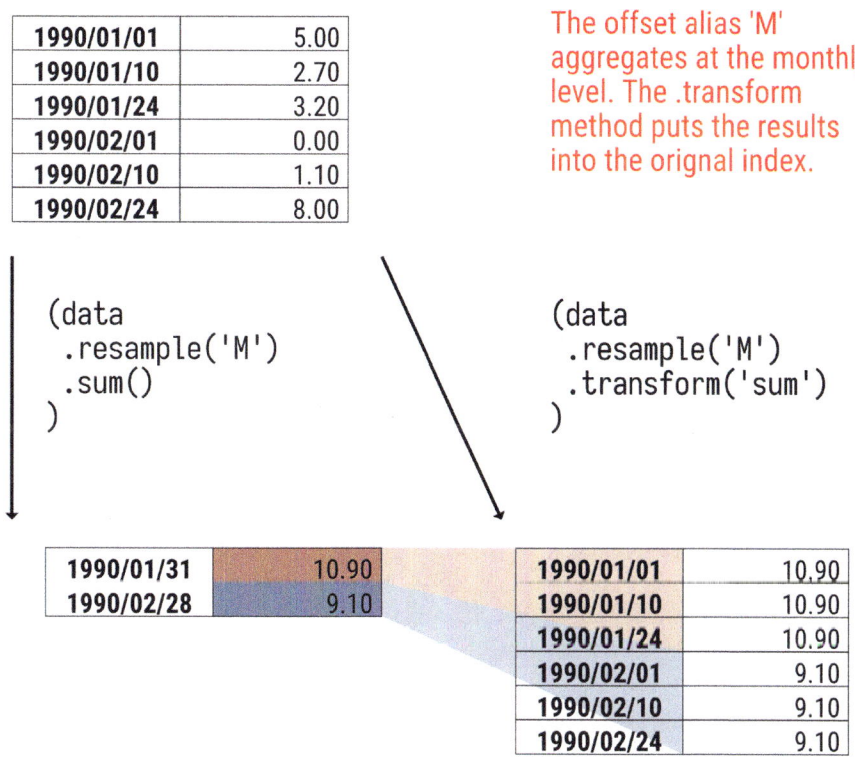

Figure 13.4: If you have dates in the index, you can use the .resample method to aggregate at date frequencies. The .transform method will take the resulting aggregates and place them back in the cell that contributed to the value (with the original index).

```
>>> season2017 = snow.loc['2016-10':'2017-05']
>>> (season2017
...        .resample('M')
...        .sum()
...        .div(season2017
...                .sum())
...        .mul(100)
... )
2016-10-31     2.153969
2016-11-30     9.772637
2016-12-31    15.715995
2017-01-31    25.468688
2017-02-28    21.041085
2017-03-31     9.274033
2017-04-30    14.738732
2017-05-31     1.834862
Freq: M, Name: SNOW, dtype: float64
```

Here is a table of the operations you can use on a resample object.

Method	Description
.agg(func, *args, **kwargs)	Apply a function (to the group), string function name, list of functions, or dictionary (mapping column names to previous function/string/list). Returns a series if called with a single function, otherwise return a dateframe for multiple functions.
.aggregate(func, *args, **kwargs)	Same as .agg
.apply(func, *args, **kwargs)	Same as .agg
.asfreq(fill_value=None)	Return values at frequency (like .reindex)
.backfill(limit=None)	Backfill the missing values.
.bfill(limit=None)	Same as .backfill
.count()	Count of non-missing items in group.
.ffill(limit=None)	Forward fill the missing values.
.fillna(method, limit=None)	Method ('ffill', 'bfill', or 'nearest') to use for filling in missing data for upsampling.
.first()	Return a series with the first value of each group.
.get_group(name, obj=None)	Return the series for grouping frequency of name.

`.interpolate(method='linear', axis=0, limit=None, limit_direction='forward', limit_area=None, downcast=None, **kwargs,)`	Return a series with interpolated values.
`.last()`	Return a series with the final value from each group.
`.max()`	Return a series with maximum value from each group.
`.mean()`	Return a series with mean value from each group.
`.median()`	Return a series with median value from each group.
`.min()`	Return a series with minimum value from each group.
`.nearest(limit=None)`	Fill the missing values with nearest.
`.ngroups`	Property with number of groups in aggregation.
`.nunique()`	Return a series with the number of unique values from each group.
`.ohlc()`	Return a dataframe with columns for open, high, low, close.
`.pad(limit=None)`	Same as `.ffill`.
`.pipe(func, *args, **kwargs)`	Apply function to resampler object.
`.plot()`	Plot the groups.
`.prod()`	Return a series with the product of each group.
`.quantile(q=0.5)`	Return a series with the quantile. If q is a list, return a multi-index series.
`.sem()`	Return a series with the standard error of mean of each group.
`.size()`	Return a series with the size of each group (number of rows including missing values).
`.std()`	Return a series with the standard deviation of each group.
`.sum()`	Return a series with the sum of each group.

| `.transform(function, *args, **kwargs)` | Return a series with the same index as the original (not grouped series). Function takes a group and returns a group with the same index. |
| `.var()` | Return a series with the variance of each group. |

Table 13.3: Resampler Methods on a Series

13.9 Groupby Operations

There is also a .groupby method that acts as a generic sort of .resample, and I use this more on dataframes than series. But here is an example of creating a function that will determine ski season by looking at the index with date information. It considers a season to be from October to September:

```
>>> def season(idx):
...     year = idx.year
...     month = idx.month
...     return year.where((month < 10), year+1)
```

We can now use this function with the .groupby method to aggregate all values for a season. Here we calculate total snowfall for each season:

```
>>> (snow
...     .groupby(season)
...     .sum()
... )
1980    457.5
1981    503.0
1982    842.5
1983    807.5
1984    816.0
         ...
2015    284.3
2016    354.6
2017    524.0
2018    308.8
2019    504.5
Name: SNOW, Length: 40, dtype: float64
```

Note

We could also do the above with `.resample` using an anchored offset alias.
The index would be a date instead of an integer:

```
>>> (snow
...     .resample('A-SEP')
...     .sum()
... )
1980-09-30    457.5
1981-09-30    503.0
1982-09-30    842.5
1983-09-30    807.5
1984-09-30    816.0
                ...
2015-09-30    284.3
2016-09-30    354.6
2017-09-30    524.0
2018-09-30    308.8
2019-09-30    504.5
Freq: A-SEP, Name: SNOW, Length: 40, dtype: float64
```

We will show more grouping operations like this when we dive into
dataframes. Mastering these operations takes some time, but it has huge
payoffs as it makes many calculations that would require creating a lot of
declarative code easy.

13.10 Cumulative Operations

There are also a handful of cumulative methods that work well with sequence
data. These are `.cummin`, `.cummax`, `.cumprod`, and `.cumsum`. They return the
cumulative minimum, maximum, product, and sum respectively. To calculate
the snowfall in a season, we can combine `.cumsum` with slicing:

```
>>> (snow
...     .loc['2016-10':'2017-09']
...     .cumsum()
... )
2016-10-01    0.0
2016-10-02    0.0
2016-10-03    4.9
2016-10-04    4.9
2016-10-05    5.5
                ...
```

```
2017-09-26    524.0
2017-09-27    524.0
2017-09-28    524.0
2017-09-29    524.0
2017-09-30    524.0
Name: SNOW, Length: 364, dtype: float64
```

Alternatively, it we wanted to do this calculation for every year, we can combine .resample with .transform and 'cumsum':

```
>>> (snow
...      .resample('A-SEP')
...      .transform('cumsum')
... )
1980-01-01     2.0
1980-01-02     5.0
1980-01-03     6.0
1980-01-04     6.0
1980-01-05     6.0
              ...
2019-09-03   504.5
2019-09-04   504.5
2019-09-05   504.5
2019-09-06   504.5
2019-09-07   504.5
Name: SNOW, Length: 14160, dtype: float64
```

Method	Description

pd.to_datetime(arg,
  errors='raise',
  dayfirst=False,
  yearfirst=False, utc=None,
  format=None, exact=True,
  unit='ns',
  infer_datetime_format=False,
  origin='unix', cache=True)
	Convert arg to date index, series, or timestamp for list, series, or scalar. Set errors to 'coerce' to have invalid be NaT, 'ignore' to leave. Specify strftime format with format or set infer_datetime_format to True if only one format type.

.isna()	Return boolean array (series) indicating where values are missing.
.fillna(value=None, method=None, limit=None, downcast=None)	Return series with missing values set to value (scalar, dict, series). Use method to fill additional holes ('bfill' or 'ffill') only limit times. Provide downcast='infer' to convert float to int if possible.

`.loc`	If index is datetime, can use partial string indexing. `'2010'` to select all of 2010. `'2010-10'` to select Oct 2010. Stop index includes that stopping period. Indexing with `Timestamp` and `datetime` objects is not partial.
`.ffill(limit=None)`	Forward fill the missing values.
`.bfill(limit=None)`	Forward fill the missing values.

`.interpolate(method='linear',`
`  axis=0, limit=None,`
`  inplace=False,`
`  limit_direction='forward',`
`  limit_area=None,`
`  downcast=None, **kwargs,)`
	Return a series with interpolated values.

`.where(cond, other=nan,`
`  level=None, errors='raise',`
`  try_cast=False)`
	Return a series with values replaced with other where cond is `False`. cond can be boolean array or function (series passed in, return boolean array). other can be scalar, series, or function (series passed in, return scalar or series).

`.dropna()`	Return a series with missing values removed.
`.shift(periods=1, freq=None,` `  fill_value=None)`	Return a series with data shifted forward by periods (can be negative). If time series and freq is offset alias, index values are shifted to offset alias. Fill in empty values with fill_value.

`.rolling(window,`
`  min_periods=None,`
`  center=False, win_type=None,`
`  closed='right')`
	Return a `Window` or `Rolling` class to aggregate. window is number windows, offset alias (for time series), or `BaseIndexer`. Set center=True to label at center of window. To use non-evenly weighted window, set win_type to string with Scipy window type.

`.resample(rule, closed='left',`
`  label='left',`
`  convention='start', kind=None,`
`  level=None,`
`  origin='start_day',`
`  offset=None)`
	Return Resampler object to aggregate on. Use rule to specify DateOffset, TimeDelta, or offset alias string.

`.transform(func)`	Return a series with same index but with transformed values. Best when used on a `.groupby` or `.resample` result. func may be an aggregation function or string when called on groupby or resample.
`.groupby(by=None, level=None, sort=True, group_keys=True, observed=False, dropna=True)`	Return a groupby object to aggregate on. by may be a function (pass the index, return label), mapping (dict or series that maps index to label), or a sequence of labels. Use observed=True to limit combinatoric explosion with categorical series.
`.cummax(skipna=True)`	Return cumulative maximum of series
`.cummin(skipna=True)`	Return cumulative minimum of series
`.cumprod(skipna=True)`	Return cumulative product of series
`.cumsum(skipna=True)`	Return cumulative sum of series

Table 13.4: Date Manipulation Methods

13.11 Summary

In this chapter, we explored many options for manipulating date information in pandas. Depending on whether you are manipulating dates in a series or dates in an index (time series), there are different options.

13.12 Exercises

With a dataset of your choice:

1. Convert a column with date information to a date.

2. Put the date information into the index for a numeric column.

3. Calculate the average value of the column for each month.

4. Calculate the average value of the column for every 2 months.

5. Calculate the percentage of the column out of the total for each month.

6. Calculate the average value of the column for a rolling window of size 7.

7. Using `.loc` pull out the first 3 months of a year.

8. Using `.loc` pull out the last 4 months of a year.

Chapter 14

Plotting with a Series

Inspecting statistical summaries and tables can reveal much about your data. Another technique to understand the data at a more intuitive level is to plot it. I am a huge fan of plotting, as it has led to insights I do not believe I would have come across otherwise. I have used visualizations to debug and find errors in code. Mastering visualization will be a huge benefit to you.

In this chapter, we will explore how to create plots from series with pandas.

14.1 Plotting in Jupyter

Pandas has native integration with Matplotlib. To leverage it in Jupyter, make sure you include the following cell magic to tell Jupyter to display the plots in the browser:

```
%matplotlib inline
```

14.2 The .plot Attribute

A series object has a .plot attribute. This attribute is interesting as you can call it directly to create plots, or access sub-attributes of it. Let's load the snow data and create some plots:

```
>>> url = 'https://github.com/mattharrison/datasets/raw/master/'\
...     'data/alta-noaa-1980-2019.csv'
>>> alta_df = pd.read_csv(url)
>>> dates = pd.to_datetime(alta_df.DATE)
>>> snow = (alta_df
...     .SNOW
```

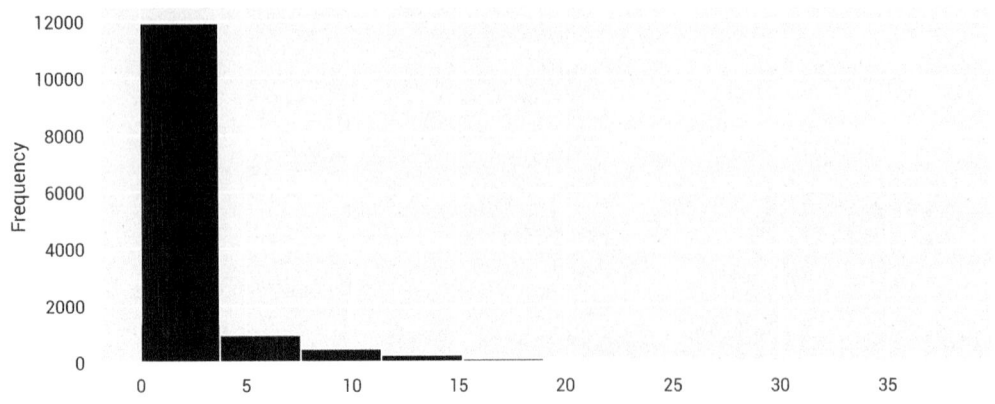

Figure 14.1: Basic histogram.

```
...        .rename(dates)
... )

>>> snow
1980-01-01    2.0
1980-01-02    3.0
1980-01-03    1.0
1980-01-04    0.0
1980-01-05    0.0
                ...
2019-09-03    0.0
2019-09-04    0.0
2019-09-05    0.0
2019-09-06    0.0
2019-09-07    0.0
Name: SNOW, Length: 14160, dtype: float64
```

The following plot attributes are available for plotting a series: bar, barh, box, hist, kde, line, and pie. The next sections will explore them.

14.3 Histograms

If you have continuous numeric data, plotting a histogram can give you insight into how the data is distributed:

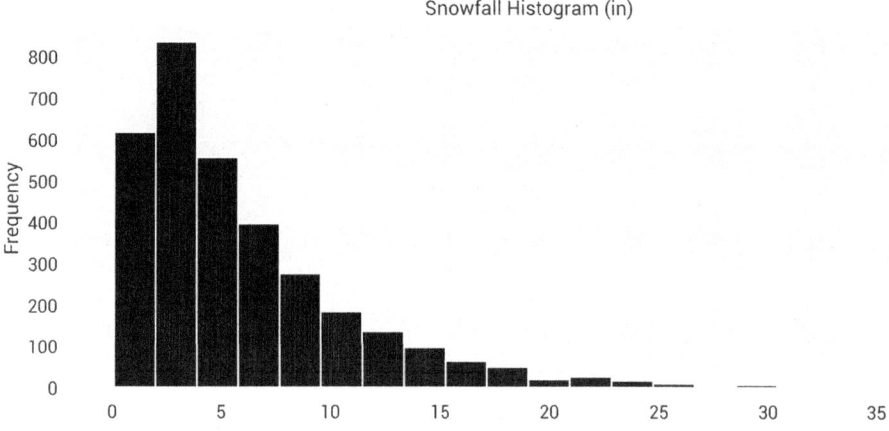

Figure 14.2: Histogram with zero values filtered out and 20 bins.

```
>>> snow.plot.hist()
```

The snow data is heavily skewed. We might want to drop the zero entries and try again. We will also change the number of bins:

```
>>> snow[snow>0].plot.hist(bins=20, title='Snowfall Histogram (in)')
```

14.4 Box Plot

You can also create a boxplot to view the distribution of the data. In this example, it does not look much like a box. This is because most of the time, it doesn't snow, so the plot shows that any time it snows is considered an outlier:

```
>>> snow.plot.box()
```

It looks more boxy if we limit it to snow amounts during January (ignoring zero):

```
>>> (snow
...     [lambda s:(s.index.month == 1) & (s>0)]
...     .plot.box()
... )
```

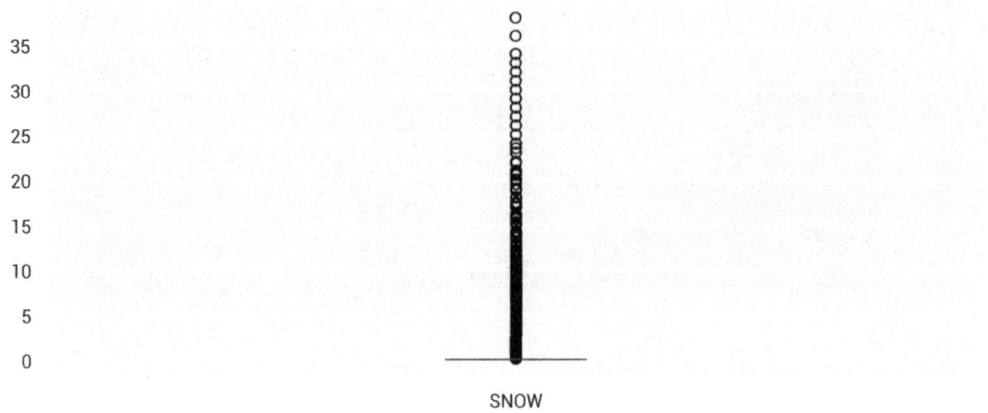

Figure 14.3: Basic boxplot.

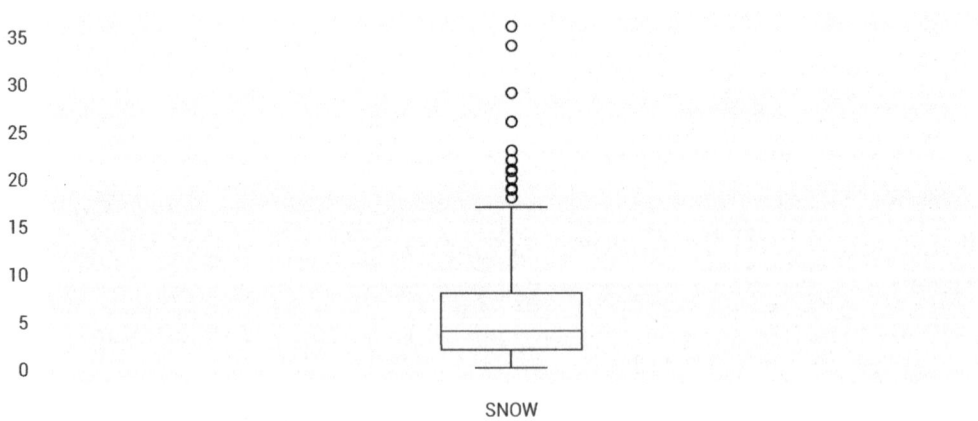

Figure 14.4: A better basic boxplot with snowfall levels for each January.

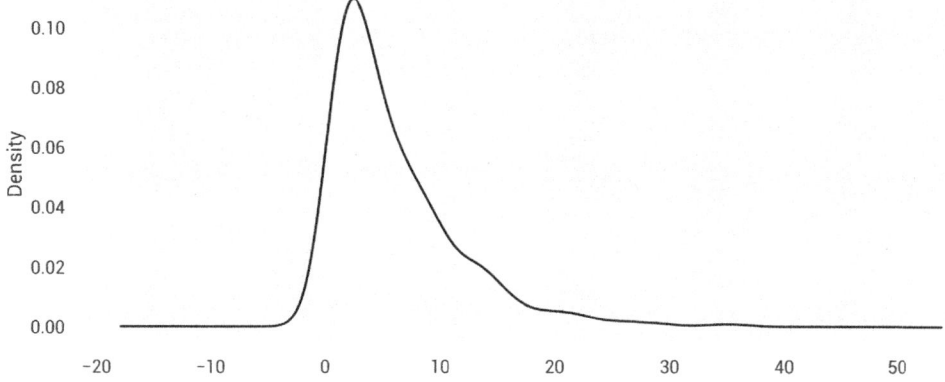

Figure 14.5: A basic kernel density estimate plot.

14.5   Kernel Density Estimation Plot

Another option to view the kernel density estimation (KDE). This is essentially a smoothed histogram:

```
>>> (snow
...      [lambda s:(s.index.month == 1) & (s>0)]
...      .plot.kde()
... )
```

14.6   Line Plots

For numeric time series values we can plot a line plot:

```
>>> snow.plot.line()
```

A line plot in pandas plots the values in the series in the y-axis and the index in the x-axis. This plot is a little crowded as we are packing daily data for 40 years into the x-axis. We can slice off the last few years to zoom in or resample to view trends. Here we pull off the last 300 values:

```
>>> (snow
...      .iloc[-300:]
...      .plot.line()
... )
```

Note that by writing the code as above, I can easily comment out the line .plot.line() and inspect the series that will be plotted.

163

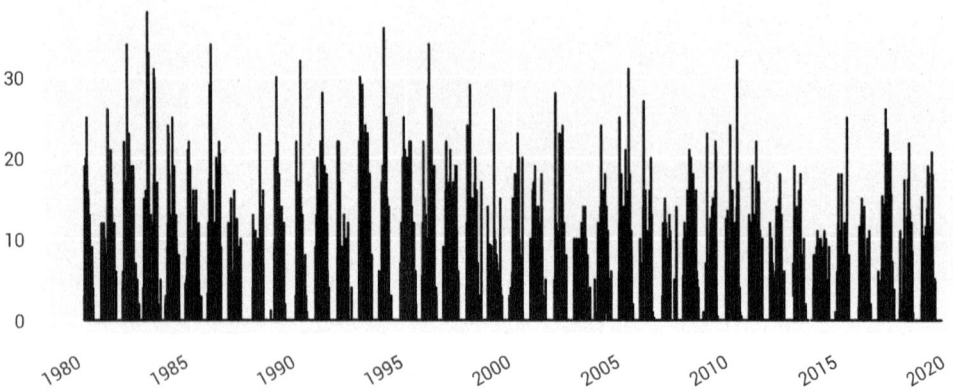

Figure 14.6: Basic line plot.

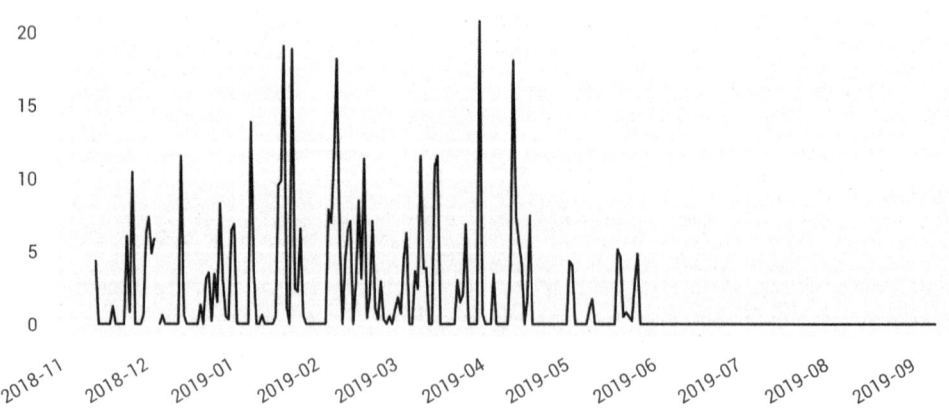

Figure 14.7: Last few values of basic line plot.

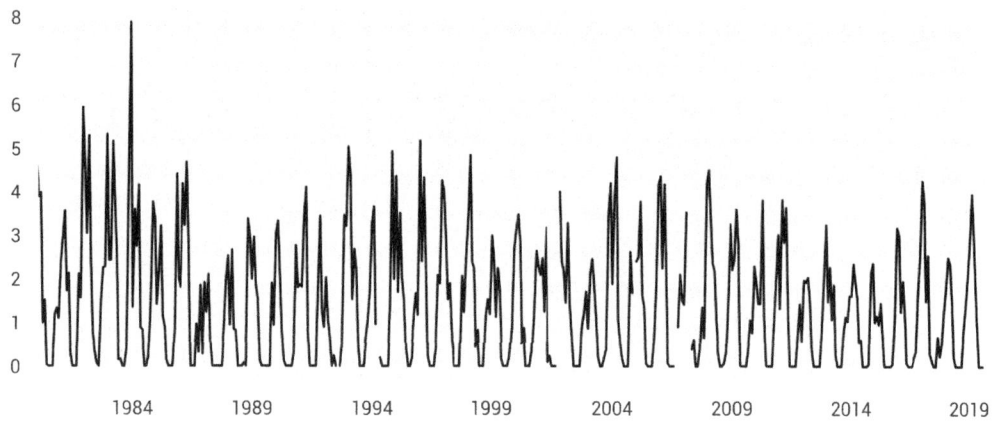

Figure 14.8: Resampled line plot.

Here I'm going to aggregate at the monthly level and look at the mean snowfall using .resample with the 'M' offset alias and the .mean aggregation method:

```
>>> (snow
...    .resample('M')
...    .mean()
...    .plot.line()
... )
```

14.7 Line Plots with Multiple Aggregations

Plotting can be even more powerful with dataframes. To give you an idea, we will use the .quantile method to pull out the 50%, 90%, and 99% values. This returns a series with multiindex (we will talk about those more later). If we chain the .unstack method, we can pull out the inner index (the one with the quantile names) into columns and create a dataframe that has a column for each quantile. If we plot this dataframe, each column will be its own line:

```
>>> (snow
...    .resample('Q')
...    .quantile([.5, .9, .99])
...    .unstack()
...    .iloc[-100:]
...    .plot.line()
... )
```

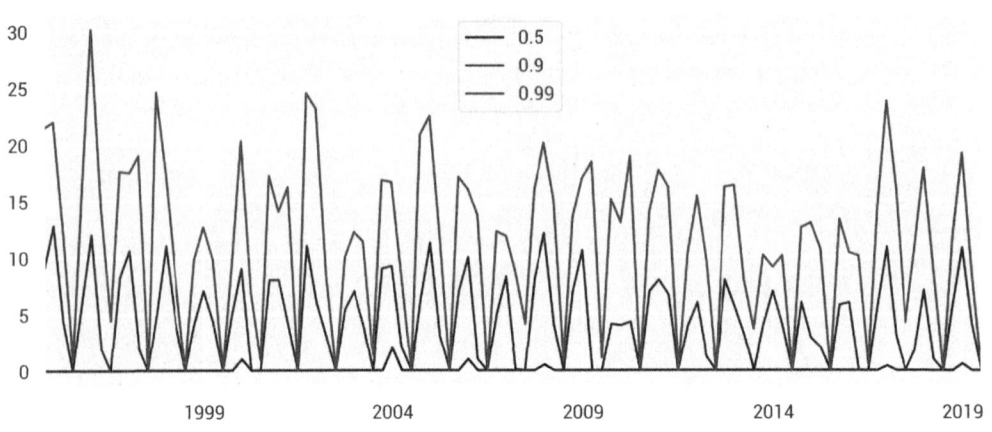

Figure 14.9: Resampled line plot from dataframe.

14.8 Bar Plots

You can also create bar plots. These are useful for comparing values. In the previous section, we looked at the percent of snow that fell during each month:

```
>>> season2017 = (snow.loc['2016-10':'2017-05'])
>>> (season2017
...     .resample('M')
...     .sum()
...     .div(season2017.sum())
...     .mul(100)
...     .rename(lambda idx: idx.month_name())
... )
October      2.153969
November     9.772637
December    15.715995
January     25.468688
February    21.041085
March        9.274033
April       14.738732
May          1.834862
Name: SNOW, dtype: float64
```

If you do a bar plot on a series it will plot the index along the x-axis and draw a bar for each value. We will add a call to .plot.bar and set the title:

166

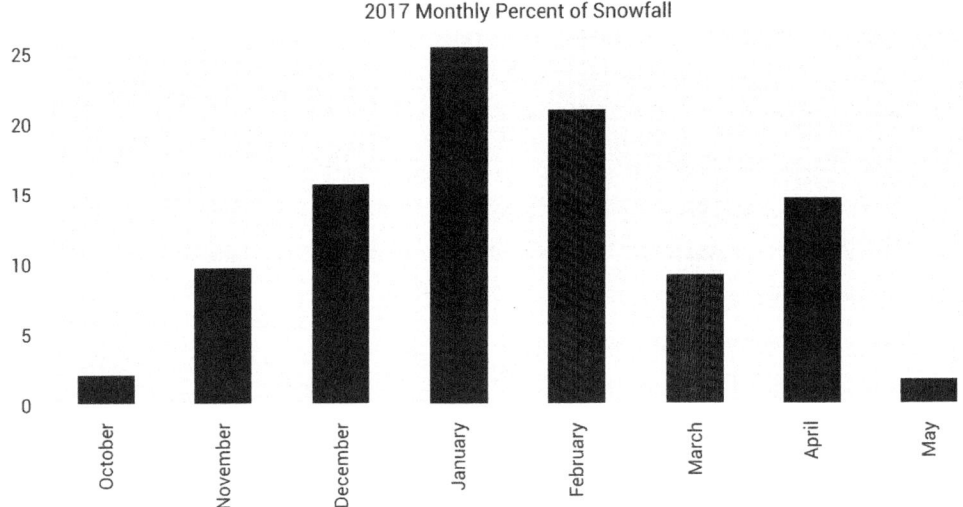

Figure 14.10: Basic series bar plot.

```
>>> (season2017
...     .resample('M')
...     .sum()
...     .div(season2017.sum())
...     .mul(100)
...     .rename(lambda idx: idx.month_name())
...     .plot.bar(title='2017 Monthly Percent of Snowfall')
... )
```

You can create a horizontal bar plot with the .barh method:

```
>>> (season2017
...     .resample('M')
...     .sum()
...     .div(season2017.sum())
...     .mul(100)
...     .rename(lambda idx: idx.month_name())
...     .plot.barh(title='2017 Monthly Percent of Snowfall')
... )
```

I like to use bar plots with categorical data. Let's pull in the makes of the auto data:

```
>>> url = 'https://github.com/mattharrison/datasets/raw/master/data/'\
...       'vehicles.csv.zip'
>>> df = pd.read_csv(url)
```

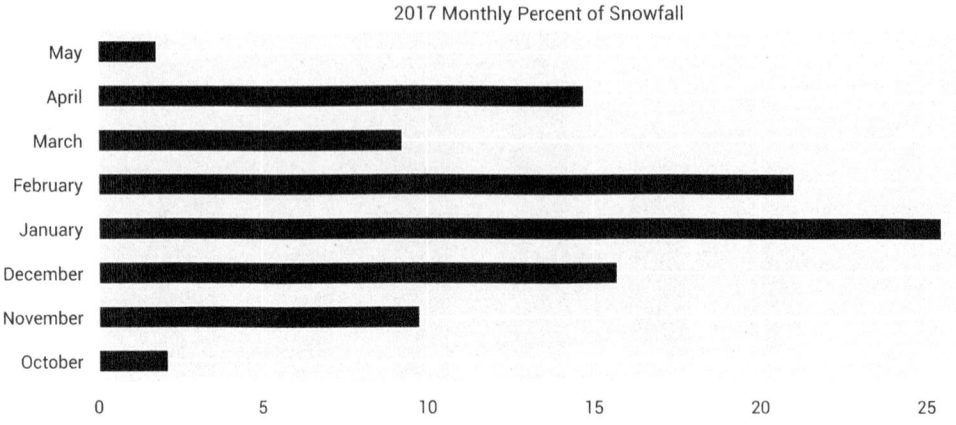

Figure 14.11: Basic series horizontal bar plot.

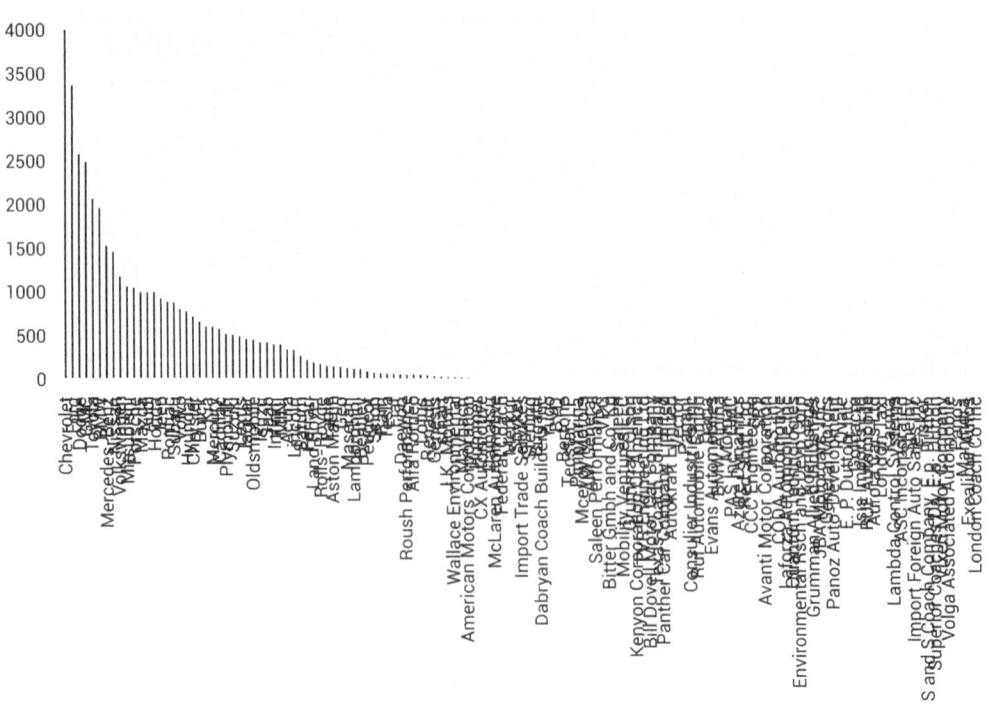

Figure 14.12: Crowded bar plot.

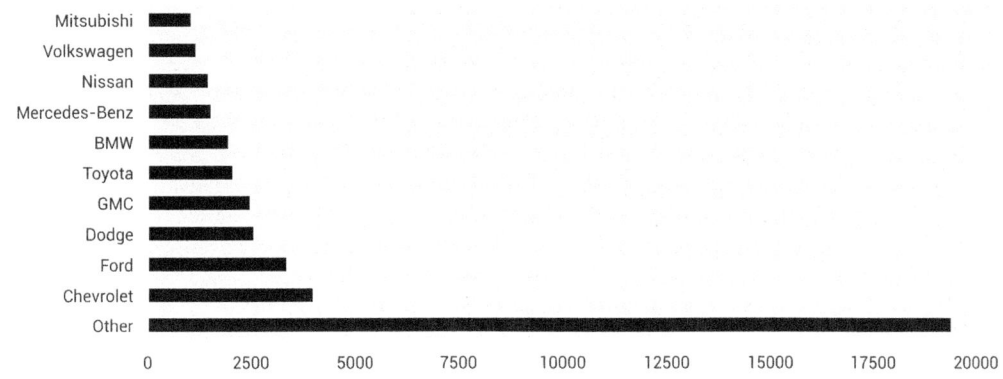

Figure 14.13: Grouping long-tail members together for legible bar plot.

```
>>> make = df.make
```

The .value_counts method is my go-to tool for understanding the values in categorical data. It puts the categories in the index and counts as the values of the series:

```
>>> make.value_counts()
Chevrolet               4003
Ford                    3371
Dodge                   2583
GMC                     2494
Toyota                  2071
                        ...
E. P. Dutton, Inc.         1
Mahindra                   1
London Taxi                1
Panos                      1
Lambda Control Systems     1
Name: make, Length: 136, dtype: int64
```

It is also easy to visualize this by tacking on .plot.bar. This will plot the categories in the x-axis:

```
>>> (make
...      .value_counts()
...      .plot.bar()
... )
```

However, you can see that the plot is very crowded. As a rough rule of thumb, I don't like to create bar plots with more than 30 bars. Let's use some pandas code to limit this to 10 makes and plot it horizontally:

```
>>> top10 = make.value_counts().index[:10]
>>> (make
...      .where(make.isin(top10), 'Other')
...      .value_counts()
...      .plot.barh()
... )
```

14.9   Pie Plots

If you are the type that prefers pie plots, you can create those as well:

```
>>> (season2017
...      .resample('M')
...      .sum()
...      .div(season2017.sum())
...      .mul(100)
...      .rename(lambda idx: idx.month_name())
...      .plot.pie(title='2017 Monthly Percent of Snowfall')
... )
```

I generally recommend using a bar plot instead of a pie plot. If you have part of a whole data, very few parts, and large differences between the parts, a pie plot might be acceptable.

14.10   Styling

You may notice that my plots don't look like the default plots of Matplotlib. I'm using the Seaborn library to set the font and color palette before plotting. Note that if you have a lot of text in the axis, you will need to use the bbox_inches='tight' option to the .savefig method or the export might be chopped off in the middle of the text. I'm also controlling the figure size with plt.subplots and passing in the resulting Matplotlib axes into the pandas .plot call. To do similar, you could use code like this:

```
import matplotlib
import seaborn as sns
color_palette = ["#440154", "#482677", "#404788", "#33638d", "#287d8e",
    "#1f968b", '#29af7f', '#55c667', '#73d055', '#b8de29', '#fde725']
fp = matplotlib.font_manager.FontProperties(
```

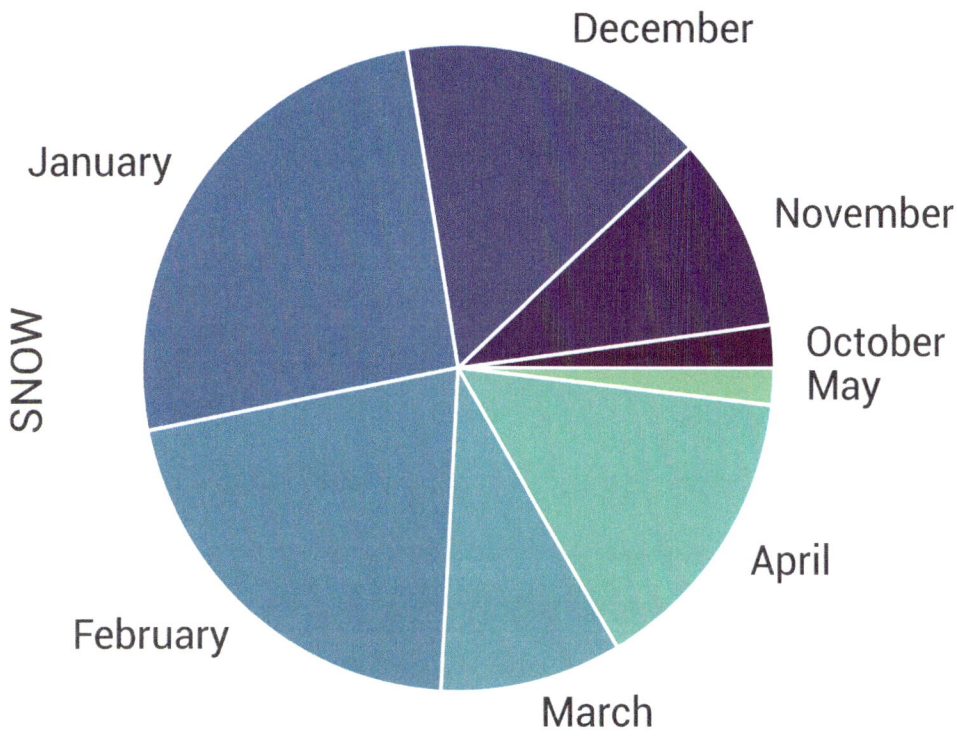

Figure 14.14: Basic series pie plot.

```
        fname='/Fonts/roboto/Roboto-Condensed.ttf')
with sns.plotting_context(rc=dict(font='Roboto', palette=color_palette)):
    fig, ax = plt.subplots(dpi=600, figsize=(10,4))
    snow.plot.hist()
    fig.savefig('snowhist.png', dpi=600, bbox_inches='tight')
```

Method	Description
s.plot(ax=None, style=None, logx=False, logy=False, xticks=None, yticks=None, xlim=None, ylim=None, xlabel=None, ylabel=None, rot=None, fontsize=None, colormap=None, table=False, **kwargs)	Common plot parameters. Use ax to use existing Matplotlib axes, style for color and marker style (see matplotlib.marker), _ticks to specify tick locations, _lim to specify tick limits, _label to specify x/y label (default to index/column name), rot to rotate labels, fontsize for tick label size, colormap for coloring, position, table to create table with data. Additional arguments are passed to plt.plot
s.plot.bar(position=.5, color=None)	Create a bar plot. Use position to specify label alignment (0-left, 1-right). Use color (string, list) to specify line color.
s.plot.barh(x=None, y=None, color=None)	Create a horizontal bar plot. Use position to specify label alignment (0-left, 1-right). Use color (string, list) to specify line color.
s.plot.hist(bins=10)	Create a histogram. Use bins to change the number of bins.
s.plot.box()	Create a boxplot.
s.plot.kde(bw_method='scott', ind=None)	Create a Kernel Density Estimate plot. Use bw_method to calculate estimator bandwidth (see scipy.stats.gaussian_kde). Use ind to specify evaluation points for PDF estimation (NumPy array of points, or integer with equally spaced points).
s.plot.line(color=None)	Create a line plot. Use color to specify line color.
s.plot.pie()	Create a pie plot.

Table 14.1: Series Plotting Methods

14.11 Summary

In this chapter, we explored basic plotting functionality with series objects. We showed a little bit of the functionality that you get when plotting with a data frame. We will explore more of this later. Also, note that because the plotting functionality is built on top of Matplotlib, you can customize the plot using Matplotlib.

14.12 Exercises

With a dataset of your choice:

1. Create a histogram from a numeric column. Change the bin size.

2. Create a boxplot from a numeric column.

3. Create a Kernel Density Estimate plot from a numeric column.

4. Create a line from a numeric column.

5. Create a bar plot from a frequency count of a categorical column.

6. Create a pie plot from a frequency count of a categorical column.

Chapter 15

Categorical Manipulation

So far, we have dealt with numeric and date data. Another common form of data is textual data, and a subset of textual data is categorical data. Categorical data is textual data that has repetitions. In this section, we will explore handling categorical data with pandas.

15.1 Categorical Data

Categories are labels that describe data. Generally, there are repeated values, and if they have an intrinsic order, they are referred to as *ordinal* values. One example is shirt sizes: small, medium, and large. Underordered values such as colors are called *nominal* values. In addition, you can convert numerical data to categories by binning them.

We will start by looking at the categorical values found in the fuel economy data set. The *make* column has categorical information:

```
>>> import pandas as pd
>>> url = 'https://github.com/mattharrison/datasets/raw/master/' \
...      'data/vehicles.csv.zip'
>>> df = pd.read_csv(url)
>>> make = df.make
>>> make
0          Alfa Romeo
1             Ferrari
2               Dodge
3               Dodge
4              Subaru
            ...
41139          Subaru
```

```
41140        Subaru
41141        Subaru
41142        Subaru
41143        Subaru
Name: make, Length: 41144, dtype: object
```

15.2 Frequency Counts

I like to use the .value_counts method to determine the *cardinality* of the values. The frequency of values will tell you if a column is categorical. If every value was unique or free form text, it is not categorical:

```
>>> make.value_counts()
Chevrolet            4003
Ford                 3371
Dodge                2583
GMC                  2494
Toyota               2071
                     ...
London Taxi             1
General Motors          1
E. P. Dutton, Inc.      1
RUF Automobile          1
JBA Motorcars, Inc.     1
Name: make, Length: 136, dtype: int64
```

We can also inspect the size and the number of unique items to infer the cardinality:

```
>>> make.shape, make.nunique()
((41144,), 136)
```

15.3 Benefits of Categories

The first benefit of categorical values is that they use less memory:

```
>>> cat_make = make.astype('category')

>>> make.memory_usage(deep=True)
2606395

>>> cat_make.memory_usage(deep=True)
95888
```

Another benefit is that categorical computations can be faster for many operations. For example, we still have access to the .str attribute on categoricals. Let's compare creating uppercase results from a string type against a categorical type:

```
>>> %%timeit
cat_make.str.upper()
1.41 ms ± 37.4 µs per loop (mean ± std. dev. of 7 runs, 1000 loops each)

>>> %%timeit
make.str.upper()
11.5 ms ± 45.7 µs per loop (mean ± std. dev. of 7 runs, 100 loops each)
```

In this case, the same operation is ten times faster with the categorical data. Note that the string operations do not return categorical series.

Also, remember that the binning functions that we showed previously, pd.cut and pd.qcut, create categorical results.

15.4 Conversion to Ordinal Categories

If we wanted to make an ordinal categorical (say alphabetic order) from the makes, we could do the following:

```
>>> make_type = pd.CategoricalDtype(
...        categories=sorted(make.unique()), ordered=True)
>>> ordered_make = make.astype(make_type)
>>> ordered_make
0           Alfa Romeo
1              Ferrari
2                Dodge
3                Dodge
4               Subaru
              ...
41139           Subaru
41140           Subaru
41141           Subaru
41142           Subaru
41143           Subaru
Name: make, Length: 41144, dtype: category
Categories (136, object): [AM General < ASC Incorporated < Acura
  < Alfa Romeo ... Volvo < Wallace Environmental < Yugo < smart]
```

A benefit of ordinal categoricals is that you can specify a lexical order to the items. If the items have an order, you can use reducing operations like maximum and minimum (where you can specify an order rather than using alphabetic order):

```
>>> ordered_make.max()
'smart'

>>> cat_make.max()
Traceback (most recent call last):
  ...
TypeError: Categorical is not ordered for operation max
you can use .as_ordered() to change the Categorical to an ordered one
```

You can also sort the series according to the order:

```
>>> ordered_make.sort_values()
20288    AM General
20289    AM General
369      AM General
358      AM General
19314    AM General
            ...
31289         smart
31290         smart
29605         smart
22974         smart
26882         smart
Name: make, Length: 41144, dtype: category
Categories (136, object): [AM General < ASC Incorporated < Acura <
    Alfa Romeo ... Volvo < Wallace Environmental < Yugo < smart]
```

15.5   The .cat Accessor

In addition, there are a few methods attached to the .cat attribute of categorical series. If you need to rename the categories, you can use the .rename_categories method. You need to pass in a list with the same length as the current categories or a dictionary mapping old values to new values. Here we will lowercase the categories using both methods:

```
>>> cat_make.cat.rename_categories(
...     [c.lower() for c in cat_make.cat.categories])
0        alfa romeo
1           ferrari
2             dodge
3             dodge
4            subaru
```

```
                   ...
41139         subaru
41140         subaru
41141         subaru
41142         subaru
41143         subaru
Name: make, Length: 41144, dtype: category
Categories (136, object): [am general, asc incorporated, acura, alfa
    romeo, ..., volvo, wallace environmental, yugo, smart]

>>> ordered_make.cat.rename_categories(
...    {c:c.lower() for c in ordered_make.cat.categories})
0        alfa romeo
1           ferrari
2             dodge
3             dodge
4            subaru
                   ...
41139         subaru
41140         subaru
41141         subaru
41142         subaru
41143         subaru
Name: make, Length: 41144, dtype: category
Categories (136, object): [am general < asc incorporated < acura
    < alfa romeo ... volvo < wallace environmental < yugo < smart]
```

The .cat attribute also allows you to add or remove categories and change the order of nominal categories.

Here we change the ordering. Previously *smart* was the maximum value because it was lowercased. Let's sort them ignoring case:

```
>>> ordered_make.cat.reorder_categories(
...      sorted(cat_make.cat.categories, key=str.lower))
0        Alfa Romeo
1           Ferrari
2             Dodge
3             Dodge
4            Subaru
                   ...
41139         Subaru
41140         Subaru
41141         Subaru
41142         Subaru
41143         Subaru
Name: make, Length: 41144, dtype: category
```

```
Categories (136, object): ['Acura' < 'Alfa Romeo' ...
    'Volvo' < 'VPG' < 'Wallace Environmental' < 'Yugo']
```

15.6   Category Gotchas

Here are a few oddities to be aware of with categorical data. Applying the
.value_counts method or .groupby to categorical data uses all of the categories
even if there were no values for them. In this example, we will look at the first
hundred entries and count the frequency of entries. Note that this returns
more than one hundred results because it includes every category!:

```
>>> ordered_make.iloc[:100].value_counts()
Dodge                              17
Oldsmobile                          8
Ford                                8
Buick                               7
Mazda                               5
                                   ..
Panos                               0
Panoz Auto-Development              0
Panther Car Company Limited         0
Peugeot                             0
AM General                          0
Name: make, Length: 136, dtype: int64
```

Similarly, using the .groupby method will use all of the categories (this is
even a bigger issue when we group by two categories with dataframes and
get a combinatoric explosion):

```
>>> (cat_make
...     .iloc[:100]
...     .groupby(cat_make.iloc[:100])
...     .first()
... )
make
AM General                           NaN
ASC Incorporated                     NaN
Acura                                NaN
Alfa Romeo                    Alfa Romeo
American Motors Corporation          NaN
                                  ...
Volkswagen                    Volkswagen
Volvo                              Volvo
Wallace Environmental                NaN
```

```
Yugo                                    NaN
smart                                   NaN
Name: make, Length: 136, dtype: category
Categories (136, object): ['AM General', 'ASC Incorporated', ...
                          'Wallace Environmental', 'Yugo', 'smart']
```

Compare this with just the result from the string series:

```
>>> (make
...    .iloc[:100]
...    .groupby(make.iloc[:100])
...    .first()
... )
make
Alfa Romeo          Alfa Romeo
Audi                      Audi
BMW                        BMW
Buick                    Buick
CX Automotive   CX Automotive
                     ...
Rolls-Royce       Rolls-Royce
Subaru                 Subaru
Toyota                 Toyota
Volkswagen         Volkswagen
Volvo                   Volvo
Name: make, Length: 25, dtype: object
```

There is an optional parameter, observed, for .groupby to tell it to only include results for which there are values:

```
>>> (cat_make
...    .iloc[:100]
...    .groupby(cat_make.iloc[:100], observed=True)
...    .first()
... )
make
Alfa Romeo          Alfa Romeo
Ferrari                Ferrari
Dodge                    Dodge
Subaru                  Subaru
Toyota                  Toyota
                     ...
Mazda                    Mazda
Oldsmobile          Oldsmobile
Plymouth              Plymouth
Pontiac                Pontiac
Rolls-Royce        Rolls-Royce
```

```
Name: make, Length: 25, dtype: object
```

Also, note that pulling out a single value with .iloc will return a scalar, but if you pass in a list, it will return a categorical even if it is a single value:

```
>>> ordered_make.iloc[0]
'Alfa Romeo'
```

```
>>> ordered_make.iloc[[0]]
0    Alfa Romeo
Name: make, dtype: category
Categories (136, object): [AM General < ASC Incorporated < Acura
    < Alfa Romeo ... Volvo < Wallace Environmental < Yugo < smart]
```

15.7 Generalization

In the manipulation methods chapter, we discussed generalizing categories when exploring the .where method. It is worth repeating similar code here since I find that I often want to limit the number of categorical values:

```
>>> def generalize_topn(ser, n=5, other='Other'):
...       topn = ser.value_counts().index[:n]
...       if isinstance(ser.dtype, pd.CategoricalDtype):
...           ser = ser.cat.set_categories(
...               topn.set_categories(list(topn)+[other]))
...       return ser.where(ser.isin(topn), other)
```

```
>>> cat_make.pipe(generalize_topn, n=20, other='NA')
0            NA
1            NA
2         Dodge
3         Dodge
4        Subaru
            ...
41139    Subaru
41140    Subaru
41141    Subaru
41142    Subaru
41143    Subaru
Name: make, Length: 41144, dtype: category
Categories (21, object): ['Chevrolet', 'Ford', 'Dodge', 'GMC', ...,
    'Volvo', 'Hyundai', 'Chrysler', 'NA']
```

Another generalization I like to do is hierarchical. Suppose I want country from make, but I only want US and German categories and I want to label everything else as "Other":

```
>>> def generalize_mapping(ser, mapping, default):
...     seen = None
...     res = ser.astype(str)
...     for old, new in mapping.items():
...         mask = ser.str.contains(old)
...         if seen is None:
...             seen = mask
...         else:
...             seen |= mask
...         res = res.where(~mask, new)
...     res = res.where(seen, default)
...     return res.astype('category')

>>> generalize_mapping(cat_make, {'Ford': 'US', 'Tesla': 'US',
...     'Chevrolet': 'US', 'Dodge': 'US',
...     'Oldsmobile': 'US', 'Plymouth': 'US',
...     'BMW': 'German'}, 'Other')
0        Other
1        Other
2           US
3           US
4        Other
         ...
41139    Other
41140    Other
41141    Other
41142    Other
41143    Other
Name: make, Length: 41144, dtype: category
Categories (3, object): ['German', 'Other', 'US']
```

Method	Description
.astype(dtype)	Return a series converted to categories. Set dtype to 'category' for unordered category, CategoricalDType for ordered category.
pd.CategoricalDtype(categories, ordered=False)	Create categorical type. Set categories to a list of categories.

183

`pd.cut(x, bins, right=True,`
`  labels=None, retbins=False,`
`  precision=3,`
`  include_lowest=False,`
`  duplicates='raise',`
`  ordered=True)`
	Bin values from x (a series). If bins is an integer, use equal-width bins. If bins is a list of numbers (defining minimum and maximum positions) use those for the edges. right defines whether the right edge is open or closed. labels allows us to specify bin names. Out of bounds values will be missing.

`pd.qcut(x, q, labels=None,`
`  retbins=False, precision=3,`
`  duplicates='raise')`
	Bin values from x (a series) into q equal-sized bins (10 for decile quantiles, 4 for quartile quantiles). Alternatively, we can pass in a list of quantile edges. Out of bounds values will be missing.

`.cat.add_categories(` `  new_categories)`	Return a series with the new categories added. If it is ordinal, the new values are added at the end (highest).
`.cat.as_ordered()`	Convert categorical series to an ordered series. Use .reorder_categories or CategoricalDtype to specify the order.
`.cat.categories`	Property with the index of categories.
`.cat.codes`	Property with a series with category codes (index into a category).
`.cat.ordered`	Boolean property if series is ordered.
`.cat.remove_categories( removals)`	Return a series with the categories removed (replace with NaN).
`.cat.remove_unused_categories()`	Return a series with the categories removed that are being used.
`.cat.rename_categories(` `  new_categories)`	Return a series with the categories replaced by a list (with new values) or a dictionary (mapping old to new values).
`.cat.reorder_categories(` `  new_categories)`	Return a series with the categories replaced by a list.

`.cat.set_categories(`
`  new_categories, ordered=False,`
`  rename=False)`
	Return a series with the categories replaced by a list.

Table 15.1: Category Attributes and Methods

15.8 Summary

If you are dealing with text data, it is worth considering whether converting the text data to categorical data makes sense. You can save a lot of memory and speed up many operations by doing so. A categorical series has a .cat attribute that will allow you to manipulate the categories.

15.9 Exercises

With a dataset of your choice:

1. Convert a text column into a categorical column. How much memory did you save?

2. Convert a numeric column into a categorical column by binning it (pd.cut). How much memory did you save?

3. Use the generalize_topn function to limit the amounts of categories in your column. How much memory did you save?

Chapter 16

Dataframes

In pandas, the two-dimensional counterpart to the one-dimensional Series is the DataFrame. If we want to understand this data structure, it helps to know how it is constructed. This chapter will introduce the dataframe.

16.1 Database and Spreadsheet Analogues

If you think of a dataframe as row-oriented, the interface will feel wrong. Many tabular data structures are row-oriented. Perhaps this is due to spreadsheets and CSV files dealt with on a row by row basis. Perhaps it is due to the many OLTP[9] databases that are row-oriented out of the box. A DataFrame, is often used for analytical purposes and is better understood when thought of as column-oriented, where each column is a Series.

> **Note**
>
> In practice, many highly optimized analytical databases (those used for OLAP cubes) are also column-oriented. Laying out the data in a columnar manner can improve performance and require fewer resources. Columns

---

[9]*OLTP* (On-line Transaction Processing) characterizes databases that are meant for transactional data. Bank accounts are an example where data integrity is imperative, yet multiple users might need concurrent access. In contrast with *OLAP* (On-line Analytical Processing), which is optimized for complex querying and aggregation. Typically, reporting systems use these types of databases, which might store data in a denormalized form to speed up access.

of a single type can be compressed easily. Performing analysis on a column requires loading only that column, whereas a row-oriented database would require reading the complete database to access an entire column.

16.2   A Simple Python Version

Below is a simple attempt to create a tabular Python data structure that is column-oriented. It has a 0-based integer index, but that is not required, the index could be string based. Each column is similar to the Series-like structure developed previously:

```
>>> df = {
...     'index':[0,1,2],
...     'cols': [
...        { 'name':'growth',
...          'data':[.5, .7, 1.2] },
...        { 'name':'Name',
...          'data':['Paul', 'George', 'Ringo'] },
...     ]
... }
```

Rows are accessed via the index, and columns are accessible from the column name. Below are simple functions for accessing rows and columns:

```
>>> def get_row(df, idx):
...     results = []
...     value_idx = df['index'].index(idx)
...     for col in df['cols']:
...         results.append(col['data'][value_idx])
...     return results

>>> get_row(df, 1)
[0.7, 'George']

>>> def get_col(df, name):
...     for col in df['cols']:
...         if col['name'] == name:
...             return col['data']

>>> get_col(df, 'Name')
['Paul', 'George', 'Ringo']
```

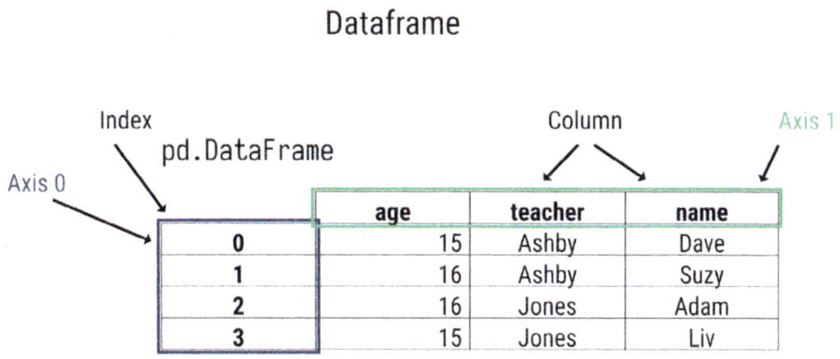

Dataframe

Figure 16.1: Figure showing column-oriented nature of Dataframe. (Note that a column can be pulled off as a Series)

16.3 Dataframes

Using the pandas DataFrame object, the previous data structure could be created like this:

```
>>> import pandas as pd
>>> df = pd.DataFrame({
...     'growth':[.5, .7, 1.2],
...     'Name':['Paul', 'George', 'Ringo'] })

>>> df
   growth     Name
0     0.5     Paul
1     0.7   George
2     1.2    Ringo
```

The leftmost values, 0, 1, and 2, are the index. There are two columns, *growth* and *Name*. This data structure (like a series) has hundreds of attributes and methods. We will highlight many of the main features below.

One of the ways we can access a row is by location-indexing off of the .iloc attribute:

```
>>> df.iloc[2]
growth      1.2
Name      Ringo
Name: 2, dtype: object
```

Columns are also accessible via multiple methods. One is indexing the column name directly off of the object:

189

```
>>> df['Name']
0       Paul
1     George
2      Ringo
Name: Name, dtype: object
```

Note the type of column is a pandas `Series` instance. Any operation that can be done to a series can be applied to a column:

```
>>> type(df['Name'])
<class 'pandas.core.series.Series'>

>>> df['Name'].str.lower()
0       paul
1     george
2      ringo
Name: Name, dtype: object
```

Note

The `DataFrame` overrides `__getattr__` to allow access to columns as attributes. This tends to work ok, but will fail if the column name conflicts with an existing method or attribute. It will also fail if the column has a non-valid attribute name (such as a column name with a space):

```
>>> df.Name
0       Paul
1     George
2      Ringo
Name: Name, dtype: object
```

You will find many who advise never to use attribute access to pull out a column, and they prefer using the index lookup. While the index lookup will work even with columns that do not have proper Python attribute names (alpha-numeric or underscore), I find that I often use attribute access when using Jupyter! Why is that? Because tab completion works better when using attribute access. (I also tend to clean up my column names to non-conflicting Python attribute names.)

The above should provide clues as to why the `Series` was covered in such detail. When column operations are required, a series method is often involved. Also, the index behavior across both data structures is the same.

16.4 Construction

dataframes can be created from many types of input:

- columns (dicts of lists)

- rows (list of dicts)

- CSV files (pd.read_csv)

- NumPy ndarrays

- other: SQL, HDF5, arrow, etc

The previous creation of df illustrated making a dataframe from columns. Below is an example of creating a dataframe from rows:

```
>>> pd.DataFrame([
...     {'growth':.5, 'Name':'Paul'},
...     {'growth':.7, 'Name':'George'},
...     {'growth':1.2, 'Name':'Ringo'}])
    Name  growth
0   Paul     0.5
1   George   0.7
2   Ringo    1.2
```

Similarly, here is an example of loading this data from a CSV file (I will mock out a file with StringIO):

```
>>> from io import StringIO
>>> csv_file = StringIO("""growth,Name
... .5,Paul
... .7,George
... 1.2,Ringo""")

>>> pd.read_csv(csv_file)
   growth    Name
0     0.5    Paul
1     0.7    George
2     1.2    Ringo
```

The pd.read_csv function tries to be smart about its input. If you pass it a URL, it will download the file. If the extension ends in .xz, .bz2, or .zip, it will decompress the file automatically (you can provide a compression='bz2' parameter to explicitly force decompression of a file that has a different extension).

191

After parsing the CSV file, pandas makes a best-effort to give a type to each column. A "best-effort" means it will convert numerics to int64 if the column is whole numbers and not missing values. Other numeric columns are converted to float64 (if they have decimals or are missing values). If there are non-numeric values, pandas will use the object type. Usually object means that the column has string type data, though it might be mixed-typed column that has string data and nan values stored as floats.

One parameter to the pd.read_csv function is dtypes. It accepts a dictionary mapping column names to types. You can use the types listed below:

Type	Description
float64	Floating point. Can specify different sizes, ie: float16, float32 or float64.
int64	Integer number. Can put u in front for unsigned. Can specify size, ie: int8, int16, int32, or int64. Does not support missing values.
Int64	Nullable integer number. Supports <NA> for integer columns. Can put U in front for unsigned. Can specify size, ie: Int16, Int32, or Int64.
datetime64[ns]	Datetime number
datetime64[ns, tz]	Datetime number with timezone
timedelta[ns]	A difference between datetimes
category	Used to specify categorical columns
object	Used for other columns such as strings, or Python objects
string	Used for text data. Supports <NA> for missing values.

Figure 16.2: Data types in pandas

Tip

Having said this, my experience with the dtype parameter is that it is easier to convert many types after they are loaded into a dataframe. I work on each column as a series and use the .astype method or one of the to_* functions at that point.

A dataframe can be instantiated from a NumPy array as well. The column names will need to be passed in as the columns parameter to the constructor:

```
>>> import numpy as np
>>> np.random.seed(42)
>>> pd.DataFrame(np.random.randn(10,3),
...     columns=['a', 'b', 'c'])
          a         b         c
0  0.496714 -0.138264  0.647689
1  1.523030 -0.234153 -0.234137
2  1.579213  0.767435 -0.469474
3  0.542560 -0.463418 -0.465730
4  0.241962 -1.913280 -1.724918
5 -0.562288 -1.012831  0.314247
6 -0.908024 -1.412304  1.465649
7 -0.225776  0.067528 -1.424748
8 -0.544383  0.110923 -1.150994
9  0.375698 -0.600639 -0.291694
```

16.5 Dataframe Axis

Unlike a series, which has one axis, there are two axes for a dataframe. They are commonly referred to as axis 0 and 1, or the "index" (or 'rows') axis and the "columns" axis respectively:

```
>>> df.axes
[RangeIndex(start=0, stop=3, step=1),
Index(['growth', 'Name'], dtype='object')]
```

For example, we can sum a dataframe along the index or along the columns using the labels 0 and 1:

```
>>> df.sum(axis=0)
growth                2.4
Name        PaulGeorgeRingo
dtype: object
```

```
>>> df.sum(axis=1)
0    0.5
1    0.7
2    1.2
dtype: float64
```

We can also spell out the axis. This is my preferred method because it is easier to read:

```
>>> df.sum(axis='index')
growth                2.4
Name        PaulGeorgeRingo
```

```
dtype: object
```

```
>>> df.sum(axis='columns')
0    0.5
1    0.7
2    1.2
dtype: float64
```

As many operations take an `axis` parameter, it is important to remember that 0 is the index and 1 is the columns:

```
>>> df.axes[0]
RangeIndex(start=0, stop=3, step=1)
```

```
>>> df.axes[1]
Index(['growth', 'Name'], dtype='object')
```

Tip

Here is a clue to help remember which axis is 0 and which is 1. Think back to a `Series`. It, like a `DataFrame`, has an index. *Axis 0 is along the index*. A mnemonic to aid in remembering is that the 1 looks like a column (axis 1 is across columns):

```
>>> df = pd.DataFrame({'Score1': [None, None],
...                    'Score2': [85, 90]})
>>> df
   Score1  Score2
0    None      85
1    None      90
```

If we want to sum up each of the columns, then we sum down the index or row axis (`axis=0`):

```
>>> df.apply(np.sum, axis=0)
Score1      0
Score2    175
dtype: int64
```

To sum along every row, we sum across the columns axis (`axis=1`):

```
>>> df.apply(np.sum, axis=1)
0    85
1    90
dtype: int64
```

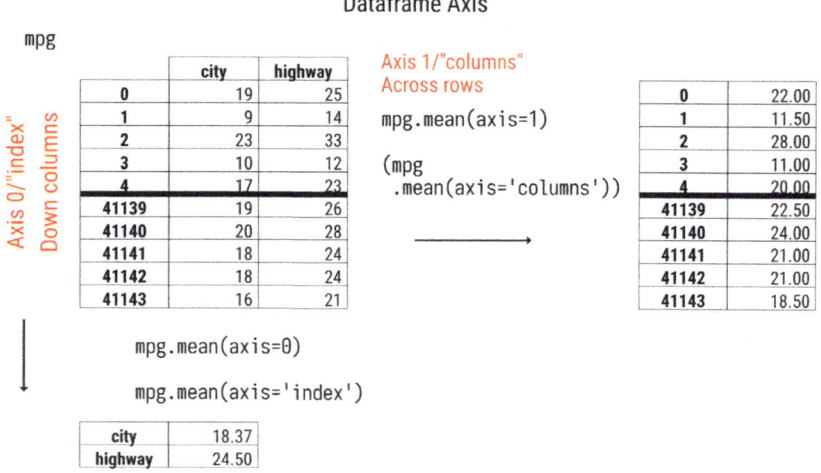

Figure 16.3: Figure showing the relation between axis 0 and axis 1. Note that when an operation is applied along axis 0, it is applied down the column. Likewise, operations along axis 1 operate across the values in the row.

Code	Description
`pd.DataFrame(data=None,` `index=None, columns=None)`	Create a dataframe from scalar, sequence, dict, ndarry or dataframe.
`.axes`	Tuple of index and columns.

Table 16.1: Dataframe creation

16.6 Summary

In this chapter, we introduced a Python data structure that is similar to how the pandas dataframe is implemented. It illustrated the index and the columnar nature of the dataframe. Then we looked at the main components of the dataframe and how columns are really just series objects. We saw various ways to construct dataframes. Finally, we looked at the two axes of the dataframe.

In future chapters, we will dig in more and see the dataframe in action.

16.7   Exercises

1. Create a dataframe with the names of your colleagues, their age (or an estimate), and their title.

2. Capitalize the values in the name column.

3. Sum up the values of the age column.

Chapter 17

Similarities with `Series` and `DataFrame`

We've spent a good portion of this book introducing the `Series` while mostly ignoring the other pandas class that you will use a lot, the `DataFrame`. Not to worry! Much of what we have discussed about series objects are directly applicable to dataframes.

In the next few chapters, we will explore the similarities between the two classes, before diving into unique features of dataframes in the following chapters.

We will be exploring a dataset from a Siena College Poll in 2018. This data has rankings of United States Presidents in various attributes.

I was made aware of this dataset when one of my children pointed me to a visualization made from it. I'm going to pull the raw data and show how to recreate the visualization first. Then we will demonstrate more features of dataframes with the presidential data.

17.1 Getting the Data

Wikipedia has the data[10] from Siena College. I scraped the data using the following commands. (Given that Wikipedia can change at any time, there is no guarantee that this code will work for you.):

```
url = 'https://en.wikipedia.org/wiki/'\
      'Historical_rankings_of_presidents_of_the_United_States'
pres_dfs = pd.read_html(url)
df = pres_dfs[-4]
```

---

[10]https://en.wikipedia.org/wiki/Historical_rankings_of_presidents_of_the_United_States

After I loaded the data, I removed some rows (the first and last), renamed the "Political Party" column to "Party", and then converted it to a categorical column type:

```
(df
 .iloc[1:-1]
 .rename(columns={'Political party': 'Party'})
 .assign(Party=lambda df_:df_
      .Party
      .str.replace(r'\[.*\]', '')
      .astype('category'))
)
```

Here are the column names with their associated explanation:

- Bg = Background

- Im = Imagination

- Int = Integrity

- IQ = Intelligence

- L = Luck

- WR = Willing to take risks

- AC = Ability to compromise

- EAb = Executive ability

- LA = Leadership ability

- CAb = Communication ability

- OA = Overall ability

- PL = Party leadership

- RC = Relations with Congress

- CAp = Court appointments

- HE = Handling of economy

- EAp = Executive appointments

- DA = Domestic accomplishments

- FPA = Foreign policy accomplishments

- AM = Avoid crucial mistakes

- EV = Experts' view

- O = Overall

At this point, I exported my data and saved it to a CSV (to avoid possible future changes at Wikipedia). You can load the data from my GitHub account:

```
>>> import pandas as pd
>>> url = 'https://github.com/mattharrison/datasets/raw/master/data/'\
...       'siena2018-pres.csv'
>>> df = pd.read_csv(url, index_col=0)

>>> df
            President              Party  Bg  ...  AM  EV   O
Seq.                                     ...
1      George Washington      Independent   7  ...   1   2   1
2            John Adams       Federalist   3  ...  16  10  14
3       Thomas Jefferson  Democratic-Republican   2  ...   7   5   5
4         James Madison  Democratic-Republican   4  ...  11   8   7
5          James Monroe  Democratic-Republican   9  ...   6   9   8
...                ...              ...  ..  ...  ..  ..  ..
41    George H. W. Bush       Republican  10  ...  17  21  21
42         Bill Clinton       Democratic  21  ...  30  14  15
43        George W. Bush       Republican  17  ...  36  34  33
44         Barack Obama       Democratic  24  ...  10  11  17
45         Donald Trump       Republican  43  ...  41  42  42

[44 rows x 23 columns]
```

Note that we lose fancy pandas types when we load from CSV, so I will need to set those up again:

```
>>> df.dtypes
President    object
Party        object
Bg            int64
Im            int64
Int           int64
             ...
```

```
DA               int64
FPA              int64
AM               int64
EV               int64
O                int64
Length: 23, dtype: object
```

Here is a function, tweak_siena_pres, to clean up this data:

```
>>> def tweak_siena_pres(df):
...     def int64_to_uint8(df_):
...         cols = df_.select_dtypes('int64')
...         return (df_
...                 .astype({col:'uint8' for col in cols}))
...
...     return (df
...        .rename(columns={'Seq.':'Seq'})     # 1
...        .rename(columns={k:v.replace(' ', '_') for k,v in
...           {'Bg': 'Background',
...            'PL': 'Party leadership', 'CAb': 'Communication ability',
...            'RC': 'Relations with Congress', 'CAp': 'Court appointments',
...            'HE': 'Handling of economy', 'L': 'Luck',
...            'AC': 'Ability to compromise', 'WR': 'Willing to take risks',
...            'EAp': 'Executive appointments', 'OA': 'Overall ability',
...            'Im': 'Imagination', 'DA': 'Domestic accomplishments',
...            'Int': 'Integrity', 'EAb': 'Executive ability',
...            'FPA': 'Foreign policy accomplishments',
...            'LA': 'Leadership ability',
...            'IQ': 'Intelligence', 'AM': 'Avoid crucial mistakes',
...            'EV': "Experts' view", 'O': 'Overall'}.items()})
...        .astype({'Party':'category'})   # 2
...        .pipe(int64_to_uint8)   # 3
...        .assign(Average_rank=lambda df_:(df_.select_dtypes('uint8') # 4
...                   .sum(axis=1).rank(method='dense').astype('uint8')),
...              Quartile=lambda df_:pd.qcut(df_.Average_rank, 4,
...                 labels='1st 2nd 3rd 4th'.split()))
...           )
...        )
```

We will go over all of the functionality exposed in the tweak_siena_pres function in detail in later chapters. I will briefly explain the chained operations.

The first call to .rename (#1) removes the period from the column named *Seq.*. The next .rename call uses a dictionary comprehension to replace the shorted column names with the longer names but also replaces spaces with

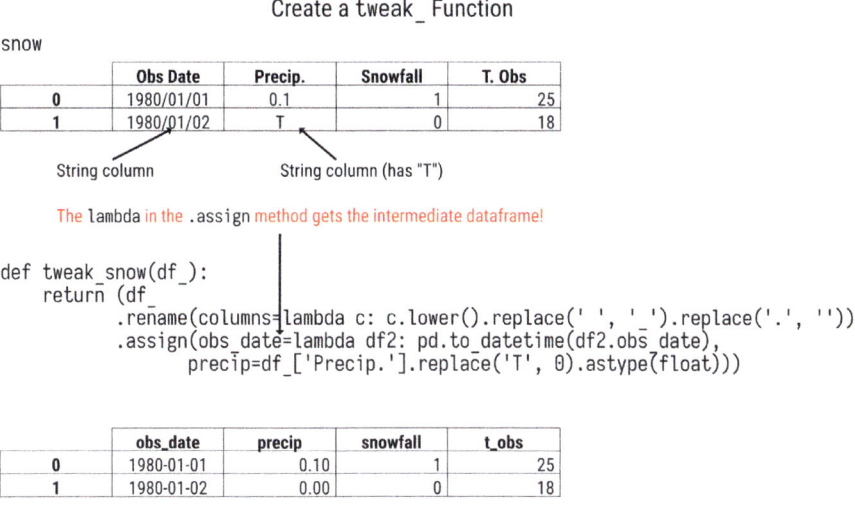

Figure 17.1: A tweak function is useful for maintaining order and sanity when working in Jupyter.

underscores. The call to .astype (#2) sets the type of the *Party* column to category. The resulting dataframe is passed to the int64_to_uint8 function with the .pipe call (#3). This converts all the int64 columns to unsigned 8-bit columns (since all of the numeric data is below 44 we can store this information in a smaller type). The final call to .assign creates an *Average_rank* column by summing all of the numeric values of a row and then taking the *dense* rank of the resulting values. It also creates a *Quartile* column by binning the *Average_rank* column into four bins.

Note

You will see many examples of "tweak" functions later in this book. This is a pattern I like to follow. At the top of my Jupyter notebook, I will load the raw data into a dataframe. Then in the cell below that, I will make a tweak function (usually written with this chain style) that takes the raw data and returns a cleaned-up dataset.

This is advantageous for a few reasons. If you have used Jupyter for a while, then you will know that your notebook may get unwieldy, it has many cells, and you may have executed them in an arbitrary order as you were working. When you come back to your notebook, it can be hard to get back to the state where your data is in the form that you want it to be. If you follow this pattern, it makes it easy to open up a notebook, load the raw data, and then clean it up in the next cell.

Another advantage of writing this as a function is that you can pull this out and leverage it in production code.

I strongly recommend that you start adopting this practice in your notebooks, and it will provide a big improvement to your data workflow.

With this cleaned up data, we can combine it with the Seaborn library to visualize the data. We will make a heatmap with Seaborn, then we will right align the labels, rotate them, and add a title to the plot:

```
>>> import matplotlib.pyplot as plt
>>> import seaborn as sns
>>> fig, ax = plt.subplots(figsize=(10,10), dpi=600)
>>> g = sns.heatmap((tweak_siena_pres(df)
...     .set_index('President')
...     .iloc[:,2:-1]
...     ),annot=True, cmap='viridis', ax=ax)
>>> g.set_xticklabels(g.get_xticklabels(), rotation=45, fontsize=8,
...     ha='right')
>>> _ = plt.title('Presidential Ranking')
>>> fig.savefig('img/pandas2/20-pres.png', bbox_inches='tight')
```

But the purpose of this chapter is not to look at visualizations, rather to see that most of what you can do with a series you can do with a dataframe. Let's start comparing.

17.2 Viewing Data

Dataframes have .head and .tail methods to view the first or last few rows of the data. I also like to use .sample, as my experience is that the first few rows of data often do not represent the data as a whole. The rows at the top may be missing some entries or are test data:

```
>>> pres = tweak_siena_pres(df)
>>> pres.head(3)
```

Seq.	President	Party	...	Average_rank	Quartile
1	George Washington	Independent	...	1	1st
2	John Adams	Federalist	...	13	2nd

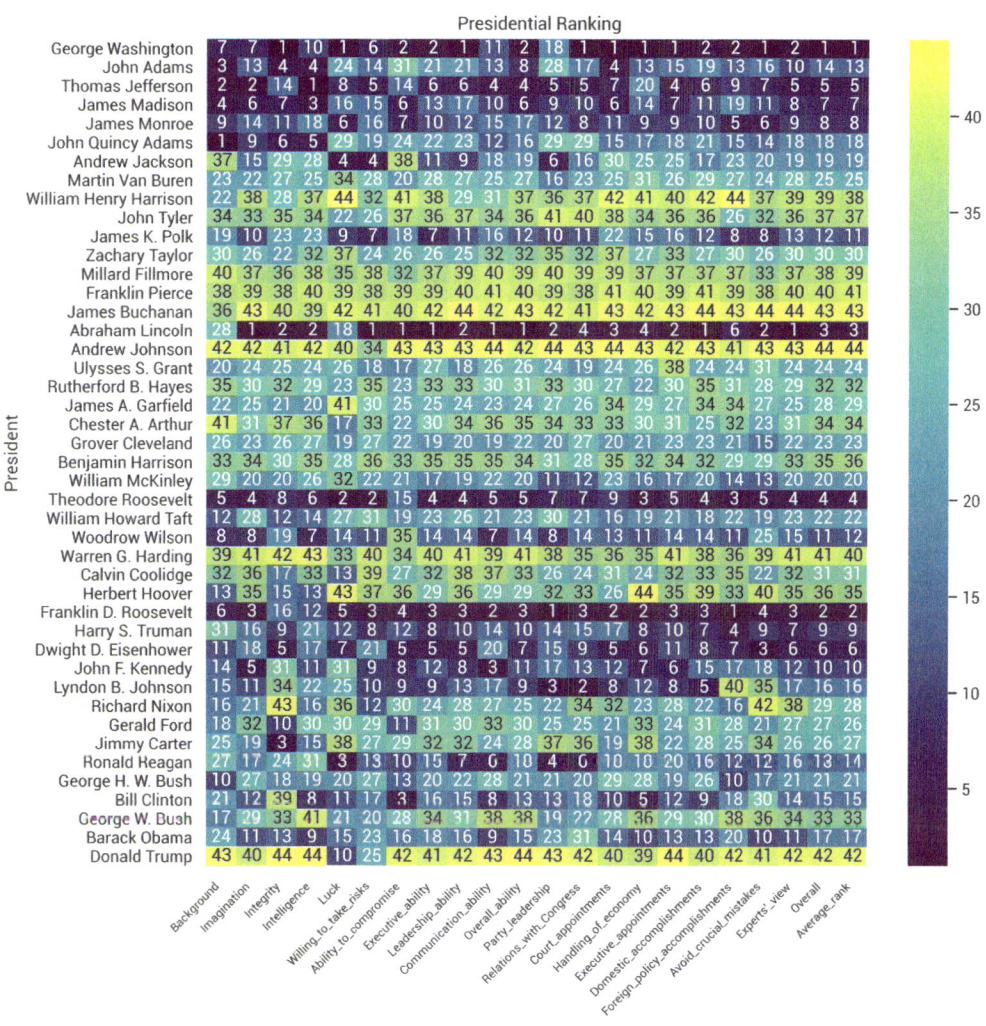

Figure 17.2: Visualization of United States presidential attributes.

```
3        Thomas Jefferson  Democratic-Republican  ...                5        1st

[3 rows x 25 columns]

>>> pres.sample(3)
            President        Party   ...   Average_rank  Quartile
Seq.                                  ...
18      Ulysses S. Grant  Republican  ...            24      3rd
36      Lyndon B. Johnson  Democratic  ...           16      2nd
21      Chester A. Arthur  Republican  ...           34      4th

[3 rows x 25 columns]
```

Method	Description
.head(n=5)	Return a dataframe with the first n values.
.tail(n=5)	Return a dataframe with the last n values.
s.sample(n=None, frac=None, replace=False, weights=None, random_state=None, axis=None)	Return a dataframe with n random entries. Can also specify a fraction with frac (if frac > 1, my specify replace=True).

Table 17.1: Dataframe viewing Methods

17.3 Summary

This chapter demonstrated loading data from Wikipedia and then cleaned up the data, creating a "tweak" function. If you follow this pattern of making a function to clean up your data, it will make your life much easier when using pandas.

17.4 Exercises

With a tabular dataset of your choice:

1. Create a dataframe from the data.

2. View the first 20 rows of data.

3. Sample 30 rows from your data.

Chapter 18

Math Methods in DataFrames

We have seen that you can perform math operations on Series objects in pandas. In this chapter, we will show that you can also do math on dataframes.

We will begin by looking at the basic math operations. We will use a cleaned up version of the data:

```
>>> url = 'https://github.com/mattharrison/datasets/raw/master/data/'\
...      'siena2018-pres.csv'
>>> df = pd.read_csv(url, index_col=0)

>>> pres = tweak_siena_pres(df)
```

18.1 Index Alignment

We can perform math operations of the dataframe. There are the math methods like .add and .div and we also have dunder methods that allow us to use the operators like +, -, /, and *.

Note that the index will *align* when we perform math. To demonstrate alignment, I will add the values from index values at rows 0-2 and column positions at index 0-3 and add then to the index values from rows 1-5 and 0-4:

```
>>> scores = (pres
...   .loc[:,'Background':'Average_rank']
... )
>>> scores
      Background  Imagination  ...  Overall  Average_rank
Seq.                           ...
1              7            7  ...        1             1
2              3           13  ...       14            13
```

3	2	2	...	5	5
4	4	6	...	7	7
5	9	14	...	8	8
...	...	...	...	...	...
41	10	27	...	21	21
42	21	12	...	15	15
43	17	29	...	33	33
44	24	11	...	17	17
45	43	40	...	42	42

```
[44 rows x 22 columns]
```

We will pull out two sections of the data:

```
>>> s1 = scores.iloc[:3, :4]
>>> s1
      Background  Imagination  Integrity  Intelligence
Seq.
1              7            7          1            10
2              3           13          4             4
3              2            2         14             1

>>> s2 = scores.iloc[1:6, :5]
>>> s2
      Background  Imagination  Integrity  Intelligence  Luck
Seq.
2              3           13          4             4    24
3              2            2         14             1     8
4              4            6          7             3    16
5              9           14         11            18     6
6              1            9          6             5    29
```

Now let's add these together.

```
>>> s1 + s2
      Background  Imagination  Integrity  Intelligence  Luck
Seq.
1            NaN          NaN        NaN           NaN   NaN
2            6.0         26.0        8.0           8.0   NaN
3            4.0          4.0       28.0           2.0   NaN
4            NaN          NaN        NaN           NaN   NaN
5            NaN          NaN        NaN           NaN   NaN
6            NaN          NaN        NaN           NaN   NaN
```

Only the overlapping rows (rows 2 and 3) and columns (*Background* through *Intelligence*) get added together. The other values are missing!

18.2 Duplicate Index Entries

If you have duplicate index values, each index value in the left dataframe will match up with the index in the right dataframe. You should be aware if you have repeated index values before performing operations that align the index.

Lets add a dataframe that has duplicated values in the index (created by concatenating the dataframe with itself):

```
>>> scores.iloc[:3, :4] + pd.concat([scores.iloc[1:6, :5]]*2)
      Background  Imagination  Integrity  Intelligence  Luck
Seq.
1            NaN          NaN        NaN           NaN   NaN
2            6.0         26.0        8.0           8.0   NaN
2            6.0         26.0        8.0           8.0   NaN
3            4.0          4.0       28.0           2.0   NaN
3            4.0          4.0       28.0           2.0   NaN
...          ...          ...        ...           ...   ...
4            NaN          NaN        NaN           NaN   NaN
5            NaN          NaN        NaN           NaN   NaN
5            NaN          NaN        NaN           NaN   NaN
6            NaN          NaN        NaN           NaN   NaN
6            NaN          NaN        NaN           NaN   NaN

[11 rows x 5 columns]

>>> pd.concat([scores.iloc[1:6, :5]]*2).index.duplicated().any()
True
```

Method	Description
.add(other, axis='columns', level=None, fill_value=None)	Add other to dataframe across axis. Unlike operator, can specify fill_value.
.sub(other, axis='columns', level=None, fill_value=None)	Subtract other from dataframe across axis. Unlike operator, can specify fill_value.
.mul(other, axis='columns', level=None, fill_value=None)	Multiply other with dataframe across axis. Unlike operator, can specify fill_value.
.div(other, axis='columns', level=None, fill_value=None)	Divide dataframe by other across axis. Unlike operator, can specify fill_value.

`.truediv(other, axis='columns', level=None, fill_value=None)`	Same as `.div`.
`.floordiv(other, axis='columns', level=None, fill_value=None)`	Integer divide dataframe by other across axis. Unlike operator, can specify `fill_value`.
`.mod(other, axis='columns', level=None, fill_value=None)`	Perform modulo operation with other across axis. Unlike operator, can specify `fill_value`.
`.pow(other, axis='columns', level=None, fill_value=None)`	Raise to other power across axis. Unlike operator, can specify `fill_value`.

Table 18.1: Dataframe Math Methods

18.3 Summary

In this chapter, we demonstrated math operations on dataframes. I generally perform math operations on series but it is nice to have the capability in dataframes. We also demonstrated index alignment.

18.4 Exercises

With a tabular dataset of your choice:

1. Create a dataframe from the data and add it to itself.

2. Create a dataframe from the data and multiply it by two.

3. Are the results from the previous exercises equivalent?

Chapter 19

Looping and Aggregation

Often we want to apply operations over items in a dataframe. We may want to use looping, the .apply method, or an aggregation method to do this.

19.1   For Loops

You can use a for loop with a dataframe, though you generally want to avoid for loops when doing numerical manipulation. When I see a for loop with pandas code, it means this is a slow operation, and you are not able to take advantage of the vectorization that speeds up many operations. However, sometimes a for loop is appropriate (I use them when labeling plots).

If you need to loop over a dataframe, here are three methods for doing it. The .iteritems method gives you a tuple with the column name and the column (a series). The .iterrows method gives you a tuple with the index value and the row (converted into a series). Finally, the .itertuples method gives you a row represented as a named tuple (with the index in position 0):

```
>>> import pandas as pd
>>> url = 'https://github.com/mattharrison/datasets/raw/master/data/'\
...      'siena2018-pres.csv'
>>> df = pd.read_csv(url, index_col=0)
>>> pres = tweak_siena_pres(df)

>>> # iteration over columns (col_name, series) tuple
>>> for col_name, col in pres.iteritems():
...      print(col_name, type(col))
...      break
Seq <class 'pandas.core.series.Series'>
```

```
>>> # iteration over rows (index, row(as a series)) tuple
>>> for idx, row in pres.iterrows():
...     print(idx, type(row))
...     break
1 <class 'pandas.core.series.Series'>

>>> # iteration over rows as namedtuple (index as first item)
>>> for tup in pres.itertuples():
...     print(tup[0], tup.Party)
...     break
1 Independent
```

19.2 Aggregations

The aggregations that are found in a series are also applicable to a dataframe. You need to keep in mind that a dataframe has two dimensions. This means you can aggregate across both dimensions. So you can sum along axis 0 (the index) or axis 1 (the columns). In this example, we will calculate the average of each row. We will isolate the numeric columns using .loc, then we will sum along the columns and divide the result by the length of the columns:

```
>>> scores = (pres
...     .loc[:,'Background':'Average_rank']
... )
>>> scores.sum(axis='columns') / len(scores.columns)
Seq.
1        3.681818
2       14.454545
3        6.545455
4        9.636364
5       10.454545
          ...
41      20.818182
42      14.636364
43      30.363636
44      15.818182
45      39.772727
Length: 44, dtype: float64
```

(Note we could also use .mean(axis=1) to do the above.)

We can use multiple aggregations with the .agg method. Below, we will count the number of non-missing values for each column, the number of entries for each column (including the missing values), the sum of each

column, and run a custom aggregation (that just returns the value for index
1):

```
>>> pres.agg(['count', 'size', 'sum', lambda col: col.loc[1]])
                                                  Seq  ...  Quartile
count                                              44  ...        44
size                                               44  ...        44
sum        12345678910111213141516171819202122/2423252627...  ...       NaN
<lambda>                                            1  ...       1st

[4 rows x 26 columns]
```

We can pass in a dictionary to perform multiple aggregations on a column:

```
>>> pres.agg({'Luck': ['count', 'size'], 'Overall': ['count', 'max']})
       Luck  Overall
count  44.0     44.0
size   44.0      NaN
max     NaN     44.0
```

You can use a keyword argument with a tuple to specify the index value
of the resultant aggregation:

```
>>> pres.agg(Intelligence_count=('Intelligence', 'count'),
...          Intelligence_size=('Intelligence', 'size')
...          )
                    Intelligence
Intelligence_count            44
Intelligence_size             44
```

The .describe method is a meta-aggregation that returns a dataframe with
summary statistics for each numeric columns:

```
>>> pres.describe()
       Background  Imagination  ...    Overall  Average_rank
count   44.000000    44.000000  ...  44.000000     44.000000
mean    22.000000    21.750000  ...  22.500000     22.500000
std     12.409674    12.519984  ...  12.845233     12.845233
min      1.000000     1.000000  ...   1.000000      1.000000
25%     11.750000    11.000000  ...  11.750000     11.750000
50%     22.000000    21.500000  ...  22.500000     22.500000
75%     32.250000    32.250000  ...  33.250000     33.250000
max     43.000000    43.000000  ...  44.000000     44.000000

[8 rows x 22 columns]
```

The .describe Method

mpg

	make	year	city08	highway08
0	Alfa Romeo	1985	19	25
1	Ferrari	1985	9	14
2	Dodge	1985	23	33
3	Dodge	1985	10	12
4	Subaru	1993	17	23
41139	Subaru	1993	19	26
41140	Subaru	1993	20	28
41141	Subaru	1993	18	24
41142	Subaru	1993	18	24
41143	Subaru	1993	16	21

mpg.describe()

- Summary statistics for numeric columns
- Use include='all' to show other types
- Count is non-NA values

	year	city08	highway08
count	41144.00	41144.00	41144.00
mean	2001.54	18.37	24.50
std	11.14	7.91	7.73
min	1984.00	6.00	9.00
25%	1991.00	15.00	20.00
50%	2002.00	17.00	24.00
75%	2011.00	20.00	28.00
max	2020.00	150.00	124.00

Figure 19.1: The .describe method provides the count of non-missing values, the mean, standard deviation, minimum, maximum, and quartiles.

Note

The *count* row in the summary statistics has a particular meaning in pandas. It is not the count of the rows, rather it is the count of the non-missing (not na) rows.

19.3 The .apply Method

Like the series, the dataframe has an .apply method. Like the series method, you should be wary of using the dataframe method. More specifically, if you are dealing with numbers, you might want to see if you can operate in a vectorized way.

Also, keep in mind that a dataframe is two-dimensional. So rather than applying a function to a single value, when you call .apply on a dataframe, you work on a whole row or a whole column. Because of that, I find that I rarely use this method.

Most of the .apply examples you find in the wild are silly examples that show how .apply works, but also give a false impression that you should be everywhere, including using it for these silly examples.

For example, if you wanted to calculate the spread of the presidential rankings for each row, I would do this:

```
>>> (pres
...     .select_dtypes('number')
...     .pipe(lambda df_:df_.max(axis='columns')
...         - df_.min(axis='columns'))
... )
Seq.
1       17
2       28
3       19
4       16
5       13
        ..
41      19
42      36
43      24
44      22
45      34
Length: 44, dtype: uint8
```

The .apply version looks like this:

```
>>> (pres
...     .select_dtypes('number')
...     .apply(lambda row: row.max()-row.min(), axis='columns')
... )
Seq.
1       17
2       28
3       19
4       16
5       13
        ..
41      19
```

```
42    36
43    24
44    22
45    34
Length: 44, dtype: int8
```

They look pretty similar but the former does an optimized max and min calculation, while the latter does a separate calculation for each row.

Or you might see an example showing how to use .apply on the index axis. If you use .apply with axis='index', it calls the function on each column. You might encounter silly examples like calculating the sum of each column:

```
>>> pres.select_dtypes('number').apply('sum')  # axis=0
Background                        968
Imagination                      957
Integrity                        990
Intelligence                     990
Luck                             990
                                 ...
Foreign_policy_accomplishments   990
Avoid_crucial_mistakes           990
Experts'_view                    990
Overall                          990
Average_rank                     990
Length: 22, dtype: int64
```

In this case, it will calculate a sum on each column, but why not just do one call and get the same result?

```
>>> pres.select_dtypes('number').sum()  # axis=0
Background                       968
Imagination                      957
Integrity                        990
Intelligence                     990
Luck                             990
                                 ...
Foreign_policy_accomplishments   990
Avoid_crucial_mistakes           990
Experts'_view                    990
Overall                          990
Average_rank                     990
Length: 22, dtype: int64
```

I have used .apply when replicating complicated logic from spreadsheets. Here is a snippet of sample data:

```
>>> import io
>>> billing_data = \
... '''cancel_date,period_start,start_date,end_date,rev,sum_payments
... 12/1/2019,1/1/2020,12/15/2019,5/15/2020,999,50
... ,1/1/2020,12/15/2019,5/15/2020,999,50
... ,1/1/2020,12/15/2019,5/15/2020,999,1950
... 1/20/2020,1/1/2020,12/15/2019,5/15/2020,499,0
... ,1/1/2020,12/24/2019,5/24/2020,699,100
... ,1/1/2020,11/29/2019,4/29/2020,799,250
... ,1/1/2020,1/15/2020,4/29/2020,799,250'''

>>> bill_df = pd.read_csv(io.StringIO(billing_data),
...       parse_dates=['cancel_date', 'period_start', 'start_date',
...                    'end_date'])

>>> bill_df
  cancel_date period_start start_date   end_date  rev  sum_payments
0  2019-12-01   2020-01-01 2019-12-15 2020-05-15  999            50
1         NaT   2020-01-01 2019-12-15 2020-05-15  999            50
2         NaT   2020-01-01 2019-12-15 2020-05-15  999          1950
3  2020-01-20   2020-01-01 2019-12-15 2020-05-15  499             0
4         NaT   2020-01-01 2019-12-24 2020-05-24  699           100
5         NaT   2020-01-01 2019-11-29 2020-04-29  799           250
6         NaT   2020-01-01 2020-01-15 2020-04-29  799           250
```

Here is some logic. If the start and end dates bound the period start date, we calculate if the revenue is greater than the sum of the payments:

```
>>> def calc_unbilled_rec(vals):
...     cancel_date, period_start, start_date, end_date, rev, \
...          sum_payments = vals
...     if cancel_date < period_start:
...         return
...     if start_date < period_start and end_date > period_start:
...         if rev > sum_payments:
...             return rev - sum_payments
...         else:
...             return 0
```

We can use .apply to call this function with the values from each row. Note that to apply it to a row we need to pass in axis='columns':

```
>>> bill_df.apply(calc_unbilled_rec, axis='columns')
0      NaN
1    949.0
2      0.0
3    499.0
```

```
4      599.0
5      549.0
6       NaN
dtype: float64
```

Below is an attempt to vectorize this with np.select. Sadly this runs about twice as slow on my machine on this small dataset. However, if the dataset has a hundred thousand rows, it runs about 200 times faster!

```
>>> import numpy as np
>>> pd.Series(np.select([
...         (bill_df.cancel_date < bill_df.period_start),   # 1
...         ((bill_df.start_date < bill_df.period_start) &   # 2
...          (bill_df.end_date > bill_df.period_start) &
...          (bill_df.rev > bill_df.sum_payments)),
...         ((bill_df.start_date < bill_df.period_start) &   # 3
...          (bill_df.end_date > bill_df.period_start) &
...          (bill_df.rev <= bill_df.sum_payments))
...         ],
...         [np.nan, bill_df.rev - bill_df.sum_payments, 0],   # 1, 2, 3
...         np.nan))  # default
0       NaN
1     949.0
2       0.0
3     499.0
4     599.0
5     549.0
6       NaN
dtype: float64
```

Note

Be careful with your timing. It is not necessarily the case that code that is slower on small datasets is slower on larger datasets!

Method	Description
.iteritems()	Iterate over a tuple of column name and series.
.iterrows()	Iterate over tuple of index name and row (presented as a series). Type information not preserved.

`.itertuples(index=True, name="Pandas")`	Iterate over a namedtuples of rows. Include index by default. Use name to specify the classname of the namedtuple (or set to None to return normal tuples).
`.sum(axis=0, skipna=True, level=None, numeric_only=None, min_count=0`	Return sum over axis. Default of empty sequence is 0, set min_count=1 to return nan.
`.min(axis=0, skipna=True, level=None, numeric_only=None`	Return minimum over the axis.
`.max(axis=0, skipna=True, level=None, numeric_only=None`	Return maximum over the axis.
`.idxmin(axis=0, skipna=True)`	Return the index of first minimum value over the axis.
`.idxmax(axis=0, skipna=True)`	Return the index of first maximum value over the axis.
`.agg(func=None, axis=0, *args, **kwargs)`	Aggregate using func over the axis. The func can be a function that collapses a column (or row), string, list of functions (or strings), dictionary of axis to function, list, or string.
`.describe(percentiles=[.25, .5, .75], include=None, exclude=None, datetime_is_numeric=False)`	Return summary statistics for dataframe.
`.apply(func-None, axis=0, raw=False, result_type=None, *args, **kwargs)`	Apply func over the axis. If func returns a sequence then return a dataframe. If func returns a scalar, then return a series.
`np.select(condlist, choicelist, default=0)`	Simulate an if then statement. Pass in a list of boolean arrays to condlist and the corresponding value in the list choicelist.

Table 19.1: Dataframe Looping Methods

19.4 Summary

In this chapter, we demonstrated looping and aggregation methods of dataframes. We also demonstrated the .apply method.

19.5   Exercises

With a tabular dataset of your choice:

1. Loop over each of the rows and calculate the maximum and minimum value.

2. Calculate the maximum and minimum value of each row and column using the .agg method.

3. Calculate the maximum and minimum value of each row and column using the .apply method.

Chapter 20

Columns Types, `.assign`, and Memory Usage

In this chapter, we will explore updating columns, creating columns, and changing the types of columns. We will show how to see how this impacts memory usage.

20.1   Conversion Methods

There are various methods and functions for changing the types of a series in pandas. We can all `.astype` to update column types. Or we can use the `.assign` method to return a new dataframe with the updated type.

The `.astype` method allows us to specify the types of each column with a dictionary.

The `.assign` method is a key method to master. You specify the name of a column with a keyword argument. If the argument name is an existing column, it will change the values of the column. If the argument name is a new column, it creates a new column. One caveat is that this method returns a new dataframe, it does not mutate the existing dataframe.

You should also know that you can pass in a scalar value, a series, or a callable as the value for the keyword argument. The callable (a function or `lambda`) should accept the current state of the dataframe (this is important when chaining because each step returns a new dataframe), and should return a scalar or series.

We saw some examples of these methods in the `tweak_siena_pres` and `int64_to_uint8` functions. Here are the relevant snippets:

```
def tweak_siena_pres(df):
    def int64_to_uint8(df_):
        # ....
        return (df_
                ...
                .astype({col:'uint8' for col in cols}))
    return (df
     # ...
     .astype({'Party':'category'})
     .pipe(int64_to_uint8)
     .assign(Average_rank=lambda df_:(df_.select_dtypes('uint8')
             .sum(axis=1).rank(method='dense').astype('uint8')),
         )
    )
```

20.2 Memory Usage

One thing to be aware of is memory usage. You can often shrink the memory usage of a dataframe by changing the type while not losing any data.

Here is the original column sizes of the presidential data:

```
>>> import pandas as pd
>>> url = 'https://github.com/mattharrison/datasets/raw/master/data/'\
...     'siena2018-pres.csv'
>>> df = pd.read_csv(url, index_col=0)
>>> pres = tweak_siena_pres(df)

>>> df.memory_usage(deep=True)
Index        3662
President    3175
Party        2976
Bg            352
Im            352
             ...
DA            352
FPA           352
AM            352
EV            352
O             352
Length: 24, dtype: int64
```

Here are the sizes of the columns where the numeric values have been optimized:

```
>>> pres.memory_usage(deep=True)
Index                   3662
President               3175
Party                    624
Background                44
Imagination               44

                        ...
Avoid_crucial_mistakes    44
Experts'_view             44
Overall                   44
Average_rank              44
Quartile                 456
Length: 26, dtype: int64
```

You can see that the ranking columns use less memory because they are stored as uint8 values instead of int64.

If you are in a REPL and do not need to manipulate the results of the .memory_usage, an alternative is to call .info, which does not return a series, but prints the result to the screen:

```
>>> pres.info(memory_usage='deep')
<class 'pandas.core.frame.DataFrame'>
Index: 44 entries, 1 to 45
Data columns (total 25 columns):
 #   Column                    Non-Null Count  Dtype
---  ------                    --------------  -----
 0   President                 44 non-null     object
 1   Party                     44 non-null     category
 2   Background                44 non-null     uint8
 3   Imagination               44 non-null     uint8
 4   Integrity                 44 non-null     uint8
 5   Intelligence              44 non-null     uint8
 6   Luck                      44 non-null     uint8
 7   Willing_to_take_risks     44 non-null     uint8
 8   Ability_to_compromise     44 non-null     uint8
 9   Executive_ability         44 non-null     uint8
 10  Leadership_ability        44 non-null     uint8
 11  Communication_ability     44 non-null     uint8
 12  Overall_ability           44 non-null     uint8
 13  Party_leadership          44 non-null     uint8
 14  Relations_with_Congress   44 non-null     uint8
 15  Court_appointments        44 non-null     uint8
 16  Handling_of_economy       44 non-null     uint8
 17  Executive_appointments    44 non-null     uint8
 18  Domestic_accomplishments  44 non-null     uint8
```

```
19  Foreign_policy_accomplishments  44 non-null  uint8
20  Avoid_crucial_mistakes          44 non-null  uint8
21  Experts'_view                   44 non-null  uint8
22  Overall                         44 non-null  uint8
23  Average_rank                    44 non-null  uint8
24  Quartile                        44 non-null  category
dtypes: category(2), object(1), uint8(22)
memory usage: 8.7 KB
```

Method	Description
.astype(dtype, copy=True, errors='raise')	Cast dataframe into dtype. (More common to use this on series.)
.assign(**kwargs)	Return a new dataframe with updated or new columns. kwargs maps column name to function, scalar, or series. If using a function, it is passed in the current state of the dataframe and should return a scalar or series. Subsequent columns may reference earlier columns in kwargs if you use a function.
.memory_usage(index=True, deep=False)	Return a series with the memory usage of each column in bytes. By default includes index. Use deep=True to show how much space object columns consume.
.info(verbose=None, buf=None, max_cols=None, memory_usage=None, show_counts=None)	Print summary of dataframe to stdout. Use memory_usage='deep' to show object column memory usage.

Table 20.1: Dataframe Methods from this Chapter

20.3 Summary

The series chapters showed how to convert the type of a series from one type to another. With a dataframe, we want to optimize the types of each column. To create a dataframe with the newer columns, we use the .assign method. If you master this method you will eliminate many bugs that pandas users encounter when they try to change columns using other methods.

20.4 Exercises

With a tabular dataset of your choice:

1. Find a numeric column and change the type of it. Did you save memory? Did you lose precision?

2. Find a string column and convert it to a category. What happened to the memory usage? Time a few string operations. Are they faster on the categorical column or string column?

Chapter 21

Creating and Updating Columns

This chapter explores the "one true way" to create and update columns in pandas. This is potentially the most controversial subject of this book, probably because it is not talked about very often, and the syntax might be unclear at first.

21.1   Loading the Data

We will be looking at a dataset of Python users from JetBrains[11].
    Let's load the data:

```
>>> import pandas as pd
>>> url = 'https://github.com/mattharrison/datasets/raw/master/data/'\
...       '2020-jetbrains-python-survey.csv'
>>> jb = pd.read_csv(url)
>>> jb
      is.python.main other.lang.None  ...      age      country.live
0                Yes             NaN  ...   30-39               NaN
1                Yes             NaN  ...   21-29             India
2                Yes             NaN  ...   30-39     United States
3                Yes             NaN  ...     NaN               NaN
4                Yes             NaN  ...   21-29             Italy
...              ...             ...  ...     ...               ...
54457            Yes             NaN  ...   21-29  Russian Federation
54458            Yes             NaN  ...     NaN               NaN
54459            Yes             NaN  ...   21-29  Russian Federation
54460            Yes             NaN  ...   30-39             Spain
```

[11]https://www.jetbrains.com/lp/python-developers-survey-2020/

```
54461              Yes              NaN  ...  21-29          Algeria

[54462 rows x 264 columns]
```

This is a pretty good dataset. It has over 50,000 rows and 264 columns. However, we will need to clean it up to perform exploratory analysis.

Some of the columns have a dummy-like encoding. For example, the columns starting with *database.* end with a database name. In the values for those columns, the database name is included. Because a user might use multiple databases, that is a mechanism to encode this. However, it also creates many columns, one per database. To keep the data for the book manageable, I'm going to filter out columns like the database columns.

Below is code that determines whether a feature can have multiple values (like database) and removes those:

```
>>> import collections
>>> counter = collections.defaultdict(list)
>>> for col in sorted(jb.columns):
...     period_count = col.count('.')
...     if period_count >= 2:
...         part_end = 2
...     else:
...         part_end = 1
...     parts = col.split('.')[:part_end]
...     counter['.'.join(parts)].append(col)
>>> uniq_cols = []
>>> for cols in counter.values():
...     if len(cols) == 1:
...         uniq_cols.extend(cols)

>>> uniq_cols
['age', 'are.you.datascientist', 'company.size',
 'country.live', 'employment.status', 'first.learn.about.main.ide',
 'how.often.use.main.ide', 'ide.main', 'is.python.main', 'job.team',
 'main.purposes', 'missing.features.main.ide', 'nps.main.ide',
 'python.years', 'python2.version.most', 'python3.version.most',
 'several.projects', 'team.size', 'use.python.most', 'years.of.coding']
```

Note that these column names have a period in them. I'm going to replace those with an underscore as it will allow us to access the names of the columns via attributes (with a period).

Let's look at the age column:

```
>>> (jb
...  [uniq_cols]
```

```
...     .rename(columns=lambda c: c.replace('.', '_'))
...     .age
...     .value_counts(dropna=False)
... )
NaN              29701
21-29             9710
30-39             7512
40-49             3010
18-20             2567
50-59             1374
60 or older        588
Name: age, dtype: int64
```

I'm going to pull out the first two characters from the *age* column and convert it to numbers. We will have to convert to float because there are missing values:

```
>>> (jb
...     [uniq_cols]
...     .rename(columns=lambda c: c.replace('.', '_'))
...     .age
...     .str.slice(0,2)
...     .astype(float)
... )
0           30.0
1           21.0
2           30.0
3            NaN
4           21.0
           ...
54457       21.0
54458        NaN
54459       21.0
54460       30.0
54461       21.0
Name: age, Length: 54462, dtype: float64
```

Note

You can also write .str.slice(0,2) as .str[0:2].

Note that currently, pandas (here is the bug[12]) can't convert strings directly to 'Int64', you need to convert to float first.

---

[12]https://github.com/pandas-dev/pandas/issues/33254

```
>>> (jb
...  [uniq_cols]
...  .rename(columns=lambda c: c.replace('.', '_'))
...  .age
...  .str.slice(0,2)
...  .astype('Int64')
... )
Traceback (most recent call last):
  ...
TypeError: object cannot be converted to an IntegerDtype

>>> (jb
...  [uniq_cols]
...  .rename(columns=lambda c: c.replace('.', '_'))
...  .age
...  .str.slice(0,2)
...  .astype(float)
...  .astype('Int64')
... )
0           30
1           21
2           30
3          <NA>
4           21
          ...
54457       21
54458      <NA>
54459       21
54460       30
54461       21
Name: age, Length: 54462, dtype: Int64
```

Now that this column is cleaned up, let's put it in a dataframe. This is where .assign comes in. As a reminder, none of the operations we have looked at in this book mutate or update a series or dataframe. Instead, they return new series or dataframes. This is what enables the chaining style we have seen throughout this book.

Sometimes (actually quite often) you will see the internet telling you to do something like this:

```
>>> jb2 = jb[uniq_cols]
>>> age_slice = jb.age.str.slice(0, 2)
>>> age_float = age_slice.astype(float)
```

```
>>> age_int = age_float.astype('Int64')
>>> jb2['age'] = age_int
SettingWithCopyWarning:
A value is trying to be set on a copy of a slice from a DataFrame.
Try using .loc[row_indexer,col_indexer] = value instead

See the caveats in the documentation: https://pandas.pydata.org/pandas-docs/
  stable/user_guide/indexing.html#returning-a-view-versus-a-copy

  jb2['age'] = age_int
```

Sometimes the above code works, but you can see the infamous SettingWithCopyWarning warning telling you that it might not be working. However, if you use .assign, you sidestep this issue completely.

Also note that line jb2['age'] = age_int does not return anything. You cannot chain on it! The .assign method will let you get update or add a column and will also return a dataframe for chaining:

```
>>> (jb
...   [uniq_cols]
...   .rename(columns=lambda c: c.replace('.', '_'))
...   .assign(age=lambda df_:df_.age
...       .str.slice(0,2)
...       .astype(float)
...       .astype('Int64'))
... )
        age  ...   years_of_coding
0        30  ...           1-2 years
1        21  ...           3-5 years
2        30  ...           3-5 years
3      <NA>  ...           11+ years
4        21  ...     Less than 1 year
...     ...  ...               ...
54457    21  ...           1-2 years
54458  <NA>  ...           1-2 years
54459    21  ...          6-10 years
54460    30  ...           3-5 years
54461    21  ...           1-2 years

[54462 rows x 20 columns]
```

Note

When you call .assign you generally pass in a keyword argument corresponding to the column name to create or update. You can assign the argument to a series, a scalar, or a function. You will see that many of my examples use lambda functions.

Using a function (it can be a normal function, but often we use a lambda to have the logic inline) has an unseen benefit. This function will accept the *current state* of the dataframe. If you have done any filtering or manipulation in the chain before calling .assign, it will be represented in this dataframe.

In the example above, my lambda looked like this:

```
.assign(age=lambda df_:df_.age
```

I could have gotten away without a lambda in this case because the *age* column was not renamed. The code could have been this:

```
.assign(age=jb.age
```

Later on, we will see updating the *country.live* and *python.years* columns. Because we have a .rename in our chain, we will use a lambda to refer to the new column names, *country_live* and *python_years* respectively.

Another benefit of chaining is that this code reads like a step-by-step recipe. First, we pull out the columns we want, then rename the columns, and finally update the age column (with its own recipe).

Once you get used to this style of programming, you will start to think of making step by step changes to your data. This will make your code easier to read and understand.

Finally, some complain that working from the source data is slow, tedious, and repetitive. Maybe it is. But, in almost every data project I've been involved with, the boss has come around and asked for an explanation of the data. Using chaining makes stepping through the explanation easy. Using the style of pandas espoused by most of the internet makes this a huge headache.

Ok, one more point. Chaining also will enable (future) query engine optimizers to speed up chained pandas code. Much like SQL optimizers can do predicate pushdown, one could envision optimizers (or a future tool that supports that pandas API) that work on chains. The use of chain would enable this.

I'll get off my .assign soapbox here. It appears that many have an almost allergic reaction to this style of coding. Yet, they aren't able to present anything better, but the spaghetti code found everywhere else.

21.2 More Column Cleanup

The *are_you_datascientist* column can be converted to a boolean column with the .replace method:

```
>>> import numpy as np
>>> (jb
...    [uniq_cols]
...    .rename(columns=lambda c: c.replace('.', '_'))
...    .assign(age=lambda df_:df_.age.str.slice(0,2)
...                            .astype(float).astype('Int64'),
...            are_you_datascientist=lambda df_: df_.are_you_datascientist
...                .replace({'Yes': True, 'No': False, np.nan: False})
...            )
...    .are_you_datascientist
... )
0        False
1         True
2        False
3        False
4        False
          ...
54457    False
54458    False
54459    False
54460     True
54461    False
Name: are_you_datascientist, Length: 54462, dtype: object
```

On to the next column. Let's look at *company_size*. I'll use the .value_counts method to see unique values:

```
>>> (jb
...    [uniq_cols]
...    .rename(columns=lambda c: c.replace('.', '_'))
...    .assign(age=lambda df_:df_.age.str.slice(0,2)
...                            .astype(float).astype('Int64'),
...            are_you_datascientist=lambda df_: df_.are_you_datascientist
...                .replace({'Yes': True, 'No': False, np.nan: False})
...            )
...    .company_size
```

```
...    .value_counts(dropna=False)
... )
NaN                  35037
51-500                4608
More than 5,000       3635
11-50                 3507
2-10                  2558
1,001-5,000           1934
Just me               1492
501-1,000             1165
Not sure               526
Name: company_size, dtype: int64
```

I'm going to do replacements here as well. It would be possible to split or use a regular expression to pull out these values. I'm going to pull off the left value of the interval. The code will look like this:

```
company_size=lambda df_:df_.company_size.replace({'Just me': 1,
    'Not sure': np.nan, 'More than 5,000': 5000,
    '2-10': 2, '11-50':11,'51-500': 51, '501-1,000':501,
    '1,001-5,000':1001}).astype('Int64'),
```

I'm not going to show the code for each column individually, but here is an overview of the steps I will take to the columns:

- *country_live* - Convert to categorical.

- *employment_status* - Fill missing values with 'Other' and convert to categorical.

- *is_python_main* - Convert to categorical.

- *team_size* - Split on en-dash, pull out the first column, replace 'More than 40' with 41, replace values where *company_size* is 1 with 1, and convert it to a float.

- *years_of_coding* - Replace 'Less than 1 year' with .5, then pull out any numbers with a regular expression, and convert them to floats.

- *python_years* - Replace '_' with '.', then pull out any numbers with a regular expression, and convert them to floats.

- *use_python_most* - Replace missing values with 'Unknown'.

After the column manipulation, we will drop the *python2_version_most* column:

```
>>> jb2 = (jb
...   [uniq_cols]
...   .rename(columns=lambda c: c.replace('.', '_'))
...   .assign(age=lambda df_:df_.age.str.slice(0,2).astype(float)
...               .astype('Int64'),
...           are_you_datascientist=lambda df_:df_.are_you_datascientist
...               .replace({'Yes': True, 'No': False, np.nan: False}),
...           company_size=lambda df_:df_.company_size.replace({
...               'Just me': 1, 'Not sure': np.nan,
...               'More than 5,000': 5000, '2-10': 2, '11-50':11,
...               '51-500': 51, '501-1,000':501,
...               '1,001-5,000':1001}).astype('Int64'),
...           country_live=lambda df_:df_.country_live.astype('category'),
...           employment_status=lambda df_:df_.employment_status
...               .fillna('Other').astype('category'),
...           is_python_main=lambda df_:df_.is_python_main
...               .astype('category'),
...           team_size=lambda df_:df_.team_size
...               .str.split(r'-', n=1, expand=True)
...               .iloc[:,0].replace('More than 40 people', 41)
...               .where(df_.company_size!=1, 1).astype(float),
...           years_of_coding=lambda df_:df_.years_of_coding
...               .replace('Less than 1 year', .5).str.extract(r'(\d+)')
...               .astype(float),
...           python_years=lambda df_:df_.python_years
...               .replace('Less than 1 year', .5).str.extract(r'(\d+)')
...               .astype(float),
...           python3_ver=lambda df_:df_.python3_version_most
...               .str.replace('_', '.').str.extract(r'(\d\.\d)')
...               .astype(float),
...           use_python_most=lambda df_:df_.use_python_most
...               .fillna('Unknown')
...          )
...       .drop(columns=['python2_version_most'])
... )
```

The resulting dataframe has clean column names and data that is more amenable to analysis:

```
>>> jb2
      age are_you_datascientist  ...  years_of_coding python3_ver
0      30                 False  ...              1.0         3.7
1      21                  True  ...              3.0         3.6
2      30                 False  ...              3.0         3.6
3    <NA>                 False  ...             11.0         3.8
4      21                 False  ...              NaN         3.8
```

```
...      ...            ...  ...         ...          ...
54457    21           False  ...         1.0          3.6
54458    <NA>         False  ...         1.0          3.7
54459    21           False  ...         6.0          3.7
54460    30            True  ...         3.0          3.7
54461    21           False  ...         1.0          3.8
```

```
[54462 rows x 20 columns]
```

Upon inspection, the *team_size* column is still missing quite a few entries. It looks like there are over 5,000 respondents that are employed but neglected to enter a team size:

```
>>> (jb2
...    .query('team_size.isna()')
...    .employment_status
...    .value_counts(dropna=False)
... )
Fully employed by a company / organization       5279
Working student                                   696
Partially employed by a company / organization    482
Self-employed                                     430
Freelancer                                          0
Other                                               0
Retired                                             0
Student                                             0
Name: employment_status, dtype: int64
```

I'm going to use another call to .assign to use machine learning to predict the missing values for that column. I will leverage the CatBoost[13] library to do that. A nice feature of this library is that it will accept missing values and also accept string values (hence the name Category Boosting). Many machine learning libraries require that all data be numeric and that none of the values are missing.

While CatBoost works with data from pandas dataframes, it doesn't like native pandas types (like 'Int64' or 'category'), so I'm going to make a function, prep_for_ml, that uses two dictionary comprehensions to change the column types when we make our predictions.

Since this is not a book about machine learning, I will not go deep into what is going on, other than to say we are training the model on all the rows where *team_size* is not missing and using the trained model to predict the missing

---

[13]https://catboost.ai/

values. You may wish to use a simpler method like .fillna to impute these missing values. (You can see I'm kind of punting on the remaining missing values and just calling .dropna at the end. Also, note that summary statistics might be biased after filling in the values.)

```
>>> import catboost as cb
>>> import numpy as np

>>> def prep_for_ml(df):
...         # remove pandas types
...         return (df
...          .assign(**{col:df[col].astype(float)
...                 for col in df.select_dtypes('number')},
...              **{col:df[col].astype(str).fillna('')
...                 for col in df.select_dtypes(['object', 'category'])})
...         )

>>> def predict_col(df, col):
...         df = prep_for_ml(df)
...         missing = df.query(f'~{col}.isna()')
...         cat_idx = [i for i,typ in enumerate(df.drop(columns=[col]).dtypes)
...                   if str(typ) == 'object']
...         X = (missing
...             .drop(columns=[col])
...             .values
...             )
...         y = missing[col]
...         model = cb.CatBoostRegressor(iterations=20, cat_features=cat_idx)
...         model.fit(X,y, cat_features=cat_idx)
...         pred = model.predict(df.drop(columns=[col]))
...         return df[col].where(~df[col].isna(), pred)
```

With the function to predict the missing values ready let's give it a try:

```
>>> jb2 = (jb
...     [uniq_cols]
...     .rename(columns=lambda c: c.replace('.', '_'))
...     .assign(age=lambda df_:df_.age.str.slice(0,2).astype(float)
...                 .astype('Int64'),
...          are_you_datascientist=lambda df_:df_.are_you_datascientist
...                 .replace({'Yes': True, 'No': False, np.nan: False}),
...          company_size=lambda df_:df_.company_size.replace({
...              'Just me': 1, 'Not sure': np.nan,
...              'More than 5,000': 5000, '2-10': 2, '11-50':11,
...              '51-500': 51, '501-1,000':501,
...              '1,001-5,000':1001}).astype('Int64'),
```

```
...              country_live=lambda df_:df_.country_live.astype('category'),
...              employment_status=lambda df_:df_.employment_status
...                  .fillna('Other').astype('category'),
...              is_python_main=lambda df_:df_.is_python_main
...                  .astype('category'),
...              team_size=lambda df_:df_.team_size
...                  .str.split(r'-', n=1, expand=True)
...                  .iloc[:,0].replace('More than 40 people', 41)
...                  .where(df_.company_size!=1, 1).astype(float),
...              years_of_coding=lambda df_:df_.years_of_coding
...                  .replace('Less than 1 year', .5).str.extract(r'(\d+)')
...                  .astype(float),
...              python_years=lambda df_:df_.python_years
...                  .replace('Less than 1 year', .5).str.extract(r'(\d+)')
...                  .astype(float),
...              python3_ver=lambda df_:df_.python3_version_most
...                  .str.replace('_', '.').str.extract(r'(\d\.\d)')
...                  .astype(float),
...              use_python_most=lambda df_:df_.use_python_most
...                  .fillna('Unknown')
...          )
...      .assign(team_size=lambda df_:predict_col(df_, 'team_size')
...              .astype(int))
...      .drop(columns=['python2_version_most'])
...      .dropna()
... )
>>> jb2
        age are_you_datascientist  ...  years_of_coding python3_ver
1        21                  True  ...              3.0         3.6
2        30                 False  ...              3.0         3.6
10       21                 False  ...              1.0         3.8
11       21                  True  ...              3.0         3.9
13       30                  True  ...              3.0         3.7
...     ...                   ...  ...              ...         ...
54456    30                 False  ...              6.0         3.6
54457    21                 False  ...              1.0         3.6
54459    21                 False  ...              6.0         3.7
54460    30                  True  ...              3.0         3.7
54461    21                 False  ...              1.0         3.8

[13711 rows x 20 columns]
```

At this point, I'm pretty satisfied with my chain (I would generally develop and debug this chain link by link using Jupyter). What I like to do is create a function (I generally name it *tweak_**) and put it right at the top of my Jupyter notebook, in the cell below the cell where I load the raw data. This makes it easy to open up a notebook, load the raw data and then run my tweak function to clean it up. After that, I'm off and running. If I find that I need to modify my dataframe further, I will update the tweak function, so all of my changes can be found in one place. This takes a little discipline to program pandas in this way, but you will reap benefits as your code will be easier to use, understand, and debug!

Here is my what my cleaned up code will look like:

```python
>>> import catboost as cb
>>> import numpy as np
>>> import pandas as pd

>>> import collections

>>> def get_uniq_cols(jb):
...     counter = collections.defaultdict(list)
...     for col in sorted(jb.columns):
...         period_count = col.count('.')
...         if period_count >= 2:
...             part_end = 2
...         else:
...             part_end = 1
...         parts = col.split('.')[:part_end]
...         counter['.'.join(parts)].append(col)
...     uniq_cols = []
...     for cols in counter.values():
...         if len(cols) == 1:
...             uniq_cols.extend(cols)
...     return uniq_cols

>>> def prep_for_ml(df):
...     # remove pandas types
...     return (df
...     .assign(**{col:df[col].astype(float)
...             for col in df.select_dtypes('number')},
...         **{col:df[col].astype(str).fillna('')
...             for col in df.select_dtypes(['object', 'category'])})
...     )

>>> def predict_col(df, col):
...     df = prep_for_ml(df)
...     missing = df.query(f'~{col}.isna()')
...     cat_idx = []
```

```
...        for i,typ in enumerate(df.drop(columns=[col]).dtypes):
...            if str(typ) == 'object':
...                cat_idx.append(i)
...        X = (missing
...             .drop(columns=[col])
...             .values
...            )
...        y = missing[col]
...        model = cb.CatBoostRegressor(iterations=20, cat_features=cat_idx)
...        model.fit(X, y, cat_features=cat_idx)
...        pred = model.predict(df.drop(columns=[col]))
...        return df[col].where(~df[col].isna(), pred)

>>> def tweak_jb(jb):
...        uniq_cols = get_uniq_cols(jb)
...        return (jb
...            [uniq_cols]
...            .rename(columns=lambda c: c.replace('.', '_'))
...            .assign(age=lambda df_:df_.age.str.slice(0,2).astype(float)
...                        .astype('Int64'),
...                    are_you_datascientist=lambda df_:df_
...                        .are_you_datascientist
...                        .replace({'Yes': True, 'No': False, np.nan: False}),
...                    company_size=lambda df_:df_.company_size.replace({
...                        'Just me': 1, 'Not sure': np.nan,
...                        'More than 5,000': 5000, '2-10': 2, '11-50':11,
...                        '51-500': 51, '501-1,000':501,
...                        '1,001-5,000':1001}).astype('Int64'),
...                    country_live=lambda df_:df_.country_live
...                        .astype('category'),
...                    employment_status=lambda df_:df_.employment_status
...                        .fillna('Other').astype('category'),
...                    is_python_main=lambda df_:df_.is_python_main
...                        .astype('category'),
...                    team_size=lambda df_:df_.team_size
...                        .str.split(r'-', n=1, expand=True)
...                        .iloc[:,0].replace('More than 40 people', 41)
...                        .where(df_.company_size!=1, 1).astype(float),
...                    years_of_coding=lambda df_:df_.years_of_coding
...                        .replace('Less than 1 year', .5)
...                        .str.extract(r'(\d+)').astype(float),
...                    python_years=lambda df_:df_.python_years
...                        .replace('Less than 1 year', .5)
...                        .str.extract(r'(\d+)').astype(float),
...                    python3_ver=lambda df_:df_.python3_version_most
```

```
...                        .str.replace('_', '.').str.extract(r'(\d\.\d)')
...                        .astype(float),
...               use_python_most=lambda df_:df_.use_python_most
...                        .fillna('Unknown')
...             )
...         .assign(team_size=lambda df_:predict_col(df_, 'team_size')
...              .astype(int))
...         .drop(columns=['python2_version_most'])
...         .dropna()
...     )
>>> url = 'https://github.com/mattharrison/datasets/raw/master/data/'\
...       '2020-jetbrains-python-survey.csv'
>>> jb = pd.read_csv(url)
>>> jb2 = tweak_jb(jb)
```

Method	*Description*
.rename(mapper=None, index=None, columns=None, axis=0, copy=True, level=None, errors='ignore')	Change axis labels. Pass columns or index as a dictionary (mapping old values to new values) or a function (accepting the old value and returning the new value).
.replace(to_replace=None, value=None, limit=None, regex=False, method='pad')	Replace values from to_replace (string, regular expression, number, series or list of previous, dictionary (mapping replacement if value is None), series, or None) with value. If to_replace is a list and there is no value you can bfill or ffill with method.
.drop(labels=None, axis=0, index=None, columns=None, level=None, errors='raise')	Drop rows or columns with specified labels. Use columns='age' rather than labels='age', axis='1'.
.dropna(axis=0, how='any', thresh=None, subset=None)	Drop rows (axis=0) or columns (axis=1) with missing values. Require certain amount missing with thresh. Limit columns with subset.
.query(expr)	Evaluate expr to filter dataframe. Refer to variables by prefixing with @. Use backticks around column names with spaces.

| .assign(**kwargs) | Return a new dataframe with updated or new columns. kwargs maps column name to function, scalar, or series. If using a function, it is passed in the current state of the dataframe and should return a scalar or series. Subsequent columns may reference earlier columns in kwargs if you use a function. |

Table 21.1: Dataframe Chapter Methods

21.3 Summary

If you need to update a column or add a new column, use the .assign method. If the .assign method is part of a chain, you may want to couple it with a function to have the current state of the dataframe you are working with. I generally will make a function to clean up my data and then put it right at the top of my notebook below where I load my data, so I can load the raw data and then clean it up in two steps.

21.4 Exercises

With a dataset of your choice:

1. Create a "tweak" function to clean up the data.

2. Explore the memory usage of the raw data and the tweaked data.

Chapter 22

Dealing with Missing and Duplicated Data

We have seen how to find missing and duplicated data with a series, and let's apply it to a dataframe. If you are doing analysis or creating machine learning models on your data, you will want to make sure that your data is complete before you start to report on it. Also, many machine learning models will fail to train if you try to train them on dataframes with missing values.

We are going to jump back to the Presidential data for this chapter.

22.1 Missing Data

Determining where data is missing involves the same methods we saw on a series. We just need to remember that a dataframe has an extra dimension. The dataframe has an `.isna` method that returns a dataframe with true and false values indicating whether values are missing:

```
>>> import pandas as pd
>>> url = 'https://github.com/mattharrison/datasets/raw/master/data/'\
...      'siena2018-pres.csv'
>>> df = pd.read_csv(url, index_col=0)
>>> pres = tweak_siena_pres(df)

>>> pres.isna()
      President  Party  ...  Average_rank  Quartile
Seq.                    ...
1         False  False  ...         False     False
2         False  False  ...         False     False
3         False  False  ...         False     False
4         False  False  ...         False     False
5         False  False  ...         False     False
```

```
...          ...     ...    ...          ...          ...
41        False   False    ...        False        False
42        False   False    ...        False        False
43        False   False    ...        False        False
44        False   False    ...        False        False
45        False   False    ...        False        False

[44 rows x 25 columns]
```

Because each of these columns is a boolean array, you can use them to select rows where values are missing.

Let's look as rows where *Integrity* is missing:

```
>>> pres[pres.Integrity.isna()]
```

It looks like there are no missing values for this column.

We can sum the results to get the counts of columns with missing values:

```
>>> pres.isna().sum()
President                  0
Party                      0
Background                 0
Imagination                0
Integrity                  0
                          ..
Avoid_crucial_mistakes     0
Experts'_view              0
Overall                    0
Average_rank               0
Quartile                   0
Length: 25, dtype: int64
```

We can take the mean of them to get the fraction missing. In this case none of them are missing:

```
>>> pres.isna().mean()
President                  0.0
Party                      0.0
Background                 0.0
Imagination                0.0
Integrity                  0.0
                          ...
Avoid_crucial_mistakes     0.0
Experts'_view              0.0
Overall                    0.0
Average_rank               0.0
Quartile                   0.0
```

Missing Data

auto

	make	year	cylinders	drive
0	Alfa Romeo	1985	4.00	Rear-Wheel
1	Ferrari	1985	12.00	Rear-Wheel
2	Dodge	1985	4.00	Front-Whee
3	Dodge	1985	8.00	Rear-Wheel
4	Subaru	1993	4.00	4-Wheel or
41139	Subaru	1993	4.00	Front-Whee
41140	Subaru	1993	4.00	Front-Whee
41141	Subaru	1993	4.00	4-Wheel or
41142	Subaru	1993	4.00	4-Wheel or
41143	Subaru	1993	4.00	4-Wheel or

auto.isna()

	make	year	cylinders	drive
0	False	False	False	False
1	False	False	False	False
2	False	False	False	False
3	False	False	False	False
4	False	False	False	False
41139	False	False	False	False
41140	False	False	False	False
41141	False	False	False	False
41142	False	False	False	False
41143	False	False	False	False

auto.isna().any()

(auto
.isna()
.sum())   Counts

(auto
.isna()
.mean()
.mul(100))   Percent

make	False
year	False
cylinders	True
drive	True

make	0
year	0
cylinders	206
drive	1189

make	0.00
year	0.00
cylinders	0.50
drive	2.89

Figure 22.1: Using .isna to create a boolean array of missing values, counting them, or getting the percent of them.

Missing Data for DataFrames

data

	day	snow
0	Mon	0.00
1	Tue	nan
2	Wed	18.00
3	Thu	12.00
4	Fri	nan
5	Sat	7.00
6	Sun	8.00

```
(data
 .assign(snow=
    data.snow.where(
      cond=~((data.day=='Tue') &
      (data.snow.isna())),
      other=10),
   s_missing=data.snow.isna()
 )
```

Where keeps values if cond is true

	day	snow	s_missing
0	Mon	0.00	False
1	Tue	10.00	True
2	Wed	18.00	False
3	Thu	12.00	False
4	Fri	nan	True
5	Sat	7.00	False
6	Sun	8.00	False

Figure 22.2: A more complicated example of filling in missing values using .where.

```
Length: 25, dtype: float64
```

With these tools, you should be able to diagnose and locate missing data. Once you have found out where the data is missing, you need to determine what actions to take. You can drop missing values with .dropna. There is a .fillna and an .interpolate method on the dataframe. But often, those are too rough of tools when dealing with multiple columns as the columns represent different things. (I do find them useful after grouping the data). I generally do that at the series level and then use .assign to update the column, filling in the missing values.

22.2 Duplicates

Like the series .drop_duplicates method, the same method is available to the dataframe. When called without any parameters, it is often too blunt of a tool to use on a dataframe. However, the subset parameter allows you to specify which columns you want it to consider dropping:

```
>>> pres.drop_duplicates()
            President                 Party  ... Average_rank  Quartile
                                             ...
Seq.
1     George Washington         Independent  ...            1       1st
2           John Adams          Federalist   ...           13       2nd
3      Thomas Jefferson  Democratic-Republican  ...         5       1st
4        James Madison  Democratic-Republican  ...            7       1st
5         James Monroe  Democratic-Republican  ...            8       1st
```

```
    ...              ...                    ...    ...         ...        ...
41        George H. W. Bush        Republican   ...           21        2nd
42              Bill Clinton        Democratic   ...           15        2nd
43           George W. Bush        Republican   ...           33        3rd
44              Barack Obama        Democratic   ...           17        2nd
45              Donald Trump        Republican   ...           42        4th

[44 rows x 25 columns]
```

Because none of the rows are complete copies, the above call does nothing. If we wanted to keep only the first president from each party, we can do the following:

```
>>> pres.drop_duplicates(subset='Party')
                 President   ...  Quartile
Seq.                        ...
1         George Washington   ...       1st
2              John Adams   ...       2nd
3         Thomas Jefferson   ...       1st
7           Andrew Jackson   ...       2nd
9     William Henry Harrison   ...       4th
16        Abraham Lincoln   ...       1st

[6 rows x 25 columns]
```

You can use the keep parameter to specify how to drop values. The default value, 'first', will keep the first value. You can use 'last' or False to keep the last value or to drop all duplicates respectively:

```
>>> pres.drop_duplicates(subset='Party', keep='last')
             President                  Party   ...  Average_rank   Quartile
Seq.                                           ...
2            John Adams              Federalist   ...           13        2nd
6     John Quincy Adams  Democratic-Republican   ...           18        2nd
10           John Tyler             Independent   ...           37        4th
13      Millard Fillmore                   Whig   ...           39        4th
44         Barack Obama              Democratic   ...           17        2nd
45         Donald Trump              Republican   ...           42        4th

[6 rows x 25 columns]

>>> pres.drop_duplicates(subset='Party', keep=False)
        President        Party   ...  Average_rank   Quartile
Seq.                            ...
2     John Adams   Federalist   ...           13        2nd
```

```
[1 rows x 25 columns]
```

To drop duplicates if only the previous row is a duplicate (rather than any row), we need a little more logic. We do this by creating a column that indicates whether it is not the same as the next value. This indicates whether it is the first entry in a sequence. Then we can combine this with a lambda function and .loc:

```
>>> (pres
...    .assign(first_in_party_seq=lambda df_: df_.Party != df_.Party.shift(1),
...            )
...    .loc[lambda df_:df_.first_in_party_seq]
... )
                       President   ... first_in_party_seq
Seq.                              ...
1             George Washington   ...                True
2                   John Adams   ...                True
3              Thomas Jefferson   ...                True
7               Andrew Jackson   ...                True
9        William Henry Harrison   ...                True
...                        ...   ...                 ...
40                Ronald Reagan   ...                True
42                 Bill Clinton   ...                True
43               George W. Bush   ...                True
44                Barack Obama   ...                True
45                Donald Trump   ...                True

[26 rows x 26 columns]
```

Method	Description
.isna()	Return boolean dataframe with same dimensions with True values where cells are missing.
.sum(axis=0, skipna=True, level=None, numeric_only=None, min_count=0	Return sum over axis. Default of empty sequence is 0, set min_count=1 t
.mean(axis=0, skipna=True, level=None, numeric_only=None, min_count=0	Return mean over axis.

`.drop_duplicates(subset=None,`
  `keep='first',`
  `ignore_index=False)`
	Return dataframe that has duplicated rows removed. Indicate certain columns to consider with subset. keep can be 'first', 'last', or False (drop all dupes). Set ignore_index=True to reset index.

Table 22.1: Dataframe Chapter Methods

22.3 Summary

In this chapter, we saw how you could diagnose how much data is missing in a dataframe. In a later chapter, we will see how to fill in missing data on JetBrains survey data. In the time series chapter, we will look at methods for dealing with missing data in sequential data sets.

22.4 Exercises

With a dataset of your choice:

1. Find out which columns have missing data.

2. Count the number of missing values for each column.

3. Find the percentage of missing values for each column.

4. Find the rows with missing data.

5. Find the rows that are duplicated.

Chapter 23

Sorting Columns and Indexes

In this chapter, we will explore sorting columns and index values.

23.1 Sorting Columns

The .sort_values method will allow you to sort the rows of a dataframe by arbitrary columns. In this example, we sort by the political party in alphabetic order:

```
>>> import pandas as pd
>>> url = 'https://github.com/mattharrison/datasets/raw/master/data/'\
...       'siena2018-pres.csv'
>>> df = pd.read_csv(url, index_col=0)
>>> pres = tweak_siena_pres(df)

>>> pres.sort_values(by='Party')
                   President  ... Quartile
Seq.                         ...
22/24        Grover Cleveland ...      3rd
32     Franklin D. Roosevelt ...      1st
17           Andrew Johnson  ...      4th
33          Harry S. Truman  ...      1st
15           James Buchanan  ...      4th
...                      ...  ...      ...
18        Ulysses S. Grant   ...      3rd
45            Donald Trump   ...      4th
13         Millard Fillmore  ...      4th
12          Zachary Taylor   ...      3rd
9     William Henry Harrison ...      4th
```

```
[44 rows x 25 columns]
```

You can also sort by multiple columns, as well as specifying whether each column should be sorted in ascending (the default) or descending order. Here we sort by the *Party* column in ascending alphabetic order and *Average_rank* in descending order:

```
>>> (pres
...    .sort_values(by=['Party', 'Average_rank'],
...       ascending=[True, False])
... )
                  President        Party  ...  Average_rank  Quartile
Seq.                                      ...
17          Andrew Johnson   Democratic  ...            44       4th
15          James Buchanan   Democratic  ...            43       4th
14         Franklin Pierce   Democratic  ...            41       4th
39            Jimmy Carter   Democratic  ...            27       3rd
8         Martin Van Buren   Democratic  ...            25       3rd
...                    ...          ...  ...           ...       ...
26      Theodore Roosevelt   Republican  ...             4       1st
16         Abraham Lincoln   Republican  ...             3       1st
13        Millard Fillmore         Whig  ...            39       4th
9    William Henry Harrison         Whig  ...            38       4th
12          Zachary Taylor         Whig  ...            30       3rd

[44 rows x 25 columns]
```

Like the built-in sorted function, you can supply a key function to the .sort_values method to determine how to sort the by column. Let's sort the rows by the last name of the president. We will use .str.split to separate the parts of the name:

```
>>> (pres
...    .President
...    .str.split()
... )
Seq.
1         [George, Washington]
2                [John, Adams]
3          [Thomas, Jefferson]
4            [James, Madison]
5             [James, Monroe]
                   ...
41    [George, H., W., Bush]
42             [Bill, Clinton]
43        [George, W., Bush]
```

```
44          [Barack, Obama]
45          [Donald, Trump]
Name: President, Length: 44, dtype: object
```

This is a case where `.apply` might be appropriate (another hint is that we are manipulating strings which are not vectorized operations.) Each value is a Python list and we need the last value:

```
>>> (pres
...     .President
...     .str.split()
...     .apply(lambda val: val[-1])
... )
Seq.
1       Washington
2           Adams
3        Jefferson
4         Madison
5          Monroe
            ...
41          Bush
42        Clinton
43          Bush
44         Obama
45         Trump
Name: President, Length: 44, dtype: object
```

Awesome, we just need to put this logic into the key function:

```
>>> (pres
...     .sort_values(by='President',
...         key=lambda name_ser: name_ser
...             .str.split()
...             .apply(lambda val:val[-1]))
... )
                        Party   ...   Quartile
President                       ...
Abraham Lincoln         Republican  ...      1st
Andrew Jackson          Democratic  ...      2nd
Andrew Johnson          Democratic  ...      4th
Barack Obama            Democratic  ...      2nd
Benjamin Harrison       Republican  ...      4th
...                             ...  ...      ...
William Henry Harrison        Whig  ...      4th
William Howard Taft     Republican  ...      2nd
William McKinley        Republican  ...      2nd
Woodrow Wilson          Democratic  ...      2nd
```

```
Zachary Taylor                   Whig  ...        3rd

[44 rows x 24 columns]
```

23.2   Sorting Column Order

If you want to sort the columns, you can use the .sort_index method and set the axis value appropriately:

```
>>> pres.sort_index(axis='columns')
      Ability_to_compromise  ...  Willing_to_take_risks
Seq.                         ...
1                         2  ...                      6
2                        31  ...                     14
3                        14  ...                      5
4                         6  ...                     15
5                         7  ...                     16
...                     ...  ...                    ...
41                       13  ...                     27
42                        3  ...                     17
43                       28  ...                     20
44                       16  ...                     23
45                       42  ...                     25

[44 rows x 25 columns]
```

I don't find myself using this very often unless I have an index with string values (as we will see later).

23.3   Setting and Sorting the Index

You can stick a column into the index with .set_index. You may want to follow that up with sorting the index:

```
>>> (pres
...     .set_index('President')
...     .sort_index()
... )
                     Party  Background  ...  Average_rank  Quartile
President                               ...
Abraham Lincoln  Republican         28  ...             3       1st
Andrew Jackson   Democratic         37  ...            19       2nd
Andrew Johnson   Democratic         42  ...            44       4th
Barack Obama     Democratic         24  ...            17       2nd
```

Benjamin Harrison	Republican	33	...	36	4th
...	...	...	...	...	...
William Henry Harrison	Whig	22	...	38	4th
William Howard Taft	Republican	12	...	22	2nd
William McKinley	Republican	29	...	20	2nd
Woodrow Wilson	Democratic	8	...	12	2nd
Zachary Taylor	Whig	30	...	30	3rd

```
[44 rows x 24 columns]
```

If you sort an index that has string index values that are duplicated, then you can slice on the index. If you did not sort the index, you will get a KeyError:

```
>>> (pres
...    .set_index('Party')
...    .loc['Democratic':'Republican']
... )
Traceback (most recent call last):
  ...
KeyError: "Cannot get left slice bound for non-unique label: 'Democratic'"
```

Sorting the index allows us to slice the index by name:

```
>>> (pres
...    .set_index('Party')
...    .sort_index()
...    .loc['Democratic':'Republican']
... )
```

	President	Background	...	Average_rank	Quartile
Party			...		
Democratic	Grover Cleveland	26	...	23	3rd
Democratic	Franklin D. Roosevelt	6	...	2	1st
Democratic	Andrew Johnson	42	...	44	4th
Democratic	Harry S. Truman	31	...	9	1st
Democratic	James Buchanan	36	...	43	4th
...	...	...	...	...	...
Republican	Theodore Roosevelt	5	...	4	1st
Republican	William McKinley	29	...	20	2nd
Republican	Benjamin Harrison	33	...	36	4th
Republican	Ulysses S. Grant	20	...	24	3rd
Republican	Donald Trump	43	...	42	4th

```
[41 rows x 24 columns]
```

Method	Description

`.sort_values(by, axis=0,`
`  ascending=True,`
`  kind='quicksort',`
`  na_position='last',`
`  ignore_index=False, key=None))`
	Return dataframe with values sorted along the axis. Use by to specify column (string) or a list of columns (for axis=0). Can use `kind='mergesort'` or `kind='stable'` for a stable sort if only sorting one column. A key function accepts a series and should return a series with the same index.

`.sort_index(axis=0, level=None,`
`  ascending=True,`
`  kind='quicksort',`
`  na_position='last',`
`  sort_remaining=True,`
`  ignore_index=False, key=None))`
	Return dataframe with index (axis=0) or columns (axis=1) sorted. Can specify a single level or multiple levels with `levels`. Can specify the direction of each level sort with `ascending`. along the axis (default is 0). Use by to specify column (string) or a list of columns (for axis=0). Can use `kind='mergesort'` or `kind='stable'` for a stable sort if only sorting one column. Can reset the index with `ignore_index`. A key function accepts an index and should return an index. For multi-level indexes, each index is passed in independently to the function.

`.set_index(keys, drop=True,`
`  append=False,`
`  verify_integrity=False)`
	Return dataframe with the new index. The keys argument can be a column name, a series (or numpy array) of labels for the index, or a list of column names or series. The drop parameter indicates whether to remove columns used for the index. The append parameter allows you to add additional index levels. You can check for duplicate index values by setting `verify_integrity=True`.

`.loc`	Attribute to index off of by index and column names. Slices use the closed interval (include start and end).

Table 23.1: Dataframe Sorting and Indexing Methods

23.4 Summary

In this chapter, we showed how to sort both the index and the columns. If you want to sort based on arbitrary values, you can use the key parameter to determine how sorting occurs. You can also sort by various columns as well as control the direction of the sort. Sorting the index is particularly useful if it contains strings because you can slice on the string values (or substrings) after the index is sorted.

23.5 Exercises

With a dataset of your choice:

1. Sort the index.

2. Set the index to a string column, sort the index, and slice by a substring of index values.

3. Sort by a single column.

4. Sort by a single column in descending order.

5. Sort by two columns.

6. Sort by the last letter of a string column.

Chapter 24

Filtering and Indexing Operations

I like to keep my data in the columns, not in the index. Occasionally you will need to manipulate the index. This chapter will explore some of the operations to change the index and operations that result from that. Then we will look at pulling data out based on index names and locations (as well as column names and positions).

24.1 Renaming an Index

In this example, we will use the `.rename` method to update the index values. This method will accept a function that takes the current value and will return a new value. Here we will use the first initial of the president:

```
>>> def name_to_initial(val):
...     names = val.split()
...     return ' '.join([f'{names[0][0]}.', *names[1:]])

>>> (pres
...   .set_index('President')
...   .rename(name_to_initial)
... )
                        Party     ...   Quartile
President                         ...
G. Washington           Independent  ...      1st
J. Adams                 Federalist  ...      2nd
T. Jefferson  Democratic-Republican  ...      1st
J. Madison    Democratic-Republican  ...      1st
J. Monroe     Democratic-Republican  ...      1st
...                             ...  ...      ...
```

```
G. H. W. Bush           Republican   ...      2nd
B. Clinton              Democratic   ...      2nd
G. W. Bush              Republican   ...      3rd
B. Obama                Democratic   ...      2nd
D. Trump                Republican   ...      4th

[44 rows x 24 columns]
```

24.2   Resetting the Index

If you want a monotonically increasing integer index for a dataframe, use the
.reset_index method:

```
>>> (pres
...    .set_index('President')
...    .reset_index()
... )
              President               Party  ... Average_rank  Quartile
0      George  Washington        Independent  ...            1       1st
1            John  Adams          Federalist  ...           13       2nd
2      Thomas  Jefferson  Democratic-Republican  ...         5       1st
3          James  Madison  Democratic-Republican  ...         7       1st
4          James  Monroe  Democratic-Republican  ...         8       1st
..            ...                      ...  ...          ...       ...
39  George H. W. Bush            Republican  ...           21       2nd
40          Bill Clinton          Democratic  ...           15       2nd
41        George W. Bush          Republican  ...           33       3rd
42          Barack Obama          Democratic  ...           17       2nd
43          Donald Trump          Republican  ...           42       4th

[44 rows x 25 columns]
```

24.3   Dataframe Indexing, Filtering, & Querying

We have already looked at how to use boolean arrays to index a series and
limit what it returns. We can also do this with dataframes. Let's look at
the presidents with an *Average_rank* below 10. First, we will make a boolean
array where the column *Average_rank* is below 10. Then we will index into the
dataframe with this boolean array:

```
>>> lt10 = pres.Average_rank < 10
>>> pres[lt10]
                President  ... Quartile
```

```
Seq.                             ...
1              George Washington  ...        1st
3              Thomas Jefferson   ...        1st
4                 James Madison   ...        1st
5                 James Monroe    ...        1st
16             Abraham Lincoln    ...        1st
26             Theodore Roosevelt ...        1st
32          Franklin D. Roosevelt ...        1st
33             Harry S. Truman    ...        1st
34          Dwight D. Eisenhower  ...        1st

[9 rows x 25 columns]
```

Let's add in another option, if they are a Republican:

```
>>> pres[lt10 & (pres.Party == 'Republican')]
                  President         Party  ... Average_rank  Quartile
Seq.                                       ...
16             Abraham Lincoln  Republican ...            3       1st
26             Theodore Roosevelt Republican ...          4       1st
34          Dwight D. Eisenhower Republican ...           6       1st

[3 rows x 25 columns]
```

Note

Be careful when combining conditions in indexing operations. If we inline the above operation, we get a different result:

```
>>> pres[pres.Average_rank < 10 & pres.Party == 'Republican']
Traceback (most recent call last):
  ...
TypeError: unsupported operand type(s) for &: 'int' and 'Categorical'
```

This is because the & operator has higher precedence than >=. So in effect the above is doing pres.Average_rank < (10 & pres.Party == 'Republican'). Let's look at what that does:

```
>>> 10 & pres.Party == 'Republican'
Traceback (most recent call last):
  ...
TypeError: unsupported operand type(s) for &: 'int' and 'Categorical'
```

Sometimes you will get back an answer here (if you are not comparing to a categorical), but you might not get the answer you wanted due to precedence.

The .query Method

mpg

	make	year	city08	highway08
0	Alfa Romeo	1985	19	25
1	Ferrari	1985	9	14
2	Dodge	1985	23	33
3	Dodge	1985	10	12
4	Subaru	1993	17	23
41139	Subaru	1993	19	26
41140	Subaru	1993	20	28
41141	Subaru	1993	18	24
41142	Subaru	1993	18	24
41143	Subaru	1993	16	21

```
makes = ['Ford', 'Toyota']          Use @ for variables
(mpg
  .query("make.isin(@makes) and city08 > 50"))
```

	make	year	city08	highway08
7139	Toyota	2000	81	64
8143	Toyota	2001	81	64
8144	Ford	2001	74	58
9212	Toyota	2002	87	69
10329	Toyota	2003	87	69
34286	Toyota	2019	52	48
34287	Toyota	2019	58	53
34307	Toyota	2019	55	53
34341	Toyota	2020	53	52
34644	Toyota	2020	55	53

Does not exist for Series!

Figure 24.1: The .query method allows you to call methods, include variables, and combine conditional expressions inside a string.

The takeaway here is that you should always put parentheses around multiple conditions in index operations if you inline them:

```
>>> pres[(pres.Average_rank < 10) & (pres.Party == 'Republican')]
              President        Party  ...  Average_rank  Quartile
Seq.                                  ...
16        Abraham Lincoln  Republican  ...             3       1st
26     Theodore Roosevelt  Republican  ...             4       1st
34  Dwight D. Eisenhower  Republican  ...             6       1st

[3 rows x 25 columns]
```

One method that is unique to the dataframe (not found on a series) is the .query method. Instead of creating boolean arrays, we create a string, similar to SQL, with the conditions we want:

```
>>> pres.query('Average_rank < 10 and Party == "Republican"')
                President        Party  ...  Average_rank  Quartile
Seq.                                    ...
16           Abraham Lincoln  Republican  ...             3  1st
26        Theodore Roosevelt  Republican  ...             4  1st
34      Dwight D. Eisenhower  Republican  ...             6  1st

[3 rows x 25 columns]
```

In the case of .query, we can use and or &, in contrast to when we want to combine boolean arrays we need to use & (likewise we can use or and not in .query). We also do not need to worry as much about precedence and parentheses.

If you have an existing variable and want to refer to it inside of the string, you can prefix the variable with a @:

```
>>> lt10 = pres.Average_rank < 10
>>> pres.query('@lt10 and Party == "Republican"')
                President        Party  ...  Average_rank  Quartile
Seq.                                    ...
16           Abraham Lincoln  Republican  ...             3  1st
26        Theodore Roosevelt  Republican  ...             4  1st
34      Dwight D. Eisenhower  Republican  ...             6  1st

[3 rows x 25 columns]
```

24.4 Indexing by Position

The .iloc attribute gives us the ability to pull out rows and columns from a dataframe. Here we pull out row position 1. Note that this returns the result as a series (even though it represents a row):

```
>>> pres.iloc[1]
President                John Adams
Party                    Federalist
Background                        3
Imagination                      13
Integrity                         4
                            ...
Avoid_crucial_mistakes           16
```

The .iloc Attribute for Dataframes

mpg

	make	year	city08	highway08
0	Alfa Romeo	1985	19	25
1	Ferrari	1985	9	14
2	Dodge	1985	23	33
3	Dodge	1985	10	12
4	Subaru	1993	17	23
41139	Subaru	1993	19	26
41140	Subaru	1993	20	28
41141	Subaru	1993	18	24
41142	Subaru	1993	18	24
41143	Subaru	1993	16	21

(mpg.iloc[[0,10,100], [2, 0]])

	city08	make
0	19	Alfa Romeo
10	23	Toyota
100	10	Rolls-Royce

Figure 24.2: Using .iloc to select rows and columns by position. Note that Python is 0-based indexing, so 0 is the first entry, 1 is the second, etc.

```
Experts'_view          10
Overall                14
Average_rank           13
Quartile              2nd
Name: 2, Length: 25, dtype: object
```

In the next example, instead of passing in scalar position, we are going to pass in row position 1 in a list. Sometimes you will hear people say to use a "nested list". To be pedantic, this is not a nested list. It is an indexing operation (the outer brackets) with a list (the inner brackets). This does not return a series but a dataframe with a single row:

```
>>> pres.iloc[[1]]
        President        Party  ...  Average_rank  Quartile
Seq.                            ...
2     John Adams  Federalist  ...            13       2nd

[1 rows x 25 columns]
```

We can also pass in slices and lists:

```
>>> pres.iloc[[0, 5, 10]]
           President   ...   Quartile
Seq.                   ...
1      George Washington   ...        1st
6      John Quincy Adams   ...        2nd
11          James K. Polk   ...        1st

[3 rows x 25 columns]

>>> pres.iloc[0:11:5]
           President   ...   Quartile
Seq.                   ...
1      George Washington   ...        1st
6      John Quincy Adams   ...        2nd
11          James K. Polk   ...        1st

[3 rows x 25 columns]
```

Finally, you can pass a function into the index operation. The function takes a dataframe and should return valid options for .iloc. The two following operations should give the same results:

```
>>> pres.iloc[[0, 5, 10]]
           President   ...   Quartile
Seq.                   ...
1      George Washington   ...        1st
6      John Quincy Adams   ...        2nd
11          James K. Polk   ...        1st

[3 rows x 25 columns]

>>> pres.iloc[lambda df: [0,5,10]]
           President   ...   Quartile
Seq.                   ...
1      George Washington   ...        1st
6      John Quincy Adams   ...        2nd
11          James K. Polk   ...        1st

[3 rows x 25 columns]
```

So far, this looks very similar to indexing on a series. But remember, a data frame is two-dimensional. We have been passing in a *row indexer*, but we can also pass in a *column indexer*. You put the column indexer after the row indexer following a comma.

Here we will just pull out the second column (index position 1). Because we are using a scalar for the column indexer, it will return a series:

```
>>> pres.iloc[[0, 5, 10], 1]
Seq.
1               Independent
6       Democratic-Republican
11              Democratic
Name: Party, dtype: category
Categories (6, object): ['Democratic', 'Democratic-Republican', ...
                         'Republican', 'Whig']
```

If we want to get a dataframe as a result (even if it only has one column), we need to pass in a list for the column indexer:

```
>>> pres.iloc[[0, 5, 10], [1]]
                     Party
Seq.
1               Independent
6       Democratic-Republican
11              Democratic
```

We can also pass in a list of columns or a slice to the column indexer. If we want to include all rows, but just filter columns, pass in : as the row indexer to select all rows:

```
>>> pres.iloc[:, [1, 2]]
                     Party   Background
Seq.
1               Independent           7
2                Federalist           3
3       Democratic-Republican         2
4       Democratic-Republican         4
5       Democratic-Republican         9
...                    ...          ...
41               Republican          10
42               Democratic          21
43               Republican          17
44               Democratic          24
45               Republican          43

[44 rows x 2 columns]

>>> pres.iloc[:, 1:3]
                     Party   Background
Seq.
1               Independent           7
```

```
2                  Federalist              3
3        Democratic-Republican            2
4        Democratic-Republican            4
5        Democratic-Republican            9
...                       ...            ...
41                  Republican            10
42                  Democratic            21
43                  Republican            17
44                  Democratic            24
45                  Republican            43

[44 rows x 2 columns
```

24.5 Indexing by Name

Let's explore indexing by the name of index entries on a dataframe. This is done by indexing on .loc. If you are confused between .loc and .iloc, just remember that .iloc indexes on position and that computer programs generally use the variable i to represent an index position.

One thing to be aware of is the difference between .iloc and .loc when dealing with integer indexes. In particular, slicing has different behavior. Slicing with .iloc follows the half-open interval (includes the first index but not the last). Slicing with .loc follows the closed interval (includes both the start and end index). (I know we mentioned this in the series chapter, but it bears repeating because it can be confusing).

I will try to slice off index names from *1* through *5* in the following example. Because I'm using .loc, this will match the names. However, the index is not an integer index, so this fails (we set the *Seq* column to the index, and it had the entry "22/24" causing pandas to leave it as string):

```
>>> pres.loc[1:5]
Traceback (most recent call last):
  ...
TypeError: cannot do slice indexing on Index with these
indexers [1] of type int
```

Let's try it again with strings:

```
>>> pres.loc['1':'5']
            President  ...  Quartile
Seq.                   ...
1      George Washington  ...      1st
2            John Adams  ...      2nd
```

The `.loc` Attribute for Dataframes

mpg

	make	year	city08	highway08
0	Alfa Romeo	1985	19	25
1	Ferrari	1985	9	14
2	Dodge	1985	23	33
3	Dodge	1985	10	12
4	Subaru	1993	17	23
41139	Subaru	1993	19	26
41140	Subaru	1993	20	28
41141	Subaru	1993	18	24
41142	Subaru	1993	18	24
41143	Subaru	1993	16	21

```
(mpg
 .loc[[0,10,100], ['year', 'make']])
```
0, 10, 100 are labels not positions

	year	make
0	1985	Alfa Romeo
10	1993	Toyota
100	1993	Rolls-Royce

Figure 24.3: Selecting rows and columns by name. You can pass in a list of index names and column names. Note that 0, 10, and 100 are the names, not the positions of the rows.

```
3        Thomas Jefferson   ...      1st
4           James Madison   ...      1st
5           James Monroe    ...      1st

[5 rows x 25 columns]
```

Contrast this with position slicing. This will return the four rows starting at the second position (by position and ignoring the names):

```
>>> pres.iloc[1:5]
             President   ... Quartile
Seq.                     ...
2             John Adams   ...      2nd
3       Thomas Jefferson   ...      1st
4          James Madison   ...      1st
5          James Monroe    ...      1st

[4 rows x 25 columns]
```

Let's shift gears for a little bit and look at a dataframe that has string entries in the columns. I'm going to stick the political party into the index and then pull out all of the Whig entries:

```
>>> (pres
...     .set_index('Party')
...     .loc['Whig']
... )
                    President  Background  ...  Average_rank  Quartile
Party                                      ...
Whig    William Henry Harrison         22  ...            38       4th
Whig             Zachary Taylor         30  ...            30       3rd
Whig            Millard Fillmore        40  ...            39       4th

[3 rows x 24 columns]
```

Note that this returns a dataframe, even though we used a scalar value for the index name. In fact, it returns the same result if we pass in a list:

```
>>> (pres
...     .set_index('Party')
...     .loc[['Whig']]
... )
                    President  Background  ...  Average_rank  Quartile
Party                                      ...
Whig    William Henry Harrison         22  ...            38       4th
Whig             Zachary Taylor         30  ...            30       3rd
Whig            Millard Fillmore        40  ...            39       4th

[3 rows x 24 columns]
```

This is because there are multiple entries for *Whig*. This is one of those areas to tread with caution. For example, the *Federalist* party only has one entry. So if you index with that name, you get back a series if you use a scalar, and a dataframe if you use a list:

```
>>> (pres
...     .set_index('Party')
...     .loc['Federalist']
... )
President        John Adams
Background                3
Imagination              13
Integrity                 4
Intelligence              4
            ...
```

```
Avoid_crucial_mistakes              16
Experts'_view                       10
Overall                             14
Average_rank                        13
Quartile                            2nd
Name: Federalist, Length: 24, dtype: object

>>> (pres
...     .set_index('Party')
...     .loc[['Federalist']]
... )
              President  Background  ...  Average_rank  Quartile
Party                                ...
Federalist  John Adams           3  ...            13       2nd

[1 rows x 24 columns]
```

One more thing is slicing with string indexes. Two things to remember:

- Sort the index if you want to slice it.

- You can slice with partial values.

If you don't sort the index before slicing it, you will get an error:

```
>>> (pres
...     .set_index('Party')
...     .loc['Democratic':'Independent']
... )
Traceback (most recent call last):
    ...
KeyError: "Cannot get left slice bound for non-unique label: 'Democratic'"
```

If you sort the index, you will get results:

```
>>> (pres
...     .set_index('Party')
...     .sort_index()
...     .loc['Democratic':'Independent']
... )
                          President  ...  Quartile
Party                                ...
Democratic          Grover Cleveland  ...       3rd
Democratic     Franklin D. Roosevelt  ...       1st
Democratic            Andrew Johnson  ...       4th
Democratic            Harry S. Truman  ...       1st
Democratic            James Buchanan  ...       4th
```

```
...                                    ...  ...          ...
Democratic-Republican      James Madison  ...          1st
Democratic-Republican   Thomas Jefferson  ...          1st
Federalist                   John Adams   ...          2nd
Independent           George Washington   ...          1st
Independent                  John Tyler   ...          4th

[22 rows x 24 columns]
```

Note that you can also use partial strings on sorted indexes:

```
>>> (pres
...    .set_index('President')
...    .sort_index()
...    .loc['C':'Thomas Jefferson', 'Party':'Integrity']
... )
                                  Party   ...   Integrity
President                                  ...
Calvin Coolidge                Republican  ...          17
Chester A. Arthur              Republican  ...          37
Donald Trump                   Republican  ...          44
Dwight D. Eisenhower           Republican  ...           5
Franklin D. Roosevelt          Democratic  ...          16
...                                   ...  ...          ...
Richard Nixon                  Republican  ...          43
Ronald Reagan                  Republican  ...          24
Rutherford B. Hayes            Republican  ...          32
Theodore Roosevelt             Republican  ...           8
Thomas Jefferson    Democratic-Republican  ...          14

[31 rows x 4 columns]
```

You cannot use partial strings on categorical indexes:

```
>>> (pres
...    .set_index('Party')
...    .sort_index()
...    .loc['D':'J']
... )
Traceback (most recent call last):
  ...
KeyError: 'D'
```

If you convert the categorical index to a string index then you can use partial strings:

```
>>> (pres
...    .assign(Party=pres.Party.astype(str))
```

```
...     .set_index('Party')
...     .sort_index()
...     .loc['D':'J']
... )
                              President   ...   Quartile
Party                                     ...
Democratic           Grover Cleveland    ...        3rd
Democratic     Franklin D. Roosevelt     ...        1st
Democratic             Andrew Johnson    ...        4th
Democratic             Harry S. Truman   ...        1st
Democratic             James Buchanan    ...        4th
...                               ...    ...        ...
Democratic-Republican    James Madison   ...        1st
Democratic-Republican  Thomas Jefferson  ...        1st
Federalist                 John Adams    ...        2nd
Independent          George Washington   ...        1st
Independent                John Tyler    ...        4th

[22 rows x 24 columns]
```

You can also slice columns (if you sort the columns):

```
>>> (pres
...     .set_index('President')
...     .sort_index()
...     .sort_index(axis='columns')
...     .loc['C':'Thomas Jefferson', 'B':'D']
... )
                        Background  ...  Court_appointments
President                          ...
Calvin Coolidge             32     ...                  31
Chester A. Arthur           41     ...                  33
Donald Trump                43     ...                  40
Dwight D. Eisenhower        11     ...                   5
Franklin D. Roosevelt        6     ...                   2
...                        ...     ...                 ...
Richard Nixon               16     ...                  32
Ronald Reagan               27     ...                  18
Rutherford B. Hayes         35     ...                  27
Theodore Roosevelt           5     ...                   9
Thomas Jefferson             2     ...                   7

[31 rows x 3 columns]
```

24.6 Filtering with Functions & `.loc`

You should be aware that you can pass in a boolean array and a function into
`.loc`. Here, I select rows with *Average_rank* less than ten and the first three
columns:

```
>>> (pres
...    .loc[pres.Average_rank < 10, lambda df_: df_.columns[:3]]
... )
```

Seq.	President	Party	Background
1	George Washington	Independent	7
3	Thomas Jefferson	Democratic-Republican	2
4	James Madison	Democratic-Republican	4
5	James Monroe	Democratic-Republican	9
16	Abraham Lincoln	Republican	28
26	Theodore Roosevelt	Republican	5
32	Franklin D. Roosevelt	Democratic	6
33	Harry S. Truman	Democratic	31
34	Dwight D. Eisenhower	Republican	11

An advantage of passing a function into `.loc` is that the function will
receive the current state of the dataframe. If you have `.loc` in a chain of
operations, the column names or rows might have changed, so if you filter
based on the original dataframe that began the chain, you might not be able
to get the data you need.

24.7 `.query` vs `.loc`

There is often more than one way to do things in pandas. You may be
wondering if you should use `.query` or `.loc`.

If you do a lot of chaining (which I recommend), `.query` has the advantage
of working on the intermediate dataframe. One could argue that `.loc` does as
well, but often when using boolean arrays with `.loc`, users insert a boolean
array based on the original data, not the intermediate data. You need to use a
function with `.loc` to get access to the original dataframe.

On the flipside, `.query` does not support column selection, but `.loc` does.
I don't think this is a situation where you should only learn one of these
constructs and neglect the other. Learn them both and figure out which one is
appropriate given your requirements.

24. Filtering and Indexing Operations

Method	Description
`.rename(mapper=None, index=None, columns=None, axis=0, copy=True, level=None, errors='ignore')`	Change axis labels. Pass the `columns` or `index` as a dictionary (mapping old values to new values) or a function (accepting the old value and returning the new value).
`.reset_index(level=None, drop=False, col_level=0, col_fill='')`	Return a dataframe with the new index (or new level). To remove a level, specify that with `level` (by position or name). Position 0 is the outermost level, and it goes up. Alternatively, -1 is the innermost level. Index values are moved to columns or dropped if `drop=True`. `col_level` determines where the index label goes with multiple column levels, other levels will get the value of `col_fill`.
`.set_index(keys, drop=True, append=False, verify_integrity=False)`	Return a dataframe with a new index. The `keys` argument can be a column name, a series (or numpy array) of labels for the index, or a list of column names or series. The drop parameter indicates whether to remove columns used for the index. The append parameter allows you to add additional index levels. You can check for duplicate index values by setting `verify_integrity=True`.

`.sort_index(axis=0, level=None,`
`    ascending=True,`
`    kind='quicksort',`
`    na_position='last',`
`    sort_remaining=True,`
`    ignore_index=False, key=None))`
	Return a dataframe with the index (axis=0) or columns (axis=1) sorted. Can specify a single level or multiple levels with levels. Can specify the direction of each level sort with ascending. Choose the axis (default is axis 0). Use by to specify a column (string) or a list of columns (for axis=0). Can use kind='mergesort' or kind='stable' for a stable sort if only sorting one column. Can reset the index with ignore_index. A key function accepts an index and should return an index, for multi-level indexes each index is passed in independently to the function.

`.query(expr)`	Evaluate expr to filter the dataframe. Refer to variables by prefixing them with @. Use backticks around the column names with spaces.
`.iloc`	Attribute to index off of by index and column positions. Slices use the half-open interval (include start but not end).
`.loc`	Attribute to index off of by index and column names. Slices use the closed interval (include start and end).

Table 24.1: Dataframe Filtering and Indexing Methods

24.8 Summary

In this chapter, we explored renaming the index. Then we saw how you can pull out rows and columns based on names or positions.

24.9 Exercises

With a dataset of your choice:

1. Pull out the first two rows by name.

2. Pull out the first two rows by position.

3. Pull out the last two columns by name.

4. Pull out the last two columns by position.

Chapter 25

Plotting with Dataframes

One feature I like about pandas is the integration with Matplotlib. This integration makes it easy to create various plots if you understand what type of plot you want. In this chapter, we will explore the built-in plotting capabilities of pandas.

25.1   Lines Plots

The dataframe has a `.plot` attribute that you can use to plot. Line plots are easy to create. Remember that pandas will plot the index in the x-axis, and each column will be its own line. Here is a default plot. It is a little hard to process, but along the x-axis is the president (from the first to the last). Each line represents what happens to the score from president to president:

```
>>> import pandas as pd
>>> url - 'https://github.com/mattharrison/datasets/raw/master/data/'\
...      'siena2018-pres.csv'
>>> df = pd.read_csv(url, index_col=0)
>>> pres = tweak_siena_pres(df)

>>> pres.plot().legend(bbox_to_anchor=(1,1))
```

Let's make another line plot that is more involved. Each line will track the scores for a single president. If we want each line to be a president then each column needs to represent president's data.

I'll show you how I will build this up. Let's chain up the operations. We will need to put the president's name in the index:

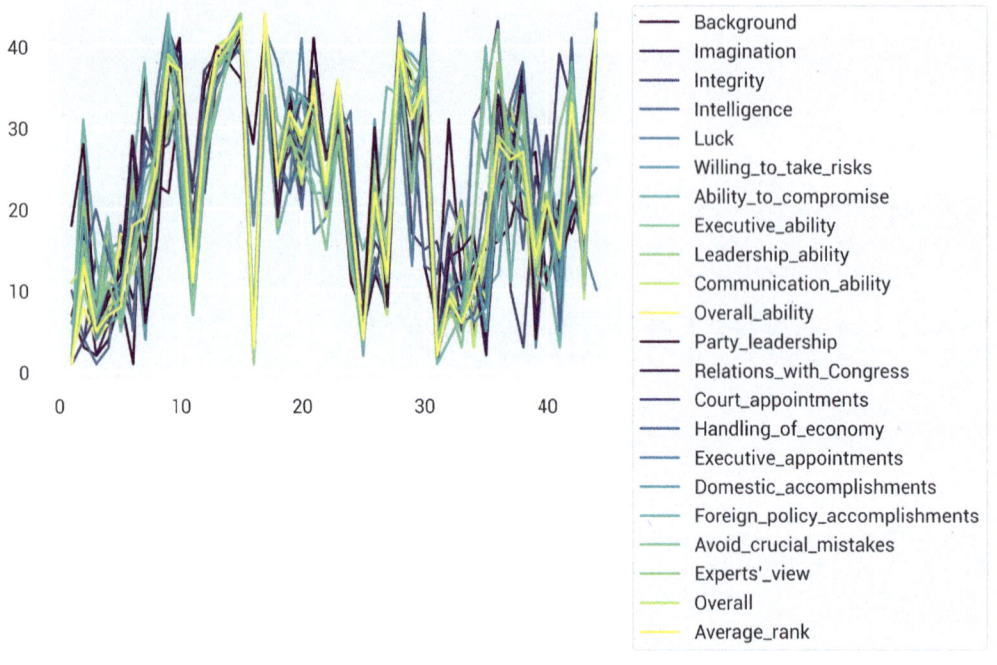

Figure 25.1: A line for each category, showing how it changed from president to president.

```
>>> (pres
...   .set_index('President')
... )
                         Party  ...  Quartile
President                         ...
George Washington         Independent  ...      1st
John Adams                 Federalist  ...      2nd
Thomas Jefferson  Democratic-Republican  ...      1st
James Madison     Democratic-Republican  ...      1st
James Monroe      Democratic-Republican  ...      1st
...                               ...  ...       ...
George H. W. Bush          Republican  ...      2nd
Bill Clinton                Democratic  ...      2nd
George W. Bush             Republican  ...      3rd
Barack Obama                Democratic  ...      2nd
Donald Trump               Republican  ...      4th

[44 rows x 24 columns]
```

The .plot Method

mpg

	make	year	city08	highway08
0	Alfa Romeo	1985	19	25
1	Ferrari	1985	9	14
2	Dodge	1985	23	33
3	Dodge	1985	10	12
4	Subaru	1993	17	23
41139	Subaru	1993	19	26
41140	Subaru	1993	20	28
41141	Subaru	1993	18	24
41142	Subaru	1993	18	24
41143	Subaru	1993	16	21

```
(mpg                         Plots each column against the index!
 .groupby('year')
 .mean()
 .plot())
```

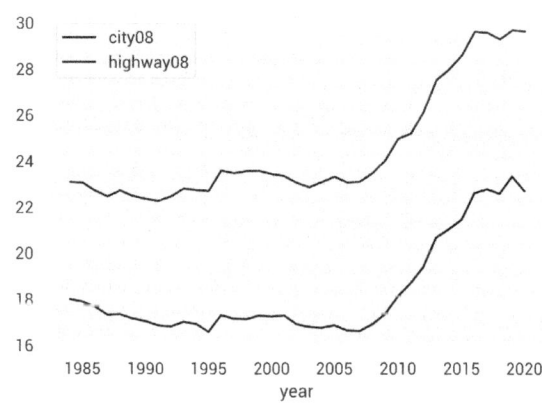

Figure 25.2: You can also call the .plot attribute. By default, it will create a line plot, plotting each numeric column against the index. The kind attribute specifies the type of plot. Rather than using kind, I recommend using the specific plot type attribute.

Next, we will filter out the columns we want (we will also remove every other president to give the plot some breathing room):

```
>>> (pres
...    .set_index('President')
...    .loc[::2,'Background':'Overall']
... )
                          Background  ...  Overall
President                             ...
George Washington                7   ...        1
Thomas Jefferson                 2   ...        5
James Monroe                     9   ...        8
Andrew Jackson                  37   ...       19
William Henry Harrison          22   ...       39
...                             ...  ...      ...
Lyndon B. Johnson               15   ...       16
Gerald Ford                     18   ...       27
Ronald Reagan                   27   ...       13
Bill Clinton                    21   ...       15
Barack Obama                    24   ...       17

[22 rows x 21 columns]
```

Next, let's transpose the result with .T:

```
>>> (pres
...    .set_index('President')
...    .loc[::2,'Background':'Overall']
...    .T
... )
President                     George Washington  ...  Barack Obama
Background                                    7  ...            24
Imagination                                   7  ...            11
Integrity                                     1  ...            13
Intelligence                                 10  ...             9
Luck                                          1  ...            15
...                                         ...  ...           ...
Domestic_accomplishments                      2  ...            13
Foreign_policy_accomplishments                2  ...            20
Avoid_crucial_mistakes                        1  ...            10
Experts'_view                                 2  ...            11
Overall                                       1  ...            17

[21 rows x 22 columns]
```

This data looks good. Each column will be its own line. Let's plot it:

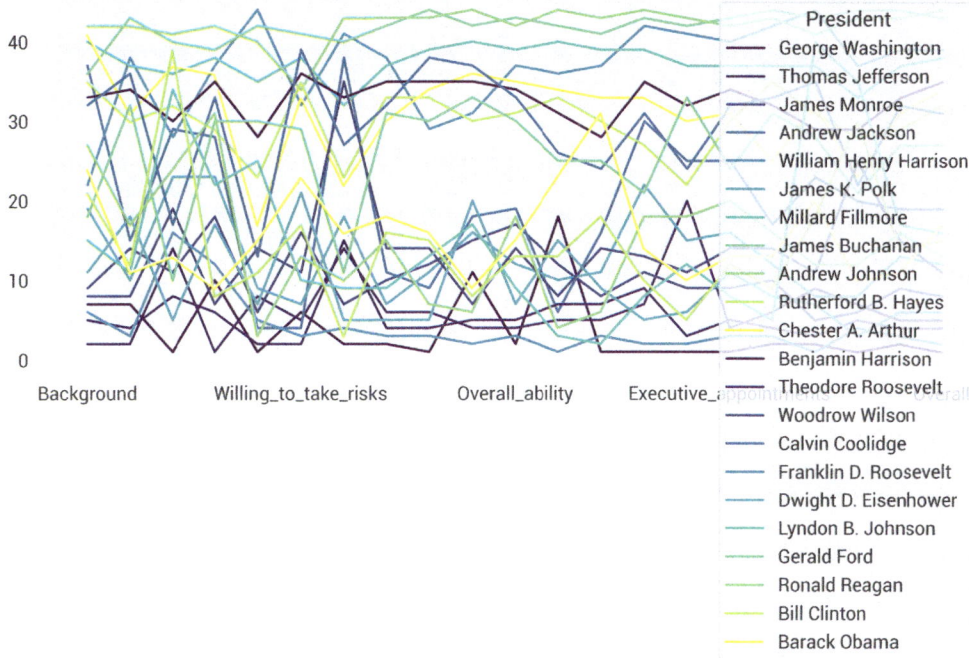

Figure 25.3: A basic line plot for each president.

```
>>> (pres
...    .set_index('President')
...    .loc[::2,'Background':'Overall']
...    .T
...    .plot()
... )
```

This is a good start, but we can make it better. Let's clean the plot up. Because pandas leverages Matplotlib, I will use some of that library:

- Label every attribute

- Rotate the attribute labels

- Move the legend

- Add a label to the y-axis

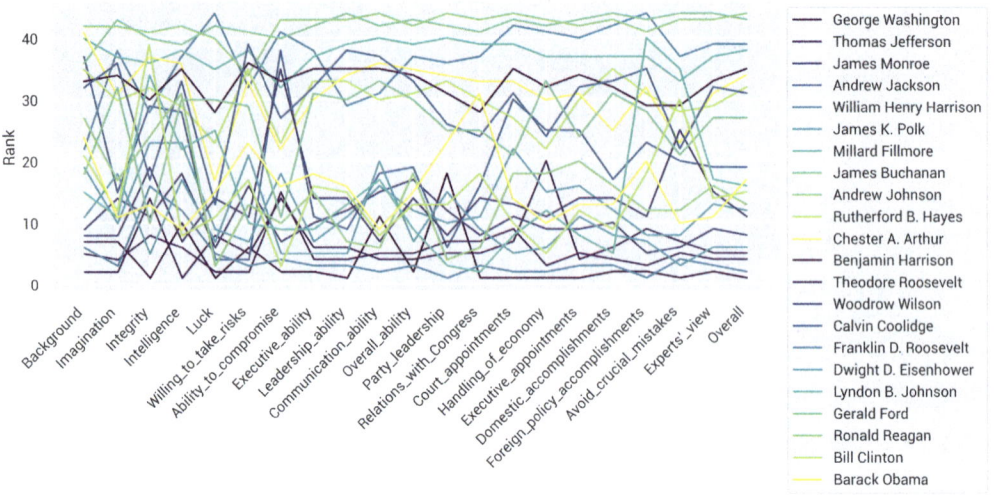

Figure 25.4: A cleaned-up line plot for each president.

```
>>> import matplotlib.pyplot as plt
>>> fig, ax = plt.subplots(dpi=600, figsize=(10,4))
>>> (pres
...    .set_index('President')
...    .loc[::2,'Background':'Overall']
...    .T
...    .plot(ax=ax, rot=45).legend(bbox_to_anchor=(1,1))
... )
>>> ax.set_xticks(range(21))
>>> ax.set_xticklabels(pres
...     .loc[:,'Background':'Overall'].columns, ha='right')
>>> ax.set_ylabel('Rank')
```

This is still a little hard to read. Generally, we want to pull attention to a single line. Let's highlight Washington. A trick that visualization experts use is to mute the other colors. I will use the .pipe method to create a colors list to indicate the colors for each line:

```
>>> fig, ax = plt.subplots(dpi=600, figsize=(10,4))
>>> colors = []
>>> def set_colors(df):
...     for col in df.columns:
...         if 'George' in col:
...             colors.append('#990000')
...         else:
```

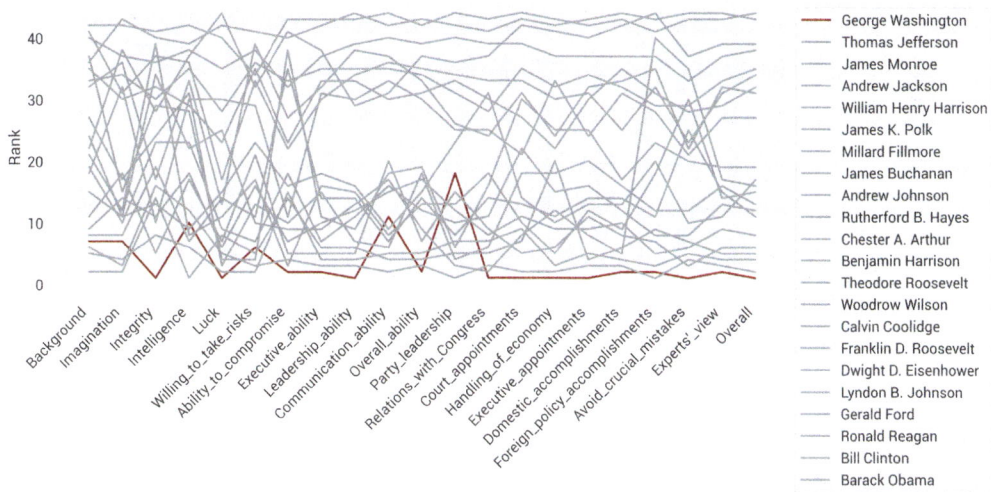

Figure 25.5: A cleaned-up line plot for each president highlighting George Washington.

```
...                colors.append('#999999')
...         return df

>>> (pres
...     .set_index('President')
...     .loc[::2,'Background':'Overall']
...     .T
...     .pipe(set_colors)
...     .plot(ax=ax, rot=45, color=colors)
...     .legend(bbox_to_anchor=(1,1))
... )
>>> ax.set_xticks(range(21))
>>> ax.set_xticklabels(pres
...     .loc[:,'Background':'Overall'].columns, ha='right')
>>> ax.set_ylabel('Rank')
```

25.2 Bar Plots

Let's make a bar plot comparing 4 attributes for each president. Again remember that pandas will plot the index on the x-axis. Here's the data:

```
>>> (pres
...     .set_index('President')
```

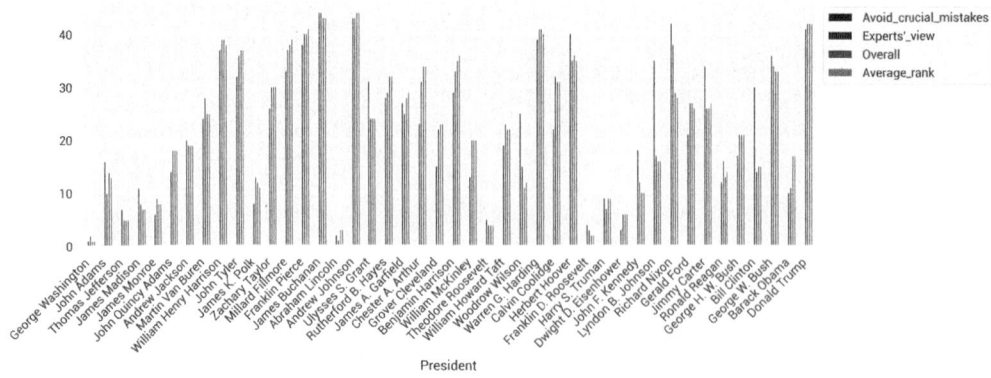

Figure 25.6: Bar plot for 4 attributes.

```
...     .iloc[:, -5:-1]
... )
                     Avoid_crucial_mistakes  ...  Average_rank
President                                    ...
George Washington                         1  ...             1
John Adams                               16  ...            13
Thomas Jefferson                          7  ...             5
James Madison                            11  ...             7
James Monroe                              6  ...             8
...                                     ...  ...           ...
George H. W. Bush                        17  ...            21
Bill Clinton                             30  ...            15
George W. Bush                           36  ...            33
Barack Obama                             10  ...            17
Donald Trump                             41  ...            42

[44 rows x 4 columns]
```

Here's the plot. Each value will be its own bar above the president label:

```
>>> fig, ax = plt.subplots(dpi=600, figsize=(10,4))
>>> (pres
...     .set_index('President')
...     .iloc[:, -5:-1]
...     .plot.bar(rot=45, ax=ax)
... )
>>> ax.set_xticklabels(labels=ax.get_xticklabels(), ha='right')
>>> ax.legend(bbox_to_anchor=(1,1))
```

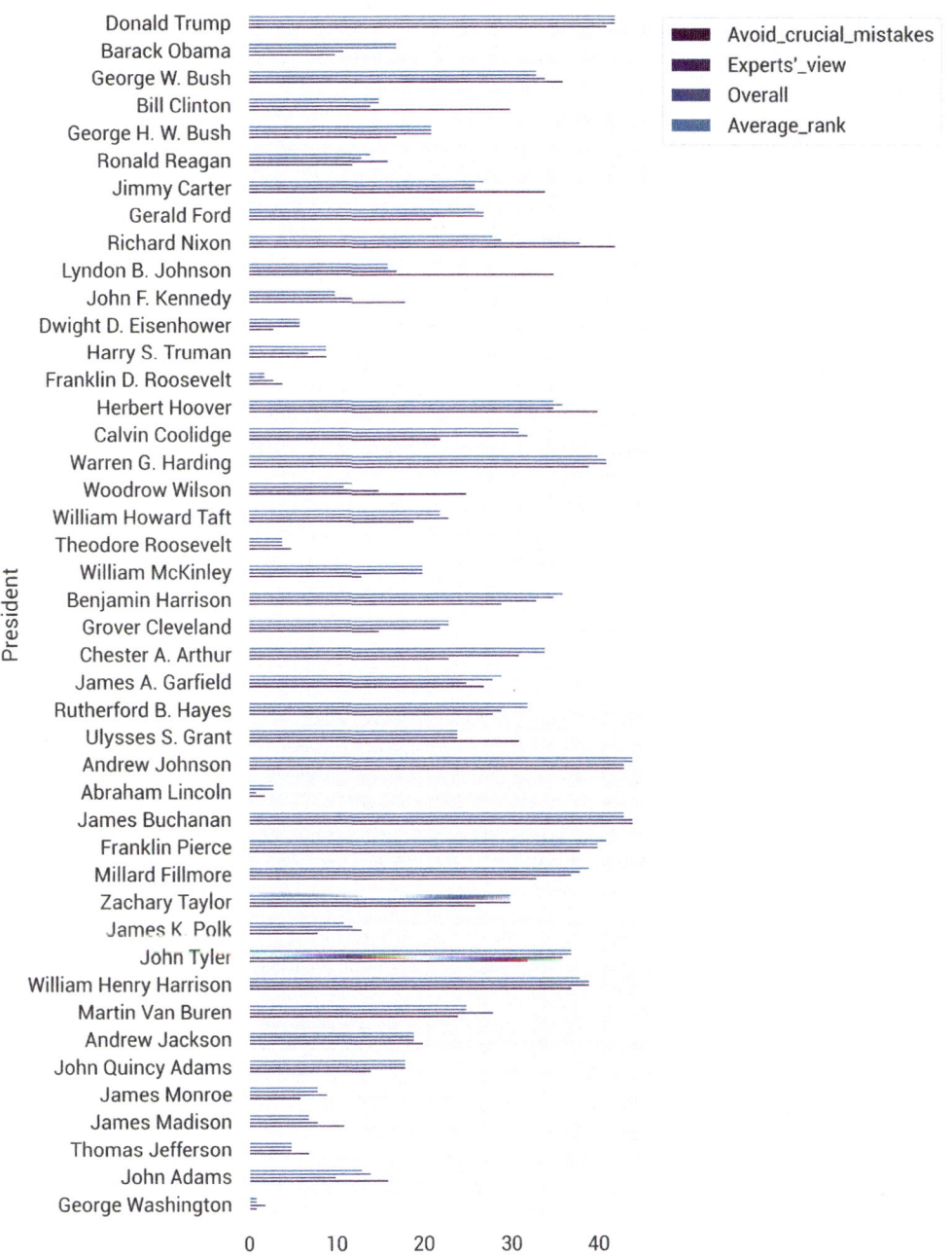

Figure 25.7: Horizontal bar plot for 4 attributes.

The .plot.barh Method

mpg

	make	year	city08	highway08
0	Alfa Romeo	1985	19	25
1	Ferrari	1985	9	14
2	Dodge	1985	23	33
3	Dodge	1985	10	12
4	Subaru	1993	17	23
41139	Subaru	1993	19	26
41140	Subaru	1993	20	28
41141	Subaru	1993	18	24
41142	Subaru	1993	18	24
41143	Subaru	1993	16	21

Plots each column as a bar!

```
def topn(ser, n=5):
    vals = ser.value_counts().index[:n]
    return ser.where(ser.isin(vals), 'Other')

(mpg
 .make
 .pipe(topn)
 .value_counts()
 .plot.barh())
```

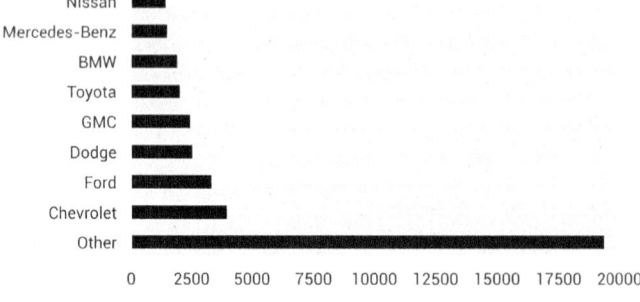

Figure 25.8: The .plot.barh method will plot each column as a bar plot. Because it is a horizontal bar plot, it will place the index in the y-axis.

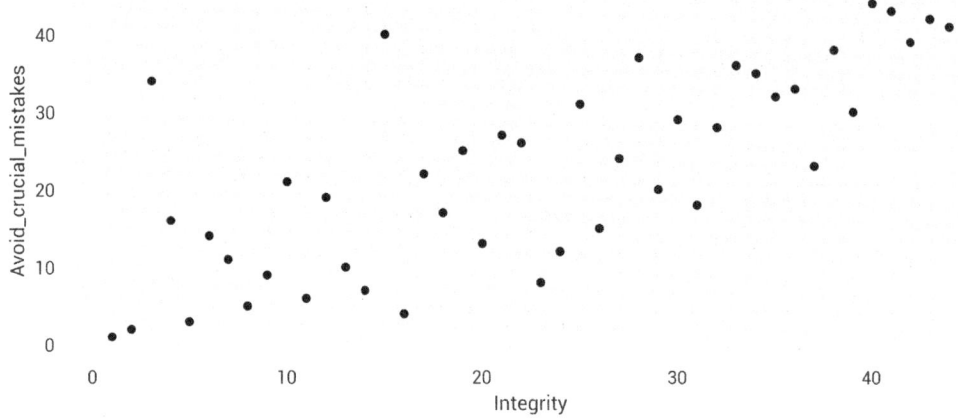

Figure 25.9: Scatter plot for Integrity and Avoid crucial mistakes.

Often it is easier to read a *horizontal bar plot*. We don't need to turn our head sideways to read the labels. By changing .bar to .barh we create a horizontal bar plot:

```
>>> (pres
...    .set_index('President')
...    .iloc[:, -5:]
...    .plot.barh(figsize=(4,12))
...    .legend(bbox_to_anchor=(1,1))
... )
```

25.3 Scatter Plots

A scatter plot is useful to determine the relationship between two columns that are numeric. We can evaluate what tends to happen to one value as the other value changes. Here is a scatter plot to example the relationship between *Integrity* and *Avoid crucial mistakes*:

```
>>> (pres
...    .plot.scatter(x='Integrity', y='Avoid_crucial_mistakes')
... )
```

It appears that as the rank for integrity falls, so does the rank for avoiding crucial mistakes. Indeed, the Pearson correlation coefficient also seems to indicate this:

Figure 25.10: Scatter plot for Integrity and Avoid crucial mistakes, colored by Luck.

```
>>> pres.Integrity.corr(pres.Avoid_crucial_mistakes)
0.7455954897815362
```

I like to add other dimensions and color by them. Let's color this by *Luck* using the c parameter to specify the column to color by:

```
>>> (pres
...     .plot.scatter(x='Integrity', y='Avoid_crucial_mistakes',
...          c='Luck', cmap='viridis')
... )
```

Another mechanism to visualize relationships between two continuous values as well as density (where the values overlap), is a hexbin plot. You should choose an appropriate colormap that is continuous and increasing from white to dark for this plot:

```
>>> (pres
...     .plot.hexbin(x='Integrity', y='Avoid_crucial_mistakes',
...          cmap='Greens')
... )
```

25.4   Area Plots and Stacked Bar Plots

A dataframe can create stacked area plots with the .area method. This plot is useful when you want to understand each column's relative contribution

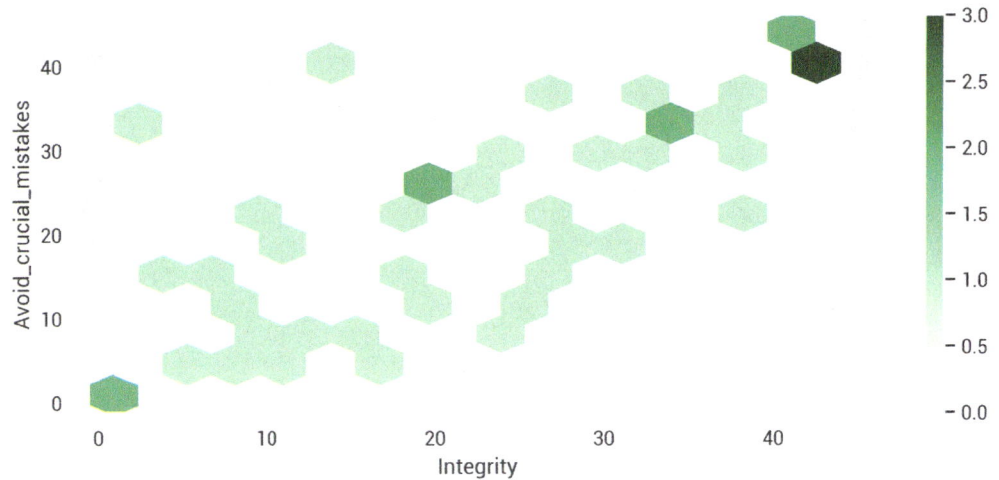

Figure 25.11: Hexbin plot for Integrity and Avoid crucial mistakes, showing where the density of values occur.

and the order of the data is important. If there is not a relationship and order between the values, I prefer a stacked bar plot.

Below, I specify the numeric columns I want with the y parameter. After plotting, I adjust the number of ticks and labels:

```
>>> (pres
...    .plot.area(x='President',
...       y='Background Imagination Integrity Intelligence Luck '\
...          'Willing_to_take_risks Ability_to_compromise'.split(),
...       rot=45)
... )
>>> ax.set_xticks(range(len(pres)))
>>> ax.set_xticklabels(labels=pres.President, ha='right')
```

In this case, using a line plot indicates some continuity from one president to the next. As presidential behavior should be somewhat independent from previous administrations, I prefer a stacked bar plot instead:

```
>>> (pres
...    .plot.bar(x='President',
...       y='Background Imagination Integrity Intelligence Luck '\
...          'Willing_to_take_risks Ability_to_compromise'.split(),
...       rot=45, stacked=True)
... )
>>> ax.set_xticks(range(len(pres)))
```

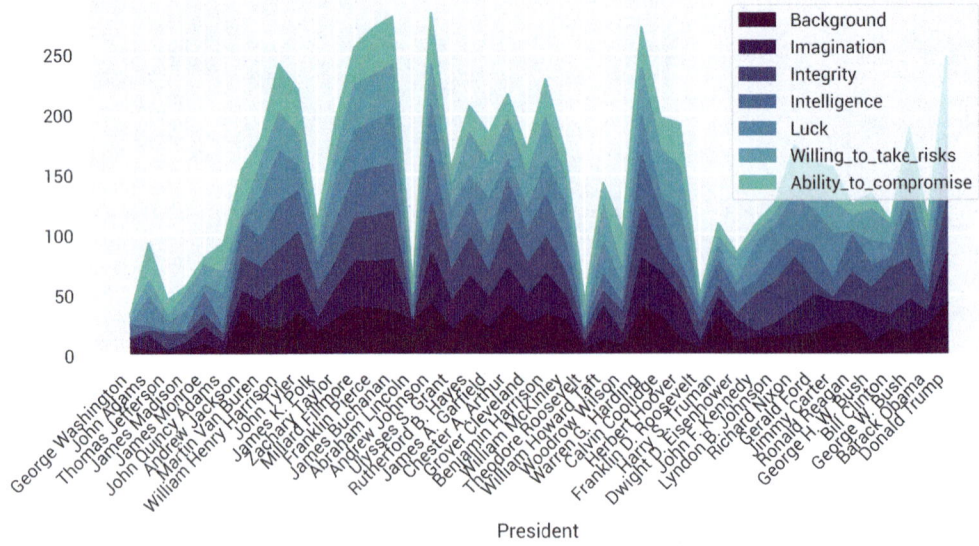

Figure 25.12: Stacked area plot.

```
>>> ax.set_xticklabels(labels=pres.President, ha='right')
```

25.5   Column Distributions with KDEs, Histograms, and Boxplots

If you have numeric information in columns, you can run summary statistics on the columns with .describe. To visualize the distribution for each column, you can plot with .hist or .density.

I'm going to shuffle the presidential data around and put the president's name in the columns, with the numeric ratings in the index. I'm going to limit this to nine presidents:

```
>>> (pres
...     .set_index('President')
...     .loc[:, 'Background':'Average_rank']
...     .iloc[:9]
...     .T
... )
President               George Washington  ...  William Henry Harrison
Background                              7  ...                      22
Imagination                             7  ...                      38
Integrity                               1  ...                      28
```

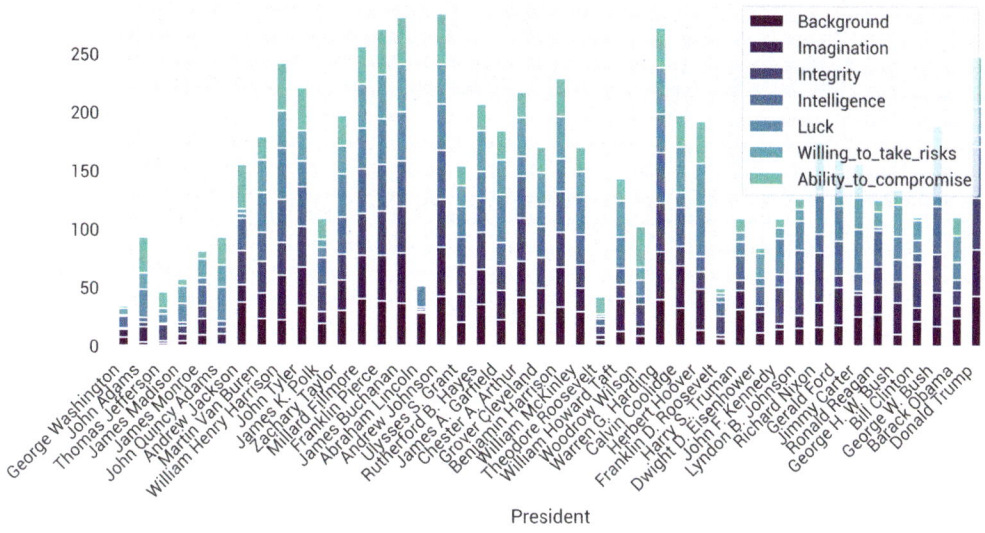

Figure 25.13: Stacked bar plot.

Intelligence	10	...		37
Luck	1	...		44
...	...	...		...
Foreign_policy	2	...		44
Avoid_crucial_mistakes	1	...		37
Experts'_view	2	...		39
Overall	1	...		39
Average_rank	1	...		38

```
[22 rows x 9 columns]
```

The .describe method summarizes each column, in this case the scores for each president:

```
>>> (pres
...     .set_index('President')
...     .loc[:, 'Background':'Average_rank']
...     .iloc[:9]
...     .T
...     .describe()
... )
count         22.000000    ...    22.000000
mean           3.681818    ...    36.909091
std            4.444219    ...     5.485124
```

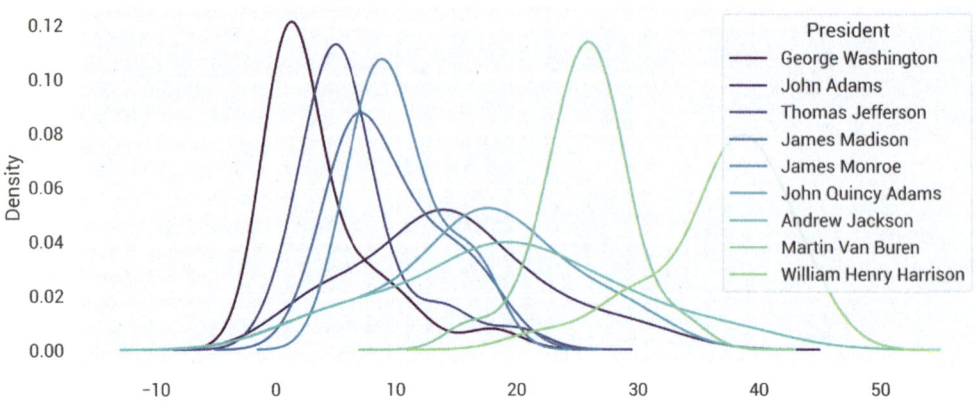

Figure 25.14: Kernel density estimation showing the distribution of scores for each president.

min	1.000000	...	22.000000
25%	1.000000	...	36.250000
50%	2.000000	...	38.000000
75%	5.000000	...	40.750000
max	18.000000	...	44.000000

```
[8 rows x 9 columns]
```

Let's visualize each president's scores with a Kernel Density Estimation (KDE):

```
>>> (pres
...     .set_index('President')
...     .loc[:, 'Background':'Average_rank']
...     .iloc[:9]
...     .T
...     .plot.density()
... )
```

You can also create a histogram. This data does not create very pretty histograms because there are not many scores:

```
>>> (pres
...     .set_index('President')
...     .loc[:, 'Background':'Average_rank']
...     .iloc[:9]
...     .T
...     .plot.hist()
... )
```

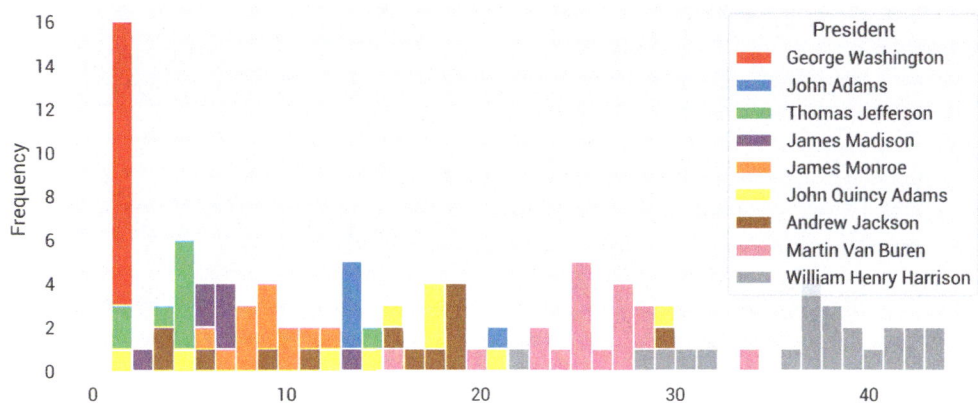

Figure 25.15: Histogram showing the distribution of scores for each president.

...)

Finally, you can create boxplots to summarize the distributions of the columns:

```
>>> ax = (pres
...      .set_index('President')
...      .loc[:, 'Background':'Average_rank']
...      .iloc[:9]
...      .T
...      .plot.box()
... )
>>> ax.set_xticklabels(labels=(pres.President[:9]), ha='right')
```

Method	Description
.plot(ax=None, style=None, subplots=False, logx=False, logy=False, xticks=None, yticks=None, xlim=None, ylim=None, xlabel=None, ylabel=None, rot=None, fontsize=None, colormap=None, table=False, **kwargs)	Common plot parameters. Use ax to use existing Matplotlib axes, style for color and marker style (see matplotlib.marker), subplots to create a new plot for each column, _ticks to specify tick locations, _lim to specify tick limits, _label to specify x/y label (default to index/column name), rot to rotate labels, fontsize for tick label size, colormap for coloring, position, table to create a table with data. Additional arguments are passed to plt.plot.

`.plot.area(x=None, y=None, stacked=True)`	Create a stacked area plot. Use column x for x-axis. Plot each y (can be a list) column as a bar. Use stack=False to create an unstacked plot.
`.plot.bar(x=None, y=None, stacked=False)`	Create a bar plot. Use column x for x-axis. Plot each y (can be a list) column as a bar. Use stack=True to stack bars for each x value.
`.plot.barh(x=None, y=None, stacked=False)`	Create a horizontal bar plot. Use column y for x-axis. Plot each x (can be a list) column as a bar. Use stack=True to stack bars for each y value.
`.plot.kde(bw_method='scott', ind=None)`	Create a Kernel Density Estimate plot. Each column of the dataframe will get its own plot. Use bw_method to calculate estimator bandwidth (see `scipy.stats.gaussian_kde`). Use ind to specify evaluation points for PDF estimation (NumPy array of points, or integer with equally spaced points).
`.plot.density()`	Synonym of `.plot.kde`.
`.plot.hist(bins=10)`	Create a histogram. Each column of the dataframe will get its own plot. Use bins to change number of bins.
`.plot.box(by=None)`	Create boxplots for each column against the index.
`.plot.scatter(x=None, y=None, c=None, s=None, **kwargs)`	Create a scatter plot. y can only be a single column name, not a list. Can use c parameter to specify a column to color by. Can use s parameter to specify a column to size points by.
`.plot.hexbin(x=None, y=None, C=None, reduce_C_function=None, gridsize=100)`	Create a hexagonal binning plot. y can only be a single column name, not a list. C can be a column containing an x,y point. reduce_C_function is a callable that reduces values in a bin (default np.mean. gridsize is number of hexes in x direction or (x,y) pair.

`.plot.line(x=None, y=None, color=None)`	Plot all columns against the index in the x-axis. Or specify a column for the x-axis with x, and which column(s) you want to plot as line(s) with y. color can be a single string specifying a color, a list of colors to cycle over, or a dictionary mapping column to color.
`.plot.pie()`	A method you shouldn't use. (Use .bar instead.)

Table 25.1: Dataframe Plotting Methods

25.6 Summary

In this chapter, we explored basic plotting functionality with series objects. We showed a little bit of the functionality that you get when plotting with a data frame. We will explore more of this later. Also note that because the plotting functionality is built on top of Matplotlib, you can customize the plot using Matplotlib.

25.7 Exercises

With a dataset of your choice:

1. Create a histogram from a numeric column. Change the bin size.

2. Create a boxplot from a numeric column.

3. Create a Kernel Density Estimate plot from a numeric column.

4. Create a line from a numeric column.

5. Create a bar plot from a frequency count of a categorical column.

6. Create a pie plot from a frequency count of a categorical column.

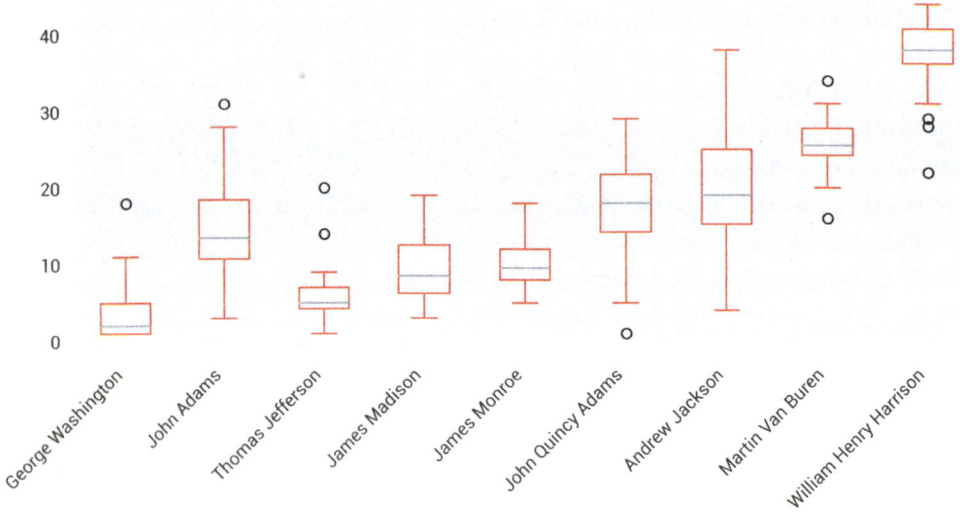

Figure 25.16: Boxplot showing the distribution of scores for each president.

Chapter 26

Reshaping Dataframes with Dummies

In this chapter, we will explore various options for manipulating and reshaping a dataframe. Various patterns will pop up when you start analyzing data, and we will give you the tools that you need to deal with them.

26.1 Dummy Columns

Creating *dummy columns* is one way to convert a categorical column into numeric columns. The process is straightforward. If you have a column that has repeated string values, create a new column for each of those values and insert a 1 or a 0 in each new column if corresponds to the original value.

We will look at a concrete example using the JetBrains Python 2020 survey data. The job columns are almost in dummy format as is. But instead of having entries of 1 and 0, they have entries of the job title and NaN:

```
>>> import pandas as pd
>>> url = 'https://github.com/mattharrison/datasets/raw/master/data/'\
...        '2020-jetbrains-python-survey.csv'
>>> jb = pd.read_csv(url)

>>> jb.filter(like='job.role')
      job.role.DBA  ... job.role.Other
0              NaN  ...            NaN
1              NaN  ...            NaN
2              NaN  ...            NaN
3              NaN  ...            NaN
4              NaN  ...            NaN
...            ...  ...            ...
54457          NaN  ...            NaN
```

```
54458        NaN  ...          NaN
54459        NaN  ...          NaN
54460        NaN  ...          NaN
54461        NaN  ...          NaN

[54462 rows x 13 columns]
```

First, we will collapse these job columns into a single column, and then I will show how to create proper dummy columns. I'm building up the chain to collapse them and walk through each link in the chain. After we have the job columns from above, we will use the .where method to insert 1 instead of the job name:

```
>>> (jb
...   .filter(like=r'job.role.*t')
...   .where(jb.isna(), 1)
... )
        job.role.DBA  ... job.role.Systems analyst job.role.Other
0               NaN  ...                      NaN            NaN
1               NaN  ...                      NaN            NaN
2               NaN  ...                      NaN            NaN
3               NaN  ...                      NaN            NaN
4               NaN  ...                      NaN            NaN
...             ...  ...                      ...            ...
54457           NaN  ...                        1            NaN
54458           NaN  ...                      NaN            NaN
54459           NaN  ...                      NaN            NaN
54460           NaN  ...                      NaN            NaN
54461           NaN  ...                      NaN            NaN

[54462 rows x 13 columns]
```

Now, we will replace NaN with 0:

```
>>> (jb
...   .filter(like=r'job.role.*t')
...   .where(jb.isna(), 1)
...   .fillna(0)
... )
        job.role.DBA  ... job.role.Systems analyst  job.role.Other
0                 0  ...                        0               0
1                 0  ...                        0               0
2                 0  ...                        0               0
3                 0  ...                        0               0
4                 0  ...                        0               0
...             ...  ...                      ...             ...
```

```
54457          0   ...                1              0
54458          0   ...                0              0
54459          0   ...                0              0
54460          0   ...                0              0
54461          0   ...                0              0

[54462 rows x 13 columns]
```

Next, we use the .idxmax method. This method scans along an axis and reports the index (or column) where the maximum value is found. In our case, each row should have a single value corresponding to the column of the job:

```
>>> (jb
...   .filter(like=r'job.role')
...   .where(jb.isna(), 1)
...   .fillna(0)
...   .idxmax(axis='columns')
... )
0                 job.role.Business analyst
1           job.role.Developer / Programmer
2           job.role.Developer / Programmer
3                           job.role.DBA
4                           job.role.DBA
                        ...
54457             job.role.Systems analyst
54458                       job.role.DBA
54459           job.role.CIO / CEO / CTO
54460     job.role.Developer / Programmer
54461                   job.role.Architect
Length: 54462, dtype: object
```

Finally, we will remove the string 'job.role.':

```
>>> job = (jb
...   .filter(like=r'job.role')
...   .where(jb.isna(), 1)
...   .fillna(0)
...   .idxmax(axis='columns')
...   .str.replace('job.role.', '', regex=False)
... )
>>> job
0                 Business analyst
1           Developer / Programmer
2           Developer / Programmer
3                           DBA
4                           DBA
```

```
                  ...
54457            Systems analyst
54458                        DBA
54459            CIO / CEO / CTO
54460    Developer / Programmer
54461                  Architect
Length: 54462, dtype: object
```

The job series now looks like a column with categorical data. This is the type of column we usually want to convert into dummy columns.

If you want to create dummy columns from a series (or a dataframe that has multiple string columns), call the `pd.get_dummies` function. Note that this is not a method on a series or a dataframe:

```
>>> dum = pd.get_dummies(job)
>>> dum
        Architect   ...   Technical writer
0               0   ...                  0
1               0   ...                  0
2               0   ...                  0
3               0   ...                  0
4               0   ...                  0
...           ...   ...                ...
54457           0   ...                  0
54458           0   ...                  0
54459           0   ...                  0
54460           0   ...                  0
54461           1   ...                  0

[54462 rows x 13 columns]
```

26.2   Undoing Dummy Columns

There are multiple ways to go from data arranged in dummy columns to a single column. The most readable is the slowest using `.idxmax`. Note you will want to execute this on a dataframe that only has the dummy columns:

```
>>> dum.idxmax(axis='columns')
0               Business analyst
1         Developer / Programmer
2         Developer / Programmer
3                            DBA
4                            DBA
                  ...
```

```
54457              Systems analyst
54458                         DBA
54459           CIO / CEO / CTO
54460     Developer / Programmer
54461                   Architect
Length: 54462, dtype: object
```

The fastest (about 8x faster on my machine) involves a little bit of NumPy:

```
>>> i, j = np.where(dum)
>>> pd.Series(dum.columns[j], i)
0              Business analyst
1         Developer / Programmer
2         Developer / Programmer
3                           DBA
4                           DBA
                  ...
54457              Systems analyst
54458                         DBA
54459           CIO / CEO / CTO
54460     Developer / Programmer
54461                   Architect
Length: 54462, dtype: object
```

Pick your poison.

Method	Description
.filter(items=None, like=None, regex=None, axis=1)	Return a dataframe filtered by index axis labels. Use items to specify a list of names. Use like to specify a substring. Use regex to specify a regular expression.
.where(cond, other=nan, axis=None, level=None, errors='raise', try_cast=None)	Replace the values where cond (a boolean array) is False. Generally I use this on series.
.fillna(value=None, method=None, axis=None, limit=None, downcast=None)	Return a dataframe with missing values filled in. value can be a scalar, dictionary (mapping column to value), series (values for index) or dataframe. Use method for 'bfill', 'pad', or 'ffill'. You can limit the replacements with limit. Use downcast to specify a dictionary mapping a column to new type (ie from float64 to int64).

`.idxmax(axis=0, skipna=True)`	Return the index of first maximum value over an axis.
`pd.get_dummies(data, prefix=None, prefix_sep='_', dummy_na=False, sparse=False, drop_first=False, dtype=None)`	Return a dataframe with string/categorical columns from data converted into dummy columns.
`np.where_dummies(condition, x=None, y=None)`	Return a numpy array where condition (boolean array) is True using value x (scalar, series) and y (scalar, series) otherwise.

Table 26.1: Dataframe Reshaping Methods

26.3 Summary

Dummy columns are one way to encode categorical variables as numbers. Many will use this option to prepare data for machine learning because many machine learning algorithms do not support string data, only numeric.

26.4 Exercises

With a dataset of your choice:

1. Create dummy columns derived from a string column.

2. Undo the dummy columns.

Chapter 27

Reshaping By Pivoting and Grouping

This chapter will explore one of the most powerful options for data manipulations, pivot tables. Pandas provides multiple syntaxes for creating them. One uses the .pivot_table method, the other common one leverages the .groupby method, you can also represent some of these operations with the pd.crosstab function.

We will explore all of these using the cleaned-up JetBrains survey data:

```
>>> jb2
        age are_you_datascientist  ...  years_of_coding python3_ver
1        21                  True  ...              3.0         3.6
2        30                 False  ...              3.0         3.6
10       21                 False  ...              1.0         3.8
11       21                  True  ...              3.0         3.9
13       30                  True  ...              3.0         3.7
...     ...                   ...  ...              ...         ...
54456    30                 False  ...              6.0         3.6
54457    21                 False  ...              1.0         3.6
54459    21                 False  ...              6.0         3.7
54460    30                  True  ...              3.0         3.7
54461    21                 False  ...              1.0         3.8

[13711 rows x 20 columns]
```

27.1 A Basic Example

When your boss asks you to get numbers "by X column", that should be a hint to pivot (or group) your data. Assume your boss asked, "What is the average age by the country for each employment status?" This is like one of those word problems that you had to learn how to do in math class, and you needed to translate the words into math operations. In this case, we need to pick a pandas operation to use and then map the problem into those operations.

I would translate this problem into:

- Put the country in the index

- Have a column for each employment status

- Put the average age in each cell

These map cleanly to the parameters of the .pivot_table method. One solution would look like this:

```
>>> (jb2
...    .pivot_table(index='country_live', columns='employment_status',
...        values='age', aggfunc='mean')
... )
employment_status    Fully employed  ...  Working student
country_live                          ...
Algeria                        31.2   ...             <NA>
Argentina                 30.632184   ...             23.0
Armenia                   22.071429   ...             <NA>
Australia                 32.935622   ...           24.125
Austria                   31.619565   ...             25.5
...                             ...   ...              ...
United States             32.429163   ...        21.842697
Uruguay                        27.0   ...             <NA>
Uzbekistan                     21.0   ...             <NA>
Venezuela                 29.769231   ...             30.0
Viet Nam                  22.857143   ...             21.0

[76 rows x 4 columns]
```

It turns out that we can use the pd.crosstab function as well. Because this is a function, we need to provide the data as series rather than the column names:

```
>>> pd.crosstab(index=jb2.country_live, columns=jb2.employment_status,
...        values=jb2.age, aggfunc='mean')
employment_status    Fully employed  ...  Working student
country_live                          ...
Algeria                        31.2   ...             <NA>
Argentina                 30.632184   ...             23.0
Armenia                   22.071429   ...             <NA>
```

Pivot Tables

auto

	make	year	cylinders	drive	city08
0	BMW	1993	8.00	Rear-Wheel	14
1	BMW	1993	8.00	Rear-Wheel	14
2	BMW	1993	12.00	Rear-Wheel	11
3	Chevrolet	1993	4.00	Front-Whee	18
4	Chevrolet	1993	6.00	Front-Whee	17
9409	Ford	1993	6.00	Front-Whee	19
9410	Chevrolet	1985	8.00	Rear-Wheel	11
9411	Chevrolet	1985	8.00	Rear-Wheel	15
9412	Chevrolet	1985	8.00	Rear-Wheel	16
9413	Chevrolet	1985	8.00	Rear-Wheel	10

```
(auto.pivot_table(aggfunc="max",
  index="year",
  columns="make",
  values="city08")
```

	BMW	Chevrolet	Ford	Tesla
1984	21.00	33.00	35.00	nan
1985	21.00	39.00	36.00	nan
1986	21.00	44.00	34.00	nan
1987	19.00	44.00	31.00	nan
1988	18.00	44.00	33.00	nan
2016	137.00	128.00	110.00	102.00
2017	137.00	128.00	118.00	131.00
2018	129.00	128.00	118.00	136.00
2019	124.00	128.00	43.00	140.00
2020	26.00	30.00	24.00	nan

Figure 27.1: The .pivot_table method allows you to pick column(s) for the index, column(s) for the column, and column(s) to aggregate. (If you specify multiple columns to aggregate, you will get hierarchical columns.)

Cross Tabulation

auto

	make	year	cylinders	drive	city08
0	BMW	1993	8.00	Rear-Wheel	14
1	BMW	1993	8.00	Rear-Wheel	14
2	BMW	1993	12.00	Rear-Wheel	11
3	Chevrolet	1993	4.00	Front-Whee	18
4	Chevrolet	1993	6.00	Front-Whee	17
9409	Ford	1993	6.00	Front-Whee	19
9410	Chevrolet	1985	8.00	Rear-Wheel	11
9411	Chevrolet	1985	8.00	Rear-Wheel	15
9412	Chevrolet	1985	8.00	Rear-Wheel	16
9413	Chevrolet	1985	8.00	Rear-Wheel	10

```
(pd.crosstab(aggfunc="max",
  index=auto.year,
  columns=auto.make,
  values=auto.city08)
```

	BMW	Chevrolet	Ford	Tesla
1984	21.00	33.00	35.00	nan
1985	21.00	39.00	36.00	nan
1986	21.00	44.00	34.00	nan
1987	19.00	44.00	31.00	nan
1988	18.00	44.00	33.00	nan
2016	137.00	128.00	110.00	102.00
2017	137.00	128.00	118.00	131.00
2018	129.00	128.00	118.00	136.00
2019	124.00	128.00	43.00	140.00
2020	26.00	30.00	24.00	nan

Figure 27.2: The pd.crosstab function allows you to pick column(s) for the index, column(s) for the column, and a column to aggregate. You cannot aggregate multiple columns (unlike .pivot_table).

```
Australia        32.935622   ...           24.125
Austria          31.619565   ...             25.5
...                     ...   ...              ...
United States    32.429163   ...        21.842697
Uruguay               27.0   ...             <NA>
Uzbekistan            21.0   ...             <NA>
Venezuela        29.769231   ...             30.0
Viet Nam         22.857143   ...             21.0

[76 rows x 4 columns]
```

Finally, we can do this with a .groupby method call. The call to .groupby returns a DataFrameGroupBy object. It is a lazy object and does not perform any calculations until we indicate which aggregation to perform. We can also pull off a column and then only perform an aggregation on that column instead of all of the non-grouped columns.

This operation is a little more involved. We pull off the *age* colum and then calculate the mean for each *country_live* and *employment_status* group. Then we leverage .unstack to pull out the inner-most index and push it up into a column (we will dive into .unstack later). You can think of .groupby and subsequent methods as the low-level underpinnings of .pivot_table and pd.crosstab:

```
>>> (jb2
...    .groupby(['country_live', 'employment_status'])
...    .age
...    .mean()
...    .unstack()
... )
employment_status    Fully employed  ...  Working student
country_live                         ...
Algeria                        31.2  ...              <NA>
Argentina                 30.632184  ...              23.0
Armenia                   22.071429  ...              <NA>
Australia                 32.935622  ...            24.125
Austria                   31.619565  ...              25.5
...                             ...  ...               ...
United States             32.429163  ...         21.842697
Uruguay                        27.0  ...              <NA>
Uzbekistan                     21.0  ...              <NA>
Venezuela                 29.769231  ...              30.0
Viet Nam                  22.857143  ...              21.0

[76 rows x 4 columns]
```

Many programmers and SQL analysts find the .groupby syntax intuitive, while Excel junkies often feel more at home with the .pivot_table method. The crosstab function works in some situations but is not as flexible. It makes sense to learn the different options. The .groupby method is the foundation of the other two, but a cross-tabulation may be more convenient.

Groupby Operation

auto

	make	year	cylinders	drive	city08
0	BMW	1993	8.00	Rear-Wheel	14
1	BMW	1993	8.00	Rear-Wheel	14
2	BMW	1993	12.00	Rear-Wheel	11
3	Chevrolet	1993	4.00	Front-Whee	18
4	Chevrolet	1993	6.00	Front-Whee	17
9409	Ford	1993	6.00	Front-Whee	19
9410	Chevrolet	1985	8.00	Rear-Wheel	11
9411	Chevrolet	1985	8.00	Rear-Wheel	15
9412	Chevrolet	1985	8.00	Rear-Wheel	16
9413	Chevrolet	1985	8.00	Rear-Wheel	10

```
(auto.groupby(['year','make'])
 .city08
 .max()
 .unstack())
```

	BMW	Chevrolet	Ford	Tesla
1984	21.00	33.00	35.00	nan
1985	21.00	39.00	36.00	nan
1986	21.00	44.00	34.00	nan
1987	19.00	44.00	31.00	nan
1988	18.00	44.00	33.00	nan
2016	137.00	128.00	110.00	102.00
2017	137.00	128.00	118.00	131.00
2018	129.00	128.00	118.00	136.00
2019	124.00	128.00	43.00	140.00
2020	26.00	30.00	24.00	nan

Figure 27.3: The .groupby method allows you to pick a column(s) for the index and column(s) to aggregate. You can .unstack the inner column to simulate pivot tables and cross-tabulation.

Grouping Data

auto

	make	year	cylinders	drive
0	Alfa Romeo	1985	4.00	Rear-Wheel
1	Ferrari	1985	12.00	Rear-Wheel
2	Dodge	1985	4.00	Front-Whee
3	Dodge	1985	8.00	Rear-Wheel
4	Subaru	1993	4.00	4-Wheel or
41139	Subaru	1993	4.00	Front-Whee
41140	Subaru	1993	4.00	Front-Whee
41141	Subaru	1993	4.00	4-Wheel or
41142	Subaru	1993	4.00	4-Wheel or
41143	Subaru	1993	4.00	4-Wheel or

```
(auto
 .groupby("make")
 .mean())
```

	year	cylinders
AM General	1984.33	5.00
ASC Incorpor	1987.00	6.00
Acura	2005.48	5.24
Alfa Romeo	1998.58	5.10
American Mot	1984.48	5.41
Volkswagen	2002.81	4.55
Volvo	2002.35	4.86
Wallace Envi	1991.50	7.81
Yugo	1988.38	4.00
smart	2013.95	3.00

Figure 27.4: When your boss asks you to get the average values by make, you should recognize that you need to pull out .groupby('make').

27.2 Using a Custom Aggregation Function

Your boss thanks you for providing insight on the age of employment status by country and says she has a more important question: "What is the percentage of Emacs users by country?"

We will need a function that takes a group (in this case, a series) of country respondents about IDE preference and returns the percent that chose emacs:

```
>>> def per_emacs(ser):
...     return ser.str.contains('Emacs').sum() / len(ser) * 100
```

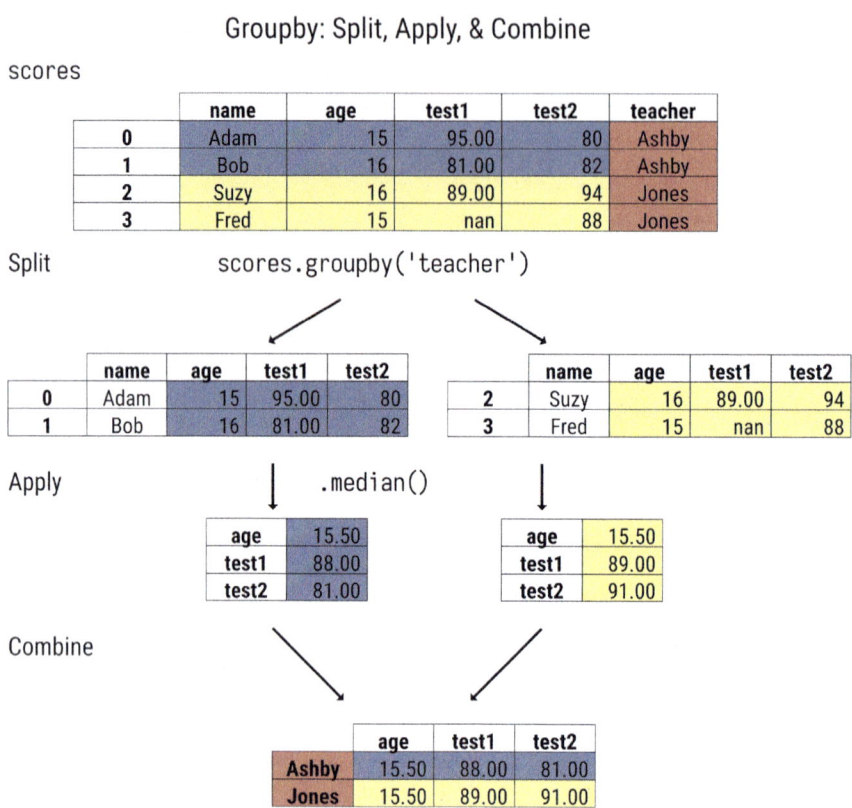

Figure 27.5: A groupby operation splits the data into groups. You can apply aggregate functions to the group. Then the results of the aggregates are combined. The column we are grouping by will be placed in the index.

Note

When you need to calculate a percentage in pandas, you can use the .mean method. The following code is equivalent to the above:

```
>>> def per_emacs(ser):
...         return ser.str.contains('Emacs').mean() * 100
```

We are now ready to pivot. In this case we still want country in the index, but we only want a single column, the emacs percentage. So we don't provide a columns parameter:

```
>>> (jb2
...   .pivot_table(index='country_live', values='ide_main', aggfunc=per_emacs)
... )
              ide_main
country_live
Algeria       0.000000
Argentina     3.669725
Armenia       0.000000
Australia     3.649635
Austria       1.562500
...                ...
United States 4.486466
Uruguay       0.000000
Uzbekistan    0.000000
Venezuela     0.000000
Viet Nam      0.000000

[76 rows x 1 columns]
```

Using pd.crosstab is a little more complicated as it expects a "cross-tabulation" of two columns, one column going in the index and the other column going in the columns. To get a "column" for the cross tabulation, we will assign a column to a single scalar value, (which will trick the cross tabulation into creating just one column with the name of the scalar value):

```
>>> pd.crosstab(index=jb2.country_live,
...       columns=jb2.assign(iden='emacs_per').iden,
...       values=jb2.ide_main, aggfunc=per_emacs)
iden          emacs_per
country_live
Algeria       0.000000
Argentina     3.669725
Armenia       0.000000
```

```
Australia      3.649635
Austria        1.562500
...                 ...
United States  4.486466
Uruguay        0.000000
Uzbekistan     0.000000
Venezuela      0.000000
Viet Nam       0.000000

[76 rows x 1 columns]
```

Finally, here is the .groupby version. I find this one very clear. Group by the *country_live* column, pull out just the *ide_main* columns. Calculate the percentage of emacs users for each of those groups:

```
>>> (jb2
...    .groupby('country_live')
...    [['ide_main']]
...    .agg(per_emacs)
... )
                 ide_main
country_live
Algeria          0.000000
Argentina        3.669725
Armenia          0.000000
Australia        3.649635
Austria          1.562500
...                   ...
United States    4.486466
Uruguay          0.000000
Uzbekistan       0.000000
Venezuela        0.000000
Viet Nam         0.000000

[76 rows x 1 columns]
```

27.3 Multiple Aggregations

Assume that your boss asked, "What is the minimum and maximum age for each country?" When you see "for each" or "by", your mind should think that whatever is following either of the terms should go in the index. This question is answered with a pivot table or using groupby. (We can use a cross-

Grouping Data with Multiple Aggregations

auto

	make	year	cylinders	drive
1	Ferrari	1985	12.00	Rear-Wheel
2	Dodge	1985	4.00	Front-Whee
3	Dodge	1985	8.00	Rear-Wheel
4	Subaru	1993	4.00	4-Wheel or
5	Subaru	1993	4.00	Front-Whee
41139	Subaru	1993	4.00	Front-Whee
41140	Subaru	1993	4.00	Front-Whee
41141	Subaru	1993	4.00	4-Wheel or
41142	Subaru	1993	4.00	4-Wheel or
41143	Subaru	1993	4.00	4-Wheel or

```
(auto
 .groupby('make')
 .agg(['min', 'max']))
```

Hierarchical columns!

	year	year	cylinders	cylinders
	min	max	min	max
Acura	1986	2020	4.00	6.00
Audi	1984	2020	4.00	12.00
BMW	1984	2020	2.00	12.00
BYD	2012	2019	nan	nan
Bentley	1998	2019	8.00	12.00
VPG	2011	2013	8.00	8.00
Vector	1992	1997	8.00	12.00
Volvo	1984	2019	4.00	8.00
Yugo	1986	1990	4.00	4.00
smart	2008	2019	3.00	3.00

Figure 27.6: You can leverage the .agg method with .groupby to perform multiple aggregations.

tabulation, but you will need to add a column to do this, and it feels unnatural to me).

Here is the .pivot_table solution. The *country_live* column goes in the index parameter. *age* is what we want to aggregate, so that goes in the values parameter. And we need to specify a sequence with min and max for the aggfunc parameter:

```
>>> (jb2
...        .pivot_table(index='country_live', values='age',
...            aggfunc=(min, max))
... )
              max  min
country_live
Algeria        60   18
Argentina      60   18
Armenia        30   18
Australia      60   18
Austria        50   18
...            ..   ..
United States  60   18
Uruguay        40   21
Uzbekistan     21   21
Venezuela      50   18
Viet Nam       60   18

[76 rows x 2 columns]
```

When you look at this using the `.groupby` method, you first determine what you want in the index, *country_live*. Then we will pull off the *age* column from each group. Finally, we will apply two aggregate functions, `min` and `max`:

```
>>> (jb2
...        .groupby('country_live')
...        .age
...        .agg([min, max])
... )
              min   max
country_live
Algeria        18    60
Argentina      18    60
Armenia        18    30
Australia      18    60
Austria        18    50
...            ...   ...
United States  18    60
Uruguay        21    40
Uzbekistan     21    21
Venezuela      18    50
Viet Nam       18    60

[76 rows x 2 columns]
```

Here is the example for `pd.crosstab`. I don't recommend this, but provide it to help explain how cross-tabulation works. Again, we want *country_live* in the index. With cross-tabulation, we need to provide a series to splay out in the columns. We cannot use the *age* column as the `columns` parameter because we want to aggregate on those numbers and hence need to set them as the `values` parameter. Instead, I will create a new column that has a single scalar value, the string `'age'`. We can provide both of the aggregations we want to use to the `aggfunc` parameter. Below is my solution. Note that is has hierarchical columns:

```
>>> pd.crosstab(jb2.country_live, values=jb2.age, aggfunc=(min, max),
...     columns=jb2.assign(val='age').val)
               max min
val            age age
country_live
Algeria         60  18
Argentina       60  18
Armenia         30  18
Australia       60  18
Austria         50  18
...             ..  ..
United States   60  18
Uruguay         40  21
Uzbekistan      21  21
Venezuela       50  18
Viet Nam        60  18

[76 rows x 2 columns]
```

27.4 Per Column Aggregations

In the previous example, we looked at applying multiple aggregations to a single column. We can also apply multiple aggregations to many columns. Here we get the minimum and maximum value of each numeric column by country:

```
>>> (jb2
...   .pivot_table(index='country_live',
...               aggfunc=(min, max))
... )
               age          ... years_of_coding
               max min      ...         max   min
country_live                ...
```

```
Algeria          60  18  ...        11.0  1.0
Argentina        60  18  ...        11.0  1.0
Armenia          30  18  ...        11.0  1.0
Australia        60  18  ...        11.0  1.0
Austria          50  18  ...        11.0  1.0
...              ..  ..  ...        ...   ...
United States    60  18  ...        11.0  1.0
Uruguay          40  21  ...        11.0  1.0
Uzbekistan       21  21  ...         6.0  1.0
Venezuela        50  18  ...        11.0  1.0
Viet Nam         60  18  ...         6.0  1.0

[76 rows x 32 columns]
```

Here is the groupby version:

```
>>> (jb2
...    .groupby('country_live')
...    .agg([min, max])
... )
                 age         ... years_of_coding
                 max min     ...             max  min
country_live                 ...
Algeria          60  18      ...            11.0  1.0
Argentina        60  18      ...            11.0  1.0
Armenia          30  18      ...            11.0  1.0
Australia        60  18      ...            11.0  1.0
Austria          50  18      ...            11.0  1.0
...              ..  ..      ...             ...   ...
United States    60  18      ...            11.0  1.0
Uruguay          40  21      ...            11.0  1.0
Uzbekistan       21  21      ...             6.0  1.0
Venezuela        50  18      ...            11.0  1.0
Viet Nam         60  18      ...             6.0  1.0

[76 rows x 32 columns]
```

I'm not going to do this with pd.crosstab, and I recommend that you don't as well.

Sometimes, we want to specify aggregations per column. With both the .pivot_table and .groupby methods, we can provide a dictionary mapping a column to an aggregation function or a list of aggregation functions.

Assume your boss asked: "What are the minimum and maximum ages and the average team size for each country?". Here is the translation to a pivot table:

```
>>> (jb2
...  .pivot_table(index='country_live',
...              aggfunc={'age': ['min', 'max'],
...                       'team_size': 'mean'})
... )
                 age       team_size
                 max min        mean
country_live
Algeria           60  18    3.722222
Argentina         60  18    4.146789
Armenia           30  18    4.235294
Australia         60  18    3.354015
Austria           50  18    3.132812
...               ..  ..         ...
United States     60  18    4.072673
Uruguay           40  21    3.700000
Uzbekistan        21  21    2.750000
Venezuela         50  18    3.227273
Viet Nam          60  18    4.666667

[76 rows x 3 columns]
```

Here is the groupby version:

```
>>> (jb2
...  .groupby('country_live')
...  .agg({'age': ['min', 'max'],
...        'team_size': 'mean'})
... )
                 age       team_size
                 min max        mean
country_live
Algeria           18  60    3.722222
Argentina         18  60    4.146789
Armenia           18  30    4.235294
Australia         18  60    3.354015
Austria           18  50    3.132812
...               ..  ..         ...
United States     18  60    4.072673
Uruguay           21  40    3.700000
Uzbekistan        21  21    2.750000
Venezuela         18  50    3.227273
Viet Nam          18  60    4.666667

[76 rows x 3 columns]
```

One nuisance of these results is that they have hierarchical columns. In general, I find these types of columns annoying and confusing to work with. They do come in useful for stacking and unstacking, which we will explore in a later section. However, I like to remove them, and I will also show a general recipe for that later.

But I want to show one last feature that is specific to .groupby and may make you favor it as there is no equivalent functionality found in .pivot_table. That feature is called *named aggregations*. When calling the .agg method on a groupby object, you can use a keyword parameter to pass in a tuple of the column and aggregation function. The keyword parameter will be turned into a (flattened) column name.

We could re-write the previous example like this:

```
>>> (jb2
...    .groupby('country_live')
...    .agg(age_min=('age', min),
...         age_max=('age', max),
...         team_size_mean=('team_size', 'mean')
...       )
... )
```

	age_min	age_max	team_size_mean
country_live			
Algeria	18	60	3.722222
Argentina	18	60	4.146789
Armenia	18	30	4.235294
Australia	18	60	3.354015
Austria	18	50	3.132812
...	...	...	...
United States	18	60	4.072673
Uruguay	21	40	3.700000
Uzbekistan	21	21	2.750000
Venezuela	18	50	3.227273
Viet Nam	18	60	4.666667

```
[76 rows x 3 columns]
```

Notice that the above result has flat columns.

27.5 Grouping by Hierarchy

I just mentioned how much hierarchical columns bothered me. I'll admit, they are sometimes useful. Now I'm going to show you how to create hierarchical indexes. Suppose your boss asked about minimum and maximum age for each country and editor. We want to have both the country and the editor in the index. We just need to pass in a list of columns we want in the index:

```
>>> (jb2.pivot_table(index=['country_live', 'ide_main'],
...     values='age', aggfunc=[min, max]))
```

		min age	max age
country_live	ide_main		
Algeria	Atom	21	60
	Eclipse + Pydev	18	18
	IDLE	40	40
	Jupyter Notebook	30	30
	Other	30	30
...		..	..
Viet Nam	Other	21	21
	PyCharm Community Edition	21	30
	PyCharm Professional Edition	21	21
	VS Code	18	30
	Vim	21	40

```
[813 rows x 2 columns]
```

Here is the groupby version:

```
>>> (jb2
...     .groupby(by=['country_live', 'ide_main'])
...     [['age']]
...     .agg([min, max])
... )
```

		age	
		min	max
country_live	ide_main		
Algeria	Atom	21	60
	Eclipse + Pydev	18	18
	Emacs	<NA>	<NA>
	IDLE	40	40
	IntelliJ IDEA	<NA>	<NA>
...		...	...
Viet Nam	Python Tools for Visual Studio (PTVS)	<NA>	<NA>
	Spyder	<NA>	<NA>
	Sublime Text	<NA>	<NA>
	VS Code	18	30
	Vim	21	40

```
[1216 rows x 2 columns]
```

Flattening Grouping Data by Multiple Columns

auto

	make	year	cylinders	drive
1	Ferrari	1985	12.00	Rear-Wheel
2	Dodge	1985	4.00	Front-Whee
3	Dodge	1985	8.00	Rear-Wheel
4	Subaru	1993	4.00	4-Wheel or
5	Subaru	1993	4.00	Front-Whee
41139	Subaru	1993	4.00	Front-Whee
41140	Subaru	1993	4.00	Front-Whee
41141	Subaru	1993	4.00	4-Wheel or
41142	Subaru	1993	4.00	4-Wheel or
41143	Subaru	1993	4.00	4-Wheel or

```
(auto
 .groupby(['make', 'year'])
 .max()
 .reset_index())
```

	make	year	cylinders
0	Acura	1986	6.00
1	Acura	1987	6.00
2	Acura	1988	6.00
3	Acura	1989	6.00
4	Acura	1990	6.00
1345	smart	2015	3.00
1346	smart	2016	3.00
1347	smart	2017	3.00
1348	smart	2018	nan
1349	smart	2019	nan

Figure 27.7: Grouping with a list of columns will create a multi-index, an index with hierarchical levels.

Those paying careful attention will note that the results of apply multiple aggregations from .groupby and .pivot_table are not exactly the same. There are a few differences:

- The hierarchical column levels are swapped (*age* is inside of *min* and *max* when pivotting, but outside when grouping)

- The row count differs

I'm not sure why pandas swaps the levels. You could use the .swaplevel method to change that. However, I would personally use a named aggregation with a groupby for flat columns:

```
>>> (jb2
...    .groupby(by=['country_live', 'ide_main'])
...    [['age']]
...    .agg([min, max])
...    .swaplevel(axis='columns')
... )
                                                      min    max
                                                      age    age
country_live ide_main
Algeria      Atom                                      21     60
             Eclipse + Pydev                           18     18
             Emacs                                    <NA>   <NA>
             IDLE                                       40     40
             IntelliJ IDEA                            <NA>   <NA>
...                                                    ...    ...
Viet Nam     Python Tools for Visual Studio (PTVS)    <NA>   <NA>
             Spyder                                   <NA>   <NA>
             Sublime Text                             <NA>   <NA>
             VS Code                                    18     30
             Vim                                        21     40

[1216 rows x 2 columns]

>>> (jb2
...    .groupby(by=['country_live', 'ide_main'])
...    .agg(age_min=('age', min), age_max=('age', max))
... )
                                                    age_min   age_max
country_live ide_main
Algeria      Atom                                        21        60
             Eclipse + Pydev                             18        18
             Emacs                                     <NA>      <NA>
             IDLE                                         40        40
             IntelliJ IDEA                             <NA>      <NA>
...                                                     ...       ...
Viet Nam     Python Tools for Visual Studio (PTVS)     <NA>      <NA>
             Spyder                                    <NA>      <NA>
             Sublime Text                              <NA>      <NA>
             VS Code                                     18        30
             Vim                                         21        40
```

```
[1216 rows x 2 columns]
```

The reason the row count is different is a little more nuanced. I have set the *country_live* and *ide_main* columns to be categorical. When you perform a groupby with categorical columns, pandas will create the cartesian product of those columns even if there is no corresponding value. You can see above a few rows with both values of <NA>. The pivot table version (at the start of the section) did not have the missing values.

> **Note**
>
> Be careful when grouping with multiple categorical columns with high cardinality. You can generate a very large (and sparse) result!

You could always call .dropna after the fact, but I prefer to use the observed parameter instead:

```
>>> (jb2
...   .groupby(by=['country_live', 'ide_main'], observed=True)
...   .agg(age_min=('age', min), age_max=('age', max))
... )
```

country_live	ide_main	age_min	age_max
India	Atom	18	40
	Eclipse + Pydev	18	40
	Emacs	21	40
	IDLE	18	40
	IntelliJ IDEA	21	30
...		...	...
Dominican Republic	Vim	21	21
Morocco	Jupyter Notebook	30	30
	PyCharm Community Edition	21	40
	Sublime Text	21	30
	VS Code	21	30

```
[813 rows x 2 columns]
```

That's looking better!

27.6 Grouping with Functions

Up until now, we have been grouping by various values found in columns. Sometimes I want to group by something other than an existing column, and I have a few options.

Often, I will create a special column containing the values I want to group by. In addition, both pivot tables and groupby operations support passing in a function instead of a column name. This function accepts a single index label and should return a value to group on. In the example below we group based on whether the index value is even or odd. We then calculate the size of each group. Here is the grouper function and the .pivot_table implementation:

```
>>> def even_grouper(idx):
...     return 'odd' if idx % 2 else 'even'

>>> jb2.pivot_table(index=even_grouper, aggfunc='size')
even    6849
odd     6862
dtype: int64
```

And here is the .groupby version:

```
>>> (jb2
...  .groupby(even_grouper)
...  .size()
... )
even    6849
odd     6862
dtype: int64
```

When we look at time series manipulation later, we will see that pandas provides a handy pd.Grouper class to allow us to easily group by time attributes.

Method	Description
pd.crosstab(index, columns, values=None, rownames=None, colnames=None, aggfunc=None, margins=False, margins_name='All', dropna=True, normalize=False)	Create a cross-tabulation (counts by default) from an index (series or list of series) and columns (series or list of series). Can specify a column (series) to aggregate values along with a function, aggfunc. Using margins=True will add subtotals. Using dropna=False will keep columns that have no values. Can normalize over 'all' values, the rows ('index'), or the 'columns'.

`.pivot_table(values=None, index=None, columns=None, aggfunc='mean', fill_value=None, margins=False, margins_name='All', dropna=True, observed=False, sort=True)`	Create a pivot table. Use `index` (series, column name, `pd.Grouper`, or list of previous) to specify index entries. Use `columns` (series, column name, `pd.Grouper`, or list of previous) to specify column entries. The `aggfunc` (function, list of functions, dictionary (column name to function or list of functions) specifies function to aggregate values. Missing values are replaced with `fill_value`. Set `margins=True` to add subtotals/totals. Using `dropna=False` will keep columns that have no values. Use `observed=True` to only show values that appeared for categorical groupers.
`.groupby(by=None, axis=0, level=None, as_index=True, sort=True, group_keys=True, observed=False, dropna=True)`	Return a grouper object, grouped using by (column name, function (accepts each index value, returns group name/id), series, `pd.Grouper`, or list of column names). Use `as_index=False` to leave grouping keys as columns. Common plot parameters. Use `observed=True` to only show values that appeared for categorical groupers. Using `dropna=False` will keep columns that have no values.
`.stack(level=-1, dropna=True)`	Push column level into the index level. Can specify a column `level` (-1 is innermost).
`.unstack(level=-1, dropna=True)`	Push index level into the column level. Can specify an index `level` (-1 is innermost).

Table 27.1: Dataframe Pivoting and Grouping Methods

Method	*Description*
Column access	Access a column by attribute or index operation.

`g.agg(func=None, *args,`
   `engine=None,`
   `engine_kwargs=None, **kwargs)`
	Apply an aggregate func to groups. func can be string, function (accepting a column and returning a reduction), a list of the previous, or a dictionary mapping column name to string, function, or list of strings and/or functions.

`g.aggregate`	Same as `g.agg`.
`g.all(skipna=True)`	Collapse each group to True if all the values are truthy.
`g.any(skipna=True)`	Collapse each group to True if any the values are truthy.
`g.apply(func, *args, **kwargs)`	Apply a function to each group. The function should accept the group (as a dataframe) and return scalar, series, or dataframe. These return a series, dataframe (with each series as a row), and a dataframe (with the index as an inner index of the result) respectively.
`g.count()`	Count of non-missing values for each group.
`g.ewm(com=None, span=None,` `halflife=None)`	Return an Exponentially Weighted grouper. Can specify center of mass (`com`), decay span, or `halflife`. Will need to apply further aggregation to this.

`g.expanding(min_periods=1,`
   `center=False, axis=0,`
   `method='single')`
	Return an expanding Window object. Can specify minimum number of observations per period (`min_periods`), set label at center of window, and whether to execute over `'single'` column or whole group (`'table'`). Will need to apply further aggregation to this.

`g.filter(func, dropna=True,` `*args, **kwargs)`	Return the original dataframe but with filtered groups removed. func is a predicate function that accepts a group and returns True to keep values from group. If `dropna=False`, groups that evaluate to False are filled with NaN.

`g.first(numeric_only=False, min_count=-1)`	Return the first row of each group. If `min_count` set to positive value, then group must have that many rows or values are filled with NaN.
`g.get_group(name, obj=None)`	Return a dataframe with named group.
`g.groups`	Property with dictionary mapping group name to list of index values. (See `.indices`.)
`g.head(n=5)`	Return the first n rows of each group. Uses original index.
`g.idxmax(axis=0, skipna=True)`	Return an index label of maximum value for each group.
`g.idxmin(axis=0, skipna=True)`	Return an index label of minimum value for each group.
`g.indices`	Property with a dictionary mapping group name to `np.array` of index values. (See `.groups`.)
`g.last(numeric_only=False, min_count=-1)`	Return the last row of each group. If `min_count` set to positive value, then group must have that many rows or values are filled with NaN.
`g.max(numeric_only=False, min_count=-1)`	Return the maximum row of each group. If `min_count` set to positive value, then group must have that many rows or values are filled with NaN.
`g.mean(numeric_only=True)`	Return the mean of each group.
`g.min(numeric_only=False, min_count=-1)`	Return the minimum row of each group. If `min_count` set to positive value, then group must have that many rows or values are filled with NaN.
`g.ndim`	Property with the number of dimensions of result.
`g.ngroup(ascending=True)`	Return a series with original index and values for each group number.
`g.ngroups`	Property with the number of groups.
`g.nth(n, dropna=None)`	Take the nth row from each group.
`g.nunique(dropna=True)`	Return a dataframe with unique counts for each group.
`g.ohlc()`	Return a dataframe with open, high, low, and close values for each group.

`g.pipe(func, *args, **kwargs)`	Apply the func to each group.
`g.prod(numeric_only=True, min_count=0)`	Return a dataframe with product of each group.
`g.quantile(q=.5, interpolation='linear')`	Return a dataframe with quantile for each group. Can pass a list for q and get inner index for each value.
`g.rank(method='average', na_option='keep', ascending=True, pct=False, axis=0)`	Return a dataframe with numerical ranks for each group. method allows to specify tie handling. 'average', 'min', 'max', 'first' (uses order they appear in series), 'dense' (like 'min', but rank only increases by one after tie). na_option allows you to specify NaN handling. 'keep' (stay at NaN), 'top' (move to smallest), 'bottom' (move to largest).
`g.resample(rule, *args, **kwargs)`	Create a resample object with offset alias frequency specified by rule. Will need to apply further aggregation to this.
`g.rolling(window_size)`	Create a rolling grouper. Will need to apply further aggregation to this.
`g.sample(n=None, frac=None, replace=False, weights=None, random_state=None)`	Return a dataframe with sample from each group. Uses original index.
`g.sem(ddof=1)`	Return the mean of standard error of mean each group. Can specify degrees of freedom (ddof).
`g.shift(periods=1, freq=None, axis=0, fill_value=None`	Create a shifted values for each group. Uses original index.
`g.size()`	Return a series with size of each group.
`g.skew(axis=0, skipna=True, level=None, numeric_only=False)`	Return a series with numeric columns inserted as inner level of grouped index with unbiased skew.
`g.std(ddof=1)`	Return the standard deviation of each group. Can specify degrees of freedom (ddof).
`g.sum(numeric_only=True, min_count=0)`	Return a dataframe with the sum of each group.
`g.tail(n=5)`	Return the last n rows of each group. Uses original index.

g.take(indices, axis=0)	Return a dataframe with the index positions (indices) from each group. Positions are relative to group.
g.transform(func, *args, **kwargs)	Return a dataframe with the original index. The function will get passed a group and should return dataframe with same dimensions as group.
g.var(ddof=1)	Return the variance of each group. Can specify degrees of freedom (ddof).

Table 27.2: Groupby Methods and Operations

27.7 Summary

Grouping is one of the most powerful tools that pandas provides. It is the underpinning of the .pivot_table method, which in turn implements the pd.crosstab function. These constructs can be hard to learn because of the inherent complexity of the operation, the hierarchical nature of the result, and the syntax. If you are using .groupby remember to write out your chains and step through them one step at a time. That will help you understand what is going on. You will also need to practice these. Once you learn the syntax, practicing will help you master these concepts.

27.8 Exercises

With a dataset of your choice:

1. Group by a categorical column and take the mean of the numeric columns.

2. Group by a categorical column and take the mean and max of the numeric columns.

3. Group by a categorical column and apply a custom aggregation function that calculates the mode of the numeric columns.

4. Group by two categorical columns and take the mean of the numeric columns.

5. Group by binned numeric column and take the mean of the numeric columns.

Chapter 28

More Aggregations

In the previous chapter, we introduced grouping and the related pivoting and cross-tabulation functionality of pandas. We will dive in a little deeper and explore the .transform method and the .filter method of a groupby object.

28.1 Aggregations while Keeping Rows

Let's assume we are still looking at the JetBrains dataset and wanted to add a new column, the count of responses from a country. One way to do that would be to create a pivot table (or groupby) of the count of responses for each country and then merge that data back into the original dataframe. However, if we use the .transform method following .groupby we get the aggregation, but they are not collapsed. The result is in terms of the original index.

This is one of the reasons I gravitate towards .groupby instead of .pivot_table, the flexibility. (Coming from a software backward and familiarity with SQL probably doesn't hurt either).

Here is the count of the country for each original row. We can provide our own function to the .transform method, or take advantage of existing functions. We want to use the 'size' function to get new counts. However, we just want to apply it to a single column, it doesn't matter which column we choose, so I will use *age*:

```
>>> import pandas as pd
>>> url = 'https://github.com/mattharrison/datasets/raw/master/data/'\
...        '2020-jetbrains-python-survey.csv'
>>> jb = pd.read_csv(url)
>>> jb2 = tweak_jb(jb)
```

Transform Operation

auto

	make	year	cylinders	drive	city08
0	BMW	1984	4.00	nan	21
1	BMW	1984	4.00	nan	21
2	Chevrolet	1984	8.00	nan	13
3	Chevrolet	1984	8.00	nan	13
4	Ford	1984	4.00	nan	21
232	BMW	2020	4.00	Rear-Wheel	21
233	Chevrolet	2020	4.00	Front-Whee	22
234	Chevrolet	2020	4.00	Front-Whee	30
235	Ford	2020	4.00	Front-Whee	24
236	Ford	2020	4.00	Front-Whee	24

```
(auto
  .groupby(['year', 'make'])
  .city08
  .mean())
```

```
(auto
  .groupby(['year', 'make'])
  .city08
  .transform('mean'))
```

.transform preserves original index

1984	BMW	21.00
1984	Chevrolet	13.00
1984	Ford	21.00
1985	BMW	19.50
1985	Chevrolet	11.50
2019	Ford	16.00
2019	Tesla	132.00
2020	BMW	22.50
2020	Chevrolet	26.00
2020	Ford	24.00

0	21.00
1	21.00
2	13.00
3	13.00
4	21.00
232	22.50
233	26.00
234	26.00
235	24.00
236	24.00

Figure 28.1: The .transform method allows us to perform aggregations on groups but returns the resulting aggregations in terms of the original index.

```
>>> (jb2
...    .groupby('country_live')
...    .age
...    .transform('size')
... )
1            1063
2            2697
10            334
11           2697
13            135
              ...
54456          99
54457         502
54459         502
54460         298
54461          18
Name: age, Length: 13711, dtype: int64
```

Here is the code to create a new column *country_responses*:

```
>>> (jb2
...    .assign(country_responses=(jb2
...        .groupby('country_live')
...        .age
...        .transform('size')))
... )
      age are_you_datascientist  ... python3_ver country_responses
1      21                  True  ...         3.6              1063
2      30                 False  ...         3.6              2697
10     21                 False  ...         3.8               334
11     21                  True  ...         3.9              2697
13     30                  True  ...         3.7               135
...   ...                   ...  ...         ...               ...
54456  30                 False  ...         3.6                99
54457  21                 False  ...         3.6               502
54459  21                 False  ...         3.7               502
54460  30                  True  ...         3.7               298
54461  21                 False  ...         3.8                18

[13711 rows x 21 columns]
```

Below is a table with the strings that `.transform` accepts (you can find these in `pd.core.groupby.generic.base.transform_kernel_allowlist`). Those that return a series are marked with (S).

String	Description
'all'	Returns True for every value if every value is truthy.
'any'	Returns True for every value if any value is truthy.
'backfill'	Backfills values for group.
'bfill'	Backfills values for group.
'count'	Count of non-NA values for group.
'cumcount'	Number of each item in group starting at 0 (S).
'cummax'	Cumulative maximum for each group.
'cummin'	Cumulative minimum for each group.
'cumprod'	Cumulative product for each group.
'cumsum'	Cumulative sum for each group.
'diff'	Subtract the previous row from each row. Group needs to be numeric.
'ffill'	Forward fill each group.
'fillna'	Fill missing values for each group. Must specify method ('ffill' or 'bfill') or value parameter.
'first'	First row for each group.
'idxmax'	Index of maximum value for each group.
'idxmin'	Index of minimum value for each group.
'last'	Last row for each group.
'mad'	Mean absolute deviation for each group.
'max'	Maximum value for each group.
'mean'	Mean value for each group.
'median'	Mean value for each group.
'min'	Minimum value for each group.
'nth'	Nth value for each group. Must specify n parameter.
'nunique'	Number of unique values for each group.
'pad'	Synonym for 'ffill'.
'pct_change'	Percent change from current row and previous for each group. Group needs to be numeric.
'prod'	Product of each group.
'quantile'	Median of each group. Specify q (0-1) to change quantile. Group needs to be numeric.

`'rank'`	Rank of each group.
`'sem'`	Unbiased standard error of each group.
`'shift'`	Shift each group row down. Can specify `periods` (default 1), or `freq` with date index.
`'size'`	Size of each group. Only works for a group with a single column (not dataframe).
`'skew'`	Skew of each group.
`'std'`	Standard deviation of each group.
`'sum'`	Sum of each group. (Will add strings!)
`'var'`	Variance of each group.

Table 28.1: Groupby Transform String

28.2 Filtering Parts of Groups

Our treatment of grouping operations has shown us how to aggregate by certain columns. In the previous section, we explored the `.transform` method of a groupby object and saw that we can calculate aggregations on groups but retain the original index. In this section, we will explore how to filter parts of groups by an aggregation but return the result with the original index.

Using the cleaned up JetBrains data, let's remove any row where the size of the country is less than the median size of countries. It looks like the median value is 60.5:

```
>>> (jb2
...    .country_live
...    .value_counts())
United States      2697
Germany            1137
India              1063
United Kingdom      699
France              674
                    ...
Saudi Arabia         12
Sri Lanka            10
Morocco               9
Tunisia               7
Uzbekistan            4
Name: country_live, Length: 76, dtype: int64
```

```
>>> (jb2
...    .country_live
...    .value_counts()
...    .median())
60.5
```

With our existing pandas knowledge, we could calculate the median size and then filter out countries below those sizes:

```
>>> countries_to_remove = (jb2
...    .country_live
...    .value_counts()
...    .lt(60.5)
...    .index)
```

Here is the result. Note that the index values are skipping, hinting that some filtering is going on:

```
>>> (jb2
...    .query('~country_live.isin(@countries_to_remove)')
...    )
        age are_you_datascientist  ...  years_of_coding python3_ver
1        21                  True  ...              3.0         3.6
2        30                 False  ...              3.0         3.6
10       21                 False  ...              1.0         3.8
11       21                  True  ...              3.0         3.9
13       30                  True  ...              3.0         3.7
...     ...                   ...  ...              ...         ...
54450    30                 False  ...             11.0         3.8
54456    30                 False  ...              6.0         3.6
54457    21                 False  ...              1.0         3.6
54459    21                 False  ...              6.0         3.7
54460    30                  True  ...              3.0         3.7

[12635 rows x 20 columns]
```

The .filter method of the groupby object makes the previous few lines a single operation. The .filter method accepts a function that takes the current group. If the function returns True (it must return a scalar, not a series or dataframe), the rows are kept for the result:

```
>>> (jb2
...    .groupby('country_live')
...    .filter(lambda g: g.country_live.size >= 60.5)
...    )
        age are_you_datascientist  ...  years_of_coding python3_ver
1        21                  True  ...              3.0         3.6
```

2	30	False	...		3.0	3.6
10	21	False	...		1.0	3.8
11	21	True	...		3.0	3.9
13	30	True	...		3.0	3.7
...	...	...	...		...	...
54450	30	False	...		11.0	3.8
54456	30	False	...		6.0	3.6
54457	21	False	...		1.0	3.6
54459	21	False	...		6.0	3.7
54460	30	True	...		3.0	3.7

```
[12635 rows x 20 columns]
```

Method	Description
g.filter(func, dropna=True, *args, **kwargs)	Return the original dataframe but with filtered groups removed. func is a predicate function that accepts a group and returns True to keep values from group. If dropna=False, groups that evaluate to False are filled with NaN.
g.transform(func, *args, **kwargs)	Return a dataframe with the original index. The function will get passed a group and should return dataframe with same dimensions as group.

Table 28.2: Chapter Groupby Methods

28.3 Summary

You often group and aggregate, but want to get the result in terms of the original index, not the aggregated index. The .transform method will allow you to preserve the original index. If you want to filter based on aggregated data but keep the original index (sans filtered rows), use the .filter method on the groupby object.

28.4 Exercises

With a dataset of your choice:

1. Add a new column that is the sum of a numeric column that was grouped by a string column.

Filter Operation

auto

	make	year	cylinders	drive	city08
0	BMW	1984	4.00	nan	21
1	BMW	1984	4.00	nan	21
2	Chevrolet	1984	8.00	nan	13
3	Chevrolet	1984	8.00	nan	13
4	Ford	1984	4.00	nan	21
232	BMW	2020	4.00	Rear-Wheel	21
233	Chevrolet	2020	4.00	Front-Whee	22
234	Chevrolet	2020	4.00	Front-Whee	30
235	Ford	2020	4.00	Front-Whee	24
236	Ford	2020	4.00	Front-Whee	24

```
(auto
  .groupby(['year', 'make'])
  .city08
  .mean() > 20)
```

```
(auto
  .groupby(['year', 'make'])
  .city08
  .filter(lambda g:g.mean() > 20)
)
```
Removed because filter was false

1984	BMW	True
1984	Chevrolet	False
1984	Ford	True
1985	BMW	False
1985	Chevrolet	False
2019	Ford	False
2019	Tesla	True
2020	BMW	True
2020	Chevrolet	True
2020	Ford	True

0	21
1	21
4	21
5	21
16	21
232	21
233	22
234	30
235	24
236	24

Figure 28.2: The .filter method allows us to filter in terms of the original data based on aggregations on groups.

2. Filter out the rows that have less than 3 entries when grouped by a string column.

Chapter 29

Cross-tabulation Deep Dive

We have seen that you can emulate some of the groupby and pivot table actions with the crosstab function. (In fact, if you look at the source code for crosstab, you will see that it calls .pivot_table under the covers. And .pivot_table calls .groupby under the covers!)

Let's explore some more of the cross-tabulation functionality using the Presidential data.

29.1 Cross-tabulation Summaries

Using the JetBrains dataset, let us summarize the count of respondents by country and age:

```
>>> import pandas as pd
>>> url = 'https://github.com/mattharrison/datasets/raw/master/data/'\
...       '2020-jetbrains-python-survey.csv'
>>> jb = pd.read_csv(url)
>>> jb2 = tweak_jb(jb)

>>> pd.crosstab(index=jb2.country_live, columns=jb2.age)
age             18    21    30    40    50    60
country_live
Algeria          2     7     5     3     0     1
Argentina        1    38    44    20     5     1
Armenia          1    13     3     0     0     0
Australia        4    58   110    63    30     9
Austria          1    31    62    22    12     0
...             ..   ...   ...   ...   ...   ...
United States   40   753  1042   478   264   120
```

```
Uruguay          0     6    13     1     0     0
Uzbekistan       0     4     0     0     0     0
Venezuela        1    10     4     5     2     0
Viet Nam         1    26     4     1     0     1

[76 rows x 6 columns]
```

29.2 Adding Margins

Both .pivot_table and crosstab have a margins parameter that will put in a
column and row at the right and bottom respectively that summarize the data:

```
>>> pd.crosstab(index=jb2.country_live, columns=jb2.age,
...      margins=True)
age            18    21    30    40    50    60    All
country_live
Algeria         2     7     5     3     0     1     18
Argentina       1    38    44    20     5     1    109
Armenia         1    13     3     0     0     0     17
Australia       4    58   110    63    30     9    274
Austria         1    31    62    22    12     0    128
...            ...   ...   ...   ...   ...   ...    ...
Uruguay         0     6    13     1     0     0     20
Uzbekistan      0     4     0     0     0     0      4
Venezuela       1    10     4     5     2     0     22
Viet Nam        1    26     4     1     0     1     33
All           315  5270  5054  2028   822   222  13711

[77 rows x 7 columns]
```

29.3 Normalizing Results

The crosstab function has another parameter, normalize, that will calculate the
percent of each cell:

```
>>> pd.crosstab(index=jb2.country_live, columns=jb2.age,
...      normalize=True)
age                  18        21    ...        50        60
country_live                        ...
Algeria        0.000146  0.000511    ...  0.000000  0.000073
Argentina      0.000073  0.002771    ...  0.000365  0.000073
Armenia        0.000073  0.000948    ...  0.000000  0.000000
Australia      0.000292  0.004230    ...  0.002188  0.000656
```

```
Austria          0.000073  0.002261  ...  0.000875  0.000000
...                   ...       ...  ...       ...       ...
United States    0.002917  0.054919  ...  0.019255  0.008752
Uruguay          0.000000  0.000438  ...  0.000000  0.000000
Uzbekistan       0.000000  0.000292  ...  0.000000  0.000000
Venezuela        0.000073  0.000729  ...  0.000146  0.000000
Viet Nam         0.000073  0.001896  ...  0.000000  0.000073

[76 rows x 6 columns]
```

You can also normalize down the columns or across the rows. (This seems backwards compared to most axis operations to me as specifying 'columns' normally means to apply the operation across the columns axis.) Here we normalize each column to sum to one:

```
>>> pd.crosstab(index=jb2.country_live, columns=jb2.age,
...       normalize='columns')
age                    18        21  ...        50        60
country_live                            ...
Algeria          0.006349  0.001328  ...  0.000000  0.004505
Argentina        0.003175  0.007211  ...  0.006083  0.004505
Armenia          0.003175  0.002467  ...  0.000000  0.000000
Australia        0.012698  0.011006  ...  0.036496  0.040541
Austria          0.003175  0.005882  ...  0.014599  0.000000
...                   ...       ...  ...       ...       ...
United States    0.126984  0.142884  ...  0.321168  0.540541
Uruguay          0.000000  0.001139  ...  0.000000  0.000000
Uzbekistan       0.000000  0.000759  ...  0.000000  0.000000
Venezuela        0.003175  0.001898  ...  0.002433  0.000000
Viet Nam         0.003175  0.004934  ...  0.000000  0.004505

[76 rows x 6 columns]
```

If you normalize by 'index', every row will sum up to 1.0:

```
>>> pd.crosstab(index=jb2.country_live, columns=jb2.age,
...       normalize='index')
age                    18        21  ...        50        60
country_live                            ...
Algeria          0.111111  0.388889  ...  0.000000  0.055556
Argentina        0.009174  0.348624  ...  0.045872  0.009174
Armenia          0.058824  0.764706  ...  0.000000  0.000000
Australia        0.014599  0.211679  ...  0.109489  0.032847
Austria          0.007812  0.242188  ...  0.093750  0.000000
...                   ...       ...  ...       ...       ...
United States    0.014831  0.279199  ...  0.097887  0.044494
Uruguay          0.000000  0.300000  ...  0.000000  0.000000
```

```
Uzbekistan       0.000000   1.000000   ...   0.000000   0.000000
Venezuela        0.045455   0.454545   ...   0.090909   0.000000
Viet Nam         0.030303   0.787879   ...   0.000000   0.030303

[76 rows x 6 columns]
```

29.4   Hierarchical Columns with Cross Tabulations

In addition, we can create hierarchical indices and columns with crosstab. Let's look at the breakdown of country and age by where people use Python and Python version, and then focus on the United States:

```
>>> (pd.crosstab(index=[jb2.country_live, jb2.age],
...       columns=[jb2.use_python_most, jb2.python3_version_most])
...     .loc[['United States']]
... )
use_python_most            Computer graphics  ... Web development
python3_version_most Python 3_5 or lower     ...        Python 3_9
country_live   age                           ...
United States  18                         0  ...              0
               21                         0  ...              4
               30                         0  ...             14
               40                         0  ...              8
               50                         0  ...              2
               60                         0  ...              1

[6 rows x 84 columns]
```

Let's dive in a little more and just look at data analysis and web development:

```
>>> (pd.crosstab(index=[jb2.country_live, jb2.age],
...       columns=[jb2.use_python_most, jb2.python3_version_most])
...     .loc[['United States'], ['Data analysis', 'Web development']]
... )
use_python_most              Data analysis  ... Web development
python3_version_most Python 3_5 or lower   ...        Python 3_9
country_live   age                         ...
United States  18                       0  ...              0
               21                       1  ...              4
               30                       3  ...             14
               40                       0  ...              8
               50                       2  ...              2
               60                       0  ...              1
```

```
(pd.crosstab([jb2.country_live, jb2.age], [jb2.use_python_most, jb2.python3_version_most])
  .loc[['United States'], ['Data analysis', 'Web development']]
  .style.background_gradient(cmap='viridis', axis=None)
)
```

country_live	use_python_most	Data analysis					Web development				
	python3_version_most	3.5	3.6	3.7	3.8	3.9	3.5	3.6	3.7	3.8	3.9
	age										
	18.0	0	0	1	5	0	0	0	1	4	0
	21.0	1	18	48	64	11	3	28	54	81	4
United States	30.0	3	29	66	90	12	3	60	77	129	14
	40.0	0	14	30	45	3	1	14	26	66	8
	50.0	2	6	26	36	1	0	10	12	14	2
	60.0	0	1	11	11	1	0	3	5	5	1

Figure 29.1: Jupyter showing a view of dataframe with a heatmap. This pulls attention to versions and ages that are most common.

```
[6 rows x 10 columns]
```

29.5 Heatmaps

Let me show you one more trick. Remember how I said humans aren't optimized for pulling out the parts that stand out? I like to add some visualizations to make this pop. I'm going to color the background (this works great in Jupyter, if I needed to generate a plot, I would use Seaborn's heatmap function). I will use the .style attribute to change the background gradient:

```
(pd.crosstab(index=[jb2.country_live, jb2.age],
    columns=[jb2.use_python_most, jb2.python3_version_most])
  .loc[['United States'], ['Data analysis', 'Web development']]
  .style.background_gradient(cmap='viridis', axis=None)
)
```

This makes it clear that in this data Python 3.8 is the most popular, as is age 30.

Method	Description

`pd.crosstab(index, columns,`
`    values=None, rownames=None,`
`    colnames=None, aggfunc=None,`
`    margins=False,`
`    margins_name='All',`
`    dropna=True, normalize=False)`
	Create a cross tabulation (counts by default) from `index` (series or list of series) and `columns` (series or list of series). Can specify a column (series) to aggregate values along with a function, `aggfunc`. Using `margins=True` will add subtotals. Using `dropna=False` will keep columns that have no values. Can normalize over `'all'` values, the rows (`'index'`), or the `'columns'`.

`.style.background_gradient(`
`    cmap='PuBu', low=0, high=0,`
`    axis=0, subset=None,`
`    text_color_threshold=0.408,`
`    vmin=None, vmax=None,`
`    gmap=None)`
	Color a dataframe in Jupyter with Matplotlib colormap (`cmap`). Specify the ends of color map with `vmin` and `cmax`. If `axis=None` apply to whole dataframe.

Table 29.1: Chapter Methods

29.6 Summary

We could live in a world without the `pd.crosstab` function. However, for certain operations, it is much more convenient than `.groupby` or `.pivot_table`. If you master this function, you can make quick work of summarizing categoricals.

29.7 Exercises

With a dataset of your choice:

1. Summarize the count of one categorical column against another.

2. Summarize the count of one categorical column against another, adding margins.

3. Summarize the count of one categorical column against another in a heatmap.

Chapter 30

Melting, Transposing, and Stacking Data

We have shown a lot of ways to manipulate a dataframe. But we are not done yet. In this chapter, we will show some of the more complicated operations that you can do to a dataframe to bend the data to your will. You probably will not use these operations very often, but you will be grateful they are around when you need them.

30.1 Melting Data

Another transformation we can do to data is "melt" it. Before looking at the method to melt data, let's discuss the structure of data. Two ways to organize the same data are "wide" (also called *stacked* or *record* form) and "long" (sometimes called *tidy* form) data. (Note that this is different from "big data", which refers to the amount of data.)

An OLAP database is an analytical database optimized for reporting. In OLAP terms, there is a notion of a *fact* and a *dimension*. A fact is a value that is measured and reported on, and a dimension is a value that describes the conditions of the fact. There are often multiple dimensions for a fact. In a sales scenario, typical facts would be the number of sales of an item and the cost. The dimensions might include the store where the item was sold, the date, and the customer.

The dimensions can then be *sliced* to explore the data. We might want to view sales by store. A dimension may be hierarchical, a store could have a region, zip code, or state, and we could view sales by any of those dimensions.

Here is data that tracks students' ages and scores. The test columns are fact columns and the other columns are dimensions:

name	age	test1	test2	teacher
Adam	15	95	80	Ashby
Bob	16	81	82	Ashby
Dave	16	89	84	Jones
Fred	15		88	Jones

The scores data is in a wide format. In contrast to a long, where each row contains a single fact (with perhaps other variables describing the dimensions). If we consider test scores to be a fact, this wide-format has more than one fact in a row. Hence it is wide.

Often, tools require that data be stored in a long-format, and only have one fact per row. This format is *denormalized* and repeats many of the dimensions but may make analysis easier.

One long version of our scores looks like this (note that we dropped teacher information):

name	age	test	score
Adam	15	test1	95
Bob	16	test1	81
Dave	16	test1	89
Fred	15	test1	NaN
Adam	15	test2	80
Bob	16	test2	82
Dave	16	test2	84
Fred	15	test2	88

Let's show how to convert wide data to long data. We will start by creating a dataframe with scores:

```
>>> scores = pd.DataFrame({
...     'name':['Adam', 'Bob', 'Dave', 'Fred'],
...     'age': [15, 16, 16, 15],
...     'test1': [95, 81, 89, None],
...     'test2': [80, 82, 84, 88],
...     'teacher': ['Ashby', 'Ashby', 'Jones', 'Jones']})

>>> scores
    name  age  test1  test2 teacher
0   Adam   15   95.0     80   Ashby
1    Bob   16   81.0     82   Ashby
2   Dave   16   89.0     84   Jones
3   Fred   15    NaN     88   Jones
```

Melting Data

scores

	name	age	test1	test2	teacher
0	Adam	15	95.00	80	Ashby
1	Bob	16	81.00	82	Ashby
2	Suzy	16	89.00	94	Jones
3	Fred	15	nan	88	Jones

```
pd.melt(scores, id_vars=['name', 'age'],
        value_vars=['test1', 'test2'])
```

	name	age	variable	value
0	Adam	15	test1	95.00
1	Bob	16	test1	81.00
2	Suzy	16	test1	89.00
3	Fred	15	test1	nan
4	Adam	15	test2	80.00
5	Bob	16	test2	82.00
6	Suzy	16	test2	94.00
7	Fred	15	test2	88.00

Figure 30.1: Melting data with pandas. Melting allows you to stack columns on top of each other.

Right now, the score for each test is in its own column. If we wanted to calculate the average of all of the tests, it would require some work to pull out all of the test score columns, stack them, and calculate the mean. Let's melt the data and put it into long form. Below, we keep name and age as dimensions, and pull out the test scores as facts:

```
>>> scores.melt(id_vars=['name', 'age'],
...          value_vars=['test1', 'test2'])
   name  age variable  value
0  Adam   15    test1   95.0
1   Bob   16    test1   81.0
2  Dave   16    test1   89.0
3  Fred   15    test1    NaN
4  Adam   15    test2   80.0
5   Bob   16    test2   82.0
6  Dave   16    test2   84.0
7  Fred   15    test2   88.0
```

Using techniques that we have learned we can accomplish this by building up a chain. But the .melt method is a nice convenience method. Here is the hand-rolled non-melt version:

```
>>> (scores
...    .groupby(['name', 'age'])
...    .apply(lambda g: pd.concat([
...        g[['test1']].rename(columns={'test1':'val'}).assign(var='test1'),
...        g[['test2']].rename(columns={'test2':'val'}).assign(var='test2')]))
...    .reset_index()
...    .drop(columns='level_2')
... )
     name   age    val      var
0    Adam    15   95.0    test1
1    Adam    15   80.0    test2
2     Bob    16   81.0    test1
3     Bob    16   82.0    test2
4    Dave    16   89.0    test1
5    Dave    16   84.0    test2
6    Fred    15    NaN    test1
7    Fred    15   88.0    test2
```

As you can see, the melt version is much easier to create.

If we want to change the description of the fact column to a more descriptive name, pass that as the var_name parameter. We can change the name of the value of the column (it defaults to value) by providing a value_name parameter. Here we change the description to *test* and the value to *score*:

```
>>> scores.melt(id_vars=['name', 'age'],
...             value_vars=['test1', 'test2'],
...             var_name='test', value_name='score')
     name   age    test    score
0    Adam    15   test1     95.0
1     Bob    16   test1     81.0
2    Dave    16   test1     89.0
3    Fred    15   test1      NaN
4    Adam    15   test2     80.0
5     Bob    16   test2     82.0
6    Dave    16   test2     84.0
7    Fred    15   test2     88.0
```

If we want to preserve the teacher information, we would need to include it in the id_vars parameter:

```
>>> scores.melt(id_vars=['name', 'age', 'teacher'],
...        value_vars=['test1', 'test2'],
...        var_name='test', value_name='score')
   name  age teacher    test  score
0  Adam   15   Ashby   test1   95.0
1   Bob   16   Ashby   test1   81.0
2  Dave   16   Jones   test1   89.0
3  Fred   15   Jones   test1    NaN
4  Adam   15   Ashby   test2   80.0
5   Bob   16   Ashby   test2   82.0
6  Dave   16   Jones   test2   84.0
7  Fred   15   Jones   test2   88.0
```

Note

Long data is also referred to as *tidy* data. See the Tidy Data paper[14] by Hadley Wickham.

30.2 Un-melting Data

Using a pivot table, we can go from long format to wide format. Here is our melted data from the previous section:

```
>>> melted = scores.melt(id_vars=['name', 'age', 'teacher'],
...        value_vars=['test1', 'test2'],
...        var_name='test', value_name='score')
>>> melted
   name  age teacher    test  score
0  Adam   15   Ashby   test1   95.0
1   Bob   16   Ashby   test1   81.0
2  Dave   16   Jones   test1   89.0
3  Fred   15   Jones   test1    NaN
4  Adam   15   Ashby   test2   80.0
5   Bob   16   Ashby   test2   82.0
6  Dave   16   Jones   test2   84.0
7  Fred   15   Jones   test2   88.0
```

It is a little more involved going in the reverse direction because we will put the id variables that we kept from the original data in a hierarchical index.

---

[14]http://vita.had.co.nz/papers/tidy-data.html

I generally flatten hierarchical indices with the .reset_index method. You can use .pivot_table or .groupby to do this:

```
>>> (melted
...   .pivot_table(index=['name','age', 'teacher'],
...               columns='test', values='score')
...   .reset_index())
test  name  age teacher   test1   test2
0     Adam   15   Ashby    95.0    80.0
1      Bob   16   Ashby    81.0    82.0
2     Dave   16   Jones    89.0    84.0
3     Fred   15   Jones     NaN    88.0

>>> (melted
...   .groupby(['name', 'age', 'teacher', 'test'])
...   .score
...   .mean()
...   .unstack()
...   .reset_index()
... )
test  name  age teacher   test1   test2
0     Adam   15   Ashby    95.0    80.0
1      Bob   16   Ashby    81.0    82.0
2     Dave   16   Jones    89.0    84.0
3     Fred   15   Jones     NaN    88.0
```

30.3 Transposing Data

We have been exploring reshaping data. We have already seen and used a common method to reshape data, the .transpose method or the .T property. Remember, this flips rows and columns.

I find that I use transposition mostly in two places:

- Viewing more data in Jupyter

- Swapping axis for plotting

Transposition often works for viewing more data because pandas uses numeric index values by default. When the numeric index goes into the column, it takes up less horizontal space, and you can see more data without having to scroll around.

I have some thoughts on viewing data. Often when I'm teaching, a student will ask how to turn off the default behavior of pandas in Jupyter

Undoing Melting

melted

	name	age	variable	value
0	Adam	15	test1	95.00
1	Bob	16	test1	81.00
2	Suzy	16	test1	89.00
3	Fred	15	test1	nan
4	Adam	15	test2	80.00
5	Bob	16	test2	82.00
6	Suzy	16	test2	94.00
7	Fred	15	test2	88.00

```
(melted
 .pivot_table(index=['name', 'age'],
              columns='variable', values='value')
 .reset_index()
)
```

	name	age	test1	test2
0	Adam	15	95.00	80.00
1	Bob	16	81.00	82.00
2	Fred	15	nan	88.00
3	Suzy	16	89.00	94.00

Figure 30.2: Unmelting data with pandas. By pivoting the data, you can specify the label column (columns) for the stacked columns (values).

to only show a limited number of rows and columns. (You can change pd.options.display.max_columns and pd.options.display.min rows to modify these if you really want to.) I generally try to dissuade them from changing these settings.

However, if you change these settings to view more data and find yourself scrolling through a million rows of data, your spidey sense should be going off telling you that you are doing things the wrong way. Humans are not made for looking for interesting data by scrolling through rows of data. It is better to use a computer (which is optimized to search through data) to find rows you might be interested in. My two favorite methods of leveraging a computer to search for us are visualization and filtering the data.

On that note, if you use the .transpose method to view more data on your screen, you might not want to transpose your whole data set. Remember that pandas stores and optimizes data by column types. If you make a row that

```
In [189]: jb2
```

Out[189]:

	age	are_you_datascientist	company_size	country_live	employment_status	first_learn_about_main_ide	how_often_use_main_ide	ide_main	is_python_main	job_team	mai
1	21.0	True	5000.0	India	Fully employed by a company / organization	School / University	Daily	VS Code	Yes	Work in a team	Bc a
2	30.0	False	5000.0	United States	Fully employed by a company / organization	Friend / Colleague	Daily	Vim	Yes	Work on your own project(s) independently	Bc a
10	21.0	False	51.0	Other country	Fully employed by a company / organization	School / University	Daily	IntelliJ IDEA	Yes	Work in a team	Bc a
11	21.0	True	51.0	United States	Fully employed by a company / organization	Online learning platform / Online course	Daily	PyCharm Community Edition	Yes	Work in a team	Bc a
13	30.0	True	5000.0	Belgium	Fully employed by a company / organization	Social network	Daily	VS Code	Yes	Work in a team	Bc a
...	...	...	...	...	...	...	...	...	...	...	...
54456	30.0	False	1001.0	Turkey	Fully employed by a company / organization	Friend / Colleague	Daily	PyCharm Community Edition	Yes	Work on your own project(s) independently	Bc a
54457	21.0	False	2.0	Russian Federation	Fully employed by a company / organization	School / University	Daily	Vim	Yes	Work on your own project(s) independently	Bc a
54459	21.0	False	1.0	Russian Federation	Self-employed (a person earning income directi...	Friend / Colleague	Daily	PyCharm Professional Edition	Yes	Work in a team	Bc a
54460	30.0	True	51.0	Spain	Fully employed by a company / organization	Search engines	Daily	Other	Yes	Work on your own project(s) independently	Bc a
54461	21.0	False	11.0	Algeria	Fully employed by a company / organization	Online learning platform / Online course	Daily	VS Code	Yes	Work in a team	Bc a

13711 rows × 19 columns

Figure 30.3: Jupyter showing default view of dataframe. We have ten rows but need to scroll to see all of the data.

contains different data types (strings, dates, numbers) into a column that can be a slow and memory-loving operation. It is better to pull off the head, tail, or take a sample of the data and then transpose it.

When we explored line plots in the plotting section, we showed an example of transposing the data. We had a presidential data set with the names of the president in the index and ratings for various skills in the columns. When we did a line plot of this data, each characteristic was its own line. Instead, we wanted each president to be its own line, so we transposed the data.

30.4 Stacking & Unstacking

I have used the .unstack method previously but not discussed it. It (along with its complement, .stack) is a powerful method to reshape your data.

At a high level, .unstack moves an index level into the columns. Usually we use this operation on multi-index data, moving one of the indices into the

```
In [190]: (jb2
          .head(18)
          .T
          )
```

Out[190]:

	1	2	10	11	13	14	15	17	22	25
age	21.0	30.0	21.0	21.0	30.0	30.0	50.0	30.0	40.0	50.0
are_you_datascientist	True	False	False	True	True	True	False	True	False	True
company_size	5000.0	5000.0	51.0	51.0	5000.0	501.0	1001.0	2.0	51.0	11.0
country_live	India	United States	Other country	United States	Belgium	Ecuador	Germany	Chile	Australia	United States
employment_status	Fully employed by a company / organization	Fully employed by a company / organization	Fully employed by a company / organization	Fully employed by a company / organization	Fully employed by a company / organization	Fully employed by a company / organization	Fully employed by a company / organization	Fully employed by a company / organization	Fully employed by a company / organization	Fully employed by a company / organization
first_learn_about_main_ide	School / University	Friend / Colleague	School / University	Online learning platform / Online course	Social network	Other	Friend / Colleague	Social network	Technical review / Forum / Blog	Search engines
how_often_use_main_ide	Daily	Daily	Daily	Daily	Daily	Weekly	Daily	Daily	Daily	Daily
ide_main	VS Code	Vim	IntelliJ IDEA	PyCharm Community Edition	VS Code	VS Code	Vim	VS Code	VS Code	PyCharm Professional Edition
is_python_main	Yes	Yes	Yes	Yes	Yes	Yes	No, I use Python as a secondary language	Yes	No, I use Python as a secondary language	Yes
job_team	Work in a team	Work on your own project(s) Independently	Work in a team	Work in a team	Work in a team	Work on your own project(s) Independently	Work in a team	Work on your own project(s) independently	Work in a team	Work on your own project(s) Independently
main_purposes	Both for work and personal	Both for work and personal	Both for work and personal	Both for work and personal	Both for work and personal	For work	For work	Both for work and personal	Both for work and personal	Both for work and personal
missing_features_main_ide	No, it has all the features I need	No, it has all the features I need	No, it has all the features I need	No, it has all the features I need	No, it has all the features I need	No, It has all the features I need	Yes – Please list:	No, It has all the features I need	No, it has all the features I need	Yes – Please list:
nps_main_ide	8.0	10.0	10.0	9.0	10.0	10.0	5.0	10.0	10.0	9.0
python_years	3.0	3.0	1.0	3.0	6.0	3.0	1.0	1.0	6.0	11.0
python3_version_most	3.6	3.6	3.8	3.9	3.7	3.8	3.6	3.8	3.7	3.8
several_projects	Yes, I work on one main and several side projects	Yes, I work on one main and several side projects	Yes, I work on one main and several side projects	Yes, I work on many different projects	Yes, I work on many different projects	Yes, I work on many different projects	Yes, I work on many different projects	Yes, I work on many different projects	Yes, I work on one main and several side projects	Yes, I work on one main and several side projects
team_size	2	5	2	2	2	5	2	0	2	2
use_python_most	Software prototyping	DevOps / System administration / Writing autom...	Web development	Data analysis	Data analysis	Programming of web parsers / scrapers / crawlers	Web development	Machine learning	Software prototyping	Data analysis
years_of_coding	3.0	3.0	1.0	3.0	3.0	3.0	11.0	1.0	11.0	11.0

Figure 30.4: Jupyter showing a transposed view of dataframe. Notice that we see ten complete samples of data showing on the screen without scrolling.

columns (creating hierarchical columns). The .stack method does the reverse, moving a multi-level column into the index.

Let's look at an example using the JetBrains data:

```
>>> import pandas as pd
>>> url = 'https://github.com/mattharrison/datasets/raw/master/data/'\
...       '2020-jetbrains-python-survey.csv'
>>> jb = pd.read_csv(url)
>>> jb2 = tweak_jb(jb)

>>> jb2
      age are_you_datascientist  ...  years_of_coding python3_ver
1      21                  True  ...              3.0         3.6
2      30                 False  ...              3.0         3.6
```

10	21	False	...	1.0	3.8
11	21	True	...	3.0	3.9
13	30	True	...	3.0	3.7
...	...	...	...	...	...
54456	30	False	...	6.0	3.6
54457	21	False	...	1.0	3.6
54459	21	False	...	6.0	3.7
54460	30	True	...	3.0	3.7
54461	21	False	...	1.0	3.8

```
[13711 rows x 20 columns]
```

We will create a hierarchical or multi-index by grouping with multiple columns. Let's take the size of responses to *are_you_datascientist* column by country:

```
>>> (jb2
...     .groupby(['country_live', 'are_you_datascientist'])
...     .size()
... )
country_live  are_you_datascientist
Algeria       False                    12
              True                      5
              Other                     1
Argentina     False                    89
              True                     16
                                       ..
Venezuela     True                      4
              Other                     2
Viet Nam      False                    16
              True                     14
              Other                     3
Length: 228, dtype: int64
```

Notice that the result is a series with a multi-index. This result is useful but a little hard to scan through. It would be easier if we had countries in the index and each of the responses to *are_you_datascientist* as their own column. We can do that by unstacking the inner index into a column (note that you could also do this operation with pd.crosstab):

```
>>> (jb2
...     .groupby(['country_live', 'are_you_datascientist'])
...     .size()
...     .unstack()
... )
are_you_datascientist  False   True   Other
```

```
country_live
Algeria                   12       5       1
Argentina                 89      16       4
Armenia                   15       2       0
Australia                210      50      14
Austria                   93      32       3
...                      ...     ...     ...
United States           2008     589     100
Uruguay                   10       9       1
Uzbekistan                 3       1       0
Venezuela                 16       4       2
Viet Nam                  16      14       3

[76 rows x 3 columns]
```

By default, `.unstack` moves the inner index up to the columns. Because this operation was performed on a series, it is changed to a dataframe. (If we perform `.unstack` on a dataframe, we will get a dataframe with nested columns.)

If we wanted to pull up the country index (which is the outer index), we could specify it by name or by position. The position is 0 for the outer index, *country_live*, and 1 for *are_you_datascientist*:

```
>>> (jb2
...    .groupby(['country_live', 'are_you_datascientist'])
...    .size()
...    .unstack(0)
... )
country_live          Algeria   Argentina  ...  Venezuela  Viet Nam
are_you_datascientist                       ...
False                      12          89  ...         16        16
True                        5          16  ...          4        14
Other                       1           4  ...          2         3

[3 rows x 76 columns]
```

I would prefer to use the index name (rather than the index position) in this case as it is easier to understand (and one less thing you need to memorize):

```
>>> (jb2
...    .groupby(['country_live', 'are_you_datascientist'])
...    .size()
...    .unstack('country_live')
... )
country_live          Algeria   Argentina  ...  Venezuela  Viet Nam
are_you_datascientist                       ...
```

False	12	89	...	16	16
True	5	16	...	4	14
Other	1	4	...	2	3

```
[3 rows x 76 columns]
```

30.5 Stacking

Let's look at stacking. Previously we saw that we could specify multiple aggregation functions with the .pivot_table method. The result is a dataframe with hierarchical columns:

```
>>> (jb2
...    .pivot_table(index='country_live',
...                 aggfunc={'age': ['min', 'max'],
...                          'company_size': ['min', 'max']})
... )
               age      company_size
               max min          max min
country_live
Algeria         60  18          5000   1
Argentina       60  18          5000   1
Armenia         30  18          5000   1
Australia       60  18          5000   1
Austria         50  18          5000   1
...             ..  ..          ...   ..
United States   60  18          5000   1
Uruguay         40  21          5000   2
Uzbekistan      21  21          5000   1
Venezuela       50  18          5000   1
Viet Nam        60  18          5000   1

[76 rows x 4 columns]
```

In a prior example, we saw that we could unstack the index by the name of the index (the name of the column before it was put in the index) or by the position. In this example we want to stack one of the hierarchical columns into the index. The columns do not have a name, so we will have to use the position. The outermost column level is 0. Stacking by this level will move *age* and *company_size* into the index:

```
>>> (jb2
...    .pivot_table(index='country_live',
...                 aggfunc={'age': ['min', 'max'],
```

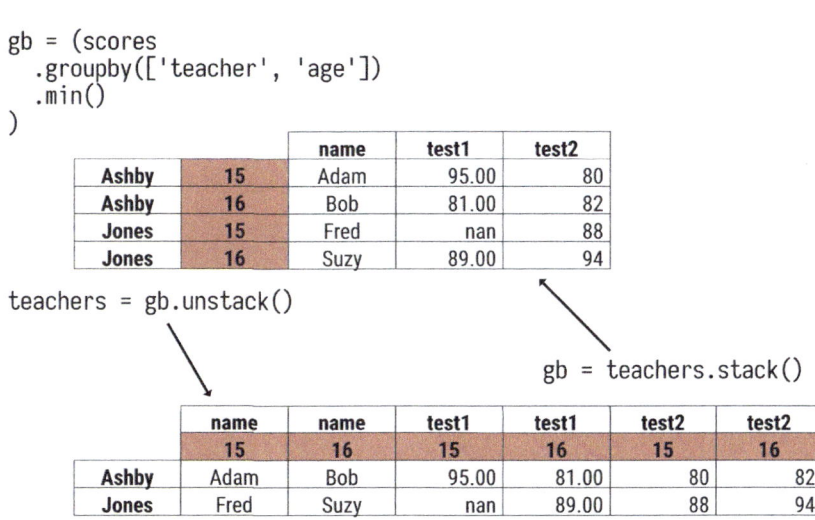

Figure 30.5: Stacking and unstacking data with pandas. Stacking puts column labels into the index. Unstacking moves index labels into columns.

```
...                    'company_size': ['min', 'max']})
...    .stack(0)
... )
                       max min
country_live
Algeria     age         60  18
            company_size 5000  1
Argentina   age         60  18
            company_size 5000  1
Armenia     age         30  18
...                     ...  ..
Uzbekistan  company_size 5000  1
Venezuela   age         50  18
```

```
               company_size  5000   1
Viet Nam       age                 60  18
               company_size  5000   1
```

`[152 rows x 2 columns]`

If we want to move the inner columns, *max* and *min*, into the index this is the default behavior. Alternatively, we can specify level 1 as an argument for .stack:

```
>>> (jb2
...   .pivot_table(index='country_live',
...               aggfunc={'age': ['min', 'max'],
...                        'company_size': ['min', 'max']})
...   .stack(1)
... )
                    age company_size
country_live
Algeria      max    60          5000
             min    18             1
Argentina    max    60          5000
             min    18             1
Armenia      max    30          5000
...                 ..           ...
Uzbekistan   min    21             1
Venezuela    max    50          5000
             min    18             1
Viet Nam     max    60          5000
             min    18             1
```

`[152 rows x 2 columns]`

Finally, if you want to change the order of the levels in a hierarchical index or columns, you can use the .swaplevel method:

```
>>> (jb2
...   .pivot_table(index='country_live',
...               aggfunc={'age': ['min', 'max'],
...                        'company_size': ['min', 'max']})
...   .stack(1)
...   .swaplevel()
... )
                    age company_size
    country_live
max Algeria          60          5000
min Algeria          18             1
max Argentina        60          5000
```

```
min  Argentina      18              1
max  Armenia        30           5000
...                 ..            ...
min  Uzbekistan     21              1
max  Venezuela      50           5000
min  Venezuela      18              1
max  Viet Nam       60           5000
min  Viet Nam       18              1

[152 rows x 2 columns]
```

30.6 Flattening Hierarchical Indexes and Columns

When you start applying grouping operations, you can end up with a hierarchical index or columns. In practice, I find these nested structures difficult to deal with and often want to remove (or flatten them).

Let's start by discussing removing the hierarchical index as that is simple. We use the .reset_index method. Here is a dataframe with a hierarchical index:

```
>>> (jb2
...    .groupby(['country_live', 'age'])
...    .mean()
... )
                    company_size  ...  python3_ver
country_live age                  ...
Algeria      18              2.0  ...     3.650000
             21       725.428571  ...     3.757143
             30              1.6  ...     3.700000
             40           1674.0  ...     3.766667
             50             <NA>  ...          NaN
...                           ...  ...          ...
Viet Nam     21       348.346154  ...     3.711538
             30           266.25  ...     3.750000
             40             51.0  ...     3.800000
             50             <NA>  ...          NaN
             60              1.0  ...     3.900000

[456 rows x 6 columns]
```

We can use .reset_index to push each index level into a column:

```
>>> (jb2
...    .groupby(['country_live', 'age'])
...    .mean()
...    .reset_index()
```

357

```
...  )
       country_live    age  ...  years_of_coding  python3_ver
0          Algeria      18  ...         6.000000     3.650000
1          Algeria      21  ...         2.428571     3.757143
2          Algeria      30  ...         3.800000     3.700000
3          Algeria      40  ...         6.666667     3.766667
4          Algeria      50  ...              NaN          NaN
..             ...     ...  ...              ...          ...
451       Viet Nam      21  ...         1.923077     3.711538
452       Viet Nam      30  ...         3.500000     3.750000
453       Viet Nam      40  ...         6.000000     3.800000
454       Viet Nam      50  ...              NaN          NaN
455       Viet Nam      60  ...         1.000000     3.900000

[456 rows x 8 columns]
```

Alternatively, when using .groupby, you can set the as_index parameter to False and the result not insert the grouping columns in the index, they will stay as columns:

```
>>> (jb2
...    .groupby(['country_live', 'age'], as_index=False)
...    .mean()
...  )
       country_live    age  ...  years_of_coding  python3_ver
0          Algeria      18  ...         6.000000     3.650000
1          Algeria      21  ...         2.428571     3.757143
2          Algeria      30  ...         3.800000     3.700000
3          Algeria      40  ...         6.666667     3.766667
4          Algeria      50  ...              NaN          NaN
..             ...     ...  ...              ...          ...
451       Viet Nam      21  ...         1.923077     3.711538
452       Viet Nam      30  ...         3.500000     3.750000
453       Viet Nam      40  ...         6.000000     3.800000
454       Viet Nam      50  ...              NaN          NaN
455       Viet Nam      60  ...         1.000000     3.900000

[456 rows x 8 columns]
```

Now let's explore flattening hierarchical columns. Sadly, the .reset_index method won't work for the column names. We don't want to push the column names into a row, generally, but want to combine them into a single level of column names. And there is no convenience method to do that in pandas.

Here is an example of data with a hierarchical column. For every country we have the mean values for each numeric column broken down by age:

```
>>> (jb2
...    .groupby(['country_live', 'age'])
...    .mean()
...    .unstack()
... )
               company_size              ... python3_ver
age                  18          21       ...        50        60
country_live                             ...
Algeria              2.0    725.428571   ...       NaN   3.900000
Argentina           51.0    459.789474   ...  3.720000   3.800000
Armenia             11.0   1015.461538   ...       NaN        NaN
Australia            4.25  1055.689655   ...  3.756667   3.777778
Austria             11.0    785.258065   ...  3.700000        NaN
...                  ...           ...   ...       ...        ...
United States      707.4   1640.298805   ...  3.742045   3.742500
Uruguay             <NA>         31.0    ...       NaN        NaN
Uzbekistan          <NA>       1265.75   ...       NaN        NaN
Venezuela            2.0         25.1    ...  3.800000        NaN
Viet Nam            51.0    348.346154   ...       NaN   3.900000

[76 rows x 36 columns]
```

In addition to the lack of a convenience method to flatten columns being a gaping hole in the pandas API, to add insult to injury you have to mutate the dataframe to update the columns. Remember, mutation generally throws a wrench in our chaining operations.

To get around this, I make a function that will flatten columns. The function joins each level of columns with an underscore. Then I combine that function with the .pipe method. This lets me do a column flattening operation in a chain:

```
>>> def flatten_cols(df):
...     cols = ['_'.join(map(str, vals))
...             for vals in df.columns.to_flat_index()]
...     df.columns = cols
...     return df

>>> (jb2
...    .groupby(['country_live', 'age'])
...    .mean()
...    .unstack()
...    .pipe(flatten_cols)
... )
               company_size_18   ... python3_ver_60
country_live                     ...
```

359

Flattening Grouping Data with Multiple Aggregations

auto

	make	year	cylinders	drive
1	Ferrari	1985	12.00	Rear-Wheel
2	Dodge	1985	4.00	Front-Whee
3	Dodge	1985	8.00	Rear-Wheel
4	Subaru	1993	4.00	4-Wheel or
5	Subaru	1993	4.00	Front-Whee
41139	Subaru	1993	4.00	Front-Whee
41140	Subaru	1993	4.00	Front-Whee
41141	Subaru	1993	4.00	4-Wheel or
41142	Subaru	1993	4.00	4-Wheel or
41143	Subaru	1993	4.00	4-Wheel or

```
def flatten(df_):
    cols = ['_'.join(cs) for cs in df_.columns.to_flat_index()]
    df_.columns = cols
    return df_
(auto
 .groupby('make')
 .agg(['min', 'max'])
 .pipe(flatten))
```

	year_min	year_max	cylinders_min	cylinders_max
Acura	1986	2020	4.00	6.00
Audi	1984	2020	4.00	12.00
BMW	1984	2020	2.00	12.00
BYD	2012	2019	nan	nan
Bentley	1998	2019	8.00	12.00
VPG	2011	2013	8.00	8.00
Vector	1992	1997	8.00	12.00
Volvo	1984	2019	4.00	8.00
Yugo	1986	1990	4.00	4.00
smart	2008	2019	3.00	3.00

Figure 30.6: Grouping and then flattening hierarchical columns.

360

```
Algeria              2.0  ...       3.900000
Argentina           51.0  ...       3.800000
Armenia             11.0  ...            NaN
Australia           4.25  ...       3.777778
Austria             11.0  ...            NaN
...                  ...  ...            ...
United States      707.4  ...       3.742500
Uruguay            <NA>   ...            NaN
Uzbekistan         <NA>   ...            NaN
Venezuela            2.0  ...            NaN
Viet Nam            51.0  ...       3.900000

[76 rows x 36 columns]
```

Method	Description

`.melt(id_vars=None,`
`    value_vars=None,`
`    var_name=None,`
`    value_name='value',`
`    col_level=None,`
`    ignore_index=True)`
	Return an unpivoted dataframe. With each column in value_vars stack on top of each other. Keep the id_vars columns.

`g.transform(func, *args,` `    **kwargs)`	Return a dataframe with original index. The function will get passed a group and should return a dataframe with same dimensions as group.
`pd.options.display.max_columns`	Property to set to configure pandas to show at most this amount of columns.
`pd.options.display.min_rows`	Property to set to configure pandas to show at most this amount of row.
`.stack(level=-1, dropna=True)`	Push a column level into an index level. Can specify the column level (-1 is innermost).
`.unstack(level=-1, dropna=True)`	Push an index level into a column level. Can specify an index level (-1 is innermost).
`.swaplevel(i=-2, j=-1, axis=0)`	Swap the levels of multi-indexed object (0 is outermost, -1 (or length of multi-index) is innermost). Can specify the name for i and j.

`.reset_index(level=None,`
`  drop=False, col_level=0,`
`  col_fill='')`
	Return a dataframe with new a index (or new level). To remove a level, specify that with level (by position or name). Position 0 is the outermost level, and it goes up. Alternatively, -1 is the innermost level. Index values are moved to columns or dropped if drop=True. col_level determines where index label goes with multiple column levels, other levels will get value of col_fill.

`.pipe(func, *args, **kwargs)`	Apply a function to a dataframe. Return the result of function.

Table 30.1: Chapter Methods

30.7 Summary

In this chapter, we showed how to melt and un-melt data. If you use the Seaborn library for plotting, you might need to transform your data so that you can plot with this library. We also explored stacking and unstacking data. Finally, we showed how to remove nested columns and indexes.

30.8 Exercises

With a dataset of your choice:

1. Melt two numeric columns values into a single column. Add a new column to indicate what the values mean.

2. Un-melt the above.

3. Group by two columns, take the mean and unstack the result.

4. Group by two columns, take the mean, and unstack the result, and flatten the columns.

Chapter 31

Working with Time Series

In this chapter, we will explore how to manipulate and work with time-series data. One thing to note, when we say "time-series", we are not talking about the pandas Series object, but rather data that has a date component. Often we will have that date component in the index of a pandas series or dataframe because that allows us to do time aggregations easily.

31.1 Loading the Data

For this section, I'm going to explore a dataset from the US Geologic Survey that deals with river flow of a river in Utah called the Dirty Devil river[15].

This data is a tab-delimited ASCII file in detail described here[16].

The columns are:

- *agency_cd* - Agency collecting data

- *site_no* - USGS identification number of site

- *datetime* - Date

- *tz_cd* - Timezone

[15]https://nwis.waterdata.usgs.gov/usa/nwis/uv/?cb_00060=on&cb_00065=on-&format=rdb&site_no=09333500&period=&begin_date-=2000-01-01&end_date=2020-09-28

[16]https://help.waterdata.usgs.gov/faq/about-tab-delimited-output Also see this link for a description of the spelling of "gage" https://www.usgs.gov/faqs/why-does-usgs-use-spelling-gage-instead-gauge

- *144166_00060* - Discharge (cubic feet per second)

- *144166_00060_cd* - Status of discharge. "A" (approved), "P" (provisional), "e" (estimate).

- *144167_00065* - Gage height (feet)

- *144167_00065_cd* - Status of gage_height. "A" (approved), "P" (provisional), "e" (estimate).

Here is my code to load the data. I have also included a tweak function that converts the date information to actual dates and renames some columns. Note that the file is not a CSV file, but we can specify tab as a separator. Also, we need to skip a few of the rows:

```
>>> import pandas as pd
>>> url = 'https://github.com/mattharrison/datasets/raw/master'\
...       '/data/dirtydevil.txt'
>>> df = pd.read_csv(url, skiprows=lambda num: num <34 or num == 35,
...                  sep='\t')
>>> def tweak_river(df_):
...     return (df_
...     .assign(datetime=pd.to_datetime(df_.datetime))
...     .rename(columns={'144166_00060': 'cfs',
...                      '144167_00065': 'gage_height'})
...     .set_index('datetime')
... )

>>> dd = tweak_river(df)
>>> dd
                     agency_cd  site_no  ... gage_height  144167_00065_cd
datetime                                 ...
2001-05-07 01:00:00       USGS  9333500  ...         NaN              NaN
2001-05-07 01:15:00       USGS  9333500  ...         NaN              NaN
2001-05-07 01:30:00       USGS  9333500  ...         NaN              NaN
2001-05-07 01:45:00       USGS  9333500  ...         NaN              NaN
2001-05-07 02:00:00       USGS  9333500  ...         NaN              NaN
...                        ...      ...  ...         ...              ...
2020-09-28 08:30:00       USGS  9333500  ...        6.16                P
2020-09-28 08:45:00       USGS  9333500  ...        6.15                P
2020-09-28 09:00:00       USGS  9333500  ...        6.15                P
2020-09-28 09:15:00       USGS  9333500  ...        6.15                P
2020-09-28 09:30:00       USGS  9333500  ...        6.15                P

[539305 rows x 7 columns]
```

31.2   Adding Timezone Information

Many times the date column is missing timezone information. In the Dirty Devil dataset, the *tz_cd* column has offset abbreviations:

```
>>> dd.tz_cd
datetime
2001-05-07 01:00:00    MDT
2001-05-07 01:15:00    MDT
2001-05-07 01:30:00    MDT
2001-05-07 01:45:00    MDT
2001-05-07 02:00:00    MDT
                        ...
2020-09-28 08:30:00    MDT
2020-09-28 08:45:00    MDT
2020-09-28 09:00:00    MDT
2020-09-28 09:15:00    MDT
2020-09-28 09:30:00    MDT
Name: tz_cd, Length: 539305, dtype: object
```

I ignored it above and have "naive" time data. Getting timezone information into a date column can be slow, buggy, or frustrating. I spent a few hours messing around with trying to add timezone information to this dataset.

My takeaway is that although the documentation and API make it appear that pd.to_datetime should handle timezone data, I would not go down that path. Generally, you should use pd.to_datetime to get a naive time and then convert the naive times to timezones with .dt.tz_localize.

I tried concatenating the *datetime* and *tz_cd* columns together and passing that into pd.to_datetime. That worked but took two minutes, whereas code to convert into a naive date column in a fraction of that time (54 ms). I tried using format strings, replacing the timezones with alternate spelling and using offsets with pd.to_datetime[17] in an attempt to speed up the conversion. They silently failed or errored out.

With the help of the pandas core developers, I was able to get that 2 minutes down to 15 seconds with this code. The key points below are using numeric date offsets (not timezone abbreviations) and utc=True:

```
>>> def tweak_river(df_):
...     return (df_
```

---

[17]https://github.com/pandas-dev/pandas/issues/43140

```
...              .assign(datetime=lambda df_:
...                  pd.to_datetime(df_.datetime + " " +
...                      df_.tz_cd.str.replace('MST', '-0700')
...                          .str.replace('MDT', '-0600'),
...                      format='%Y-%m-%d %H:%M %z', utc=True))
...              .rename(columns={'144166_00060': 'cfs',
...                               '144167_00065': 'gage_height'})
...              .set_index('datetime')
...          )
```

However, I was able to get the runtime down to 1 second. The code is more involved, but this is 15-120x faster than the other code.

For my dataset, I wrote the following function, to_america_denver_time, to get my date parsing with timezone information down from 2 minutes to 2 seconds. I group by the offset column and then use the grouping name (the offset name) to call .dt.tz_localize. This creates a date with local times. However, they are using offsets and not timezones.

To add timezone, you need to use .dt.tz_convert after creating the local time:

```
>>> def to_america_denver_time(df_, time_col, tz_col):
...     return (df_
...             .assign(**{tz_col: df_[tz_col].replace('MDT', 'MST7MDT')})
...             .groupby(tz_col)
...             [time_col]
...             .transform(lambda s: pd.to_datetime(s)
...                 .dt.tz_localize(s.name, ambiguous=True)
...                 .dt.tz_convert('America/Denver'))
...         )
```

```
>>> def tweak_river(df_):
...     return (df_
...         .assign(datetime=to_america_denver_time(df_, 'datetime',
...                 'tz_cd'))
...         .rename(columns={'144166_00060': 'cfs',
...                          '144167_00065': 'gage_height'})
...         .set_index('datetime')
...         )
```

```
>>> dd = tweak_river(df)
```

Here is the resulting data:

```
>>> dd
                          agency_cd  ...  gage_height  144167_00065_cd
datetime                            ...
2001-05-07 01:00:00-06:00      USGS  ...          NaN              NaN
2001-05-07 01:15:00-06:00      USGS  ...          NaN              NaN
2001-05-07 01:30:00-06:00      USGS  ...          NaN              NaN
2001-05-07 01:45:00-06:00      USGS  ...          NaN              NaN
2001-05-07 02:00:00-06:00      USGS  ...          NaN              NaN
...                             ...  ...          ...              ...
2020-09-28 08:30:00-06:00      USGS  ...         6.16                P
2020-09-28 08:45:00-06:00      USGS  ...         6.15                P
2020-09-28 09:00:00-06:00      USGS  ...         6.15                P
2020-09-28 09:15:00-06:00      USGS  ...         6.15                P
2020-09-28 09:30:00-06:00      USGS  ...         6.15                P

[539305 rows x 7 columns]
```

Note

One thing that bit me was I was trying to use `'MST'` and `'MDT'` as offset names. The underlying pytz library that handles timezone information didn't like them. (For a list of valid names inspect `pytz.all_timezones`.) The timezone for this data is *America/Denver*.

31.3 Exploring the Data

I'm going to visualize the flow (cfs) of the river over time:

```
>>> import matplotlib.pyplot as plt
>>> fig, ax = plt.subplots(dpi=600)
>>> dd.cfs.plot()
```

From looking at this visualization, it looks like there are some pretty big outliers. (Looking at a histogram or calling `.describe` would also confirm this.):

```
>>> dd.cfs.describe()
count    493124.000000
mean        104.460537
std         477.341329
min           0.000000
25%          34.700000
50%          81.000000
75%         115.000000
max       35800.000000
Name: cfs, dtype: float64
```

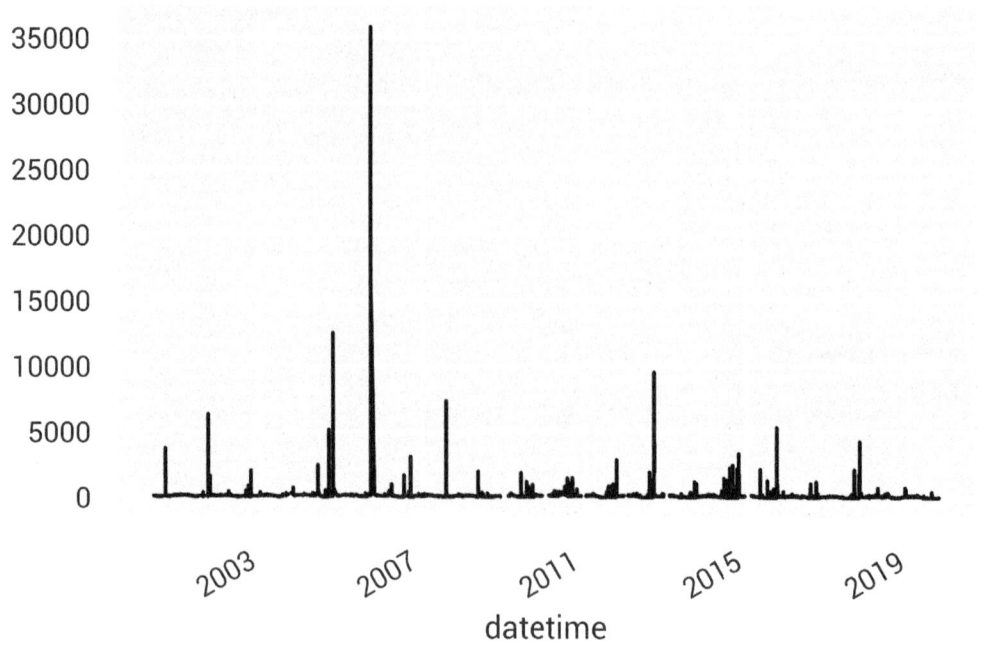

Figure 31.1: Visualization of flow of Dirty Devil river.

31.4 Slicing Time Series

Because the dataframe has datetime data in the index, we get some special slicing abilities. We can slice with strings that represent dates (or parts of dates). Below we will slice out the rows from 2018 onward:

```
>>> (dd
...   .cfs
...   .loc['2018':]
... )
datetime
2018-01-01 00:00:00-07:00    92.80
2018-01-01 00:15:00-07:00    88.30
2018-01-01 00:30:00-07:00    90.50
2018-01-01 00:45:00-07:00    90.50
2018-01-01 01:00:00-07:00    94.00
                              ...
2020-09-28 08:30:00-06:00     9.53
2020-09-28 08:45:00-06:00     9.20
2020-09-28 09:00:00-06:00     9.20
```

```
2020-09-28 09:15:00-06:00       9.20
2020-09-28 09:30:00-06:00       9.20
Name: cfs, Length: 95886, dtype: float64
```

We can include month information as well. When you specify just the month on an end slice, it includes all entries from that month on both the start and end slices (which has different behavior than both partial string slicing with .loc and position slicing with .iloc):

```
>>> (dd
...    .cfs
...    .loc['2018/3':'2019/5']
... )
datetime
2018-03-01 00:00:00-07:00       104.0
2018-03-01 00:15:00-07:00       107.0
2018-03-01 00:30:00-07:00       107.0
2018-03-01 00:45:00-07:00       105.0
2018-03-01 01:00:00-07:00       103.0
                                ...
2019-05-31 22:45:00-06:00       121.0
2019-05-31 23:00:00-06:00       123.0
2019-05-31 23:15:00-06:00       123.0
2019-05-31 23:30:00-06:00       125.0
2019-05-31 23:45:00-06:00       123.0
Name: cfs, Length: 43862, dtype: float64
```

Let's visualize what that slice of data looks like:

```
>>> (dd
...    .cfs
...    .loc['2018/3':'2019/5']
...    .plot()
... )
```

I'm going to clip the visualization and limit the upper value to 400 and try the visualization again:

```
>>> (dd
...    .cfs
...    .loc['2018/3':'2019/5']
...    .clip(upper=400)
...    .plot()
... )
```

Because the index is a time series, we can leverage the ability to resample. A common operation these days is to plot rolling 7-day average data on top of

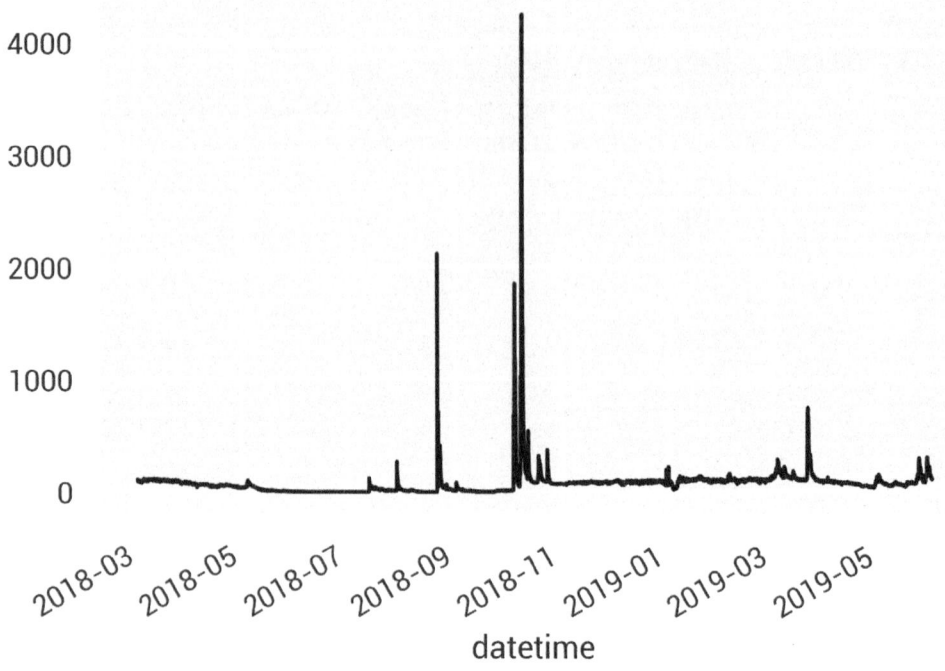

Figure 31.2: Visualization of flow of Dirty Devil river from March 2018 through May 2019.

daily data. The .rolling method accepts a moving window size, window, and like a grouping operation, you generally aggregate the result. Let's do it:

```
>>> dd2018 = (dd
...    .cfs
...    .loc['2018/3':'2019/5']
...    .clip(upper=400))

>>> ax = (dd2018
...    .resample('D')
...    .mean()
...    .plot(figsize=(10,4), alpha=.5, linewidth=1, label='Daily')
... )

>>> ax = (dd2018
...    .resample('D')
...    .mean()
...    .rolling(7)
```

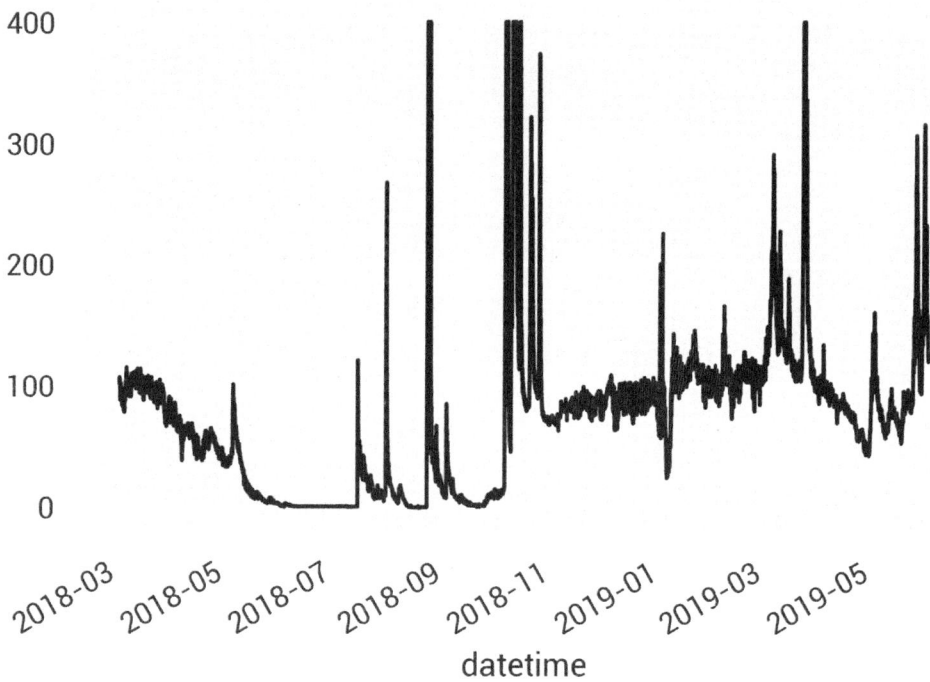

Figure 31.3: Visualization of flow of Dirty Devil river from March 2018 through May 2019 with value clipped at 400.

```
...     .mean()
...     .plot(figsize=(10,4), ax=ax, label='7-day Rolling')
... )
>>> ax.legend()
>>> ax.set_title('Dirty Devil Flow 2018 (cfs)')
```

31.5 Missing Timeseries Data

Let's look at dealing with missing data in timeseries. First we will search for it using .isna. One of the nice features of the .query method is that you can call other methods from it. Here we use .query and .isna to find missing values from the *cfs* column:

```
>>> (dd
...     [['cfs']]
...     .loc['2018/3':'2019/5']
```

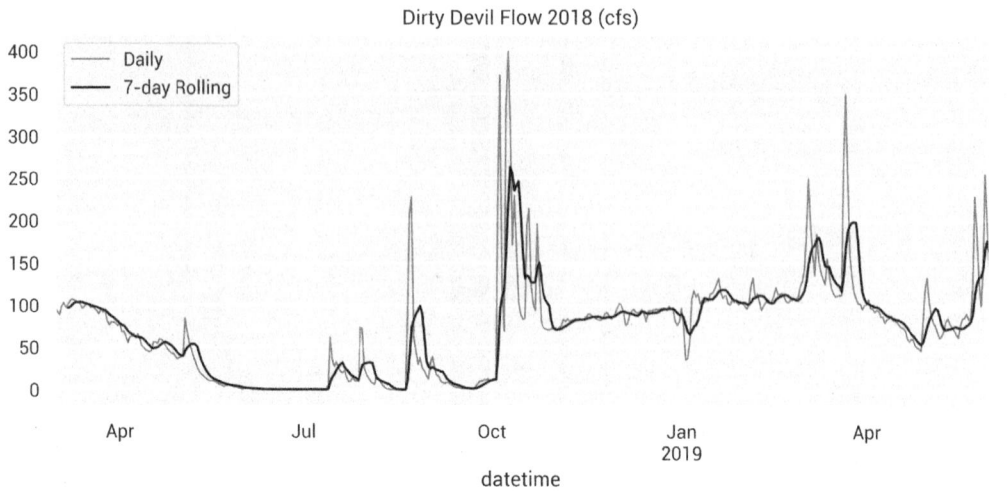

Figure 31.4: Visualization of flow of daily and weekly levels of Dirty Devil river from March 2018 through May 2019 with value clipped at 400.

```
...     .query('cfs.isna()')
... )
                                cfs
datetime
2018-07-07 13:15:00-06:00      NaN
2018-07-07 13:30:00-06:00      NaN
2018-07-07 13:45:00-06:00      NaN
2018-07-07 14:00:00-06:00      NaN
2018-07-07 14:15:00-06:00      NaN
...                            ...
2018-08-18 08:15:00-06:00      NaN
2018-08-18 08:30:00-06:00      NaN
2018-08-18 08:45:00-06:00      NaN
2018-08-18 09:15:00-06:00      NaN
2018-08-18 10:30:00-06:00      NaN

[337 rows x 1 columns]
```

Here is code to visualize the missing data from July 7-8. This will help us understand how the various methods work to deal with these missing values:

```
>>> (dd
...     [['cfs']]
...     .loc['2018/7/7':'2018/7/8']
...     .plot(figsize=(10,3))
```

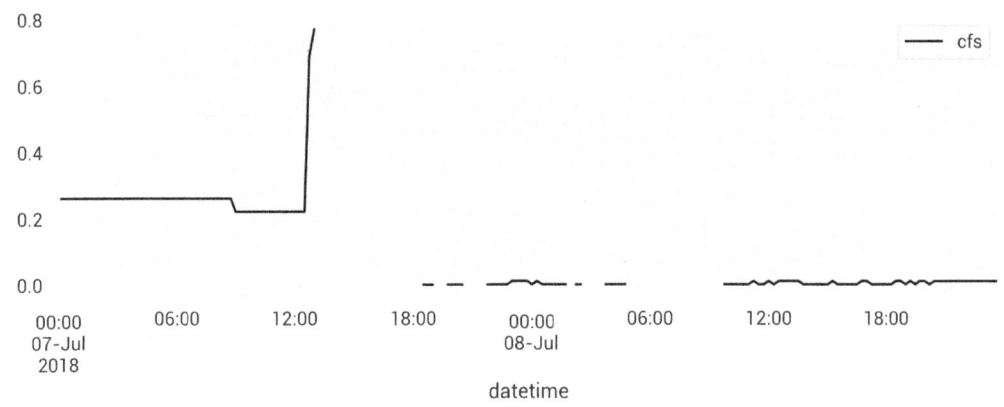

Figure 31.5: Visualization of missing data from flow of Dirty Devil river.

...)

The series chapter discussed various methods for filling in missing data. Let's visualize those below. I'm adding an offset to each line so you can see the behavior:

```
>>> fig, ax = plt.subplots(dpi=600, figsize=(10,3))
>>> dd_july = (dd
...   ['cfs']
...   .loc['2018/7/7 11:00':'2018/7/7 20:00']
... )

>>> dd_july.plot(ax=ax, label='original', linewidth=2)
>>> (dd_july
...   .bfill()
...   .add(.05)
...   .plot(label='bfill', ax=ax, linewidth=.5))

>>> (dd_july
...   .ffill()
...   .add(.1)
...   .plot(label='ffill', ax=ax, linewidth=.5))

>>> (dd_july
...   .interpolate(method='polynomial', order=3)
...   .add(.15)
...   .plot(label='interpolate poly (order 3)', ax=ax, linewidth=.5))
```

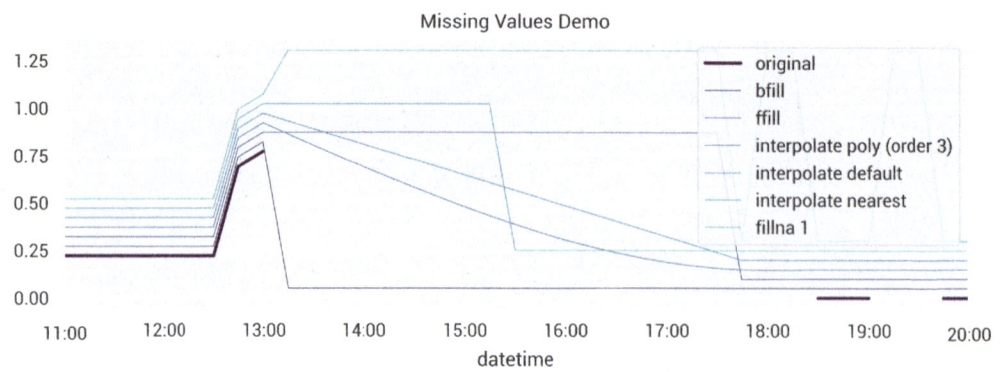

Figure 31.6: Visualization of filling in missing data from flow of Dirty Devil river.

```
>>> (dd_july
...    .interpolate()
...    .add(.2)
...    .plot(label='interpolate default', ax=ax, linewidth=.5))

>>> (dd_july
...    .interpolate(method='nearest')
...    .add(.25)
...    .plot(label='interpolate nearest', ax=ax, linewidth=.5))

>>> (dd_july
...    .fillna(1)
...    .add(.3)
...    .plot(label='fillna 1', ax=ax, linewidth=.5))

>>> ax.legend()
>>> ax.set_title('Missing Values Demo')
```

31.6   Exploring Seasonality

Time series data may have a seasonal component to it. Let's examine how to explore this with pandas (and related tools). We will explore the cubic feet per second column (*cfs*) of the Dirty Devil dataset. We can summarize monthly behavior in this column by combining .groupby and .describe. Note that we already have an index with date information in it, so one might suppose that we could use .resample with 'M' as an offset alias. However, a .resample operation will put the end date of each month in the index, while a .grouby on the month number will have only twelve entries in the index:

```
>>> (dd
...     .groupby(dd.index.month)
...     .cfs
...     .describe()
... )
          count         mean           std  ...    50%     75%       max
datetime                                     ...
1       26011.0   117.268802     29.000354  ...  114.0   132.0     265.0
2       41309.0   125.890293     24.280297  ...  125.0   141.0     303.0
3       51807.0   127.037609     48.885942  ...  116.0   136.0     750.0
4       50669.0    82.786214     74.133528  ...   70.0    97.8    2140.0
5       49507.0    63.007851     68.791835  ...   43.9    78.5    1960.0
6       41379.0    74.327241    139.857378  ...   32.0    82.5    2460.0
7       37089.0    62.775011    115.285805  ...   17.4    68.2    1660.0
8       37584.0    74.676246    247.800553  ...   25.6    59.1    7320.0
9       42272.0   128.309332    546.921269  ...   20.0    55.9    9540.0
10      44647.0   196.285529   1455.942059  ...   57.4    80.9   35800.0
11      42165.0    97.194344     39.743333  ...   89.3   105.0     766.0
12      28685.0   100.042608     26.700535  ...   97.8   113.0     407.0

[12 rows x 8 columns]
```

We can also visualize these components by plotting. Here is a chain to plot the mean for each month as a bar plot:

```
>>> fig, ax = plt.subplots(dpi=600, figsize=(10,4))
>>> (dd
...     .groupby(dd.index.month)
...     ['cfs']
...     .describe()
...     ['mean']
...     .plot.bar(ax=ax)
... )
```

We can also plot a line plot of each of the quantiles (I'm not showing the maximum value because it has so many outliers, it blows out the y-axis):

```
>>> fig, ax = plt.subplots(dpi=600, figsize=(10,4))
>>> (dd
...     .groupby(dd.index.month)
...     ['cfs']
...     .describe()
...     .loc[:, 'min':'75%']
...     .plot.bar(ax=ax)
```

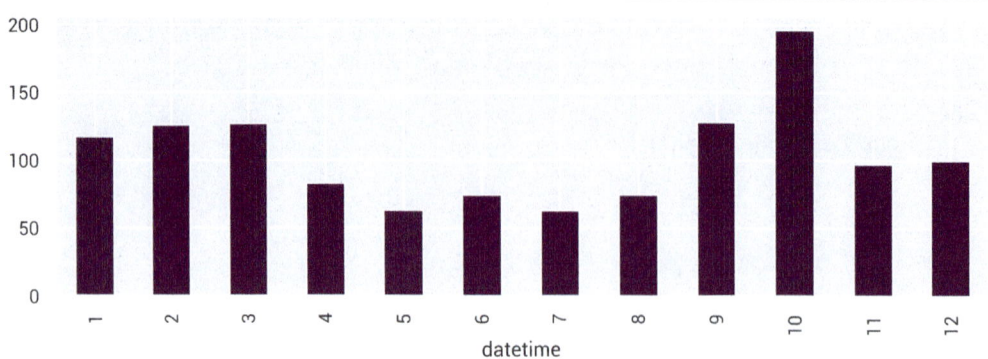

Figure 31.7: Visualization of monthly average of flow of Dirty Devil river.

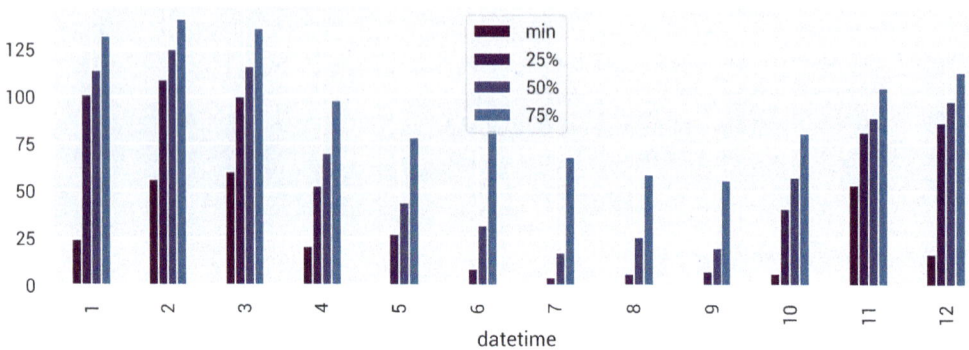

Figure 31.8: Visualization of monthly quantiles of flow of Dirty Devil river.

...)

To get much fancier we could leverage the pandas `.boxplot` method, but at that point, I would prefer using Seaborn[18] which is built on top of Matplotlib and pandas and provides a lot of power. I'm going to use the Seaborn `boxplot` function, and pass in clipped measurements to the data parameter. We also need to specify what we plot in the x and y axis. I create a column from the index with the month data (and rename it from *datetime* to *Month*), and the *cfs* column for x and y respectively:

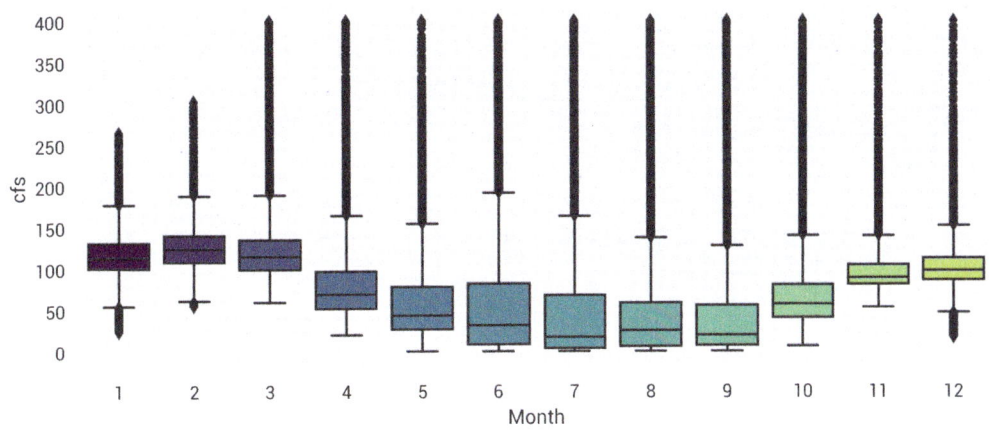

Figure 31.9: Boxplot of monthly quantiles of flow of Dirty Devil river.

```
>>> import seaborn as sns
>>> fig, ax = plt.subplots(dpi=600, figsize=(10,4))
>>> sns.boxplot(data=dd.assign(cfs=dd.cfs.clip(upper=400)),
...     x=dd.index.month.rename('Month'), y='cfs', ax=ax)
```

Plots such as these can give us an understanding of the monthly patterns we see in the data. For more complex time series analysis, I would consider using a library like Kats[19].

31.7 Resampling Data

We explored resampling in the series section, but I want to show some of the power that you get by using offset aliases. We will be using the flow data from the Dirty Devil dataset to dive into resampling. This data has information sampled at a 15-minute interval:

```
>>> dd.cfs
datetime
2001-05-07 01:00:00-06:00    71.00
2001-05-07 01:15:00-06:00    71.00
2001-05-07 01:30:00-06:00    71.00
```

---

[18]https://seaborn.pydata.org/

[19]https://facebookresearch.github.io/Kats/

```
2001-05-07 01:45:00-06:00    70.00
2001-05-07 02:00:00-06:00    70.00
                               ...
2020-09-28 08:30:00-06:00     9.53
2020-09-28 08:45:00-06:00     9.20
2020-09-28 09:00:00-06:00     9.20
2020-09-28 09:15:00-06:00     9.20
2020-09-28 09:30:00-06:00     9.20
Name: cfs, Length: 539305, dtype: float64
```

Let's aggregate this information from a 15-minute interval to a daily interval. Because the index has date information in it, we can use .resample in combination with 'D' (daily) as the offset alias. I am going to use .median as the aggregation method because the flow data is heavily skewed:

```
>>> (dd
...     .resample('D')
...     .median()
... )
                            site_no     cfs   gage_height
datetime
2001-05-07 00:00:00-06:00   9333500.0   71.50         NaN
2001-05-08 00:00:00-06:00   9333500.0   69.00         NaN
2001-05-09 00:00:00-06:00   9333500.0   63.50         NaN
2001-05-10 00:00:00-06:00   9333500.0   55.00         NaN
2001-05-11 00:00:00-06:00   9333500.0   55.00         NaN
...                               ...     ...         ...
2020-09-24 00:00:00-06:00   9333500.0    9.53        6.16
2020-09-25 00:00:00-06:00   9333500.0   10.20        6.18
2020-09-26 00:00:00-06:00   9333500.0   10.90        6.20
2020-09-27 00:00:00-06:00   9333500.0   10.20        6.18
2020-09-28 00:00:00-06:00   9333500.0    9.53        6.16

[7085 rows x 3 columns]
```

31.8   Rules with Offset Aliases

If we wanted to combine multiple days, we can do that as well by providing a numeric *rule* before the alias. You can insert a number before the offset alias. In this example, we will aggregate every two days by using '2D'. Pay attention to the index of the result:

```
>>> (dd
...     .resample('2D')
```

```
...     .median()
... )
                               site_no     cfs   gage_height
datetime
2001-05-07 00:00:00-06:00   9333500.0   69.00           NaN
2001-05-09 00:00:00-06:00   9333500.0   56.00           NaN
2001-05-11 00:00:00-06:00   9333500.0   54.00           NaN
2001-05-13 00:00:00-06:00   9333500.0   47.00           NaN
2001-05-15 00:00:00-06:00   9333500.0   54.00           NaN
...                              ...     ...           ...
2020-09-20 00:00:00-06:00   9333500.0    6.83          6.07
2020-09-22 00:00:00-06:00   9333500.0    7.68          6.10
2020-09-24 00:00:00-06:00   9333500.0    9.86          6.17
2020-09-26 00:00:00-06:00   9333500.0   10.50          6.19
2020-09-28 00:00:00-06:00   9333500.0    9.53          6.16

[3543 rows x 3 columns]
```

31.9 Combining Offset Aliases

We can also combine offset aliases. If we want to aggregate at the three-day, 2-hour and 10-minute interval, we can combine all of these rules with the offset aliases into a single string:

```
>>> (dd
...     .resample('3D2H10min')
...     .median()
... )
                               site_no     cfs   gage_height
datetime
2001-05-07 00:00:00-06:00   9333500.0   67.00           NaN
2001 05-10 02:10:00-06:00   9333500.0   55.00           NaN
2001-05-13 04:20:00-06:00   9333500.0   49.00           NaN
2001-05-16 06:30:00-06:00   9333500.0   50.00           NaN
2001-05-19 08:40:00-06:00   9333500.0   46.00           NaN
...                              ...     ...           ...
2020-09-14 13:20:00-06:00   9333500.0    5.79         6.030
2020-09-17 15:30:00-06:00   9333500.0    6.04         6.040
2020-09-20 17:40:00-06:00   9333500.0    7.11         6.080
2020-09-23 19:50:00-06:00   9333500.0   10.03         6.175
2020-09-26 22:00:00-06:00   9333500.0    9.86         6.170

[2293 rows x 3 columns]
```

31.10 Anchored Offset Aliases

Some of the frequencies in offset aliases allow you to modify when the window for the frequency ends. You can use this operation on the weekly, quarterly, and yearly frequencies. Note that the default quarter ends in March, June, September, and December:

```
>>> (dd
...     .resample('Q')
...     .median()
... )
                            site_no    cfs  gage_height
datetime
2001-06-30 00:00:00-06:00  9333500.0   44.00          NaN
2001-09-30 00:00:00-06:00  9333500.0   27.00          NaN
2001-12-31 00:00:00-07:00  9333500.0   85.00          NaN
2002-03-31 00:00:00-07:00  9333500.0  122.00          NaN
2002-06-30 00:00:00-06:00  9333500.0   46.00          NaN
...                              ...     ...          ...
2019-09-30 00:00:00-06:00  9333500.0   13.30         6.21
2019-12-31 00:00:00-07:00  9333500.0   92.10         6.75
2020-03-31 00:00:00-06:00  9333500.0  126.00         6.99
2020-06-30 00:00:00-06:00  9333500.0   23.20         6.55
2020-09-30 00:00:00-06:00  9333500.0    5.79         5.96

[78 rows x 3 columns]
```

We can tack on -JAN to force the quarters to end in January, April, July, and October:

```
>>> (dd
...     .resample('Q-JAN')
...     .median()
... )
                            site_no    cfs  gage_height
datetime
2001-07-31 00:00:00-06:00  9333500.0   42.0          NaN
2001-10-31 00:00:00-07:00  9333500.0   39.0          NaN
2002-01-31 00:00:00-07:00  9333500.0  116.0          NaN
2002-04-30 00:00:00-06:00  9333500.0   96.0          NaN
2002-07-31 00:00:00-06:00  9333500.0   13.0          NaN
...                              ...    ...          ...
2019-10-31 00:00:00-06:00  9333500.0   12.8         6.25
2020-01-31 00:00:00-07:00  9333500.0  116.0         6.84
2020-04-30 00:00:00-06:00  9333500.0  116.0         6.98
2020-07-31 00:00:00-06:00  9333500.0   13.9         6.37
```

```
2020-10-31 00:00:00-06:00  9333500.0    0.5         5.49

[78 rows x 3 columns]
```

For annual and quarterly offset aliases, you can change the anchoring by using -JAN, -FEB, … -DEC. For weekly offset aliases, you can change the anchoring by using -SUN, -MON, … -SAT.

31.11 Resampling to Finer-grain Frequency

Remember, this river flow data is at the 15-minute frequency. If we wanted to have it at a two minute frequency, we could do the following:

```
>>> (dd
...    .resample('2min')
...    .median()
... )
                           site_no   cfs  gage_height
datetime
2001-05-07 01:00:00-06:00  9333500.0  71.0         NaN
2001-05-07 01:02:00-06:00        NaN   NaN         NaN
2001-05-07 01:04:00-06:00        NaN   NaN         NaN
2001-05-07 01:06:00-06:00        NaN   NaN         NaN
2001-05-07 01:08:00-06:00        NaN   NaN         NaN
...                              ...   ...         ...
2020-09-28 09:22:00-06:00        NaN   NaN         NaN
2020-09-28 09:24:00-06:00        NaN   NaN         NaN
2020-09-28 09:26:00-06:00        NaN   NaN         NaN
2020-09-28 09:28:00-06:00        NaN   NaN         NaN
2020-09-28 09:30:00-06:00  9333500.0   9.2        6.15

[5100736 rows x 3 columns]
```

You will notice that there is now a bunch of missing data. You will probably want to refer to the missing data section and adopt an appropriate option to deal with it. Below, we interpolate the missing values:

```
>>> (dd
...    .resample('2min')
...    .median()
...    .interpolate()
... )
                           site_no   cfs  gage_height
datetime
2001-05-07 01:00:00-06:00  9333500.0  71.0         NaN
```

```
2001-05-07 01:02:00-06:00   9333500.0   71.0          NaN
2001-05-07 01:04:00-06:00   9333500.0   71.0          NaN
2001-05-07 01:06:00-06:00   9333500.0   71.0          NaN
2001-05-07 01:08:00-06:00   9333500.0   71.0          NaN
...                               ...    ...           ...
2020-09-28 09:22:00-06:00   9333500.0    9.2          6.15
2020-09-28 09:24:00-06:00   9333500.0    9.2          6.15
2020-09-28 09:26:00-06:00   9333500.0    9.2          6.15
2020-09-28 09:28:00-06:00   9333500.0    9.2          6.15
2020-09-28 09:30:00-06:00   9333500.0    9.2          6.15

[5100736 rows x 3 columns]
```

31.12 Grouping a Date Column with pd.Grouper

The .resample method is a powerful way to aggregate data with dates in the index. But what if you want to aggregate dataframes by a column with date information? Enter the pd.Grouper class.

Here is an anchored offset alias using .resample on the Dirty Devil data. It aggregates on quarters that end in January:

```
>>> (dd
...     .resample('Q-JAN')
...     .median()
... )
                             site_no     cfs   gage_height
datetime
2001-07-31 00:00:00-06:00   9333500.0    42.0          NaN
2001-10-31 00:00:00-07:00   9333500.0    39.0          NaN
2002-01-31 00:00:00-07:00   9333500.0   116.0          NaN
2002-04-30 00:00:00-06:00   9333500.0    96.0          NaN
2002-07-31 00:00:00-06:00   9333500.0    13.0          NaN
...                               ...     ...           ...
2019-10-31 00:00:00-06:00   9333500.0    12.8          6.25
2020-01-31 00:00:00-07:00   9333500.0   116.0          6.84
2020-04-30 00:00:00-06:00   9333500.0   116.0          6.98
2020-07-31 00:00:00-06:00   9333500.0    13.9          6.37
2020-10-31 00:00:00-06:00   9333500.0     0.5          5.49

[78 rows x 3 columns]
```

Assuming that we have a date column that we want to aggregate on (I'm going to move the index into a column, *datetime*), we could perform the same aggregation using pd.Grouper. The key parameter specifies the column to group on, the freq parameter specifies the offset alias:

```
>>> (dd
...     .reset_index()
...     .groupby(pd.Grouper(key='datetime', freq='Q-JAN'))
...     .median()
... )
                               site_no     cfs   gage_height
datetime
2001-07-31 00:00:00-06:00    9333500.0    42.0          NaN
2001-10-31 00:00:00-07:00    9333500.0    39.0          NaN
2002-01-31 00:00:00-07:00    9333500.0   116.0          NaN
2002-04-30 00:00:00-06:00    9333500.0    96.0          NaN
2002-07-31 00:00:00-06:00    9333500.0    13.0          NaN
...                                ...     ...          ...
2019-10-31 00:00:00-06:00    9333500.0    12.8         6.25
2020-01-31 00:00:00-07:00    9333500.0   116.0         6.84
2020-04-30 00:00:00-06:00    9333500.0   116.0         6.98
2020-07-31 00:00:00-06:00    9333500.0    13.9         6.37
2020-10-31 00:00:00-06:00    9333500.0     0.5         5.49

[78 rows x 3 columns]
```

Method	Description
pd.to_datetime(arg, errors='raise', dayfirst=False, yearfirst=False, utc=False, format=None, exact=True, unit=None, infer_datetime format=False, origin='unix', cache=True)	Convert an arg to a datetime. Not guaranteed to return a datetime64 type. Use utc=True to convert from naive to UTC (tz-aware) time. Specify strftime string with format. When parsing time since cpoch, set unit='s' for seconds.
s.dt.tz_localize(tz, ambiguous='raise', nonexistent='raise')	Return a date converted to a timezone. Set tz=None to convert to naive time. For ambiguous times (when clocks move back for daylight savings) set to 'infer' to base on order, array of True/False for DST, non-DST time, 'NaT' to leave empty. For nonexistent times (when clock moves forward) set nonexistent to 'shift_forward', 'shift_backward', 'NaT', or timedelta object.

`s.dt.tz_convert(tz)`	Convert from an existing timezone to another timezone. Set `tz=None` to convert to UTC time.
`df.loc`	If you have a dataframe/series with a datetime index, you can slice on partial date strings.

`df.resample(rule, axis=0,`
`  closed=None, label=None,`
`  convention='start', kind=None,`
`  on=None, level=None,`
`  origin='start_day')`
	Return a resampled dataframe (with a date in the index, or specify the date column with on). Set closed to `'right'` to include the right side of interval (default is `'right'` for `M/A/Q/BM/BQ/W`). Set the label to `'right'` to use the right label for bucket. Can specify the timestamp to start origin.

`df.rolling(window,`
`  min_periods=None,`
`  center=False, win_type=None,`
`  on=None, axis=0, closed=None,`
`  method='single')`
	Return a window object to perform aggregations on.

`s.bfill(axis=0, limit=None,` `  downcast=None)`	Backward fill the missing values. Alternate syntax for `s.fillna(method='bfill')`
`s.ffill(axis=0, limit=None,` `  downcast=None)`	Forward fill the missing values. Alternate syntax for `s.fillna(method='ffill')`

`s.interpolate(method='linear',`
`  axis=0, limit=None,`
`  limit_direction='forward',`
`  limit_area=None,`
`  downcast=None, **kwargs,)`
	Return a series with interpolated values.

`s.fillna(value=None, method=None,`
`  axis=0, limit=None,`
`  downcast=None)`
	Use the value (scalar, dict, series) or method (`'ffill'`, `'bfill'`, or `'nearest'`) for filling in missing data.

`pd.Grouper(key=None, level=None,`
`  freq=None, axis=0, sort=False,`
`  closed=None, label=None,`
`  convention=None,`
`  origin='start_day',`
`  offset=None, dropna=True)`
	Return a groupby object based on the column (key) or date index (key=None) and offset alias (freq).

Table 31.1: Chapter Methods

31.13 Summary

There are many tools to manipulate time-series data in pandas. I recommend combining liberal amounts of visualizations when manipulating the data to validate the results.

31.14 Exercises

With a dataset of your choice:

1. Convert a date column from a string to a proper date.

2. Group the data by month names and look at the mean values.

3. Group the data by each month of every year and look at the mean values.

4. Insert the date column in the index and slice out a portion of the rows by date.

Chapter 32

Joining Dataframes

Dataframes hold tabular data. Databases hold tabular data. You can perform many of the same operations on dataframes that you do to database tables. In this section, we will look at the theory for joining dataframes.

Here are the two tables we will be using for examples:

Index	color	name
0	Blue	John
1	Blue	George
2	Purple	Ringo

Index	carcolor	name
3	Red	Paul
1	Blue	George
2		Ringo

32.1 Adding Rows to Dataframes

Let's assume that we have two dataframes that we want to combine into a single dataframe, with rows from both. The simplest way to do this is with the concat function. Below, we create the dataframes:

```
>>> import pandas as pd
>>> import numpy as np
>>> df1 = pd.DataFrame({'name': ['John', 'George', 'Ringo'],
...                     'color': ['Blue', 'Blue', 'Purple']})
>>> df2 = pd.DataFrame({'name': ['Paul', 'George', 'Ringo'],
```

```
...                          'carcolor': ['Red', 'Blue', np.nan]},
...                  index=[3, 1, 2])
```

The concat function in the pandas library accepts a list of dataframes to combine. This function is useful when you have multiple files that you want to combine into one dataframe. It will find any columns that have the same name and use a single column for each of the repeated columns. In this case, *name* is common to both dataframes:

```
>>> pd.concat([df1, df2])
   carcolor   color    name
0       NaN    Blue    John
1       NaN    Blue  George
2       NaN  Purple   Ringo
3       Red     NaN    Paul
1      Blue     NaN  George
2       NaN     NaN   Ringo
```

Note that .concat preserves index values, so the resulting dataframe has duplicate index values. If you would prefer an error when duplicates appear, you can pass the verify_integrity=True parameter setting:

```
>>> pd.concat([df1, df2], verify_integrity=True)
Traceback (most recent call last):
  ...
ValueError: Indexes have overlapping values:
  Int64Index([1, 2], dtype='int64')
```

Alternatively, if you would prefer that pandas create new index values for you, pass in ignore_index=True as a parameter:

```
>>> pd.concat([df1, df2], ignore_index=True)
   carcolor   color    name
0       NaN    Blue    John
1       NaN    Blue  George
2       NaN  Purple   Ringo
3       Red     NaN    Paul
4      Blue     NaN  George
5       NaN     NaN   Ringo
```

32.2 Adding Columns to Dataframes

The concat function also can align dataframes based on the index values, rather than using the columns. If you set axis=1, we get this behavior. I do not use this operation often, rather I use .assign to create columns. However, here is an example of concat along the columns axis:

```
>>> pd.concat([df1, df2], axis=1)
     name    color    name carcolor
0    John     Blue     NaN      NaN
1  George     Blue  George     Blue
2   Ringo   Purple   Ringo      NaN
3     NaN      NaN    Paul      Red
```

Note that this repeats the name column. Using SQL, we can *join* two database tables together based on common columns. If we want to perform a join similar to a database join on a dataframe, we need to use the .merge method. We will cover that in the next section.

32.3 Joins

Databases have different types of joins. The four common ones include inner, outer, left, and right. The dataframe has two methods to support these operations, .join and .merge. I prefer the .merge method.

Note

The .join method is meant for joining based on the index rather than columns. In practice, I find myself joining based on columns instead of index values.

If you want the .join method to join based on column values, you need to set that column as the index first:

```
>>> df1.set_index('name').join(df2.set_index('name'))
         color carcolor
name
John      Blue      NaN
George    Blue     Blue
Ringo   Purple      NaN
```

It is easier to just use the .merge method.

The default join type for the .merge method is an *inner join*. The .merge method looks for common column names in the dataframe it is going to join. The method aligns the values in those columns. If both columns have values that are the same, they are kept along with the remaining columns from both data

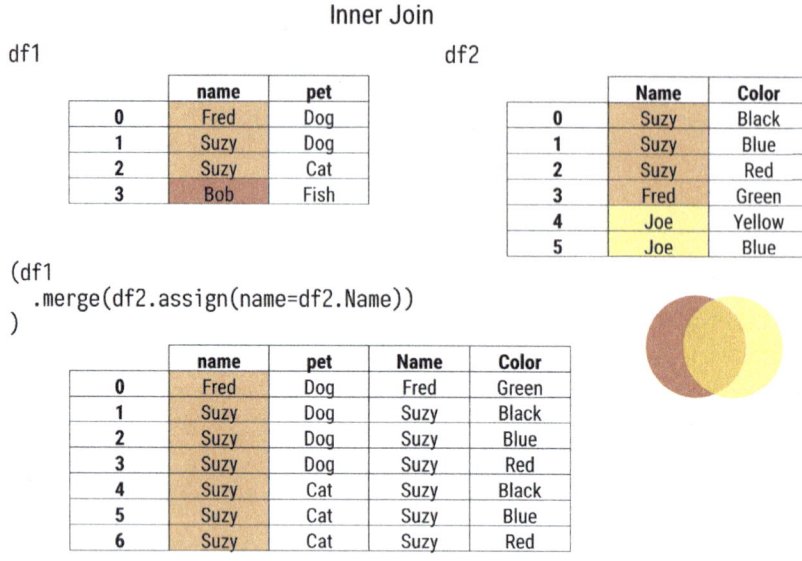

Note every Suzy row matches with every Suzy in df2!

Figure 32.1: The `.merge` method performs an inner join by default. The resulting dataframe will only have rows where the merge column value exists in both dataframes.

frames. Rows with values in the aligned columns that only appear in one data frame are discarded:

```
>>> df1.merge(df2)  # inner join
     name   color carcolor
0  George    Blue    Blue
1   Ringo  Purple     NaN
```

When the `how='outer'` parameter setting is passed in, an *outer join* is performed. Again, the method looks for common column names. It aligns the values for those columns and adds the values from the other columns of both data frames. If either dataframe had a value in the field that we join on that was absent from the other, the new columns are filled with NaN:

Left Join

df1

	name	pet
0	Fred	Dog
1	Suzy	Dog
2	Suzy	Cat
3	Bob	Fish

df2

	Name	Color
0	Suzy	Black
1	Suzy	Blue
2	Suzy	Red
3	Fred	Green
4	Joe	Yellow
5	Joe	Blue

```
(df1
  .merge(df2.assign(name=df2.Name), how='left')
)
```

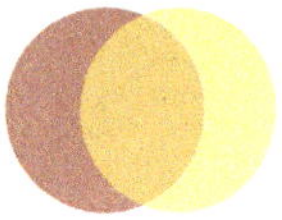

	name	pet	Name	Color
0	Fred	Dog	Fred	Green
1	Suzy	Dog	Suzy	Black
2	Suzy	Dog	Suzy	Blue
3	Suzy	Dog	Suzy	Red
4	Suzy	Cat	Suzy	Black
5	Suzy	Cat	Suzy	Blue
6	Suzy	Cat	Suzy	Red
7	Bob	Fish	nan	nan

Note every Suzy row matches with every Suzy in df2! Bob has missing values

Figure 32.2: A left join keeps all values from the left merge column (orange and red). The values that are unique to the right dataframe (yellow) are dropped. Note the combinatoric explosion for *Suzy* because each left value is matched with all the values in the right.

```
>>> df1.merge(df2, how='outer')
     name   color carcolor
0    John    Blue      NaN
1  George    Blue     Blue
2   Ringo  Purple      NaN
3    Paul     NaN      Red
```

To perform a *left join*, pass the how='left' parameter setting. A left join keeps only the values from the columns in the dataframe that the .merge method is called on. If the other dataframe is missing aligned values, NaN is used to fill in their values:

```
>>> df1.merge(df2, how='left')
     name  color carcolor
0    John   Blue      NaN
1  George   Blue     Blue
```

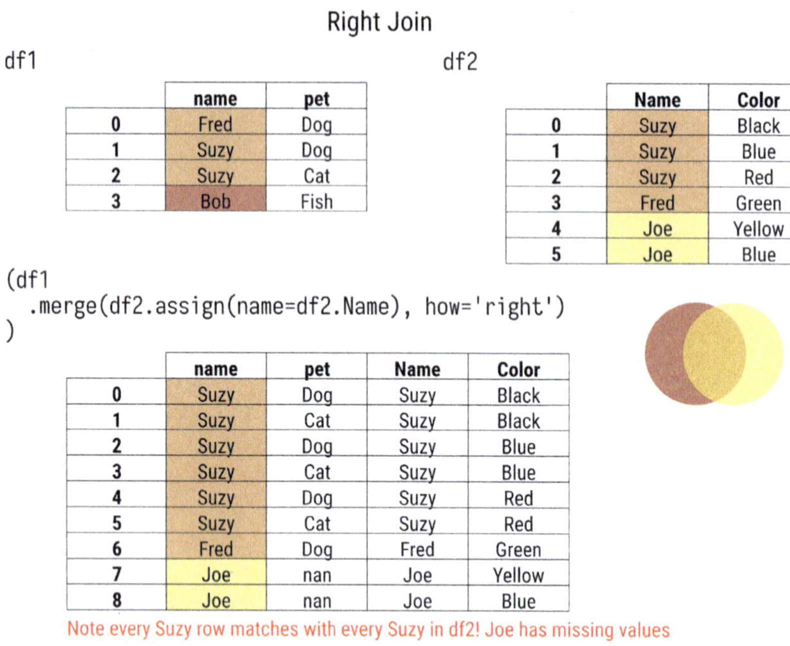

Right Join

df1

	name	pet
0	Fred	Dog
1	Suzy	Dog
2	Suzy	Cat
3	Bob	Fish

df2

	Name	Color
0	Suzy	Black
1	Suzy	Blue
2	Suzy	Red
3	Fred	Green
4	Joe	Yellow
5	Joe	Blue

```
(df1
  .merge(df2.assign(name=df2.Name), how='right')
)
```

	name	pet	Name	Color
0	Suzy	Dog	Suzy	Black
1	Suzy	Cat	Suzy	Black
2	Suzy	Dog	Suzy	Blue
3	Suzy	Cat	Suzy	Blue
4	Suzy	Dog	Suzy	Red
5	Suzy	Cat	Suzy	Red
6	Fred	Dog	Fred	Green
7	Joe	nan	Joe	Yellow
8	Joe	nan	Joe	Blue

Note every Suzy row matches with every Suzy in df2! Joe has missing values

Figure 32.3: A right join keeps all values from the right merge column (orange and yellow). The values that are unique to the left dataframe (red) are dropped.

```
2   Ringo  Purple      NaN
```

Finally, there is support for a *right join* as well. A right join keeps the values from the dataframe that is passed in as the first parameter of the .merge method. If the dataframe that .merge was called on has aligned values, they are kept, otherwise NaN is used to fill in the missing values:

```
>>> df1.merge(df2, how='right')
     name    color carcolor
0  George     Blue     Blue
1   Ringo   Purple      NaN
2    Paul      NaN      Red
```

If we want to join on columns that don't have the same name, we can use the left_on and right_on parameters. We can also specify a subset of columns if we don't want to merge on all of the common columns:

Outer Join

df1

	name	pet
0	Fred	Dog
1	Suzy	Dog
2	Suzy	Cat
3	Bob	Fish

df2

	Name	Color
0	Suzy	Black
1	Suzy	Blue
2	Suzy	Red
3	Fred	Green
4	Joe	Yellow
5	Joe	Blue

```
(df1
  .merge(df2.assign(name=df2.Name), how='outer')
)
```

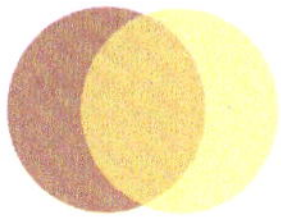

	name	pet	Name	Color
0	Fred	Dog	Fred	Green
1	Suzy	Dog	Suzy	Black
2	Suzy	Dog	Suzy	Blue
3	Suzy	Dog	Suzy	Red
4	Suzy	Cat	Suzy	Black
5	Suzy	Cat	Suzy	Blue
6	Suzy	Cat	Suzy	Red
7	Bob	Fish	nan	nan
8	Joe	nan	Joe	Yellow
9	Joe	nan	Joe	Blue

Note every Suzy row matches with every Suzy in df2! Bob and Joe have missing values

Figure 32.4: An outer join keeps all values from the left and right merge columns.

```
>>> df1.merge(df2, how='right', left_on='color',
...      right_on='carcolor')
   name_x color   name_y carcolor
0    John  Blue   George     Blue
1  George  Blue   George     Blue
2     NaN   NaN     Paul      Red
3     NaN   NaN    Ringo      NaN
```

The .merge method has a few other parameters that turn out to be useful in practice. The table below lists them:

Parameter	Meaning
on	Column names to join on. String or list. (Default is intersection of names).
left_on	Column names for left dataframe. String or list. Used when names don't overlap.
right_on	Column names for right dataframe. String or list. Used when names don't overlap.
left_index	Join based on left dataframe index. Boolean
right_index	Join based on right dataframe index. Boolean

32.4 Join Indicators

The .merge method has an option to add a column that indicates where the data in the row can come from. If you include the indicator=True parameter, pandas will create a column called _merge. The indicator parameter can also be a string, in which can the new column will be the name of the string rather than _merge.

The _merge column will have the values of left_only, right_only, or both to indicate the row came from the dataframe .merge was called on, the data frame passed in, or both of them respectively:

```
>>> df1.merge(df2, how='outer',
...       indicator=True)
     name   color carcolor      _merge
0    John    Blue      NaN   left_only
1  George    Blue     Blue        both
2   Ringo  Purple      NaN        both
3    Paul     NaN      Red  right_only
```

32.5 Merge Validation

The .merge method recently added a useful option, the validate parameter. It will raise a MergeError if the join validates a constraint. The constraint can be '1:1', '1:m', or 'm:1' for ensuring that the join keys are indeed one to one, one to many, or many to one. You can also specify 'm:m' for many to many, but that constraint is always ignored.

In the following example, the left key is *color*, which has non-unique values (many) and the right key is *carcolor* which is unique (one), so the constraint should be 'm:1'. If we pass in a wrong constraint, like a one to many constraint, the MergeError is raised:

```
>>> df1.merge(df2, how='right', left_on='color',
...     right_on='carcolor', validate='1:m')
Traceback (most recent call last):
  ...
pandas.errors.MergeError: Merge keys are not
  unique in left dataset; not a one-to-many merge
```

This parameter is useful to check that your data looks like you think it should. I recommend validating your data after merges.

32.6 Joining Data Example

In the previous section, we discussed the theory behind joining data. In this section, we will look at a concrete example.

Most of the data we have looked at in the book has been delivered in a single CSV file. Sometimes we have data from multiple sources, and we need to combine them. This section will explore joining a real-world dataset.

32.7 Dirty Devil Flow and Weather Data

In this section we will revisit the Dirty Devil data. Let's load the flow and gage height data. In this case we will leave the *datetime* column as a column and not use it for the index:

```
>>> import pandas as pd
>>> url = 'https://github.com/mattharrison/datasets/raw/master/data/'\
...         'dirtydevil.txt'
>>> df = pd.read_csv(url, skiprows=lambda num: num <34 or num == 35,
...                 sep='\t')
>>> def to_us_mountain_time(df_, time_col, tz_col):
...     return (df_
...             .assign(**{tz_col: df_[tz_col].replace('MDT',
...                         'MST7MDT')})
...             .groupby(tz_col)
...             [time_col]
...             .transform(lambda s: pd.to_datetime(s)
...                 .dt.tz_localize(s.name, ambiguous=True)
...                 .dt.tz_convert('US/Mountain'))
...             )
```

```
>>> def tweak_river(df_):
...     return (df_
...       .assign(datetime=to_us_mountain_time(df_, 'datetime', 'tz_cd'))
...       .rename(columns={'144166_00060': 'cfs',
...                        '144167_00065': 'gage_height'})
...     )

>>> dd = tweak_river(df)
>>> dd
        agency_cd  site_no  ... gage_height 144167_00065_cd
0            USGS  9333500  ...         NaN             NaN
1            USGS  9333500  ...         NaN             NaN
2            USGS  9333500  ...         NaN             NaN
3            USGS  9333500  ...         NaN             NaN
4            USGS  9333500  ...         NaN             NaN
...           ...      ...  ...         ...             ...
539300       USGS  9333500  ...        6.16               P
539301       USGS  9333500  ...        6.15               P
539302       USGS  9333500  ...        6.15               P
539303       USGS  9333500  ...        6.15               P
539304       USGS  9333500  ...        6.15               P

[539305 rows x 8 columns]
```

I'm also going to load some meteorological data[20] from Hanksville, Utah, a city nearby the river. We will then join both datasets together so we have flow data as well as temperature and precipitation information.

Some of the columns that are interesting are:

- *DATE* - Date

- *PRCP* - Precipiation in inches

- *TMIN* - Minimum temperature (F) for day

- *TMAX* - Maximum temperature (F) for day

- *TOBS* - Observed temperature (F) when measurement made

---

[20]https://www.ncdc.noaa.gov/cdo-web/

```
>>> url = 'https://github.com/mattharrison/datasets/raw/master/data/'\
...        'hanksville.csv'

>>> temp_df = pd.read_csv(url)
>>> def tweak_temp(df_):
...     return (df_
...             .assign(DATE=pd.to_datetime(df_.DATE)
...                 .dt.tz_localize('US/Mountain', ambiguous=False))
...             .loc[:,['DATE', 'PRCP', 'TMIN', 'TMAX', 'TOBS']]]
...     )

>>> temp_df = tweak_temp(temp_df)
>>> temp_df
                            DATE  PRCP  TMIN  TMAX  TOBS
0     2000-01-01 00:00:00-07:00  0.02  21.0  43.0  28.0
1     2000-01-02 00:00:00-07:00  0.03  24.0  39.0  24.0
2     2000-01-03 00:00:00-07:00  0.00   7.0  39.0  18.0
3     2000-01-04 00:00:00-07:00  0.00   5.0  39.0  25.0
4     2000-01-05 00:00:00-07:00  0.00  10.0  44.0  22.0
...                          ...   ...   ...   ...   ...
6843  2020-09-20 00:00:00-06:00  0.00  46.0  92.0  83.0
6844  2020-09-21 00:00:00-06:00  0.00  47.0  92.0  84.0
6845  2020-09-22 00:00:00-06:00  0.00  54.0  84.0  77.0
6846  2020-09-23 00:00:00-06:00  0.00  47.0  91.0  87.0
6847  2020-09-24 00:00:00-06:00  0.00  43.0  94.0  88.0

[6848 rows x 5 columns]
```

32.8 Joining Data

The pandas API provides a function for merging data, pd.merge. It also has two methods for joining data, .join and .merge that wrap that function. I will use the .merge method.

Let's try to use .merge and merge by date. This method will try to merge by columns that have the same name. The dd dataframe has a *datetime* column, and temp_df has a *DATE* column. We can use the left_on and right_on parameters to help it know how to align the data. The .merge method tries to do an *inner join* by default. That means that row with values that are the same in the merge columns will be joined together:

```
>>> (dd
...   .merge(temp_df, left_on='datetime', right_on='DATE')
... )
```

```
       agency_cd  site_no                datetime  ...  TMIN  TMAX  TOBS
0           USGS  9333500 2001-05-08 00:00:00-06:00  ...  43.0  85.0  58.0
1           USGS  9333500 2001-05-09 00:00:00-06:00  ...  36.0  92.0  64.0
2           USGS  9333500 2001-05-10 00:00:00-06:00  ...  50.0  92.0  67.0
3           USGS  9333500 2001-05-11 00:00:00-06:00  ...  46.0  87.0  60.0
4           USGS  9333500 2001-05-12 00:00:00-06:00  ...  45.0  93.0  72.0
...          ...      ...                       ...  ...   ...   ...   ...
4968        USGS  9333500 2020-09-20 00:00:00-06:00  ...  46.0  92.0  83.0
4969        USGS  9333500 2020-09-21 00:00:00-06:00  ...  47.0  92.0  84.0
4970        USGS  9333500 2020-09-22 00:00:00-06:00  ...  54.0  84.0  77.0
4971        USGS  9333500 2020-09-23 00:00:00-06:00  ...  47.0  91.0  87.0
4972        USGS  9333500 2020-09-24 00:00:00-06:00  ...  43.0  94.0  88.0

[4973 rows x 13 columns]
```

This appears to have worked but is somewhat problematic. Remember that the dd dataset has a 15-minute frequency, but temp_df only has daily data, so we are only using the value from midnight. We should probably use our resampling skills to calculate the median flow value for each date and then merge. In that case, we will want to use the index of the grouped data to merge, so we specify left_index=True:

```
>>> (dd
...     .groupby(pd.Grouper(key='datetime', freq='D'))
...     .median()
...     .merge(temp_df, left_index=True, right_on='DATE')
... )
       site_no    cfs  gage_height  ...  TMIN  TMAX  TOBS
492  9333500.0  71.50          NaN  ...  41.0  82.0  55.0
493  9333500.0  69.00          NaN  ...  43.0  85.0  58.0
494  9333500.0  63.50          NaN  ...  36.0  92.0  64.0
495  9333500.0  55.00          NaN  ...  50.0  92.0  67.0
496  9333500.0  55.00          NaN  ...  46.0  87.0  60.0
...        ...    ...          ...  ...   ...   ...   ...
6843 9333500.0   6.83         6.07  ...  46.0  92.0  83.0
6844 9333500.0   6.83         6.07  ...  47.0  92.0  84.0
6845 9333500.0   7.39         6.09  ...  54.0  84.0  77.0
6846 9333500.0   7.97         6.11  ...  47.0  91.0  87.0
6847 9333500.0   9.53         6.16  ...  43.0  94.0  88.0

[6356 rows x 8 columns]
```

That looks better (and gives us a few more rows of data).

32.9   Validating Joined Data

Let's validate that we had a one to one join, ie each date from the flow data matched up with a single date from the temperature data. We can use the `validate` parameter to do this:

```
>>> (dd
...     .groupby(pd.Grouper(key='datetime', freq='D'))
...     .median()
...     .merge(temp_df, left_index=True, right_on='DATE',
...            how='inner', validate='1:1')
... )
        site_no    cfs  gage_height  ...  TMIN  TMAX  TOBS
492   9333500.0  71.50         NaN   ...  41.0  82.0  55.0
493   9333500.0  69.00         NaN   ...  43.0  85.0  58.0
494   9333500.0  63.50         NaN   ...  36.0  92.0  64.0
495   9333500.0  55.00         NaN   ...  50.0  92.0  67.0
496   9333500.0  55.00         NaN   ...  46.0  87.0  60.0
...         ...    ...         ...   ...   ...   ...   ...
6843  9333500.0   6.83        6.07   ...  46.0  92.0  83.0
6844  9333500.0   6.83        6.07   ...  47.0  92.0  84.0
6845  9333500.0   7.39        6.09   ...  54.0  84.0  77.0
6846  9333500.0   7.97        6.11   ...  47.0  91.0  87.0
6847  9333500.0   9.53        6.16   ...  43.0  94.0  88.0

[6356 rows x 8 columns]
```

Because this did not raise a `MergeError`, we know that our data had non-repeating date fields.

32.10   Visualization of Merged Data

You know that I'm a big fan of visualization. Let's visualize the merged time series. We will add on to our merge chain, stick the date in the index, pull out the years from 2014 forward, use the *cfs, gage_height, PRCP,* and *TOBS* columns, interpolate the missing values, do a rolling 15 day average, and plot the result in their own subplot:

```
>>> fig, ax = plt.subplots(dpi=600)
>>> (dd
...     .groupby(pd.Grouper(key='datetime', freq='D'))
...     .median()
...     .merge(temp_df, left_index=True, right_on='DATE',
...            how='inner', validate='1:1')
```

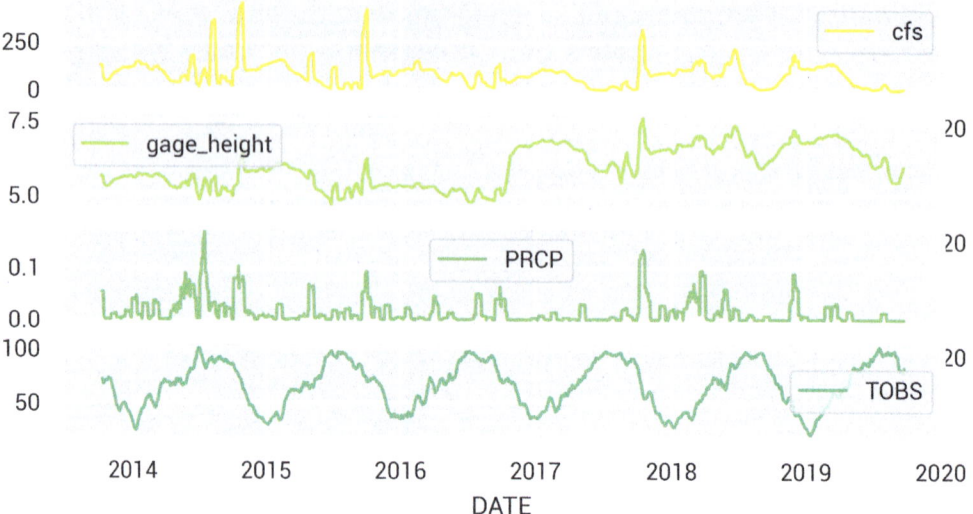

Figure 32.5: Visualization of 15-day average for Dirty Devil river metrics.

```
...     .set_index('DATE')
...     .loc['2014':,['cfs', 'gage_height', 'PRCP', 'TOBS']]
...     .interpolate()
...     .rolling(15)
...     .mean()
...     .plot(subplots=True, figsize=(10,8), ax=ax)
... )
>>> fig.suptitle('Dirty Devil Metrics (15 day average)')
```

Here's a scatterplot of temperature against river flow. I'm coloring this by month of the year:

```
>>> fig, ax = plt.subplots(dpi=600)
>>> dd2 = (dd
...     .groupby(pd.Grouper(key='datetime', freq='D'))
...     .median()
...     .merge(temp_df, left_index=True, right_on='DATE',
...             how='inner', validate='1:1')
...     .query('cfs < 400')
... )
>>> (dd2
...     .plot.scatter(x='cfs', y='TOBS', c=dd2.DATE.dt.month,
```

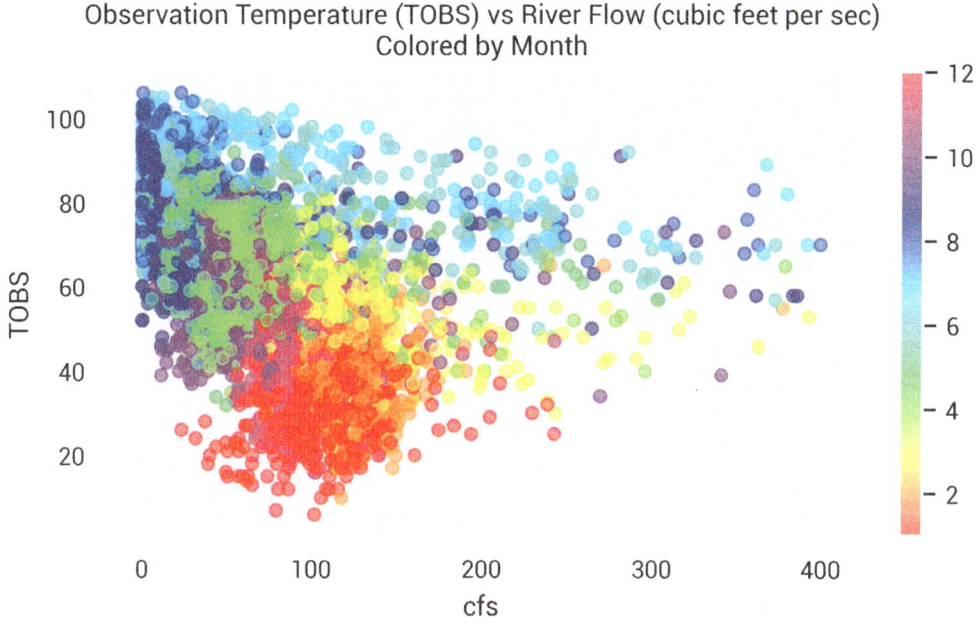

Figure 32.6: Scatterplot of temperature against river flow, colored by month.

```
...                    ax=ax, cmap='hsv', alpha=.5)
... )
>>> ax.set_title('Observation Temperature (TOBS) '
...     'vs River Flow (cubic feet per sec)\nColored by Month')
```

Method	Description

pd.concat(objs, axis=0,
  join='outer',
  ignore_index=False, keys=None,
  levels=None, names=None,
  verify_integrity=False,
  sort=False, copy=True)
	Combine a list of objs along the specified axis.

`df.set_index(keys, drop=True,`
   `append=False,`
   `verify_integrity=False)`
	Return a dataframe with a new index. The keys argument can be a column name, a series (or numpy array) of labels for the index, or a list column names or series. The drop parameter indicates whether to remove columns used for the index. The append parameter allows you to add additional index levels. You can check for duplicate index values by setting `verify_integrity=True`.

`df.join(other, on=None,`
   `how='left', lsuffix='',`
   `rsuffix='', sort=False)`
	Return a dataframe with the df joined with other by index names. Can specify how to be `'left'`, `'right'`, `'outer'`, or `'inner'`. If column names are overlapping, can specify suffix. Alternatively, can use on to specify column names from df to join with index from other. Use `df.merge` instead.

`df.merge(right, how='inner',`
   `on=None, left_on=None,`
   `right_on=None,`
   `left_index=False,`
   `right_index=False, sort=False,`
   `suffixes=('_x', '_y'),`
   `copy=True, indicator=False,`
   `validate=None)`
	Return a dataframe with the df joined with other by overlapping columns. Can specify how to be `'left'`, `'right'`, `'outer'`, `'inner'`, or `'cross'`. Can specify specific columns with on. Can specify unique columns to either dataframe with `left_on` and `right_on`. Can join on the index with `left_index` and `right_index`. Can validate merge with `'one_to_one'` (`'1:1'`), `'one_to_many'` (`'1:m'`), or `'many_to_one'` (`'m:1'`). `'many_to_many'` (`'m:m'`) doesn't do any checks.

Table 32.1: Chapter Methods

32.11 Summary

Data can often have more utility if we combine it with other data. In the '70s, *relational algebra* was invented to describe various joins among tabular data. The .merge method of the DataFrame lets us apply these operations to tabular data in the pandas world. This chapter described concatenation and the four basic joins that are possible via .merge.

32.12 Exercises

1. Create a dataframe for employees. It should have:

Index	name	company
0	Fred	AMZN
1	John	GOOG
2	Sally	GOOG
3	Annie	NFLX

Create a dataframe for location. It should have:

Index	ticker	location
0	AMZN	Seattle
1	GOOG	SF

1. What type of join do we need to do to get the location of each employee?

2. How would you validate the join?

Chapter 33

Exporting Data

Most of this book has dealt with exploring data, tweaking data, and visualizing data. In addition, you may need to share data with others. In this chapter, we will explore some of the mechanisms for exporting data.

33.1 Dirty Devil Data

In this section, we will revisit the Dirty Devil data. Let's load the flow and gage height data:

```
>>> import pandas as pd
>>> url = 'https://github.com/mattharrison/datasets/raw/master'\
...         '/data/dirtydevil.txt'
>>> df = pd.read_csv(url, skiprows=lambda num: num <34 or num == 35,
...                  sep='\t')
>>> def to_denver_time(df_, time_col, tz_col):
...     return (df_
...         .assign(**{tz_col: df_[tz_col].replace('MDT', 'MST7MDT')})
...         .groupby(tz_col)
...         [time_col]
...         .transform(lambda s: pd.to_datetime(s)
...             .dt.tz_localize(s.name, ambiguous=True)
...             .dt.tz_convert('America/Denver'))
...     )

>>> def tweak_river(df_):
...     return (df_
...         .assign(datetime=to_denver_time(df_, 'datetime', 'tz_cd'))
...         .rename(columns={'144166_00060': 'cfs',
...                          '144167_00065': 'gage_height'})
```

```
...        .set_index('datetime')
...      )

>>> dd = tweak_river(df)
>>> dd
                          agency_cd  ... gage_height  144167_00065_cd
datetime                             ...
2001-05-07 01:00:00-06:00      USGS  ...         NaN               NaN
2001-05-07 01:15:00-06:00      USGS  ...         NaN               NaN
2001-05-07 01:30:00-06:00      USGS  ...         NaN               NaN
2001-05-07 01:45:00-06:00      USGS  ...         NaN               NaN
2001-05-07 02:00:00-06:00      USGS  ...         NaN               NaN
...                             ...  ...         ...               ...
2020-09-28 08:30:00-06:00      USGS  ...        6.16                 P
2020-09-28 08:45:00-06:00      USGS  ...        6.15                 P
2020-09-28 09:00:00-06:00      USGS  ...        6.15                 P
2020-09-28 09:15:00-06:00      USGS  ...        6.15                 P
2020-09-28 09:30:00-06:00      USGS  ...        6.15                 P

[539305 rows x 7 columns]
```

33.2 Reading and Writing

There are a bunch of functions in pandas that deal with ingesting data. They all begin with read_. Similarly, there are analagous exporting methods on the dataframe object. These exporting methods start with .to_. We will talk about the common methods for exporting in this chapter.

33.3 Creating CSV Files

The Comma Separated Value (CSV) file is ubiquitous. It has been around since the early 70s. This format has the benefit of being human-readable, and that is about where the benefits end. There was no standard for CSV files for a long time. In 2005 a standard was released, but the damage was already done. As such escaping mechanisms, encoding, header handling, and data types all suffer. You can see the pandas developers' attempts to deal with all of these issues when you look at the interface for the pd.read_csv function. It has over 40 parameters!

To write our data to a file, we can use the .to_csv method. One thing to be aware of is that by default, pandas will write the index values in a CSV, but when reading a CSV it will create a new index unless we specify a column for the index:

```
>>> dd.to_csv('/tmp/dd.csv')
```

Note

If you don't provide a filename, `.to_csv` will return the string content that would go into the file rather than writing the file. We will take advantage of that in this book to examine what the export looks like.

Let's look at what the first five lines of the export looks like:

```
>>> print(dd.head(5).to_csv())
datetime,agency_cd,site_no,tz_cd,cfs,144166_00060_cd,gage_height,14416
2001-05-07 01:00:00-06:00,USGS,9333500,MDT,71.0,A:[91],,
2001-05-07 01:15:00-06:00,USGS,9333500,MDT,71.0,A:[91],,
2001-05-07 01:30:00-06:00,USGS,9333500,MDT,71.0,A:[91],,
2001-05-07 01:45:00-06:00,USGS,9333500,MDT,70.0,A:[91],,
2001-05-07 02:00:00-06:00,USGS,9333500,MDT,70.0,A:[91],,
```

If we wanted to read this and stick *datetime* in the index, we could use this code:

```
>>> dd2 = pd.read_csv('/tmp/dd.csv', index_col='datetime')
```

Note that CSV files don't do much type conversion other than trying to convert strings to numbers. You can use the `parse_dates` parameter to attempt to convert the index into proper dates, but I would recommend creating a tweak function and revisiting the section on dealing with timezones to properly handle this (hint: it will look much like the `tweak_river` function from above).

There are a bunch of optional parameters for exporting CSV files, but I normally don't adjust them.

33.4 Exporting to Excel

Another commonly used option is exporting the data frame to an Excel spreadsheet. The benefits of this method are that the world basically revolves around Excel. Everyone was taught how to use it in Kindergarten, and business schools still teach it today. As such, Excel drives most of the business world.

> **Note**
>
> You will have to make sure `openpyxl` is installed to use Excel support. Simply installing the pandas library usually will not install full Excel support.

Let's export the data to Excel:

```
>>> dd.to_excel('/tmp/dd.xlsx')
Traceback (most recent call last):
  ...
ValueError: Excel does not support datetimes with timezones.
Please ensure that datetimes are timezone unaware before writing to Excel.
```

Whoops! That didn't quite work. We will need to strip the timezone information before exporting to Excel.

Note that exporting to Excel is a bit slower than writing CSV files. (Also note that Excel reads CSV files, so if you can deal without the limited formatting and type information that pandas inserts in an xlsx file, you might be ok with sending out CSV files to your Excel-junkie friends.):

```
>>> (dd
...    .reset_index()
...    .assign(datetime=lambda df_: df_.datetime.dt.tz_convert(tz=None))
...    .set_index('datetime')
...    .to_excel('/tmp/dd.xlsx')
... )
```

Another benefit of Excel is that you can write a spreadsheet that has multiple sheets. In this example, we write 2010 data to one sheet and 2011 data to another:

```
>>> writer = pd.ExcelWriter('/tmp/dd2.xlsx')
>>> dd2 = (dd
...    .reset_index()
...    .assign(datetime=lambda df_: df_.datetime.dt.tz_convert(tz=None))
...    .set_index('datetime')
... )
>>> (dd2
...    .loc['2010':'2010-12-31']
...    .to_excel(writer, sheet_name='2010')
... )
>>> (dd2
...    .loc['2011':'2011-12-31']
...    .to_excel(writer, sheet_name='2011')
... )
```

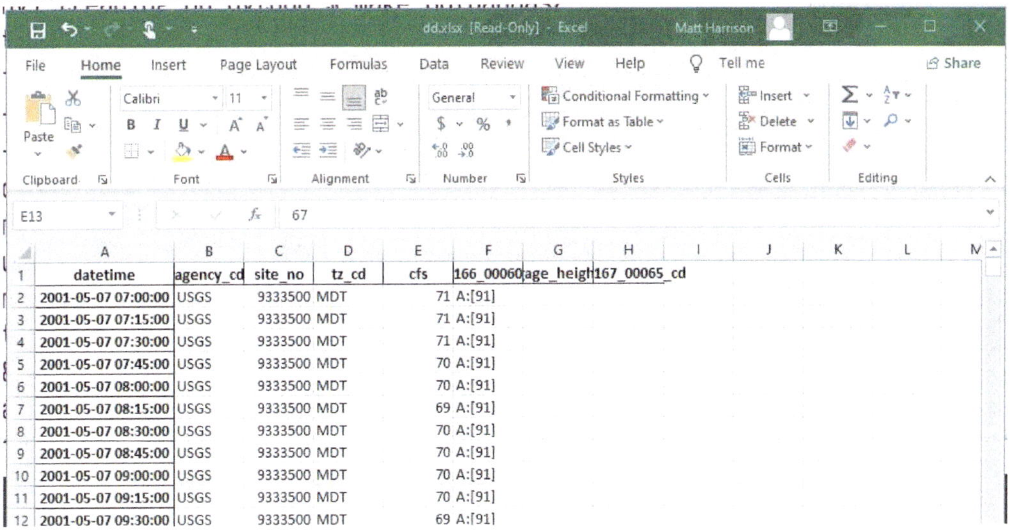

Figure 33.1: Excel export of pandas data frame.

```
>>> writer.save()
```

33.5 Feather

Here is an option that is a relative newcomer. Feather is a binary file format for persisting columnar data that is found in data frames. This is not a surprise because the creator of pandas works on it. Feather tends to be fast, and it keeps type information (for the most part). It is also supposed to be supported by other languages if you happen to have to deal with processing data in R, Julia, or others.

Note

You will need to install the feather-format library to leverage this functionality.

Let's try exporting our data:

```
>>> dd.to_feather('/tmp/dd.fea')
Traceback (most recent call last):
 ...
ValueError: feather does not support serializing
 <class 'pandas.core.indexes.datetimes.DatetimeIndex'> for the index;
```

```
you can .reset_index() to make the index into column(s)
```

Whoops. It looks like we need to convert the index to non-date types:

```
>>> (dd
...    .reset_index()
...    .to_feather('/tmp/dd.fea')
... )
```

Let's see how this did in preserving our information:

```
>>> dd2 = pd.read_feather('/tmp/dd.fea')
>>> dd2.set_index('datetime').equals(dd)
True
```

Awesome! It looks like this works (with the exception of our index issue). Feather is relatively quick and supports most datatypes.

33.6 SQL

You can stick a data frame into a SQL table with the .to_sql method. In this example, we will create a SQLite database and insert our data into a table named *dd*.

> **Note**
>
> You will need to install sqlalchemy for SQL functionality.

```
>>> import sqlite3
>>> con = sqlite3.connect('dd.db')
>>> dd.to_sql('dd', con, if_exists='replace')
```

Let's read from the database:

```
>>> import sqlalchemy as sa
>>> eng = sa.create_engine('sqlite:///dd.db')
>>> sa_con = eng.connect()
>>> dd2 = pd.read_sql('dd', sa_con, index_col='datetime')
>>> dd2.equals(dd)
False
```

```
>>> dd2
                     agency_cd  site_no  ...  gage_height  144167_00065_cd
datetime                                 ...
2001-05-07 01:00:00       USGS  9333500  ...          NaN             None
2001-05-07 01:15:00       USGS  9333500  ...          NaN             None
2001-05-07 01:30:00       USGS  9333500  ...          NaN             None
```

2001-05-07 01:45:00	USGS	9333500	...	NaN	None
2001-05-07 02:00:00	USGS	9333500	...	NaN	None
...	...	...	...	...	...
2020-09-28 08:30:00	USGS	9333500	...	6.16	P
2020-09-28 08:45:00	USGS	9333500	...	6.15	P
2020-09-28 09:00:00	USGS	9333500	...	6.15	P
2020-09-28 09:15:00	USGS	9333500	...	6.15	P
2020-09-28 09:30:00	USGS	9333500	...	6.15	P

```
[539305 rows x 7 columns]
```

It looks like we could read the table from the database, but it was not equal to the original data. Closer inspection reveals that our index with timezone aware dates was stored with timezone data, but when the data came out from the database, this information was dropped.

Here is an example of using the sqlite3 command-line tool to inspect the database:

```
$ sqlite3 dd.db
SQLite version 3.31.1 2020-01-27 19:55:54
Enter ".help" for usage hints.
sqlite> .schema
CREATE TABLE IF NOT EXISTS "dd" (
"datetime" TIMESTAMP,
  "agency_cd" TEXT,
  "site_no" INTEGER,
  "tz_cd" TEXT,
  "cfs" REAL,
  "144166_00060_cd" TEXT,
  "gage_height" REAL,
  "144167_00065_cd" TEXT
);
CREATE INDEX "ix_dd_datetime"ON "dd" ("datetime");
sqlite> SELECT * FROM dd LIMIT 1;
2001-05-07 01:00:00-06:00|USGS|9333500|MDT|71.0|A:[91]||
sqlite>
```

If we update the index with timezone information, our dataframe is equal to the original data:

```
>>> (dd2
...    .reset_index()
...    .assign(datetime=lambda df_: df_.datetime
...            .dt.tz_localize('America/Denver', ambiguous=False))
...    .set_index('datetime')
...    .equals(dd)
```

```
... )
True
```

33.7 JSON

Those who implement backend services often need to serialize data with JavaScript Object Notation (JSON). The pandas library has a .to_dict method to format data as a dictionary. It also has a .to_json method which supports exporting data formatted as JSON in multiple layouts.

Let's try out .to_dict first. While not strictly JSON, they are both dictionary representations (with JSON being serialized as a string):

```
>>> obj = dd.to_dict()
```

There is no corresponding pd.read_dict function. Rather, there is a class method on the data frame called .from_dict. Let's see how round tripping works with this method:

```
>>> dd2 = pd.DataFrame.from_dict(obj)
>>> dd.equals(dd2)
True
```

Note

Dictionary exports do not support duplicated index names. Unlike .to_json (when called with orient='columns' which raises a ValueError), it will silently drop data.

Ok, now on to .to_json:

```
>>> dd.to_json('/tmp/dd.json.gz')
>>> dd2 = pd.read_json('/tmp/dd.json')
>>> dd2
                     agency_cd  site_no  ... gage_height  144167_00065_cd
2001-05-07 07:00:00       USGS  9333500  ...         NaN             None
2001-05-07 07:15:00       USGS  9333500  ...         NaN             None
2001-05-07 07:30:00       USGS  9333500  ...         NaN             None
2001-05-07 07:45:00       USGS  9333500  ...         NaN             None
2001-05-07 08:00:00       USGS  9333500  ...         NaN             None
...                        ...      ...  ...         ...              ...
2020-09-28 14:30:00       USGS  9333500  ...        6.16                P
2020-09-28 14:45:00       USGS  9333500  ...        6.15                P
2020-09-28 15:00:00       USGS  9333500  ...        6.15                P
2020-09-28 15:15:00       USGS  9333500  ...        6.15                P
```

```
2020-09-28 15:30:00        USGS  9333500  ...        6.15              P

[539305 rows x 7 columns]

>>> dd2.equals(dd)
False
```

These are not equal because the dates in the index were exported (and converted) to UTC dates (even though they had *America/Denver* time information). Let's put them back into *America/Denver*:

```
>>> dd3 = (dd2
...     .reset_index()
...     .rename(columns={'index':'datetime'})
...     .assign(datetime=lambda df_: df_.datetime.dt.tz_localize(tz='UTC')
...             .dt.tz_convert('America/Denver'))
...     .set_index('datetime')
... )

>>> dd3
                            agency_cd  ... gage_height  144167_00065_cd
datetime                               ...
2001-05-07 01:00:00-06:00        USGS  ...         NaN              NaN
2001-05-07 01:15:00-06:00        USGS  ...         NaN              NaN
2001-05-07 01:30:00-06:00        USGS  ...         NaN              NaN
2001-05-07 01:45:00-06:00        USGS  ...         NaN              NaN
2001-05-07 02:00:00-06:00        USGS  ...         NaN              NaN
...                               ...  ...         ...              ...
2020-09-28 08:30:00-06:00        USGS  ...        6.16                P
2020-09-28 08:45:00-06:00        USGS  ...        6.15                P
2020-09-28 09:00:00-06:00        USGS  ...        6.15                P
2020-09-28 09:15:00-06:00        USGS  ...        6.15                P
2020-09-28 09:30:00-06:00        USGS  ...        6.16                P

[539305 rows x 7 columns]
```

Let's check if they are equal now:

```
>>> dd3.equals(dd)
False
```

Still not. Turns out this is a rounding issue (in the debugging chapter, we will show how to figure this out):

```
>>> dd3.round(3).equals(dd)
True
```

Note

The `.to_json` method exports dates as epoch integers:

```
>>> dd.head()
                              agency_cd  ... gage_height   144167_00065_cd
datetime                                 ...
2001-05-07 01:00:00-06:00      USGS     ...        NaN                NaN
2001-05-07 01:15:00-06:00      USGS     ...        NaN                NaN
2001-05-07 01:30:00-06:00      USGS     ...        NaN                NaN
2001-05-07 01:45:00-06:00      USGS     ...        NaN                NaN
2001-05-07 02:00:00-06:00      USGS     ...        NaN                NaN

[5 rows x 7 columns]

>>> dd.head().to_json()[:60]
'{"agency_cd":{"989218800000":"USGS","989219700000":"USGS",'
```

Pandas converts the epoch integers into naive UTC dates (they have UTC wall time, but have no timezone information).

Method	Description
df.to_csv(path_or_buf=None, sep=',', na_rep='', float_format=None, columns=None, header=True, index=True, index_label=None, mode='w', encoding='utf8', compression='infer', quoting=csv.QUOTE_MINIMAL, quotechar='"', line_terminator=os.linesep, chunksize=None, date_format=None, doublequote=True, escapechar=None, decimal='.', errors='strict', storage_options=None)	Write to a CSV file (or stdout if not specified). Can specify float_format with '%.3f' (.1234 to .123).

```
pd.read_csv(filepath_or_buffer,
    sep=',', header='infer',
    names=None, index_col=None,
    usecols=None, squeeze=False,
    prefix='',
    mangle_dupe_cols=True,
    dtype=None, engine=None,
    converters=None,
    true_values=None,
    false_values=None,
    skipinitialspace=False,
    skiprows=None, skipfooter=0,
    nrows=None, na_values=None,
    keep_default_na=True,
    na_filter=True, verbose=False,
    skip_blank_lines=True,
    parse_dates=False,
    infer_datetime_format=False,
    keep_date_col=False,
    date_parser=None,
    dayfirst=False,
    cache_dates=True,
    iterator=False,
    chunksize=None,
    compression='infer',
    thousands=None, decimal='.',
    lineterminator=None,
    quotechar='"', quoting=0,
    doublequote=True,
    escapechar=None, comment=None,
    encoding=None,
    encoding_errors='strict',
    dialect=None,
    error_bad_lines=None,
    warn_bad_lines=None,
    on_bad_lines=None,
    delim_whitespace=False,
    low_memory=True,
    memory_map=False,
    float_precision=None,
    storage_options=None)
```

Create a dataframe from a CSV file. Use sep to parse files with other delimiters. Use names to specify column names. Specify missing numeric values with na_values. Set dayfirst=True to use dates in a non US-centric environment.

```df.to_excel(excel_writer,` ` sheet_name='Sheet1',` ` na_rep='', float_format=None,` ` columns=None, header=True,` ` index=True, index_label=None,` ` startrow=0, startcol=0,` ` engine=None, merge_cells=True,` ` encoding=None, inf_rep='inf',` ` verbose=True,` ` freeze_panes=None,` ` storage_options=None)```	Write an Excel formatted file or instance `ExcelWriter`.
```pd.ExcelWriter(path, engine=None,` ` date_format=None,` ` datetime_format=None,` ` mode='w',` ` storage_options=None,` ` if_sheet_exists=None,` ` engine_kwargs=None, **kwargs)```	Create a class for writing dataframes into sheets.
```pd.read_excel(io, sheet_name=0,` ` header=0, names=None,` ` index_col=None, usecols=None,` ` squeeze=False, dtype=None,` ` engine=None, converters=None,` ` true_values=None,` ` false_values=None,` ` skiprows=None, nrows=None,` ` na_values=None,` ` keep_default_na=True,` ` na_filter=True, verbose=False,` ` parse_dates=False,` ` date_parser=None,` ` thousands=None, comment=None,` ` skipfooter=0,` ` mangle_dupe_cols=True,` ` storage_options=None)```	Create a dataframe from Excel file or dictionary (mapping sheet name to dataframe) if sheet_name is a list.
```df.to_feather(path)```	Write a Feather formatted file.
```pd.read_feather(path,` ` columns=None,` ` use_threads=True,` ` storage_options=None)```	Create a dataframe from a Feather file.

`sqlite3.connect(database,`
`  timeout=None,`
`  detect_types=None,`
`  isolation_level=None,`
`  check_same_thread=None,`
`  factory=None,`
`  cached_statements=None,`
`  uri=None)`
	Open a connection to a SQLite database. Use database=':memory:' to create RAM database.

`sa.create_engine(url, **kwargs)`	Create a SQLAlchemy engine from a database connection string.
`eng.connect()`	Get the database connection from a SQLAlchemy engine.

`df.to_sql(name, con, schema=None,`
`  if_exists='fail', index=True,`
`  index_label=None,`
`  chunksize=None, dtype=None,`
`  method=None)`
	Create a SQL table with name from the dataframe. Store the results in database specified by connection con. Can specify 'replace' or 'append' for if_exists.

`pd.read_sql(sql, con,`
`  index_col=None,`
`  coerce_float=True,`
`  params=None, parse_dates=None,`
`  columns=None, chunksize=None,)`
	Create a dataframe from a SQL query.

`df.to_dict(orient='dict',` `  into=dict)`	Serialize a dataframe into a dictionary. Orientation can be 'dict' (column to dict of index to value), 'list' (column to list of values), 'series' (column to series), 'split' (dictionary with index, columns, and data keys), 'records' (list of dictionary (column to value)), 'index' (dictionary of index to dictionary of column to value).

`pd.Dataframe.from_dict(data,`
`  orient='columns', dtype=None,`
`  columns=None)`
	Create a dataframe from a dictionary. Orientation can be 'columns' (like 'dict' in .to_dict) or 'index'.

`df.to_json(path_or_buf=None,`
`  orient=None,`
`  date_format='epoch',`
`  double_precision=10,`
`  force_ascii=True,`
`  date_unit='ms',`
`  default_handler=None,`
`  lines=False,`
`  compression='infer',`
`  index=True, indent=None,`
`  storage_options=None)`
	Serialize a dataframe to JSON. Orientation can be `'columns'` (column to dict of index to value), `'list'` (column to list of values), `'series'` (column to series), `'split'` (dictionary with index, columns, and data keys), `'records'` (list of dictionary (column to value)), `'index'` (dictionary of index to dictionary of column to value), `'data'` (list of values), `'values'` (values array), `'table'` (dictionary of schema and data). Can change date format with `'iso'` (ISO8601).

`pd.read_json(path_or_buf=None,`
`  orient=None, typ='frame',`
`  dtype=None, convert_axes=None,`
`  convert_dates=True,`
`  keep_default_dates=True,`
`  numpy=False,`
`  precise_float=False,`
`  date_unit=None,`
`  encoding='utf-8',`
`  encoding_errors='strict',`
`  lines=False, chunksize=None,`
`  compression='infer',`
`  nrows=None,`
`  storage_options=None)`
	Create a dataframe from JSON.

`df.round(decimals=0)`	Create a dataframe with decimals rounded to given places.
`df.equals(other)`	Compares two dataframes if they have the same shape and values. Columns should have the same type.

Table 33.1: Chapter Methods

33.8 Summary

There are many formats for exporting data with pandas. As I keep mentioning in this book, you will want to double-check your data after you have exported it so that you know what is in there. Some formats, like CSV, lose most type information. Others try to preserve it but may get hung up on timezones or rounding issues.

33.9 Exercises

With a dataset of your choice:

1. Export the data from a dataframe into a CSV file.

2. Export the data from a dataframe into a SQLite database.

3. Export the data from a dataframe into a Feather file.

4. Export the data from a dataframe into JSON.

Chapter 34

Styling Dataframes

In this chapter, I will demonstrate how to style a dataframe inside of Jupyter.

34.1 Loading the Data

We are going to use the Dirty Devil dataset for this section.

```
>>> import pandas as pd

>>> url = 'https://github.com/mattharrison/datasets/raw/master '\
...       '/data/dirtydevil.txt'
>>> df = pd.read_csv(url, skiprows=lambda num: num <34 or num == 35,
...                  sep='\t')
>>> def tweak_river(df_):
...     return (df_
...   .assign(datetime=pd.to_datetime(df_.datetime))
...   .rename(columns={'144166_00060': 'cfs',
...                    '144167_00065': 'gage_height'})
...   .set_index('datetime')
... )

>>> dd = tweak_river(df)
>>> dd
                    agency_cd  site_no  ... gage_height  144167_00065_cd
datetime                                ...
2001-05-07 01:00:00      USGS  9333500  ...         NaN              NaN
2001-05-07 01:15:00      USGS  9333500  ...         NaN              NaN
2001-05-07 01:30:00      USGS  9333500  ...         NaN              NaN
2001-05-07 01:45:00      USGS  9333500  ...         NaN              NaN
2001-05-07 02:00:00      USGS  9333500  ...         NaN              NaN
```

```
...               ...     ...  ...        ...              ...
2020-09-28 08:30:00  USGS 9333500 ...        6.16              P
2020-09-28 08:45:00  USGS 9333500 ...        6.15              P
2020-09-28 09:00:00  USGS 9333500 ...        6.15              P
2020-09-28 09:15:00  USGS 9333500 ...        6.15              P
2020-09-28 09:30:00  USGS 9333500 ...        6.15              P

[539305 rows x 7 columns]
```

Now that we have the basic data, I'm going to do some aggregations and column creation. See if you can go through the following code and figure out what it is doing. I'll explain right after showing it, but after going through this book you should start practicing reading code and making sure that you can understand what it is doing.

::

```
>>> import sparklines
>>> agg_flow = (dd
...    #.resample('M')  # resample .agg doesn't support named aggregations
...    .groupby(pd.Grouper(freq='M'))
...    .agg(cfs=('cfs', 'median'),
...        total_flow=('cfs', lambda ser:(ser*15*60).sum()),
...        gage_height=('gage_height', 'median'),
...        flow_trend=('cfs', lambda ser: sparklines.sparklines(
...            ser
...            .fillna(0)
...            .resample('2D')
...            .median()
...            .fillna(0))
...            [0])
...        )
...    .assign(quarterly_flow=lambda df_: df_
...            .total_flow
...            .resample('Q')
...            .transform('sum'),
...        percent_quarterly_flow=lambda df2_: df2_
...            .total_flow / df2_.quarterly_flow,
...        off_goal=lambda df3_: df3_.percent_quarterly_flow-.33,
...        cost=lambda df4_: df4_.total_flow * .0002)
...    )
>>> agg_flow
            cfs    total_flow  ...   off_goal        cost
datetime                       ...
2001-05-31  47.00  105383700.0 ...   0.525199   21076.7400
2001-06-30  23.00   17843400.0 ...  -0.185199    3568.6800
```

```
2001-07-31   17.00      7781400.0  ...  -0.298037   1556.2800
2001-08-31   52.50    192848220.0  ...   0.462151  38569.6440
2001-09-30   26.00     42819300.0  ...  -0.154114   8563.8600

...           ...           ...    ...      ...          ...
2020-05-31   21.25     60721029.0  ...  -0.098571  12144.2058
2020-06-30   10.20     24475410.0  ...  -0.236716   4895.0820
2020-07-31   10.80     67073337.0  ...   0.428016  13414.6674
2020-08-31    0.32     11042316.0  ...  -0.205207   2208.4632
2020-09-30    5.79     10369692.0  ...  -0.212809   2073.9384

[233 rows x 8 columns]
```

There might have been a curveball in here... the sparklines library. Let's skip that for now and describe the rest of the chain.

Group by the months in the index (note that I'm using named aggregations and that as the comment states, the result of the .resample method does not support named aggregations). For each group, calculate the median of the *cfs* column, calculate *total_flow* from the the *cfs* column (it is the 15 minute value, so we multiply it by 15 to get the minutes and 60 to get the seconds), and create a *flow_trend* column that uses sparklines.

After grouping, we are going to make some more columns. *quarterly_flow* resamples our monthly data to the quarterly level and sums it. *percent_quarterly_flow* divides *total_flow* by *quarterly_flow*. The *off_goal* column assumes that each month should contribute 33% of the quarterly water flow and measures how far off we are from that goal. The *cost* column calculates expense assuming it costs 2 hundredths of a cent per cubic foot of water.

34.2 Sparklines

A sparkline[21] is a small plot drawn without axes or coordinates created by Edward Tufte. The intent is to show a general tread. The sparklines[22] library in Python is a Unicode barchart implementation of this idea.

If you have a series of numbers, you can create a Unicode string that represents them:

---

[21]This creative use of embedding sparklines was inspired by this tweet https://twitter.com/pmbaumgartner/status/1084645440224559104

[22]https://github.com/deeplook/sparklines

```
>>> import sparklines
>>> sparklines.sparklines(range(10))
['▁▂▃▄▅▆▇█']
```

So let's revisit this chunk of code:

```
...        flow_trend=('cfs', lambda ser: sparklines.sparklines(
...            ser
...            .resample('2D')
...            .median()
...            .fillna(0))
...            [0])
```

We use the *cfs* column, resample to every two days (remember this series, ser, is data for every 15 minutes for a single month), calculate the median value of river flow, and fill in missing values with zero. This gives us a series with the median two-day value. We pass this data into the sparklines library to generate a Unicode bar plot. The sparklines library returns a list with the string inside of it, so we pull the chart out of the list.

The resulting column looks like this:

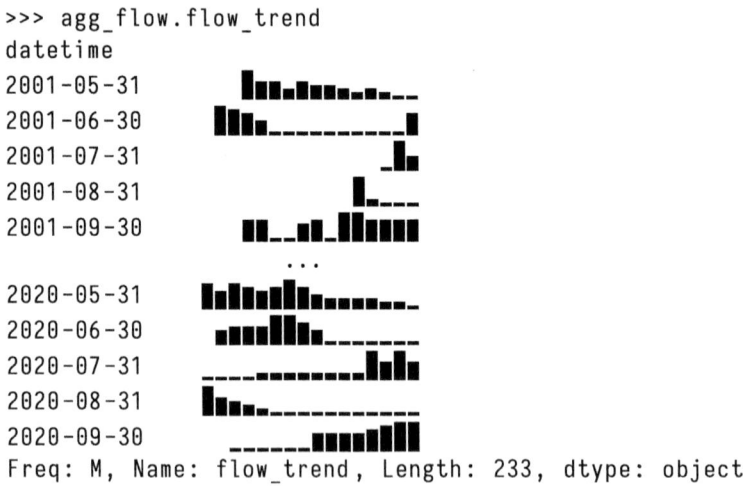

```
>>> agg_flow.flow_trend
datetime
2001-05-31
2001-06-30
2001-07-31
2001-08-31
2001-09-30
           ...
2020-05-31
2020-06-30
2020-07-31
2020-08-31
2020-09-30
Freq: M, Name: flow_trend, Length: 233, dtype: object
```

34.3 The .style Attribute

Up to this point, most of the results of our chains have been a series or dataframe. The .style attribute of a dataframe allows you to chain, but you can only chain more styling methods, you cannot update the dataframe. If you want to style the output, you should do that as the last step(s) of your chain.

```
: (agg_flow
  .reset_index()
  .style
  # after this we are not working a a dataframe but a "styler" object
  .format({'cost': '${:,.2f}', 'datetime': '{:%Y/%m}/01',
           'percent_quarterly_flow': '{:.1%}',
           'off_goal': '{:+.1%}',
           **{col: '{:.1f}' for col in ['cfs', 'total_flow', 'quarterly_flow']}},
          na_rep='Missing')
)
```

	datetime	cfs	total_flow	gage_height	flow_trend	quarterly_flow	percent_quarterly_flow	off_goal	cost
0	2001/05/01	47.0	105383700.0	Missing		123227100.0	85.5%	+52.5%	$21,076.74
1	2001/06/01	23.0	17843400.0	Missing		123227100.0	14.5%	-18.5%	$3,568.68
2	2001/07/01	17.0	7781400.0	Missing		243448920.0	3.2%	-29.8%	$1,556.28
3	2001/08/01	52.5	192848220.0	Missing		243448920.0	79.2%	+46.2%	$38,569.64
4	2001/09/01	26.0	42819300.0	Missing		243448920.0	17.6%	-15.4%	$8,563.86
5	2001/10/01	54.0	134975700.0	Missing		480483900.0	28.1%	-4.9%	$26,995.14
6	2001/11/01	104.0	203110200.0	Missing		480483900.0	42.3%	+9.3%	$40,622.04
7	2001/12/01	115.0	142398000.0	Missing		480483900.0	29.6%	-3.4%	$28,479.60
8	2002/01/01	136.0	197745300.0	Missing		638525700.0	31.0%	-2.0%	$39,549.06
9	2002/02/01	131.0	157920300.0	Missing		638525700.0	24.7%	-8.3%	$31,584.06
10	2002/03/01	107.0	282860100.0	Missing		638525700.0	44.3%	+11.3%	$56,572.02
11	2002/04/01	57.0	152018100.0	Missing		167027670.0	91.0%	+58.0%	$30,403.62
12	2002/05/01	12.0	12806010.0	Missing		167027670.0	7.7%	-25.3%	$2,561.20
13	2002/06/01	12.0	2203560.0	Missing		167027670.0	1.3%	-31.7%	$440.71
14	2002/07/01	53.5	19996200.0	Missing		405788400.0	4.9%	-28.1%	$3,999.24
15	2002/08/01	Missing	0.0	Missing		405788400.0	0.0%	-33.0%	$0.00
16	2002/09/01	80.0	385792200.0	Missing		405788400.0	95.1%	+62.1%	$77,158.44
17	2002/10/01	97.0	32053500.0	Missing		284306400.0	11.3%	-21.7%	$6,410.70
18	2002/11/01	82.0	36025200.0	Missing		284306400.0	12.7%	-20.3%	$7,205.04
19	2002/12/01	87.0	216227700.0	Missing		284306400.0	76.1%	+43.1%	$43,245.54

Figure 34.1: Changing the style of the columns.

34.4 Formatting

One thing you can do with styling is control the formatting. Let's make the *cost* column show dollar signs, change the format of the *datetime* column, convert *percent_quarterly_flow* to a percentage, and and a plus or minus to the *off_goal* column. This is done with the .format method.

```
(agg_flow
 .reset_index()
 .style
 # after this we are not working a a dataframe but a "styler" object
 .format({'cost': '${:,.2f}', 'datetime': '{:%Y/%m}/01',
          'percent_quarterly_flow': '{:.1%}',
          'off_goal': '{:+.1%}',
          **{col: '{:.1f}' for col in ['cfs', 'total_flow', 'quarterly_flow']}},
          na_rep='Missing')
 .bar(subset='cfs', color='#c07fef', vmax=agg_flow.cfs.quantile(.95))
 .bar(subset='off_goal', color=['red', 'green'], align='mid')
 .highlight_null(null_color='#fef78c')  # wish this was highlight_na
 .highlight_max(axis=0, color='green')
)
```

Figure 34.2: Adding bar plots to *cfs* and *off_goal* columns. Highlighting missing and maximum values.

34.5 Embedding Bar Plots

The next thing we are going to do is embed a bar plot in the cell background. We use the `.bar` method for that.

The *cfs* bars are clipped (via `vmax`) to the 95% quantile, otherwise they don't show up due to outliers. The *off_goal* bars specify two colors to distinguish positive from negative.

34.6 Highlighting

There are a few styling methods to highlight values. You can highlight missing, minimum, maximum, a range, or a quantile range. Our example highlights missing and maximum values.

```
(agg_flow
 .reset_index()
 .style
 # after this we are not working a a dataframe but a "styler" object
 .format({'cost': '${:,.2f}', 'datetime': '{:%Y/%m}/01',
          'percent_quarterly_flow': '{:.1%}',
          'off_goal': '{:+.1%}',
          **{col: '{:.1f}' for col in ['cfs', 'total_flow', 'quarterly_flow']}},
          na_rep='Missing')
 .bar(subset='cfs', color='#c07fef', vmax=agg_flow.cfs.quantile(.95))
 .bar(subset='off_goal', color=['red', 'green'], align='mid')
 .highlight_null(null_color='#fef70c')  # wish this was highlight_na
 .highlight_max(axis=0, color='green')
 .background_gradient(axis=0, cmap='Reds', subset='cost', vmin=1_000, vmax=25_000)
 .set_caption('Dirty Devil Summary')
)
```

Figure 34.3: Heatmaps set in the *cost* column. A caption ("Dirty Devil Summary").

34.7 Heatmaps and Gradients

You can shade the background based on the value of the cell. We demoed this in the cross-tabulation section. Here we will use a red color map to color the *cost* column. We will set vmax to indicate that anything over $25,000 is over budget. he background.

Depending on the data, you may want to choose a different colormap. For correlations, you want to use a diverging colormap. For postive numeric data, you may consider an increasing or continuous colormap. You can use a Matplotlib colormap. They are shown at the end of the chapter.

34.8 Captions

The .set_caption allows you to specify text for a caption. This will appear before the dataframe.

```
(agg_flow
 .reset_index()
 .style
 # after this we are not working a a dataframe but a "styler" object
 .format({'cost': '${:,.2f}', 'datetime': '{:%Y/%m}/01',
          'percent_quarterly_flow': '{:.1%}',
          'off_goal': '{:+.1%}',
          **{col: '{:.1f}' for col in ['cfs', 'total_flow', 'quarterly_flow']}},
          na_rep='Missing')
 .bar(subset='cfs', color='#c07fef', vmax=agg_flow.cfs.quantile(.95))
 .bar(subset='off_goal', color=['red', 'green'], align='mid')
 .highlight_null(null_color='#fef70c')  # wish this was highlight_na
 .highlight_max(axis=0, color='green')
 .background_gradient(axis=0, cmap='Reds', subset='cost', vmin=1_000, vmax=25_000)
 .set_caption('Dirty Devil Summary')
 .set_properties(**{'background-color': '#999'}, subset='datetime')
 .applymap(lambda val: f'color: "grey"; opacity: 80%; background-color:{"#4589ae" if val > 0 else "#c07fef"}' ,
          subset='cfs')
 .set_table_styles([{'selector': 'td:hover', 'props': 'background-color: pink; font-size:14pt;'}])
)
```

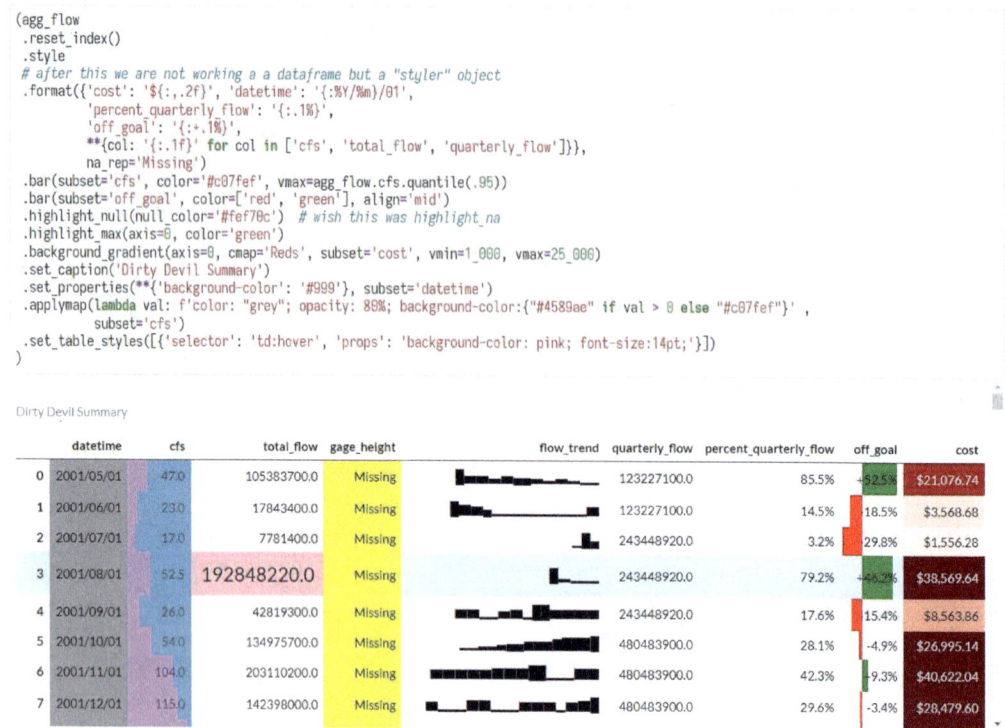

Figure 34.4: Using `.set_properties` to set CSS properties on the *datetime* column. Notice that the *datetime* column is gray. Using `.applymap` to set CSS properties on the *cfs* column. Notice that the font and background of *cfs* has changed. Using `.set_table_styles` to set CSS properties on hovering. Notice that when you hover over a cell, the style gets set.

34.9 CSS Properties

The `.set_properties` method lets you set CSS properties to each cell.

The `.applymap` method will also let you place CSS properties. You pass in a function that takes the value of the cell and return a string with the CSS properties for that cell.

Another way to set CSS styling is with the `.set_table_styles` method. This method allows you to specify the selector and the properties for the selector.

```
(agg_flow
 .reset_index()
 .style
 # after this we are not working a a dataframe but a "styler" object
 .format({'cost': '${:,.2f}', 'datetime': '{:%Y/%m}/01',
          'percent_quarterly_flow': '{:.1%}',
          'off_goal': '{:+.1%}',
          **{col: '{:.1f}' for col in ['cfs', 'total_flow', 'quarterly_flow']}},
         na_rep='Missing')
 .bar(subset='cfs', color='#c07fef', vmax=agg_flow.cfs.quantile(.95))
 .bar(subset='off_goal', color=['red', 'green'], align='mid')
 .highlight_null(null_color='#fef70c')  # wish this was highlight_na
 .highlight_max(axis=0, color='green')
 .background_gradient(axis=0, cmap='Reds', subset='cost', vmin=1_000, vmax=25_000)
 .set_caption('Dirty Devil Summary')
 .set_properties(**{'background-color': '#999'}, subset='datetime')
 .applymap(lambda val: f'color: "grey"; opacity: 80%; background-color:{"#4589ae" if val > 0 else "#c07fef"}' ,
           subset='cfs')
 # .set_table_styles breaks stick headers if it is after
 .set_table_styles([{'selector': 'td:hover', 'props': 'background-color: pink; font-size:14pt;'}])
 .set_sticky(axis="columns")
)
```

Figure 34.5: Using .set_sticky to make sure that the columns stay visible. You can see that we are looking at index value 37, but still have the column headers visible.

34.10   Stickiness

If you find it annoying to lose the column headers when scrolling down a dataframe, or losing the index when scrolling to the side, you are in luck. The .set_sticky method will make the headers stay in place when scrolling. Note however, that you should use call this method at the end of your chain because if you set some CSS styles after it, you might lose the stickiness.

34.11   Hiding the Index

Finally, you can hide the index. In the image you can see that we have made the index disappear. Through this book we have seen that unless you are doing

```
(agg_flow
 .reset_index()
 .style
 # after this we are not working a a dataframe but a "styler" object
 .format({'cost': '${:,.2f}', 'datetime': '{:%Y/%m}/01',
          'percent_quarterly_flow': '{:.1%}',
          'off_goal': '{:+.1%}',
          **{col: '{:.1f}' for col in ['cfs', 'total_flow', 'quarterly_flow']}},
         na_rep='Missing')
 .bar(subset='cfs', color='#c07fef', vmax=agg_flow.cfs.quantile(.95))
 .bar(subset='off_goal', color=['red', 'green'], align='mid')
 .highlight_null(null_color='#fef78c')  # wish this was highlight_na
 .highlight_max(axis=0, color='green')
 .background_gradient(axis=0, cmap='Reds', subset='cost', vmin=1_000, vmax=25_000)
 .set_caption('Dirty Devil Summary')
 .set_properties(**{'background-color': '#999'}, subset='datetime')
 .applymap(lambda val: f'color: "grey"; opacity: 80%; background-color:{"#4589ae" if val > 0 else "#c07fef"}',
           subset='cfs')
 # .set_table_styles breaks stick headers if it is after
 .set_table_styles([{'selector': 'td:hover', 'props': 'background-color: pink; font-size:14pt;'}])
 .set_sticky(axis="columns")
 .hide_index()
)
```

Figure 34.6: Using .hide_index to hide the index.

grouping, I recommend keeping important data out of the index (and then moving it out when you are done with grouping).

If you are displaying a dataframe, removing the index can remove a potential distraction. Use the .hide_index method accessed from the .style attribute to hide it when displaying data in Jupyter.

Method	Description

`.format(formatter=None,`
`  subset=None, na_rep=None,`
`  precision=None, decimal='.',`
`  thousands=None, escape=None)`
	Return a Styler. formatter can be a string, a callable that takes a value and returns the string representation, or a dictionary mapping column names to Python format specifiers or callables. subset is a column or list of columns to apply (if not using a dictionary formatter). Use na_rep to specify alternate representation for missing numbers. Use precision to specify floating point decimal places. Use #ecimal to change decimal separtor. Use thousands to specify character to insert for thousands separator. The escape parameter can specify 'html' or 'latex' to provide properly escaped cells.

`.bar(subset=None, axis=0,`
`  color='#d65f5f', width=100,`
`  align='left', vmin=None,`
`  vmax=None)`
	Return a Styler. Draw a bar chart in cell background. subset is a column or list of columns to apply to. If you specify a two-tuple for color, the first is for negative values. width is the percentage of the cell to use. align defaults to 'left' side, you can specify 'zero' for the center of the cell, or 'mid' for center to right aligned if all values are negative or (max-min)/2. Use vmin and vmax to clip values.

`.highlight_max(null_color='red',`
`  subset=None, axis=0,`
`  props=None)`
	Return a Styler that highlights maximum values. You can specify CSS properties with props.

`.highlight_null(null_color='red',` `  subset=None, props=None)`	Return a Styler that highlights missing values. You can specify CSS properties with props.

`.background_gradient(cmap='PuBu',`
`  low=0, high=0, axis=0,`
`  subset=None,`
`  text_color_threshold=0.408,`
`  vmin=None, vmax=None,`
`  gmap=None)`
	Return a Styler that highlights background colors based on values. Use cmap to specify a Matplotlib colormap.

`.set_caption(caption)`	Return a Styler. Create HTML caption. If using LaTex, can specify a tuple with full and short captions.
`.set_properties(subset=None, **kwargs)`	Return a Styler. Set CSS properties on each cell. You can specify them as keyword arguments, but will probably need to use an unpacked dictionary since many CSS properties have dashes in them (ie: `**{'background-color': 'red'}`).
`.applymap(func, subset=None, **kwargs)`	Return a Styler. Set CSS properties on each cell. The func takes the current value of the cell and returns a string with the CSS properties. You can pass additional arguments to func with kwargs.
`.set_table_styles(table_styles, axis=0, overwrite=True)`	Return a Styler. Set CSS properties on table, columns, rows, or HTML selectors. `table_styles` can be a list of dictionaries (mapping `'selector'` to CSS selector, and `'props'` to CSS properties) or a dictionary (mapping column names (or index names if `axis=1`) to row CSS selectors (a list of the selector and the property).
`.set_sticky(axis=0, pixel_size=None, levels=None)`	Return a Styler. Sets columns to sticky if `axis=1`. Set index to stick if `axis=0`. Make sure you call this as one of the last styling operations, otherwise it might not work.
`.hide_index(subset=None)`	Return a Styler. Hide the index or index values specified in subset.

Table 34.1: Styling Methods

34.12 Summary

In this chapter, we demonstrated many of the styling features of pandas. There are other features that we didn't demonstrate. Feel free to explore those

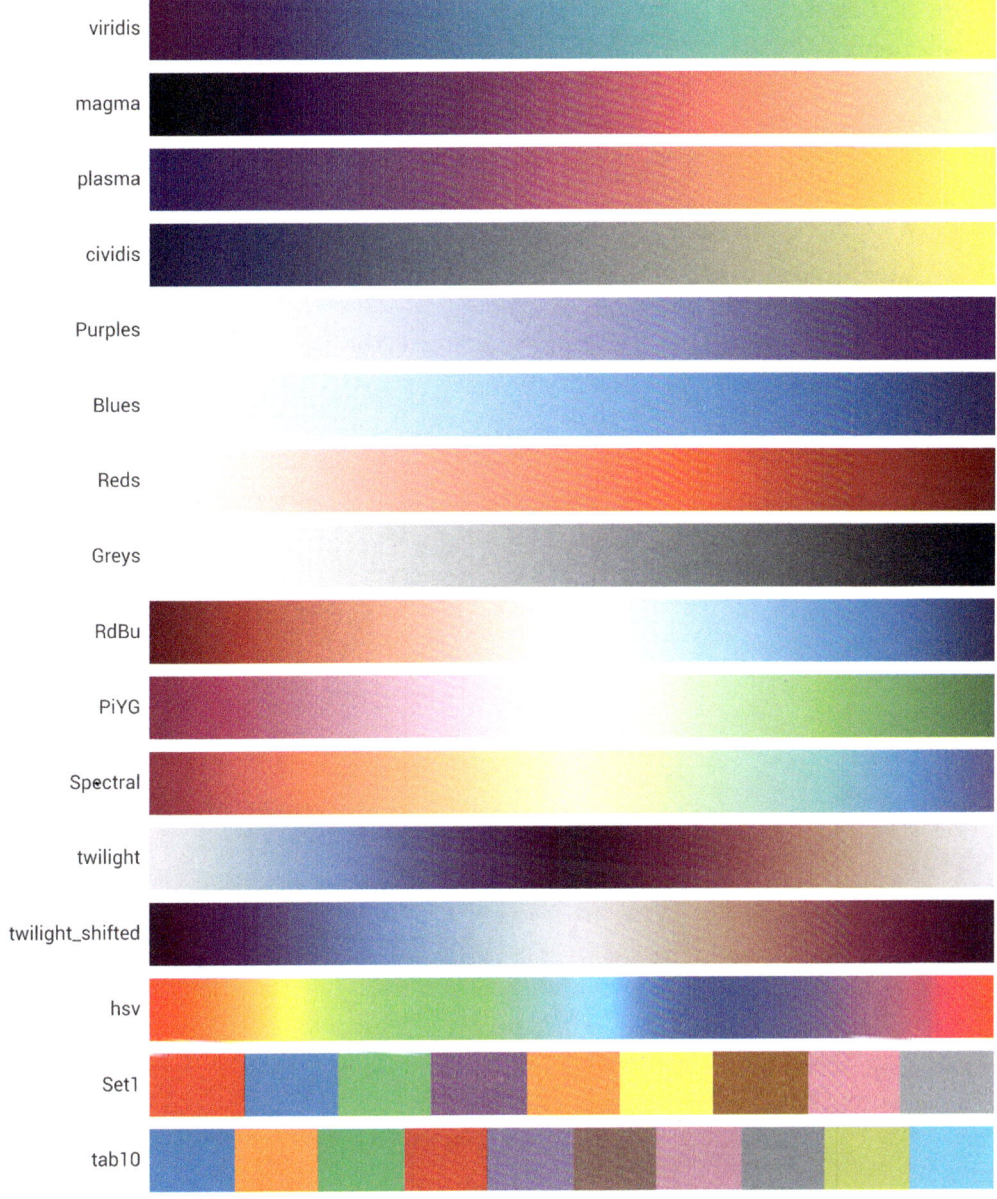

Figure 34.7: Select Matplotlib colormaps. Continuous (viridis through cividis). Increasing (Purples through Greys). Diverging (RdBu through Spectral). Cyclic (twilight through hsv). Categorical (Set1 and tab10).

and see if they will be useful to use. We also demonstrated how to create a sparkplot as Unicode.

34.13 Exercises

With a dataset of your choice:

1. Color the background of the first two columns blue.

2. Format the numeric values by specifying precision and thousands separator.

3. Include a bar plot in a column.

4. Set a background gradient for a column.

5. Make the column headers sticky.

Chapter 35

Debugging Pandas

In this chapter, we will explore various techniques for debugging Pandas.

35.1 Checking if Dataframes are Equal

The first technique we will explore is checking whether two dataframes are equal. This is especially useful after serializing and deserializing data and unfortunately, is a little more difficult than it should be. We can use the .equals method which will check if two dataframes are equal, but if they are not, diagnosing the problem is hard.

Let's step through an example with our Dirty Devil data:

```
>>> import pandas as pd
>>> url = 'https://github.com/mattharrison/datasets/raw/master'\
...       '/data/dirtydevil.txt'
>>> df = pd.read_csv(url, skiprows=lambda num: num <34 or num == 35,
...                  sep='\t')
>>> def to_denver_time(df_, time_col, tz_col):
...     return (df_
...         .assign(**{tz_col: df_[tz_col].replace('MDT', 'MST7MDT')})
...         .groupby(tz_col)
...         [time_col]
...         .transform(lambda s: pd.to_datetime(s)
...             .dt.tz_localize(s.name, ambiguous=True)
...             .dt.tz_convert('America/Denver'))
...     )
>>> def tweak_river(df_):
...     return (df_
...       .assign(datetime=to_denver_time(df_, 'datetime', 'tz_cd'))
```

```
...            .rename(columns={'144166_00060': 'cfs',
...                             '144167_00065': 'gage_height'})
...        )
...
>>> dd = tweak_river(df)
>>> dd
         agency_cd   site_no  ...  gage_height  144167_00065_cd
0             USGS   9333500  ...          NaN              NaN
1             USGS   9333500  ...          NaN              NaN
2             USGS   9333500  ...          NaN              NaN
3             USGS   9333500  ...          NaN              NaN
4             USGS   9333500  ...          NaN              NaN
...            ...       ...  ...          ...              ...
539300        USGS   9333500  ...         6.16                P
539301        USGS   9333500  ...         6.15                P
539302        USGS   9333500  ...         6.15                P
539303        USGS   9333500  ...         6.15                P
539304        USGS   9333500  ...         6.15                P

[539305 rows x 8 columns]
```

Now let's roundtrip this through JSON and evaluate whether we get the same data back:

```
>>> dd2 = pd.read_json(dd.to_json())
>>> dd.equals(dd2)
False
```

Nope, the data is different! Our task is to find out why dd and dd2 are different.

We can quantify the count of different values:

```
>>> (dd
...     .ne(dd2)
...     .sum()
... )
agency_cd                0
site_no                  0
datetime            539305
tz_cd                    0
cfs                  48048
144166_00060_cd      46181
gage_height         125656
144167_00065_cd     105928
dtype: int64
```

And we can view the percent of different values:

```
>>> (dd
...     .ne(dd2)
...     .mean()
...     .mul(100)
... )
agency_cd              0.000000
site_no                0.000000
datetime             100.000000
tz_cd                  0.000000
cfs                    8.909244
144166_00060_cd        8.563058
gage_height           23.299617
144167_00065_cd       19.641576
dtype: float64
```

The pandas library has a function hidden away in the testing namespace that helps a little, pd.testing.assert_frame_equal. This function is meant to be used for the core developers of pandas when developing and testing the library, but let's try it here:

```
>>> pd.testing.assert_frame_equal(dd, dd2)
Traceback (most recent call last):
  ...
AssertionError: Attributes of DataFrame.iloc[:, 2]
      (column name="datetime") are different

Attribute "dtype" are different
[left]:  datetime64[ns, America/Denver]
[right]: datetime64[ns]
```

Ok, it hints that the *datetime* column has different types. As we saw in the JSON serialization section, when we serialize, we lose timezone information. Let's address that and try again:

```
>>> pd.testing.assert_frame_equal(dd,
...     (dd2
...         .assign(datetime=dd2.datetime
...             .dt.tz_localize('UTC')
...             .dt.tz_convert('America/Denver')))
... )
```

In this case, no assertion is raised, it is quiet! However .equals still fails:

```
>>> dd.equals(dd2
...     .assign(datetime=dd2.datetime
...         .dt.tz_localize('UTC')
...         .dt.tz_convert('America/Denver'))
```

```
... )
False
```

Let's try the check_exact parameter for assert_frame_equals:

```
>>> pd.testing.assert_frame_equal(dd,
...    (dd2
...       .assign(datetime=dd2.datetime
...           .dt.tz_localize('UTC')
...           .dt.tz_convert('America/Denver'))),
...    check_exact=True
... )
Traceback (most recent call last):
  ...
AssertionError: DataFrame.iloc[:, 4] (column name="cfs") are different

DataFrame.iloc[:, 4] (column name="cfs") values are different (0.34619 %)
[index]: [0, 1, 2, 3, 4, 5, 6, 7, 8, 9, 10, 11, 12, 13, 14, 15, 16, ...]
[left]:  [71.0, 71.0, 71.0, 70.0, 70.0, 69.0, 70.0, 70.0, 70.0, 70.0, ...]
[right]: [71.0, 71.0, 71.0, 70.0, 70.0, 69.0, 70.0, 70.0, 70.0, 70.0, ...]
```

It looks like some of the values in the *cfs* column differ. Let's examine those with the .ne method. This method will return a boolean array where the values are not equal in a series:

```
>>> dd[dd.cfs.ne(dd2.cfs)]
        agency_cd  site_no  ...  gage_height  144167_00065_cd
96246       USGS  9333500  ...          NaN              NaN
96247       USGS  9333500  ...          NaN              NaN
96248       USGS  9333500  ...          NaN              NaN
96249       USGS  9333500  ...          NaN              NaN
96250       USGS  9333500  ...          NaN              NaN
...          ...      ...  ...          ...              ...
538678      USGS  9333500  ...         6.06                P
538728      USGS  9333500  ...         6.06                P
538735      USGS  9333500  ...         6.06                P
538739      USGS  9333500  ...         6.06                P
538753      USGS  9333500  ...         6.06                P

[48048 rows x 8 columns]
```

Ok, let's look at the values for *cfs* from row label *96246* from both of the datasets:

```
>>> dd.loc[96246].cfs, dd2.loc[96246].cfs
(1.7, 1.7000000000000002)
```

It looks like we have rounding issues. Let's address those and check again:

```
>>> dd.round(2).equals(
...    dd2
...       .assign(datetime=dd2.datetime
...               .dt.tz_localize('UTC').
...               dt.tz_convert('America/Denver'))
...       .round(2)
...    )
True
```

Here is a little function I wrote to help diagnose where dataframes are not the same:

```
>>> def cmp_dfs(df1, df2, round_amt=3):
...     diff_cols = set(df1.columns) ^ set(df2.columns)
...     if diff_cols:
...         print(f'Different columns {diff_cols}')
...     if df1.shape != df2.shape:
...         print(f'Different shapes {df1.shape} {df2.shape}')
...     bad = False
...     for col in df1.columns:
...         s1 = df1[col]
...         s2 = df2[col]
...         if s1.equals(s2):
...             continue
...         bad = True
...         if s1.dtype != s2.dtype:
...             print(f'{col} types differ {s1.dtype} vs {s2.dtype}')
...         if s1.dtype == float:
...             if s1.round(round_amt).equals(s2.round(round_amt)):
...                 print(f'{col} has rounding differences '
...                       f'{df1[s1.ne(s2)][col].dropna().iloc[0]} '
...                       f'vs {df2[s1.ne(s2)][col].dropna().iloc[0]}')
...             else:
...                 print(f'{col} differs {df1[s1.ne(s2)][col].dropna()}')
...     if not bad:
...         print('Same')

>>> cmp_dfs(dd, dd2)
datetime types differ datetime64[ns, America/Denver] vs datetime64[ns]
datetime differs 0        2001-05-07 01:00:00-06:00
1        2001-05-07 01:15:00-06:00
2        2001-05-07 01:30:00-06:00
3        2001-05-07 01:45:00-06:00
4        2001-05-07 02:00:00-06:00
                  ...
539300   2020-09-28 08:30:00-06:00
```

```
539301    2020-09-28 08:45:00-06:00
539302    2020-09-28 09:00:00-06:00
539303    2020-09-28 09:15:00-06:00
539304    2020-09-28 09:30:00-06:00
Name: datetime, Length: 539305, dtype: datetime64[ns, America/Denver]
cfs has rounding differences 1.7 vs 1.7000000000000002
gage_height has rounding differences 3.28 vs 3.2800000000000002
```

Feel free to leverage this function and the others described in this section to discover why your dataframes are not equal.

35.2 Debugging Chains

In this section, we will explore debugging chains of operations on dataframes or series. I have taught thousands of people pandas during my career. I've also seen a lot of pandas code from clients and students. Almost universally, it is messy code. I get it. I used to write pandas code that way too. Making liberal use of chaining and creating functions to tweak my data has gone a long way towards remedying my ails.

I have been a vocal proponent of chaining on social media. Occasionally, I will hear someone protest that they don't like chaining. When asked why they usually flounder. Excuses like excess code, copying data (yes, there are copies, but no more than non-chained pandas), and hard to debug popup. I don't buy excess code. In fact I think chaining produces less code. The pandas library is an in-memory library that works by copying data, this argument is a moot point. Let's address the debugging complaint.

I'm going to show a "tweak" function that I created to analyze fuel economy data[23].

Here is my tweak function:

```
>>> import pandas as pd
>>> autos = pd.read_csv('https://github.com/mattharrison/datasets/raw/'
...        'master/data/vehicles.csv.zip')
>>> def to_tz(df_, time_col, tz_offset, tz_name):
...        return (df_
...                .groupby(tz_offset)
...                [time_col]
...                .transform(lambda s: pd.to_datetime(s)
...                        .dt.tz_localize(s.name, ambiguous=True)
```

[23]https://www.fueleconomy.gov/feg/download.shtml

440

```
...                    .dt.tz_convert(tz_name))
...                )


>>> def tweak_autos(autos):
...     cols = ['city08', 'comb08', 'highway08', 'cylinders',
...             'displ', 'drive', 'eng_dscr', 'fuelCost08',
...             'make', 'model', 'trany', 'range', 'createdOn',
...             'year']
...     return (autos
...     [cols]
...     .assign(cylinders=autos.cylinders.fillna(0).astype('int8'),
...             displ=autos.displ.fillna(0).astype('float16'),
...             drive=autos.drive.fillna('Other').astype('category'),
...             automatic=autos.trany.str.contains('Auto'),
...             speeds=autos.trany.str.extract(r'(\d)+').fillna('20')
...                 .astype('int8'),
...             offset=autos.createdOn
...                 .str.extract(r'\d\d:\d\d ([A-Z]{3}?)')
...                 .replace('EDT', 'EST5EDT'),
...             str_date=(autos.createdOn.str.slice(4,19) + ' ' +
...                 autos.createdOn.str.slice(-4)),
...             createdOn=lambda df_: to_tz(df_, 'str_date',
...                 'offset', 'America/New_York'),
...             ffs=autos.eng_dscr.str.contains('FFS')
...             )
...     .astype({'highway08': 'int8', 'city08': 'int16',
...             'comb08': 'int16', 'fuelCost08': 'int16',
...             'range': 'int16', 'year': 'int16',
...             'make': 'category'})
...     .drop(columns=['trany', 'eng_dscr'])
...     )

>>> tweak_autos(autos)
        city08  comb08  highway08  ...  offset             str_date   ffs
0           19      21         25  ...     EST  Jan 01 00:00:00 2013  True
1            9      11         14  ...     EST  Jan 01 00:00:00 2013  False
2           23      27         33  ...     EST  Jan 01 00:00:00 2013  True
3           10      11         12  ...     EST  Jan 01 00:00:00 2013  NaN
4           17      19         23  ...     EST  Jan 01 00:00:00 2013  True
...        ...     ...        ...  ...     ...                   ...   ...
41139       19      22         26  ...     EST  Jan 01 00:00:00 2013  True
41140       20      23         28  ...     EST  Jan 01 00:00:00 2013  True
41141       18      21         24  ...     EST  Jan 01 00:00:00 2013  True
41142       18      21         24  ...     EST  Jan 01 00:00:00 2013  True
```

441

| 41143 | 16 | 18 | 21 | ... | EST | Jan 01 00:00:00 2013 | True |

```
[41144 rows x 17 columns]
```

Say you came across this tweak_autos function wanted to understand what it does. First of all, realize that it is written like a recipe, step by step:

- Pull out columns found in cols.

- Create various columns (.assign).

- Convert column types (.astype).

- Drop extra columns that are no longer needed after we created new columns from them (.drop).

Haters of chaining say there is no way to debug this. I have a few ways to debug the chain. The first is using comments. I comment out all of the operations and then go through them one at a time. This comes in really handy to visually see what is happening as the chain progresses. Let's look at all four steps with debugging. First pull out the columns:

```
>>> def tweak_autos(autos):
...     cols = ['city08', 'comb08', 'highway08', 'cylinders',
...             'displ', 'drive', 'eng_dscr', 'fuelCost08',
...             'make', 'model', 'trany', 'range', 'createdOn',
...             'year']
...     return (autos
...      [cols]
...      # .assign(cylinders=autos.cylinders.fillna(0).astype('int8'),
...      #         displ=autos.displ.fillna(0).astype('float16'),
...      #         drive=autos.drive.fillna('Other').astype('category'),
...      #         automatic=autos.trany.str.contains('Auto'),
...      #         speeds=autos.trany.str.extract(r'(\d)+').fillna('20')
...      #                 .astype('int8'),
...      #         offset=autos.createdOn
...      #                 .str.extract(r'\d\d:\d\d ([A-Z]{3}?)')
...      #                 .replace('EDT', 'EST5EDT'),
...      #         str_date=(autos.createdOn.str.slice(4,19) + ' ' +
...      #                 autos.createdOn.str.slice(-4)),
...      #         createdOn=lambda df_: to_tz(df_, 'str_date',
...      #                 'offset', 'America/New_York'),
...      #         ffs=autos.eng_dscr.str.contains('FFS')
...      #         )
...      # .astype({'highway08': 'int8', 'city08': 'int16',
```

```
...      #              'comb08': 'int16', 'fuelCost08': 'int16',
...      #              'range': 'int16', 'year': 'int16',
...      #              'make': 'category'})
...      # .drop(columns=['trany', 'eng_dscr'])
...      )

>>> tweak_autos(autos)
        city08  comb08  ...  range                        createdOn  year
0           19      21  ...      0  Tue Jan 01 00:00:00 EST 2013  1985
1            9      11  ...      0  Tue Jan 01 00:00:00 EST 2013  1985
2           23      27  ...      0  Tue Jan 01 00:00:00 EST 2013  1985
3           10      11  ...      0  Tue Jan 01 00:00:00 EST 2013  1985
4           17      19  ...      0  Tue Jan 01 00:00:00 EST 2013  1993
...        ...     ...  ...    ...                           ...   ...
41139       19      22  ...      0  Tue Jan 01 00:00:00 EST 2013  1993
41140       20      23  ...      0  Tue Jan 01 00:00:00 EST 2013  1993
41141       18      21  ...      0  Tue Jan 01 00:00:00 EST 2013  1993
41142       18      21  ...      0  Tue Jan 01 00:00:00 EST 2013  1993
41143       16      18  ...      0  Tue Jan 01 00:00:00 EST 2013  1993

[41144 rows x 14 columns]
```

Now let's look at what comes out after .assign:

```
>>> def tweak_autos(autos):
...      cols = ['city08', 'comb08', 'highway08', 'cylinders',
...              'displ', 'drive', 'eng_dscr', 'fuelCost08',
...              'make', 'model', 'trany', 'range', 'createdOn',
...              'year']
...      return (autos
...       [cols]
...       .assign(cylinders=autos.cylinders.fillna(0).astype('int8'),
...               displ=autos.displ.fillna(0).astype('float16'),
...               drive=autos.drive.fillna('Other').astype('category'),
...               automatic=autos.trany.str.contains('Auto'),
...               speeds=autos.trany.str.extract(r'(\d)+').fillna('20')
...                   .astype('int8'),
...               offset=autos.createdOn
...                   .str.extract(r'\d\d:\d\d ([A-Z]{3}?)')
...                   .replace('EDT', 'EST5EDT'),
...               str_date=(autos.createdOn.str.slice(4,19) + ' ' +
...                   autos.createdOn.str.slice(-4)),
...               createdOn=lambda df_: to_tz(df_, 'str_date',
...                   'offset', 'America/New_York'),
...               ffs=autos.eng_dscr.str.contains('FFS')
...               )
```

```
...        # .astype({'highway08': 'int8', 'city08': 'int16',
...        #          'comb08': 'int16', 'fuelCost08': 'int16',
...        #          'range': 'int16', 'year': 'int16',
...        #          'make': 'category'})
...        # .drop(columns=['trany', 'eng_dscr'])
...        )

>>> tweak_autos(autos)
        city08  comb08  highway08  ...  offset              str_date    ffs
0           19      21         25  ...     EST  Jan 01 00:00:00 2013    True
1            9      11         14  ...     EST  Jan 01 00:00:00 2013   False
2           23      27         33  ...     EST  Jan 01 00:00:00 2013    True
3           10      11         12  ...     EST  Jan 01 00:00:00 2013     NaN
4           17      19         23  ...     EST  Jan 01 00:00:00 2013    True
...        ...     ...        ...  ...     ...                   ...    ...
41139       19      22         26  ...     EST  Jan 01 00:00:00 2013    True
41140       20      23         28  ...     EST  Jan 01 00:00:00 2013    True
41141       18      21         24  ...     EST  Jan 01 00:00:00 2013    True
41142       18      21         24  ...     EST  Jan 01 00:00:00 2013    True
41143       16      18         21  ...     EST  Jan 01 00:00:00 2013    True

[41144 rows x 19 columns]
```

Changing columns types often doesn't have a visual impact, so I'll uncomment the last two steps together:

```
>>> def tweak_autos(autos):
...     cols = ['city08', 'comb08', 'highway08', 'cylinders',
...             'displ', 'drive', 'eng_dscr', 'fuelCost08',
...             'make', 'model', 'trany', 'range', 'createdOn',
...             'year']
...     return (autos
...       [cols]
...       .assign(cylinders=autos.cylinders.fillna(0).astype('int8'),
...               displ=autos.displ.fillna(0).astype('float16'),
...               drive=autos.drive.fillna('Other').astype('category'),
...               automatic=autos.trany.str.contains('Auto'),
...               speeds=autos.trany.str.extract(r'(\d)+').fillna('20')
...                   .astype('int8'),
...               offset=autos.createdOn
...                   .str.extract(r'\d\d:\d\d ([A-Z]{3}?)')
...                   .replace('EDT', 'EST5EDT'),
...               str_date=(autos.createdOn.str.slice(4,19) + ' ' +
...                   autos.createdOn.str.slice(-4)),
...               createdOn=lambda df_: to_tz(df_, 'str_date',
...                   'offset', 'America/New_York'),
```

444

```
...               ffs=autos.eng_dscr.str.contains('FFS')
...          )
...       .astype({'highway08': 'int8', 'city08': 'int16',
...               'comb08': 'int16', 'fuelCost08': 'int16',
...               'range': 'int16', 'year': 'int16',
...               'make': 'category'})
...       .drop(columns=['trany', 'eng_dscr'])
...       )

>>> tweak_autos(autos)
        city08  comb08  highway08  ...  offset              str_date    ffs
0           19      21         25  ...     EST  Jan 01 00:00:00 2013   True
1            9      11         14  ...     EST  Jan 01 00:00:00 2013  False
2           23      27         33  ...     EST  Jan 01 00:00:00 2013   True
3           10      11         12  ...     EST  Jan 01 00:00:00 2013    NaN
4           17      19         23  ...     EST  Jan 01 00:00:00 2013   True
...        ...     ...        ...  ...     ...                   ...    ...
41139       19      22         26  ...     EST  Jan 01 00:00:00 2013   True
41140       20      23         28  ...     EST  Jan 01 00:00:00 2013   True
41141       18      21         24  ...     EST  Jan 01 00:00:00 2013   True
41142       18      21         24  ...     EST  Jan 01 00:00:00 2013   True
41143       16      18         21  ...     EST  Jan 01 00:00:00 2013   True

[41144 rows x 17 columns]
```

Commenting out chain operations is an effective debugging technique.

35.3 Debugging Chains Part II

I won't stop with the debugging techniques. Here's another one that allows you to look at the intermediate state after any method call in a chain. Remember that the .pipe method will pass the current state of a dataframe or series into a function. This function can return anything, but it normally returns a dataframe or a series.

Imagine a function that just returns the dataframe (or series) that was passed into it, but it also prints out the representation to the screen. That is what the show function below does. This function leverages the display function in Jupyter to create an optional HTML header and display the dataframe as HTML rather than a string version:

```
>>> from IPython.display import display, HTML
>>> def show(df_, rows=20, cols=30, title=None):
...     if title:
```

```
from IPython.display import display, HTML
def show(df_, rows=20, cols=30, title=None):
    if title:
        display(HTML(f'<h2>{title}</h2>'))
    with pd.option_context('display.min_rows', rows, 'display.max_columns', cols):
        display(df_)
    return df_

def tweak_autos(autos):
    cols = ['city08', 'comb08', 'highway08', 'cylinders', 'displ', 'drive', 'eng_dscr',
        'fuelCost08', 'make', 'model', 'trany', 'range', 'createdOn', 'year']
    return (autos
        [cols]
        .assign(cylinders=autos.cylinders.fillna(0).astype('int8'),
                displ=autos.displ.fillna(0).astype('float16'),
                drive=autos.drive.fillna('Other').astype('category'),
                automatic=autos.trany.str.contains('Auto'),
                speeds=autos.trany.str.extract(r'(\d+)').fillna('20').astype('int8'),
                tz=autos.createdOn.str.extract(r'\d\d:\d\d ([A-Z]{3}?)').replace('EDT', 'EST5EDT'),
                str_date=(autos.createdOn.str.slice(4,19) + ' ' + autos.createdOn.str.slice(-4)),
                createdOn=lambda df_: to_tz(df_, 'str_date', 'tz', 'US/Eastern'),
                ffs=autos.eng_dscr.str.contains('FFS')
                )
        .pipe(show, rows=2, title='New Cols')
        .astype({'highway08': 'int8', 'city08': 'int16', 'comb08': 'int16', 'fuelCost08': 'int16',
                'range': 'int16', 'year': 'int16', 'make': 'category'})
        .drop(columns=['trany', 'eng_dscr'])
        )

tweak_autos(autos)
```

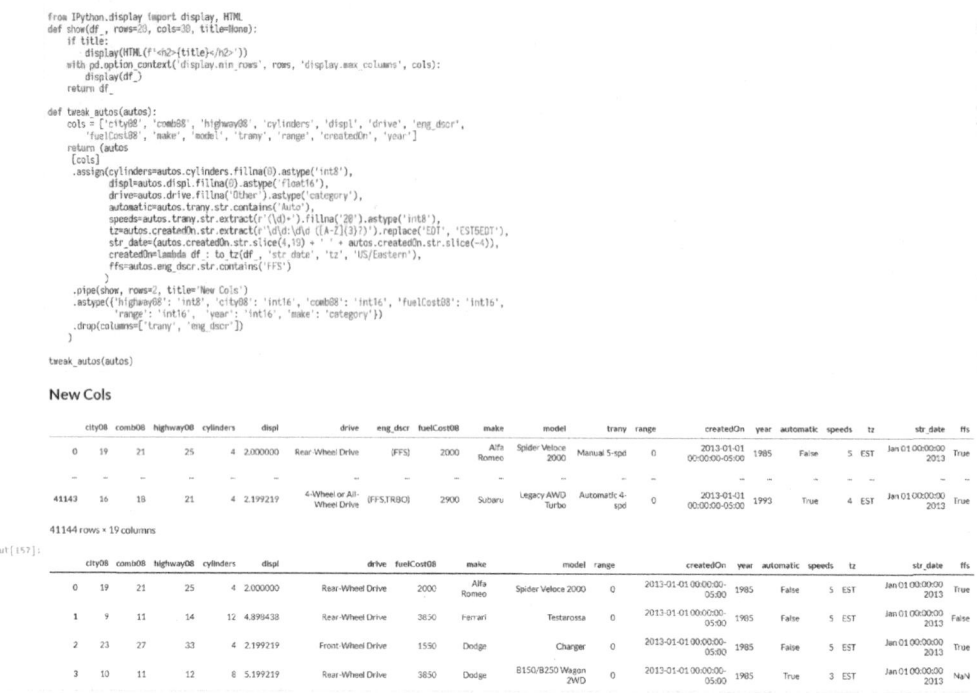

Figure 35.1: Inserting show function inside of chain to debug intermediate state.

```
...         display(HTML(f'<h2>{title}</h2>'))
...     with pd.option_context('display.min_rows', rows,
...                           'display.max_columns', cols):
...         display(df_)
...     return df_
```

Let's stick show into the tweak_autos function right after the new columns are created, but before we convert the types. The image shows the new output.

Another useful tool during chaining is to inspect the shape of the intermediate dataframes to ensure that you are not accidentally removing all the rows or that you don't have a combinatoric explosion of data following a merge. You could leverage .pipe with a function that prints out the shape of the data:

```
>>> def shape(df_):
...     print(df_.shape)
...     return df_
```

35.4 Debugging Chains Part III

We are on a roll with debugging. Let's keep going!

Another complaint that people who justify not using chains is that they really want to have the intermediate states of each operation. For example, they might write the tweak_autos chain like this:

```
cols = ['city08', 'comb08', 'highway08', 'cylinders', 'displ',
        'drive', 'eng_dscr', 'fuelCost08', 'make', 'model',
        'trany', 'range', 'createdOn', 'year']
autos2 = autos[cols]
cyl_nona = autos.cylinders.fillna(0)
cyl_int8 = cyl_nona.astype('int8')
autos2['cylinders'] = cyl_int8
displ_nona = autos.displ.fillna(0)
displ_float16 = displ_nona.astype('float16')
autos2['displ'] = displ_float16
...
autos2.drop(columns=['trany', 'eng_dscr'], inplace=True)
```

I left out much of the column updating and type changing, but I think you get the point: most users pull out a column, mess with it, and finally stick it back in. Anti-chainers claim that this ability to inspect the state using any of these variables is useful. (Nevermind that the variables just sit around in global memory wasting space.)

Admittedly, the intermediate state might be useful during development, but that utility quickly fades away during analysis and also creates a mess. It is just noise.

If you really do want the intermediate state of the dataframe, guess what? You can get that by leveraging .pipe. Below is a function, get_var, that will create a global variable with the contents of the intermediate value of a dataframe. Just shim this function into the chain with .pipe:

```
>>> def get_var(df, var_name):
...     globals()[var_name] = df
...     return df
```

Let's use get_var to create a variable, new_cols, with the state of tweak_autos immediately after creating the new columns:

```
>>> def tweak_autos(autos):
...     cols = ['city08', 'comb08', 'highway08', 'cylinders',
...             'displ', 'drive', 'eng_dscr', 'fuelCost08',
...             'make', 'model', 'trany', 'range', 'createdOn',
...             'year']
...     return (autos
...     [cols]
...     .assign(cylinders=autos.cylinders.fillna(0).astype('int8'),
...             displ=autos.displ.fillna(0).astype('float16'),
...             drive=autos.drive.fillna('Other').astype('category'),
...             automatic=autos.trany.str.contains('Auto'),
...             speeds=autos.trany.str.extract(r'(\d)+').fillna('20')
...                 .astype('int8'),
...             offset=autos.createdOn
...                 .str.extract(r'\d\d:\d\d ([A-Z]{3}?)')
...                 .replace('EDT', 'EST5EDT'),
...             str_date=(autos.createdOn.str.slice(4,19) + ' ' +
...                 autos.createdOn.str.slice(-4)),
...             createdOn=lambda df_: to_tz(df_, 'str_date',
...                 'offset', 'America/New_York'),
...             ffs=autos.eng_dscr.str.contains('FFS')
...     )
...     .pipe(get_var, 'new_cols')
...     .astype({'highway08': 'int8', 'city08': 'int16',
...              'comb08': 'int16', 'fuelCost08': 'int16',
...              'range': 'int16', 'year': 'int16',
...              'make': 'category'})
...     .drop(columns=['trany', 'eng_dscr'])
...     )
>>> res = tweak_autos(autos)
```

Let's inspect the intermediate state stored in new_cols:

```
>>> new_cols
       city08  comb08  highway08  ...  offset              str_date   ffs
0          19      21         25  ...     EST  Jan 01 00:00:00 2013  True
1           9      11         14  ...     EST  Jan 01 00:00:00 2013  False
2          23      27         33  ...     EST  Jan 01 00:00:00 2013  True
3          10      11         12  ...     EST  Jan 01 00:00:00 2013  NaN
4          17      19         23  ...     EST  Jan 01 00:00:00 2013  True
...       ...     ...        ...  ...     ...                   ...  ...
41139      19      22         26  ...     EST  Jan 01 00:00:00 2013  True
41140      20      23         28  ...     EST  Jan 01 00:00:00 2013  True
41141      18      21         24  ...     EST  Jan 01 00:00:00 2013  True
41142      18      21         24  ...     EST  Jan 01 00:00:00 2013  True
```

```
41143        16       18          21   ...   EST   Jan 01 00:00:00 2013   True

[41144 rows x 19 columns]
```

You can use the .pipe method to debug intermediate states of chained operations.

35.5 Debugging Chains Part IV

Another option for debugging code in Jupyter is to leverage the pdb debugger. In Jupyter notebook, there are two main options to do this. One is to run the command %debug command immediately after coming across an exception. The other way to invoke the debugger is to explicitly invoke the set_trace function.

Let's look at the first option. I'm going to insert a link into the chain to call an err function that raises an exception. When we run this, it will raise an exception:

```
>>> def err(*args):
...     1/0

>>> def tweak_autos(autos):
...     cols = ['city08', 'comb08', 'highway08', 'cylinders',
...             'displ', 'drive', 'eng_dscr', 'fuelCost08',
...             'make', 'model', 'trany', 'range', 'createdOn',
...             'year']
...     return (autos
...     [cols]
...     .assign(cylinders=autos.cylinders.fillna(0).astype('int8'),
...             displ=autos.displ.fillna(0).astype('float16'),
...             drive=autos.drive.fillna('Other').astype('category'),
...             automatic=autos.trany.str.contains('Auto'),
...             speeds=autos.trany.str.extract(r'(\d)+').fillna('20')
...                 .astype('int8'),
...             offset=autos.createdOn
...                 .str.extract(r'\d\d:\d\d ([A-Z]{3}?)')
...                 .replace('EDT', 'EST5EDT'),
...             str_date=(autos.createdOn.str.slice(4,19) + ' ' +
...                 autos.createdOn.str.slice(-4)),
...             createdOn=lambda df_: to_tz(df_, 'str_date',
...                 'offset', 'America/New_York'),
...             ffs=autos.eng_dscr.str.contains('FFS')
...         )
...     .pipe(err)
```

449

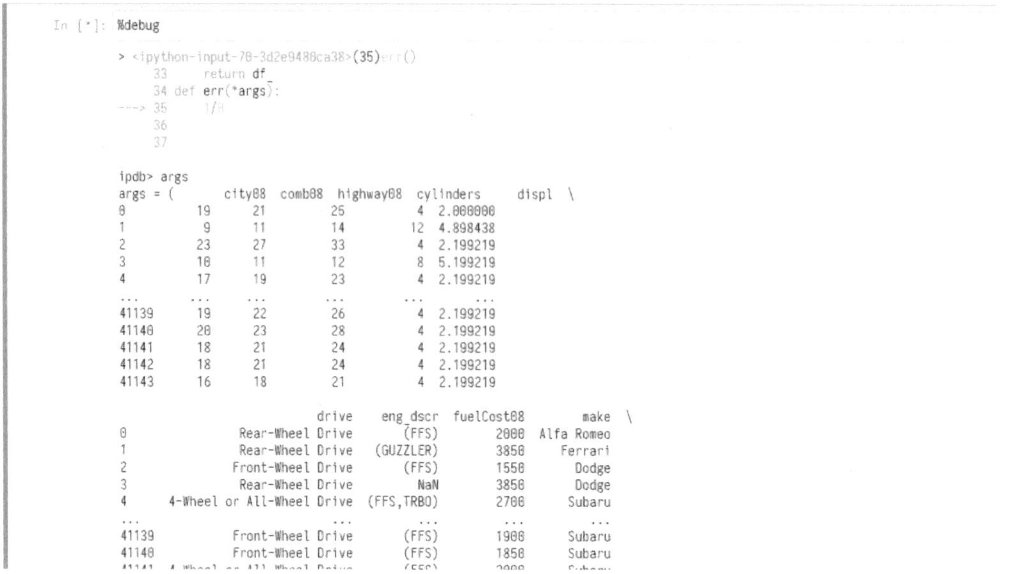

Figure 35.2: Run the %debug cell magic after executing a cell that raises and exception.

```
...            .astype({'highway08': 'int8', 'city08': 'int16',
...                     'comb08': 'int16', 'fuelCost08': 'int16',
...                     'range': 'int16',  'year': 'int16',
...                     'make': 'category'})
...            .drop(columns=['trany', 'eng_dscr'])
...        )

>>> res = tweak_autos(autos)
Traceback (most recent call last):
  ...
ZeroDivisionError: division by zero
```

This just raises an exception. But if you run this in Jupyter, you can drop into a debugger after raising the exception. In a new cell, run the command %debug.

You are now in the debugger. Here is a brief overview of the pdb commands that I find useful:

- h - (help) Show the commands.

- l - (list) List code around break.

- s - (step) Step into function/method.

- w - (where) Show where you are in stack.

- u - (up) Move up in the stack.

- d - (down) Move down in the stack.

- c - (continue) Continue running code.

- q - (quit) Quit running code.

Another mechanism to drop into the debugger is to call the set_trace function. Replace err with this function:

```
>>> from IPython.core.debugger import set_trace
>>> def err(*args):
...     set_trace()
```

Note

While the debugger is running in Jupyter, no other cells can run. Make sure you type c or q to finish your debugging session before executing other cells.

35.6 Debugging Apply (and Friends)

It can be confusing to keep track of what pandas passes around when you call .apply, .assign, .groupby(...).apply, .groupby(...).agg, .groupby(...).transform, .pipe, and others. What is getting passed in? A series, dataframe, group? One answer is to look at the documentation, which is generally good (although there are some holes). Also, it can be useful to have access to the object being passed around so you can play with it in Jupyter and figure out what you want your .apply (or .groupby(...).apply or .groupby(...).agg ...) to do.

We can take a similar approach to debugging with .pipe and create a function to help us. The debug_var function accepts an item (this is what we want to check). This function will store the item in the debug_item variable (we can overwrite this if we desire) for future inspection. Then the function raises a DebugException to prevent further processing. We will pass this function into .apply.

Here is the function:

```
>>> class DebugException(Exception):
...     pass

>>> def debug_var(thing, *, name='debug_item', raise_ex=True):
...     globals()[name] = thing
...     if raise_ex:
...         raise DebugException
...     return thing
```

Let's use this function to explore how .apply works. What gets passed into the .apply method? Plug in the function and find out. Let's use it on the Fuel Economy data:

```
>>> def tweak_autos(autos):
...     cols = ['city08', 'comb08', 'highway08', 'cylinders',
...             'displ', 'drive', 'eng_dscr', 'fuelCost08',
...             'make', 'model', 'trany', 'range', 'createdOn',
...             'year']
...     return (autos
...      [cols]
...      .assign(cylinders=autos.cylinders.fillna(0).astype('int8'),
...             displ=autos.displ.fillna(0).astype('float16'),
...             drive=autos.drive.fillna('Other').astype('category'),
...             automatic=autos.trany.str.contains('Auto'),
...             speeds=autos.trany.str.extract(r'(\d)+').fillna('20')
...                 .astype('int8'),
...             offset=autos.createdOn
...                 .str.extract(r'\d\d:\d\d ([A-Z]{3}?)')
...                 .replace('EDT', 'EST5EDT'),
...             str_date=(autos.createdOn.str.slice(4,19) + ' ' +
...                 autos.createdOn.str.slice(-4)),
...             createdOn=lambda df_: to_tz(df_, 'str_date',
...                 'offset', 'America/New_York'),
...             ffs=autos.eng_dscr.str.contains('FFS')
...         )
...      .astype({'highway08': 'int8', 'city08': 'int16',
...             'comb08': 'int16', 'fuelCost08': 'int16',
...             'range': 'int16', 'year': 'int16',
...             'make': 'category'})
...      .drop(columns=['trany', 'eng_dscr'])
...     )

>>> autos2 = tweak_autos(autos)
>>> autos2.apply(debug_var, name='this')
Traceback (most recent call last):
  ...
```

```
DebugException

>>> this
0          19
1           9
2          23
3          10
4          17
            ..
41139      19
41140      20
41141      18
41142      18
41143      16
Name: city08, Length: 41144, dtype: int16
```

Looks like this is a single column. The .apply method will call our function on every single column.

I've removed the whole stack trace from the exception above, but I try to convince my students that they should try to understand the stack trace. In a previous section, we talked about the debugger and how to step through the stack to explore what is going on.

Let's re-run this, but with the axis=1 parameter to see what gets passed into our function:

```
>>> autos2.apply(debug_var, axis=1)
Traceback (most recent call last):
  ...
DebugException

>>> debug_item
city08                             19
comb08                             21
highway08                          25
cylinders                           4
displ                             2.0
drive                 Rear-Wheel Drive
fuelCost08                       2000
make                      Alfa Romeo
model             Spider Veloce 2000
range                               0
createdOn    2013-01-01 00:00:00-05:00
year                             1985
automatic                       False
speeds                              5
```

```
tz                              EST
str_date          Jan 01 00:00:00 2013
ffs                             True
Name: 0, dtype: object
```

It looks like it is passing in a row represented as a series.

Let's try it with .assign:

```
>>> (autos2
...    .assign(new_col=debug_var)
... )
Traceback (most recent call last):
  ...
DebugException

>>> debug_item
        city08  comb08  highway08  ...   tz            str_date      ffs
0           19      21         25  ...  EST  Jan 01 00:00:00 2013    True
1            9      11         14  ...  EST  Jan 01 00:00:00 2013   False
2           23      27         33  ...  EST  Jan 01 00:00:00 2013    True
3           10      11         12  ...  EST  Jan 01 00:00:00 2013     NaN
4           17      19         23  ...  EST  Jan 01 00:00:00 2013    True
...        ...     ...        ...  ...  ...                  ...     ...
41139       19      22         26  ...  EST  Jan 01 00:00:00 2013    True
41140       20      23         28  ...  EST  Jan 01 00:00:00 2013    True
41141       18      21         24  ...  EST  Jan 01 00:00:00 2013    True
41142       18      21         24  ...  EST  Jan 01 00:00:00 2013    True
41143       16      18         21  ...  EST  Jan 01 00:00:00 2013    True

[41144 rows x 17 columns]
```

Looks like debug_item is the whole dataframe.

Let's try it when we call .groupby(...).agg with a dictionary:

```
>>> (autos2.groupby('make').agg({'city08': debug_var}))
Traceback (most recent call last):
  ...
DebugException

>>> debug_item
Series([], Name: city08, dtype: int16)
```

Looks like debug_item is the *city08* column.

You get the idea. With the intermediate variable in hand, you should be able to make progress on your analysis.

Note

In addition to creating a variable, you can also combine this technique with the %debug cell magic. This will drop you into a debugger at the point that the exception was raised.

35.7 Memory Usage

Because pandas requires that you load your data into RAM, you need to be aware of the size of your data. Because pandas doesn't mutate data (in general), you will need some overhead to be able to work with data. I typically recommend that my clients have 3-10x more memory than the size of the data they are analyzing.

One way to explore the data is to look at the `.info` method. Just remember to use the `memory_usage='deep'` option so you take into account any Python objects the dataframe might use (strings for example):

```
>>> dd.info(memory_usage='deep')
<class 'pandas.core.frame.DataFrame'>
RangeIndex: 539305 entries, 0 to 539304
Data columns (total 8 columns):
 #   Column          Non-Null Count   Dtype
---  ------          --------------   -----
 0   agency_cd       539305 non-null  object
 1   site_no         539305 non-null  int64
 2   datetime        539305 non-null  datetime64[ns, America/Denver]
 3   tz_cd           539305 non-null  object
 4   cfs             493124 non-null  float64
 5   144166_00060_cd 493124 non-null  object
 6   gage_height     433377 non-null  float64
 7   144167_00065_cd 433377 non-null  object
dtypes: datetime64[ns, America/Denver](1), float64(2), int64(1), object(4)
memory usage: 135.1 MB
```

Another option is to use the 3rd party library *memory-profiler*. You can install this with pip:

```
pip install memory-profiler
```

If you are using Jupyter, you will want to run install the extension, so you have access to the %%memit cell magic. Run this command in a cell in Jupyter:

```
%load_ext memory_profiler
```

Now you can leverage the %%memit cell magic. This will run a cell and track from the operating system's point of view how much memory the process has allocated. It also reports how much the memory usage has grown:

```
>>> %% memit
>>> dd = tweak_river(df)
peak memory: 304.42 MiB, increment: 254.99 MiB
```

If you find that you are using too much memory, consider:

- Sampling rows to limit the data

- Only loading columns you need

- Changing types to more efficient types (ie using 'int8' instead of 'int64' when representing human ages, or using 'category' for categorical data)

- Acquiring more memory (or using a machine with more memory)

35.8 Timing Information

In addition to how much memory your data is using, you probably want your code to run as fast as possible. Throughout this book, we have emphasized best practices, but we have also seen that pandas often has two (or three or four) ways of doing something.

My general response when clients ask what is faster is "it depends". And that is true. If you compare two pieces of code and benchmark them on a small amount of data, there is no guarantee that the fast code will still be faster when bombarded with more data. (Pay special attention to .apply, .query, and date conversion.)

After saying "it depends", I follow that up with "benchmark it and see". You can use the %%time cell magic to measure the clock time of a cell in Jupyter:

```
>>> %%time
>>> dd = tweak_river(df)
CPU times: user 228 ms, sys: 8.8 ms, total: 237 ms
Wall time: 235 ms
```

Another cell magic that provides timing information is %%timeit. This will run the cell a few times and give you the mean and standard deviation of the runtime:

```
>>> %%timeit
>>> dd = tweak_river(df)
233 ms ± 9.11 ms per loop (mean ± std. dev. of 7 runs, 1 loop each)
```

Method	Description
df.equals(other)	Compares two dataframes if they have the same shape and values. Columns should have the same type.
df.eq(other, axis='columns', level=None)	Return dataframe with same index and columns but boolean values indicating whether values are the same elementwise.
df.ne(other, axis='columns', level=None)	Return dataframe with same index and columns but boolean values indicating whether values are different elementwise.
pd.testing.assert_frame_equal(left, right, check_dtype=True, check_index_type='equiv', check_column_type='equiv', check_frame_type=True, check_names=True, by_blocks=False, check_exact=False, check_datetimelike_compat=False, check_categorical=True, check_like=False, check_freq=True, check_flags=True, rtol=1e-05, atol=1e-08, obj='DataFrame')	Utility function to determine if two dataframes are the same. Can change numeric tolerance with rtol (relative tolerance) and atol (absolute tolerance).
df.round(decimals=0)	Create a dataframe with decimals rounded to given places.
.pipe(func, *args, **kwargs)	Apply a function to a dataframe. Return the result of function.
IPython.display.display(*objs, include=None, exclude=None, metadata=None, transient=None, display_id=None, **kwargs)	Displays objs in Jupyter.

`df.info(verbose=None, buf=None,`
   `max_cols=None,`
   `memory_usage=None,`
   `show_counts=None)`
	Print summary of dataframe to stdout.
	Use `memory_usage='deep'` to show object
	column memory usage.

Table 35.1: Chapter Methods

35.9 Summary

In this chapter we have shown various techniques for understanding what is happening when you use pandas. One of the keys to being successful with pandas is to understand what operations do to your data and be able to validate that the operation worked as you expected it to. We also showed how to profile memory usage and timing.

35.10 Exercises

With a dataset of your choice, create a tweak function to perform a chain of operations.

1. Use the debugger to step into the chain of your tweak function.

2. Capture an intermediate state of your chain into a variable.

3. Time how long the tweak function takes to run.

4. Determine how much memory the tweak function needs to run.

Chapter 36

Summary

Thanks for learning about the pandas library. Hopefully, as you have read through this book, you have begun to appreciate the power in this library. You might be wondering what to do now that you have finished this book?

I've taught many people Python and pandas over the years, and they typically question what to do to continue learning. My answer is pretty simple: find a project that you would like to work on and find an excuse to use Python or pandas. If you are in a business setting and use Excel, try to see if you can replicate what you do in Jupyter and pandas. If you are interested in Machine Learning, check out Kaggle for projects to try out your new skills. Or simply find some data about something you are interested in and start playing around.

About the Author

Matt Harrison has been using Python since 2000. He runs MetaSnake, a Python and Data Science consultancy and corporate training shop. In the past, he has worked across the domains of search, build management and testing, business intelligence, and storage.

He has presented and taught tutorials at conferences such as Strata, SciPy, SCALE, PyCON, and OSCON as well as local user conferences. The structure and content of this book is based on first-hand experience teaching Python to many individuals.

He blogs at `hairysun.com` and occasionally tweets useful Python related information at `@__mharrison__`.

Index

Index

Also Available

If you are interested in learning Pandas in a corporate training, please reach out to MetaSnake. MetaSnake has conducted live and virtual trainings for teams all over the world. See https://metasnake.com for details.

If you are interested in on-demand training, see https://store.metasnake.com for on-demand course offerings.

One more thing

Thank you for buying and reading this book.

If you have found this book helpful, I have a big favor to ask. As a self-published author, I don't have a big Publishing House with lots of marketing power pushing my book. I also try to price my books so that they are much more affordable.

If you enjoyed this book, I hope that you would take a moment to leave an honest review on Amazon or social media. A short comment on how the book helped you and what your learned makes a huge difference. A quick review is useful to others who might be interested in the book.

Thanks again!

Printed in Great Britain
by Amazon

79545021R00282